The Ukrainian Challenge: reforming labour market and social policy

International Labour Office
Central and Eastern European Team

D1114701

Central European University Press
in association with ILO-CEET

This edition first published 1995 by the Central European University Press,
H-1051 Budapest, Nádor utca 9, Hungary,
in association with
ILO Central and Eastern European Multidisciplinary Advisory Team (CEET),
ILO-CEET, H-1066 Budapest, Mozsár utca 14, Hungary

Distributed by
Oxford University Press, Walton Street, Oxford OX2 6DP
Oxford New York Athens Auckland Bangkok Bombay Toronto
Calcutta Cape Town Dar es Salaam Delhi Florence Hong Kong
Istanbul Karachi Kuala Lumpur Madras Madrid Melbourne
Mexico City Nairobi Paris Singapore Taipei Tokyo Toronto
and associated companies in Berlin Ibadan
Distributed in the United States
by Oxford University Press Inc., New York

ISBN: 1 85866 044 0 Hbk
ISBN: 1 85866 045 9 Pbk

Typeset by SetAll, Clifton Hampden, Oxon
Printed and bound in Great Britain by Biddles of Guildford

Contents

List of Figures

List of Tables

Preface

Ukraine is a major eastern European country that only acquired independence in late 1991. It became independent in the most difficult of circumstances. Between 1991 and 1994, its economy went into what we will call a state of hyper-stagflation – a combination of massive economic decline and an inflation rate that rose to above 10,000% in 1993. Its political and social infrastructure had to emerge against the background of rapidly shrinking living standards and concern about the sustainability of the country itself.

Remarkably, Ukraine in mid-1994 seemed to have established the necessary political basis for a sustained transformation of its social and economic policies. This was epitomised by the democratic elections and by the endorsement of the Group of Seven and the International Monetary Fund, both of which committed large sums of financial assistance to facilitate the reform process.

In the coming period, it will be essential for the Government, for those agencies providing financial assistance, for the emerging employer and trade union organisations and for others involved in that process to give very high priority to the substantial reform of labour market and social policy. The importance of these spheres of policy cannot be overemphasised. Open unemployment will mount in 1994–1995, poverty is already widespread and severe, life expectancy has fallen from what was an already low level, the aftermath of the Chernobyl nuclear accident is still having profound social effects and will continue to do so for many years, and very much in the foreground is the need to address the social and labour market consequences of restructuring the economy away from its overemphasis on production for military purposes.

The following is an attempt to assess the trends in social and labour market policy in Ukraine. Although there are exceptions, relatively little analytical work has been done on those issues in the country. The initial intention of our analysis was to provide a picture of the issues and priorities in labour market, industrial relations and social policies, so as to guide the ILO in its technical work with the Ministry of Labour, the Ministry of Social Protection, the Ministry of Statistics and the trade unions and the employer organisations in Ukraine. However, encouraged by our partners in this exercise, the United Nations Development Programme office in Kiev, we have hoped that it would prove useful for other international agencies, such as the European Union (notably its TACIS programme), the IMF and the World Bank, as well as what are usually called 'bilateral donors', that is, government agencies in ILO member countries wishing to provide assistance to the emerging Ukrainian authorities.

We hope that the report is of use for those in Ukraine having to deal with novel and extremely complex policy challenges. In some respects, we have been critical of trends and policies. We hope the criticism will be perceived as constructive, for that has been our intention. Indeed, we have been helped and advised by a very large number of people in Ukraine, who have been unfailingly cooperative and supportive. We would like to thank all of them. It seems unfair to single out a few for particular thanks, yet some played crucial roles that should be acknowledged.

First, we would like to thank the Minister of Labour, Mihailo Kaskievich, who gave his support at the outset, who encouraged the Team to complete the work and who ensured that all his Ministerial colleagues were able to work with us. In his Ministry, we also thank First Deputy Minister of Labour, Anatoly Sorokin, who likewise encouraged and supported the work, Nadiya Malysh, Deputy Minister of Labour in charge of social policy, Mikola Makhnenko, Director of the Integrated Department, Viktor Yerasov, Director of the State Employment Service, Vladimir Labatyuk, Director of the Wages Department, Alexander Sintchenko, Director of the Employment Department, and Bouls Nadtochy, Chief, Dept. of Living Standards. Many others in the Ministry deserve thanks and we apologise for not mentioning them all.

We also thank the Minister of Statistics, First Deputy Minister of Statistics, Volodimir Gusakovskiy, Deputy Minister Irina Hainatska, Director of the Department of Demography and Labour Statistics, Nadezhda Grigorovich, Deputy Head of that Department, and Natalya Vlasenko for their general assistance in the collection of information, and in particular for collaborating with us on what we have called the Ukraine Labour Flexibility Survey (ULFS). This was a survey of employment and labour practices in a representative sample of 348 industrial establishments in the six largest industrial areas of the country, covering over 372,000 workers. Carried out in early 1994 to provide background information for this review, and more generally to assist the ILO in developing an empirical basis for future technical work, this survey is one of a series we have been conducting in the region. A separate report on its findings should be published at the same time as this report.

We would also like to thank the Minister of Social Protection, Arkardy Ershov, and his Deputy Minister, Valentin Gamachek, and their colleagues, who were particularly helpful in connection with Chapter 7, on social protection reform.

Throughout the work, we were assisted and encouraged by the support we received from the Social and Labour Affairs Committee of the Cabinet of Ministers, and in particular its chairman, Igor Kharchenko, and Alexander Timosheev, the Committee's wages specialist. We also benefited from meeting with members of Parliament, in particular with Mykola Biloblotsky, head of the Parliamentary Commission on Social Policy and Labour Affairs. And we are grateful to Anatoly Rybak, chairman of the National Council for Social Partnership, and his colleagues for their cooperation.

On the trade union side, we had numerous contacts with all types of trade union and with many individuals. We are grateful for the support and cooperation of Alexander Stoyan, the President of the Federation of Trade Unions of Ukraine, and his Vice-President, Grigory Osoviy. Technical contributions were made by Valentina Polynich and Sergiy Ukrainets. We also benefited from the technical report of Rodyna Svetlana, Head of the wage department and worked with numerous other trade union officials in the wide variety of unions that are emerging in Ukraine, as reviewed in Chapter 6, particularly Okeksandr Mril and Semen Karikov and Mark Tarnawsky.

On the employer side, we had valuable assistance from all groups identified as representatives of employers, and these are also identified in Chapter 6. We very much hope that those organisations will continue to become more representative of independent employers, and feel sure that the international employer organisations will wish to assist them in developing their functions and capacities. We are grateful for useful discussions with President Leonid Kuchma, at the time President of the Ukrainian League of Industrialists and Entrepreneurs, and with Volodimir Ryzhov, executive director of the ULIE. Valuable discussions were also held with the leaders of the Ukrainian National Assembly of Entrepreneurship, the Union of Leaseholders and Entrepreneurs of Ukraine and the Business Union of Crimea.

Among academic specialists, we would like to thank in particular, Demyan Boginya, Guennady Kulikov, Olina Paliy, Ella Libanova, Vladimir Shamota and Valentina Steshenko, of the Ukrainian Academy of Sciences, Vladimir Yatsenko, of the Kiev State Economics University, and Vladimir Lanovoy, Director of the Centre for Market Reform and former Minister of the Economy.

And then we come to basics. Without his support and unfailing good humour, this report would not have been possible, so it is with great pleasure that we acknowledge the support of Stephen Browne, the UN Resident

Representative in Kiev. He and his colleagues, most notably Dimitri Chernobay, enabled the Team to complete the work, and the UNDP provided essential financial assistance.

This report is the responsibility of the ILO's Central and Eastern European Team, and therefore does not formally commit the ILO to support the views and conclusions reached in the report. Of course, in practice we hope and believe that those conclusions adhere to the values of the ILO, and that the analysis will be useful for the technical departments of the ILO that will be working in Ukraine. Moreover, we have consulted our colleagues on many issues, and wish to thank them for their comments.

The report is the responsibility of ILO-CEET. Principal authors of the main chapters were Guy Standing for Chapter 1, Alena Nesporova, for Chapters 2 and 3, Daniel Vaughan-Whitehead, for Chapter 4, Robert Kyloh, for Chapter 5, Pekka Aro and Björn Grünewald, for Chapter 6 and Michael Cichon, for Chapter 7. Much appreciated assistance was provided by Igor Chernyshev, of the ILO's Statistics Department, and by Laszlo Zsoldos and Paula Repo. The latter edited the manuscript and deserves very special thanks for doing so in a short period, under difficult circumstances.

In 1994, Ukraine had just elected a new president and parliament, and there seemed a renewed determination to introduce major reforms oriented to restructuring the economy and the social infrastructure. We believe reforms are urgently required, and throughout the text of the review we have tried to highlight areas where we feel progress can and should be made. The ILO is prepared and able to provide assistance in some of those areas, and would welcome the opportunity to provide assistance and advice on others in partnership with other agencies and government organisations.

Indeed, the scope and depth of the policy needs are such that it will take a coordinated effort of the Ukrainian authorities and the international community to make sustained progress in reforming social and labour policy. We hope that as soon as practicable an international meeting of the Ukrainian authorities and foreign donors and technical assistance agencies can be convened so that such a coordinated approach is developed and implemented. Without such coordination, there is likely to be a frustrating and costly process of duplication, inefficiency and confusion.

The report was submitted to the tripartite Conference 'Reforming Labour Market and Social Policy in Ukraine' organised by the Ministry of Labour of Ukraine, ILO and the UNDP Office in Ukraine. It took place in Kiev, September 26–27, 1994. Conclusions and recommendations drawn from the Conference are included in Chapter 8. At the end of the conference, with the Minister of Labour, Mihailo Kaskievich, in the chair the conclusions and the report were endorsed.

1

From Paralysis to Progress

1. Introduction

Ukraine has struggled into independent existence with considerable economic, social and ecological difficulties, and has been plunged into a period of unparalleled hyper-stagflation. Although it helped precipitate the country's determination to achieve independence, the tragic nuclear explosion at Chernobyl on April 26, 1986 traumatised the country, has continued to affect the whole population directly or indirectly and will do so for many years.[1] Then in unfavourable economic circumstances, following the break-up of the Soviet Union the country became independent on August 24, 1991, confirmed by a referendum on December 1, 1991.

> *'The country is doomed to make a decisive jump forward.' — Victor Pynzenyk, Ukrainian economist and former Deputy Prime Minister*

The subsequent lack of political consensus on social and economic strategy for reform, coupled with the scale of the country's problems, seems to have paralysed effective restructuring. This was epitomised by the fact that in the parliamentary elections of March 1994 there were 30 political parties, and a majority of the 5,000 candidates for the 450 seats were 'independent'. The election of a new President in July 1994 raised new expectations that a coherent, sustained reform strategy would take shape soon, and that this would be backed by financial and technical assistance from the international community.

Ukraine is one of the largest countries of Europe, with over 52 million people, spread over 26 regions (24 oblasts, Kiev City and the Republic of Crimea). Ukraine emerged into independence as the world's third largest nuclear power, with a vast number of nuclear arms stationed on its

---

[1] It has been estimated that nearly 40,000 square kilometres of Ukrainian land were contaminated by radionuclides and 4.7 million hectares of farmland, 3.1 million of that arable, were lost. It is estimated to have affected at least three million people directly.

territory, as well as Europe's second largest army. Its economy was heavily skewed to military-industrial production – having accounted for an estimated 35% of the former Soviet Union's military-industrial complex, which employed 2.5 million Ukrainian workers. Its trade was heavily tied to that of Russia and production was dependent on imported oil, mainly from Russia. Trade with Russia and other parts of the Soviet Union accounted for over 80% of its total trade, and the severing of links created a huge economic shock. The country also emerged burdened by a huge external debt (over 16% of the total debt attributed to the Soviet Union). That will constrain the country's economic and social policy for many years.

Besides the aftermath of the Chernobyl accident, there has been a serious and steady deterioration in the environment – notably in the Donbas, the Dniepr area and Polissia, among others – which has surely contributed to the shrinking life expectancy of the population in the 1990s.

The country has also been faced by a need to forge a national identity and hold together its various regions, some of which have shown a tendency to prefer reintegration with Russia, notably the Crimea, populated largely by Russians and Tatars, and home of the Russian Black Sea fleet. Nationally, Russians account for over 22% of the population. In the eastern Ukraine, there is a 'pro-Russia' preference; in the western part of the country there is a much more nationalist tendency and a preference to see the future of the country in terms of a turn away from Russia towards integration with western Europe.

Increasingly, it has seemed that eastern Ukraine, whose heavy industry was most hard hit by the break-up of the Soviet Union, would be the area in greatest economic difficulties. However, it is not only an east–west split that has threatened the development of a national reform strategy. The capital city, Kiev, has appeared to have little control over the establishment of semi-autonomous local economic zones in Transcarpathia in the west, Odessa, Nikolayev and Kherson in the south and Donetsk and Lugansk in the east, while Crimea, which only became part of Ukraine in the 1950s, has become openly 'separatist'. Although decentralisation must be a major feature of economic restructuring, this political regionalisation has impeded the development of a national economic strategy, but has also reflected and been exacerbated by the lack of such a strategy.

All observers agree that, in the longer-term and if the country does not break up, Ukraine should become a prosperous country, given its potentially very fertile soil, considerable stock of raw materials, its industrial base and technically skilled workforce. It has often been described as the 'breadbasket of Europe', since until recently overtaken by Russia it produced more grain than any country in Europe. However, economic realities in the 1990s necessitate a painful and very extensive process of

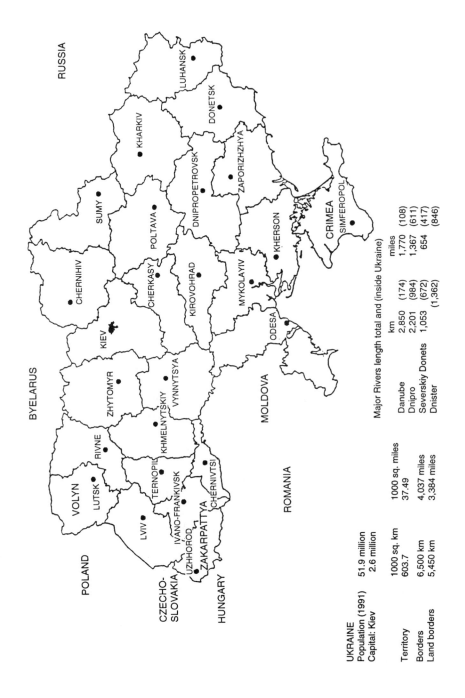

UKRAINE

RUSSIA

BYELARUS

POLAND

CZECHO-
SLOVAKIA

HUNGARY

MOLDOVA

ROMANIA

VOLYN
LUTSK ●

RIVNE ●

LVIV ●

TERNOPIL ●

IVANO-FRANKIVSK ●

UZHHOROD ●
ZAKARPATTYA

CHERNIVTSI ●

ZHYTOMYR ●

KHMELNYTSKIY ●

VYNNYTSYA ●

KIEV

CHERNIHIV ●

CHERKASY ●

KIROVOHRAD ●

SUMY ●

POLTAVA ●

KHARKIV ●

DNIPROPETROVSK ●

ZAPORIZHZHYA ●

LUHANSK ●

DONETSK ●

MYKOLAYIV ●

KHERSON ●

ODESA ●

CRIMEA
SIMFEROPOL ●

UKRAINE
Population (1991)   51.9 million
Capital: Kiev   2.6 million

	1000 sq. km	1000 sq. miles
Territory	603.7	37.49
Borders	6,500 km	4,037 miles
Land borders	5,450 km	3,384 miles

Major Rivers length total and (inside Ukraine)

	km		miles	
Danube	2,850	(174)	1,770	(108)
Dnipro	2,201	(984)	1,367	(611)
Severskiy Donets	1,053	(672)	654	(417)
Dnister		(1,362)		(846)

economic and social restructuring if that potential is to be realised. Short-term prospects look as grim as the recent economic decline has been. Although statistics are sometimes of dubious quality – a point to which we will refer in the following chapters – it is widely agreed that the economy shrank very sharply and continuously between 1991 and 1993, and continued to do so in 1994.

2. In Search of a Ukrainian Economic Strategy

2.1. Structural Constraints

To appreciate the difficulties of achieving economic and social policy reform in the 1990s in Ukraine, one must appreciate the structural features that constrained the development of an effective and coherent reform strategy after independence.

> *'Down and outs can't be independent'* — *Ukrainian plant manager, March 1994*

In the 1980s, Ukraine was fully integrated into the Soviet economic system in a subordinated way. Its productive structure was dependent on imported oil, over 90% of which came from Russia, and gas, about 70% of which came from Russia. Its trade was overwhelmingly oriented to the Soviet Union and its industrial production was largely dependent on imported inputs from Russia and other republics of the USSR. It was disproportionately a producer of armaments and although it had a trade surplus with the rest of the Soviet Union, that reflected the distorted price system in which its huge import of oil and gas was acquired at a small fraction of the world price. Recalculated at world prices, Ukraine had a structural trade deficit with the rest of the Soviet Union, which was compounded by a large trade deficit with the rest of the world.[2]

Thus, once trading links with other republics of the former Soviet Union were disrupted by the break up of the USSR and the associated trading block, the structural deficit due to the pattern of specialisation in production that had been built up since the 1950s was bound to become a huge constraint to independent economic policy, as was the essentially complementary nature of the productive structure of the Ukrainian economy. The severing of the productive links was almost certain to lead to a disintegra-

---

[2] K. Kiss and V. Sidenko, Ukraine on the Way toward Economic Stabilisation and Independence, *Eastern European Economics*, Winter 1992–1993, pp. 65–9.

tion of the production system, since most industrial production in Ukraine depended in some way on other sectors in other republics. Moreover, ironically, Ukraine's crucial hard currency exports were concentrated on products that had severe environmental consequences, so that any increased exports would mean increased environmental damage.[3]

A further constraint was that much of the production and a corresponding share of investment, credit and tax revenue were controlled by the centralised administrative apparatus based in Moscow. Thus, when the Soviet economy began to unravel in the mid and late 1980s, the burden of net transfers from Ukraine, which had long been a feature of the country's economic subordination, became a drag on economic growth. In 1990, the Ukrainian economy shrank for the first time since 1945.

Another constraint was the complex pattern of state subsidies for both production and consumption, which was to account for a large part of the government's growing budget deficit. According to some statistics, subsidies to enterprises accounted for about 12% of GNP by the end of the 1980s, and consumer subsidies on basic foodstuffs accounted for almost as much.[4]

Another structural constraint was that after many decades of subordination to Moscow, Ukraine lacked an administrative system of people capable of taking – or experienced in taking – independent decisions, let alone of implementing them. The size of the public administration was also very small, which in some respects might be an advantage, but if a central government has only a little over 12,000 employees in a country of over 52 million people, then the capacity to design and implement new national policies must be severely constrained. In judging the evident chaos of the first three years of independent policymaking, that basic fact should not be forgotten.

2.2. From Dependence into Crisis

Against that background, the first rounds of reform, beginning in 1990, involved a series of measures to secure greater control over the Ukrainian economy, notably with Ukraine's first tax law in mid-1990, which introduced a high-rated Value Added Tax and Ukrainian income tax.

Leading up to independence, during the latter period of 'perestroika' in the late 1980s, the trend to decentralisation and democratisation made it possible for politicians in Ukraine to formulate a quasi-independent economic policy. In November 1990, the Ukrainian Council of Ministers

---

[3] K. Kiss and V. Sidenko, op. cit., p. 78.

[4] E. Libanova and A. Revenko, Public Policy and Social Conditions in Ukraine during 1989–1993, paper prepared for UNICEF, Kiev, 1993, p. 9.

formulated a Programme for Transition to a Market Economy. In April 1991, the Ukrainian Parliament passed the Law on Foreign Economic Activities, extending opportunities for foreign trade and economic relations, and in June 1991, Parliament established a national institutional structure, extended legal control over all economic organisations in the country, and also acquired control of all tax revenue.

In July, 1991, Parliament adopted the Programme of Emergency Measures to Stabilise the Ukrainian Economy and Resolve the Crisis, supposedly a two-year stabilisation and restructuring Programme that combined measures to stimulate production, including tax breaks and partial price liberalisation, controls over private exports of raw materials, restrictions on exports of consumer goods, credit restrictions, a declaration that firms operating at a loss would be closed, cuts in state subsidies and cuts in public expenditure. In September 1991, just after the declaration of independence, a law was passed nationalising all Union property in Ukraine.

In October 1991, a new reform Programme was endorsed by Parliament, entitled Principles of the Economic Policy of Ukraine under Conditions of Independence. This envisaged a relative shift of production to consumer goods in national income, plus a commitment to industrial conversion from military to civilian goods, cuts in exports of raw materials and development of high tech industries, as well as economic de-regulation and anti-monopoly and pro-privatisation measures. It looked like an industrial policy for restructuring.

However, due in part to the political upheavals in Moscow in August 1991 and in part to the country's deep integration with the Russian economic and financial system, economic independence has proved a mirage. Price liberalisation and partial wage liberalisation in Moscow unleashed an inflationary spiral and the federal budget deficit grew alarmingly.[5] Both fed into the Ukrainian economy, as did Russia's policy of moving its oil price towards world levels. The inflation and inability to exert national control led to the introduction of a national currency in late 1991 – the karbovanets – and precipitated the formal declaration of independence. In 1992–1993, the inflationary pressures and the growing trade deficit worsened the Ukrainian Government's budget deficit, which was compounded by a widespread practice of enterprises to hoard stocks, partly in the expectation of price rises and partly due to the lack of demand, the hoarding being a practice financed by bank credits that were subsequently written off, and by the low revenue-raising capacity of the fiscal authorities.

[5] One of the sources of difficulty in Ukraine was that at the time the only bank in the Commonwealth of Independent States with the authority to inject money into the economy was in Russia, making Ukraine dependent on Russia's price, fiscal and incomes policies. National Institute for Strategic Studies, Strategies for the Development of Ukraine: Contemporary Challenges and Choices, Kiev, 1994, mimeo, p. 31.

Following the break-up of the Soviet Union, the authorities in Ukraine were at the forefront of promoting and founding the Commonwealth of Independent States (CIS) and the ruble zone, in large part because that seemed to offer a way of restoring a large-scale market to counteract the adverse effects of the dismantling of inter-enterprise linkages between Ukrainian and Russian and other ex-Soviet production. Unfortunately, given the parlous state of production throughout the CIS, as an entity it offered little short-term prospect of enabling the Ukrainian economy to revive.

2.3. The Governance Crisis

Despite a plethora of reform measures and pronouncements in 1991–1993, the basic issue remained that of deciding on and maintaining a national reform strategy that took account of the country's structural constraints and the feasible options. In the period around the attainment of independence, some prominent policymakers were convinced by like-minded reformers in Moscow and by the international financial agencies to press for a 'shock therapy' economic strategy. Many others believed that it would not work or that pursuing that course would lead to a break up of the country and to excessive levels of social misery. Others seemed intent on blocking reforms for as long as possible, so as to enable a minority to secure some economic 'rent' through corruption or manipulation of partial reforms for their own advantage. The lack of consensus on the direction and pace of reform was the beginning of an impasse that has lasted into 1994.

Scepticism about the feasibility or desirability of the orthodox shock therapy strategy – involving price liberalisation, followed by an economic stabilisation Programme based on tight monetary and fiscal policy, rapid privatisation and then induced industrial restructuring – may have been justified. What was not justified was the resultant inertia, with halting efforts to introduce economic reforms being followed swiftly by retreats or non-implementation of decrees and edicts.

The most basic problem has been one of governance, that is establishing policy-making and policy-implementing mechanisms that have the authority and capacity to function reasonably effectively. This unresolved issue has influenced the development of social and labour policy and should be central to debates about the future of such policy. Getting governance right is at least as important as getting prices right. One of the biggest problems in formulating a coherent reform policy was the difficulty of agreeing on the separation of powers between President and Parliament, which seems likely to persist after the 1994 elections.

Similarly, the excessive regional fragmentation of politics seems to be promoted by the electoral system adopted for the 1994 elections. Undoubtedly, the system is democratic in the conventional sense. However, it has been argued, persuasively, that in the context of Ukraine's development, the use of a single-constituency, majority voting system favours regional parties and independents rather than national political parties.[6] This could prevent the emergence of a stable and coherent reform strategy. A third and related political factor to bear in mind is the instability of the position of senior political decision-makers, since the short tenure of most senior Ministers in successive governments has both mirrored and contributed to the instability in the development and implementation of economic and social policy. Thus, for instance, it is surely no coincidence that there has been an unusually strong correlation between political instability and increases in the money supply.[7]

In the early stages of reform, it was essential to establish a legislative route to reform. Although a start was made in that direction initially, this was not what happened in 1991–1993, since policymaking seems to have devolved into a stream of decrees and edicts, often with little evidence of a commitment to implementation or a growing ability to implement them. Above all, during 1992 and 1993 there was a shift from formal parliamentary legislation to ad hoc reform by decree and edict, with the issuing of a large number of decrees that were partial, sometimes contradictory and often not implemented.[8]

Formally, from the outset, policies for economic restructuring did emerge. Thus, tentative moves to property restructuring included the establishment of a State Property Fund, to deal with privatisation, which began with some auctions of small-scale enterprises in 1993.[9] Yet it has been claimed that laws passed to introduce land reform actually obstructed it, even though defenders of the reforms might argue that they were intended as a gradual extension of private ownership in a way that would limit the likelihood of landlordism developing, and should be inclined to add that land reform was not actually put into effect.

What was most needed was enterprise restructuring, and although the 1991 and 1992 Programmes envisaged anti-monopoly measures, these were undermined by various decrees in 1992 and 1993. Thus, there was a decree

---

[6] This is the view of Myron Wasylyk, a former US State Department Official, who in 1993–1994 was Executive Director of the Council of Advisers to the Parliament of Ukraine.

[7] M. Zienchuk, Ukraine in Numbers, *The Ukrainian Legal and Economic Bulletin*, Vol. 2, No. 1, p. 35.

[8] Centre for Market Reforms, Ukraine: A Survey of Economic and Social Reforms, Kiev, mimeo, 1993.

[9] The State Property Fund claimed in February 1994 that 1,750 industrial enterprises were privatised in 1993, and 36 in 1992, Intelnews, Vol. IV, No. 56, February 26, 1994, p. 2.

that gave back managerial and administrative powers to central Ministries, weakening enterprise autonomy of management. And there was a Cabinet Resolution in 1993, entitled *On the Application of Definite Forms of Labour Agreement with Managers of Enterprises under Public Ownership*, by which managerial salaries were linked more formally to the size of enterprise, in terms of assets and number of workers, which strengthened the longstanding tendency to create – and more importantly in 1993, to preserve – mammoth, monopolistic enterprises, precisely the opposite of what was required.

By late 1993, numerous enterprises were effectively idle, reflecting a dwindling supply of raw materials and energy, excessive stocks and empty wage funds. But the Government continued to prevent bankruptcies, by providing extra subsidies and credit, even after the latest credit squeeze, of December 1993. By then, most industrial enterprises were in a parlous financial situation. The trade unions, according to the leadership's own accounts to us (January 1994), cut back on the provision of enterprise benefits to workers, notably on food and recreation vouchers and health facilities, often raising prices for such services. Enterprises in the military-industrial complex were most hard hit, although as ILO-CEET's survey of industrial establishments showed, the slump was affecting all industrial sectors.

3. The Economic Outcome

The results of the partial and contradictory reforms were disastrous. In 1992–1994, the economy drifted into hyper-stagflation. Following partial price liberalisation in conditions of state production based on huge monopolistic industrial and agricultural enterprises, enterprises found it easy to adjust prices upwards.

> 'Strict monetary policy without reform is empty. It is plain cruelty when someone has not received his salary in five months. The only way is to issue new money.' — Victor Yushchenko, National Bank Chairman, February 16, 1994.

The initial price liberalisation took place in January 1992, a further round of liberalisation occurred in mid-1993 and another in December 1993. A new currency was also introduced in January 1992, when Ukraine became the first CIS country to leave the ruble zone. Then, instead of the planned stabilisation policy, during 1992 credits to agriculture and state enterprises increased by over 40 times. During 1993, credit emissions continued to be enormous, to both the public and financial sectors.

Meanwhile, wages were raised to offset inflation, with the Government's occasional attempts to limit the flow of money to enterprise wage and consumption funds resulting in industrial tension, leading to further rises in money wages and a further twist in inflation, which simply accelerated the decline in real wages, further undermining the motivation to work and thus contributing to the sharp decline in labour productivity.[10]

In response to the supply and demand shocks and partial or non-implemented reforms, the economy suffered an extraordinary decline. Overall, production fell sharply, with agriculture being particularly badly hit, as indicated in *Table 1.1*, even though informal production and barter transactions may have been growing. Mining, construction and heavy and light industry also slumped. In 1992, industrial output declined by over 6%, and agricultural production by over 8%.[11] Industrial output declined by 8.0% in 1993.[12] And, according to the Ministry of Statistics, the output of the country's main industrial products declined by 22.0% in 1993. Within industry, consumer goods production fell by 45.9%, and sectors such as coal mining, metallurgy and the chemical industry shrunk by over 20%.

Table 1.1 *Economic Performance Indicators, Ukraine, 1991–1993 (percent change over the year)*

	1991	1992	1993
GDP growth rate	−13.5	−13.7	−14.0
Net national product	−13.4	−16.0	−15.0
Industrial production	−4.8	−6.4	−8.0
Consumer goods production:	−5.1	−9.4	−15.9
• Food	−13.5	−15.6	−10.1
• Non-food	3.1	−4.7	−25.1
Labour productivity	−11.0	−13.4	−13.0
Capital investment	−7.1	−36.1	−22.0
Inflation (Consumer price index)	327	2,095	10,255

Source: Ministry of Statistics, *Statistical Yearbook of Ukraine*, 1992, *Statistichniy Byuleten* (Statistical Bulletin), No. 1, January 1994. Several figures for 1993 have been recently precised by the Ministry of Statistics.

[10] V. Lanovoy, Ukraine: National Strategy of Technical Assistance for Reform, Report prepared for UN, mimeo, Kiev, 1993, p. 44.

[11] Some estimates have put the declines as much higher, at 9% and 14% respectively, with heavy industry declining by more than the remainder of the economy. Centre for Market Reforms, 1993, op. cit., p. 32.

[12] Others have estimated that the net material product (a measure of national income) declined by 30% between 1989 and 1992, and that industrial output declined by less (20%) than transport and communications, construction, agriculture and services in general. Libanova and Revenko, 1993, op. cit., p. 1.

The exchange rate of the new karbovanets currency plunged from 200 to the US dollar in June 1992 to over 10,000 in September 1993 and over 44,000 in mid-1994. Symbolically, in November 1993, the Government introduced a 100,000 karbovanets note, worth less than US$ 4 at the exchange rate of the time. The declining value of the currency reflected the inflationary pressures, the growing budget deficit and the release of money by the National Bank of Ukraine to fund subsidies and credits, as well as the foreign debt and the deterioration in foreign trade due to the break up of the COMECON trading system.

Foreign debt has become a major and growing constraint. The huge trade deficit and the shortage of hard currency made it extremely hard to pay off that debt, particularly to hard-pressed Russia, the government of which threatened in early 1994 to cut off oil supplies unless debt repayments were accelerated.[13] This led to Ukrainian debate on whether or not to continue with its agreement with the USA and Russia to dismantle the nuclear arms on its territory. In the light of this unresolved issue, tensions may be compounded by the fact that all oil and gas pipelines from Russia to western Europe go through Ukraine, for which Ukraine charges transit fees.

Perhaps as serious as the foreign debt is the Government's budget deficit. After being in balance in 1990, the budget moved into a deficit of enormous proportions in relation to GDP in 1992. In 1993 the deficit was 6.8% of GDP. The most immediate major cause was slack monetary policy, and the continuing flow of credit and subsidies perceived to be needed to prevent industrial collapse. Often purchasers were simply unable or unwilling to pay for goods, yet were still provided with them. For instance, by early 1994 the gas monopolist, Ukrgasprom, was owed a huge amount from domestic customers, yet was continuing to supply them.[14] In general, by then enterprise indebtedness had become critical, with fresh credit being provided for debt clearing purposes.[15] It seemed as if the discipline had snapped, and the so-called soft budget constraint of the former Soviet system had actually become softer.

A second and structural cause of the budget deficit has been the inability, or unwillingness, of central Government to cut public expenditure, particularly social expenditure, which as will be shown later has grown as a share of national income. Perhaps the most fundamental problem was that, while subsidies and capital transfers persisted without economic

---

[13] For a while in early 1994, Turkmenistan, which supplies about 30% of Ukraine's natural gas, cut off its supply. The flow recommenced when Ukraine bought grain from its state farms on credit to send to Turkmenistan, adding to the Government's budget deficit and to inflation.

[14] *Intelnews*, Vol. IV, No. 57, February 27, 1994, p. 1.

[15] *Intelnews*, Vol. IV, No. 55, February 25, 1994, p. 7.

justification, the new taxation system was simply not working, most notably the value added tax. In 1992, for instance, according to some estimates, only 38% of VAT was collected, and there was an equally low compliance rate with personal income tax.[16]

With the growing budget deficit in 1992, and in large part reflecting that monetary looseness and the absence of structural reform, price inflation accelerated through 1992 and 1993, by the end of which it was generally believed that Ukraine's inflation rate was among the highest in the world.

The data are sketchy and in need of refinement. According to the new Consumer Price Index data (based on retail prices in state, cooperative and kolkhoz markets, and thus excluding the private sector), which is generally considered to be an underestimate of inflation, prices rose by over 2,000% in 1992, with the biggest increase coming in January 1992, when partial price liberalisation boosted retail prices by 73%, which was promptly followed by a Presidential Decree that set profitability limits on those goods for which prices had been decontrolled. Most of those limits were removed in July 1992. During 1992 inflation was boosted by substantial price increases for imported oil and by the extraordinary 'emission' of domestic currency to support the government's budget deficit.[17]

In December 1992, the range of goods subject to regulated prices was expanded, so that a very mixed system emerged, with many goods subject to administered prices, many by price regulation and only about half being decontrolled. Although price inflation seemed to be stabilising in early 1993, rising prices for imported oil and gas forced up production costs, resulting in another round of retail price rises in June, and an acceleration of price inflation in the second half of 1993, fuelled by releases in money supply. By then, further price liberalisation was being introduced, and inflation soared.

In such circumstances, the economists' fear is that the higher the inflation and the longer it is allowed to continue, the more socially painful the corrective economic stabilisation and adjustment policy will be.

Using the new Consumer Price Index, which was introduced in February 1993, the Ministry of Statistics estimated in February 1994 that the rate of inflation reached 10,256% for the year of 1993, with prices nearly doubling in December alone. Inflation was 4% in 1990, about 290% in 1991 and about 2,000% in 1992.

[16] O. Havrylyshyn, M. Miller and W. Perraudin, Deficits, Inflation and the Political Economy of Ukraine, paper presented at a Conference on Societies in Transformation: Experience of Market Reforms in Ukraine, Kiev, May 20, 1994, p. 10.

[17] Between 1992 and 1993, the average price of oil rose from US$ 42 to US$ 73 per ton, the price of gas from US$ 9 to US$ 55 per thousand square metres. V. Pynzenyk, Ukrainian Economic Reforms: Reflections on the Past and the Future, paper presented at the conference Societies in Transformation: Experience of Market Reforms in Ukraine, Kiev, May 19–21, 1994.

In late November 1993, in response to the threat of hyperinflation, the Government imposed what it designated as a strict credit squeeze. In part, that was intended to impose stricter financial discipline in industrial enterprises. As the Minister of Economics, Roman Shpek, told the press in December, 1993: 'We have considerably reduced credit emissions by stopping the financing of unprofitable enterprises. Industrial enterprises will be granted complete independence.'[18]

The tightening of monetary policy did lead to a general financial squeeze on enterprises, an increasing number of which could not pay wages to their workers, who either had to work for little or no pay or were put on unpaid leave. Yet, one of the justifications given for the credit squeeze of late 1993 was the need to free funds for emergency wage and social protection payments.

In late 1993, the Government also liberalised prices on more goods, mainly basic foodstuffs, and raised prices on those items that were still subject to administered pricing, thereby raising inflation by 90.8% in a matter of days.[19]

By February 1994, with the impending elections, and no doubt fearing the economic and political consequences, the authorities relaxed the monetary squeeze, and in one week issued a new wave of credit equivalent to about 10% of the country's GNP for 1993.[20] Once again, a move in one direction had precipitated a retreat, because of the absence of a legitimised and coherent strategy for structural reform. Meanwhile, the IMF and the World Bank held back on a scheduled loan of over US$ 1 billion, due to the lack of anti-inflationary policy conditions.

Subsequently, monthly inflation declined fairly steadily in the first six months of 1994, falling from 19.2% in January to 3.9% in June, according to the Ministry of Statistics. However, the real economy continued to decline extraordinarily rapidly.

In sum, by early 1994, the economy was gripped in a state of hyper-stagflation, providing the ingredients of further economic decline and runaway inflation, overseen by a hesitant political machinery, three factors that elsewhere have proved the classic antecedents to social unrest and the undermining of democracy. The overworked word 'crisis' seemed strangely banal in the circumstances. Yet the elections of mid-1994 took place with remarkable calm, leading to a smooth transfer of power and demonstrating that political democracy was taking root. A breathing space for structural reform seemed ensured.

---

[18] Interview of December 13, 1993, as quoted in I. Brzezinski and M. Zienchuk, Political Debate on Ukraine, *The Ukrainian Legal and Economic Bulletin*, Vol. 2, No. 1, January–February, 1994, p. 26.

[19] I. Brzezinski and M. Zienchuk, op. cit., p. 27.

[20] *Financial Times*, February 3, 1994, p. 3.

4. Signs of Economic Restructuring

It would be a gross error to believe that there was no economic restructuring between 1991 and 1994. It certainly was inadequately slow and much of what took place may not have been the type of restructuring that was required. Yet a series of changes heralded an underlying transformation that will surely accelerate and become more evident in 1995.

> *'You won't believe it, but the biggest profit now comes from manufacturing children's bicycles.*
>
> *We also produce gas containers and special equipment for manufacturing sausages.'* — *Yuriy Alexeyev, Plant director of PivdenMash, formerly the world's biggest manufacturer of intercontinental ballistic missiles, answering a question in July about what the factory produced now that it no longer produced ICBMs.*

The quotation from the plant director of PivenMash is significant, even allowing for possible exaggeration. This enterprise once employed about 50,000 workers, and since 1991 has to adjust, cut jobs and convert to civilian production at a rapid rate.

Much of what has taken place has been very defensive in character. It has been widely reported that the military industry has not received any state orders since 1992. Perhaps, it has to some extent exported its former products, yet its long-term survival depends on its capacity to convert and restructure. No doubt, it has obtained large subsidies, and no doubt such enterprises have contributed to the huge chain of inter-enterprise indebtedness that could cause havoc to production and employment unless managed in a coordinated way. However, such enterprises were being forced to restructure to some extent. One sad point is that they had a high concentration of highly skilled, technically qualified workers, most of whom were seriously underutilised by 1994, performing jobs that were undermining their skills and motivation.

Besides the conversion aspect of economic restructuring, there have been others, most of which have had both negative and positive characteristics. Given the decline in living standards in 1992–1994 and the stagflation in the formal, state-dominated economy, an important trend that has yet to be integrated into policy analysis or the statistical analysis of the economy was the apparent growth of the informal economy, which in effect has grown to compensate in part for the decline in the state-dominated sphere. This has numerous implications for economic, social and labour market policy.

One should be wary about painting too rosy a picture of this, or of expecting that the informal economy will absorb all or most of those who become unemployed, since as in other countries it is likely that those people whose activities and incomes have thrived most in the informal economy have been those with relatively good incomes and security in the formal economy. However, with the haemorrhaging of the mainstream economy, the growth of what are probably mainly own-account activities has acted as a buffer to limit the fall in living standards.

The most conspicuous aspect of this process has been the growth of small-scale private agricultural production. According to official data from the Ministry of Statistics, the number of households producing vegetables on private plots increased by two-thirds between 1985 and 1993, and the number of urban households operating such plots doubled in the period *(Table 1.2)*.[21]

Table 1.2 *Households with Agricultural Production from Own Land, Ukraine, 1985–1993 (thousand)*

	1985	1993	% change
All households	10,211	13,859	35.7
Collective farmers	4,358	4,105	5.8
Workers and others:	5,852	9,754	66.7
• Rural residents	2,420	2,917	20.6
• Urban residents	3,432	6,837	100.0

Source: Ministry of Statistics, 1994.

By 1993, when the urban population was about 35.4 million, over 6.8 million urban households were producing agricultural output on their own plots. This was the outcome of the policy in the 1970s and 1980s of distributing individual plots of at least 600 square metres to individual families. What seems to have happened is that in the early 1990s the intensity of the use of those plots has increased, such that by 1993 – given that several generations have used many of the plots – in urban areas almost every second family was growing fruit, vegetables and potatoes for their own consumption, for barter or for sale in open markets or on the streets. The main crop seems to have been potatoes, and the area devoted to them rose fivefold between the two surveys carried out in 1985 and 1993.

Some aspects of the informal economy should be the source of concern among policymakers. Anecdotal evidence suggests that much of the activ-

[21] See also V. Yatsenko, Employment Policy in Ukraine in 1991–1994, paper presented to ILO Conference on Employment Policy and Programmes, Budapest, June 2–3, 1994.

ity has veered towards being black economy or illegal, and much of it has been in petty trade and services, including economic tourism, as discussed in Chapter 2. One should not belittle many of those activities, since consumer services are needed in Ukraine and because it will take time for 'petty capitalism' to evolve into mainstream legitimate business. Nevertheless, the drift into economic informalism poses challenges for policymakers that cannot be dismissed by the view that eventually the activities will become formalised as normal tax-paying, regulated work. Not only is that unlikely in the near or medium-term future, but international trends suggest that informal economic activities are expanding in most industrialised and service-based economies.

Why worry? There are many reasons for concern, of which there are two directly relevant to our analysis.

- First, protective legislation and regulations scarcely apply to many of those activities, so that those obliged to or choosing to work in them are unlikely to be protected in case of accidents, ill-health or arbitrary dismissal, or if they go bankrupt and become unemployed.
- Second, almost definitionally, the state loses tax and social security contributions, and is thus constrained in the provision of social benefits, especially as the wage share of national income declines as a result of the drift into the informal and black economy.

'Generally speaking, the drop in production has no structural features such as the controlled reduction of unprofitable, wasteful and environmentally threatening industrial activity. . . .

So far, Ukraine has experienced a catastrophic decrease in basic production – consumer goods and, first and foremost, food-stuffs.'[22] — National Institute for Strategic Studies

---

In short, ways will have to be found of legitimising and regulating the informal economy without stifling the creativity, flexibility and economic dynamism that typically characterise much of what takes place outside the mainstream economy. One avenue that should be explored is regeneration of cooperative forms of employment, which traditionally have played an important role in Ukrainian society, particularly in agricultural communities, where attempts to transform collective farms into cooperative farms (koopkhoz) deserve to be encouraged, especially as it has been reported by

---

[22] National Institute for Strategic Studies, 1994, op. cit., p. 25.

the Ministry of Labour that productivity is higher on such farms than average.[23]

Besides the growth of the informal economy, other signs of restructuring have been less encouraging. The reality with food production may be different because of the increased private production, since the statistics tend to include only the state sector. Yet the gloomy assessment of the lack of industrial restructuring seemed widely shared by Ukrainian economists.

Even so, there was some property restructuring of production and distribution, probably more than has been recognised. In 1993–1994, there was some shift from purely state enterprises to leaseholdings (orenda) and to joint-stock companies. According to the Ministry of Statistics, leaseholding enterprises accounted for one fifth (20.5%) of industrial output in late 1993, and in some sectors, notably construction, a majority of enterprises were non-state by that time.[24]

One may wonder whether leaseholdings are fundamentally different from state enterprises, but presumably there is a degree of relative autonomy that gives them more scope for other forms of restructuring. It was also apparent from the ILO's Ukraine Labour Flexibility Survey (ULFS) that many industrial establishments had changed property forms in 1993–1994 and that many more were planning to change in 1994–1995 *(Figures 1.1 and 1.2)*.

The property restructuring involved in such changes may have been limited, yet as we found in visiting factories, changes from being state-run from Kiev to being a closed or open joint stock enterprise seemed to induce behavioural changes in management and trade unions, which are likely to take several years to develop fully. As it was, sales in real terms were more likely to have fallen in state and leaseholding enterprises. So, one should not dismiss the extent or effect of property restructuring (nor, of course, should we exaggerate it).

There was also some size restructuring of enterprises. This is essential, since the large size of enterprises in the Soviet system was a major factor inducing technological stalemate and low and declining productivity. In Ukraine, the ULFS found that all size categories of factory had cut employment, and that the larger establishments had cut more in percentage terms than medium or small-scale establishments with fewer than 250 workers. And about 10% of factories had reduced their size by divesting themselves of some production units over the past two years.

[23] M. Kaskievich, The Modern State of the Cooperative Sector, paper presented to the International Seminar on Economies in Transition and the Employment Problem: The Role of Cooperatives and Associative Enterprises, organised by the ILO and the Ministry of Labour, Kiev, May 11–14, 1993.

[24] Ministry of Statistics, *Statistichniy Byuletin* (Statistical Bulletin), No. 1, January 1994.

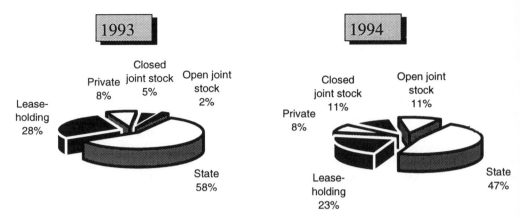

The share of joint stock increased by 15 percentage points from 1993 to 1994

Figure 1.1   *Property Form Distribution of Establishment in Industry, Ukraine, 1993–1994*
Source: ILO-CEET, Ukraine Labour Flexibility Survey, 1994.

The tendency for restructuring by divesting deserves to be encouraged, for in creating a network of enterprises of varying sizes and specialisations a more regulated economic system will emerge, in which the dichotomy of formal-informal could be reduced. That in itself could induce flexibility in the production system and help legitimise much of the informal activity that needs to be brought into the mainstream of the economy.

Finally, there were signs of technological restructuring. By all accounts, one should not become too optimistic about that. However, many managements in the ULFS reported that they had introduced some technological change over the past year, and it seemed that this was linked to property and size restructuring. We measured technological change in terms of product innovation (new, wider range or narrower range of products), capital innovation (new equipment, automatiqn, etc.) and work process innovation (reorganisation of working arrangements).

Although the data may be only proxies for technological change, they suggest that there were changes in all three respects *(Table 1.3.)*. The overall trend to a narrower range of products should not necessarily be interpreted as an adverse trend, since the former Soviet enterprises typically produced an excessive and often unlinked range of products that lowered enterprise efficiency.

In sum, there has been some move towards economic and enterprise restructuring. The signs should not distract attention from the substantial and broadly-based economic decline, and between 1991 and 1994 there

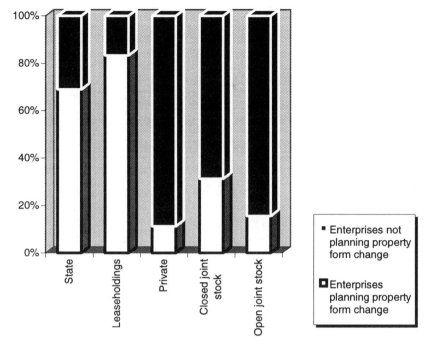

Most of the state enterprises and leaseholdings were apt to change their property form

Figure 1.2 *Establishments Planning to Change Property Form by Current Property Form, Ukraine, 1994*
Source: ILO-CEET, Ukraine Labour Flexibility Survey, 1994.

Table 1.3 *Technological Innovation in Industry by Property Form of Establishment, Ukraine, 1991–1993 (a percentage of establishments having made a change)*

	State	Lease-holding	Private	Closed joint stock	Open joint stock
Change in range of products					
• Increased	21.7	25.6	41.4	28.9	33.3
• Decreased	36.0	33.3	20.7	34.2	36.1
New technology	30.1	34.6	37.9	60.5	52.6
Change in work organisation	28.8	44.9	20.7	52.6	45.9

Source: ILO-CEET, Ukraine Labour Flexibility Survey.

were only tentative efforts to achieve the radical restructuring of the economic system that was needed. All the signs indicate that the economy has not been rigidly adhering to its former structure.

No doubt there has been technological regression, no doubt many enterprise managements have responded to stagflation by cutting back on capital investment and other forms of investment – including training, as we found in the ULFS – while trying to pay themselves reasonable salaries and providing their workforces with acceptable wages. These tendencies have been widely observed, and ultimately derive from a loss of state control over state enterprises. They raise the crucial issue of *corporate governance*. The most important need for effective enterprise and economic restructuring is independent, responsible management, which can only be achieved if managements are answerable for their enterprise's performance, whether to their boards or to their workers. In Ukraine, achieving managerial restructuring is a crucial task for the near future, and so far little progress seems to have been made.

5. The Social Predicament

> 'The currently used minimum monthly subsistence level, which amounts to 1.7 million karbovanets, is not realistic, for if the average wage is 0.7 million karbovanets, we have to realise that the majority of the Ukrainian population is living in poverty.' — Grigoriy Osoviy, Deputy President, Ukrainian Federation of Trade Unions, July 1994.

Although affected by other factors as well, notably the economic collapse, social developments since independence have to be seen in the context of the Chernobyl accident of 1986. Besides those who died, over 120,000 people had to be resettled and nearly three million people who had been directly affected were left with life-shortening illnesses and were made eligible for free medicine, subsidised food and entitlement to early retirement. Since then, no less than one-sixth of the Ukrainian national budget has been allocated to schemes to support those affected, supplemented by modest assistance provided by international agencies and foreign governments.[25]

Socio-demographic trends in Ukraine since independence have been depressing. In 1991–1993, birth rates dropped and mortality increased, not only among middle-aged men. In 1993, there were 180,000 more deaths

[25] S. Browne, *The Transition in Ukraine*, United Nations, mimeo, Kiev, September 1993, p. 9.

than births in the country.[26] Average life expectancy in 1992 was 64 for men and 74 for women, respectively two and one years less than recorded in 1989.[27]

It has been estimated that an extraordinary 402 out of every 1,000 15 year old males could not expect to reach the age of 65, compared to 257 in that age category in France and 178 in Japan. The natural decline in the population has been offset by a net immigration into Ukraine in 1992. Nevertheless, the demographic indicators were stark evidence of the declining social situation.

Table 1.4 *The Resident Population of Ukraine, by Age, 1985–2000*

	1989	1991	1992	1993	1995*	2000*
Total resident population (million)	51.7	51.7	51.8	52.0	51.7	51.0
• Under age 16 (%)	23.0	22.8	22.6	22.4	21.4	19.4
• Working ages** (%)	55.8	55.7	55.7	55.6	55.2	56.4
• Over working age (%)	21.2	21.5	21.7	22.0	23.4	24.2

*Estimate.
**Aged 16–54 for women, 16–59 for men.

Source: Ministry of Statistics, *Naselenia Ukraini, 1992 rik. Demographichniy Shchorichnik (The Population of Ukraine, 1992, Demographic Yearbook)*, Kiev, Technika, 1993; for the forecasts for 1995 and 2000, see V. Yatsenko, *Demographichni perspektivi Ukraini (Demographic Perspectives in Ukraine)*, in Commission of the Supreme Council of Ukraine, *Demographichna situatsya v Ukraini (Demographic Situation in Ukraine)*, Kiev, 1993.

By international standards, Ukraine has a relatively high dependency rate, due primarily to the low average age of pensionable retirement – age 60 for men, 55 for women – and a relatively low labour force participation rate among those aged under 20. Although pensions have been low, and have been so low that a large proportion of those receiving pensions have continued to work, they have represented a growing financial burden on the state. Despite adjustments to compensate for inflation, the real value of pensions has fallen drastically since 1991, as discussed in Chapter 7.

As far as the effectiveness of the former system of social protection in the period of reform is concerned, the general impression is that there has been an enormous increase in the rate of poverty. Estimates vary, but some have claimed that by 1993 over three-quarters of the population had incomes below the subsistence level. Perhaps indicative of the declining

[26] *Intelnews*, Kiev, June 11, 1994, p. 2.
[27] E. Libanova, Ukraine's Demographic-related Economic Problems, draft paper for UN Human Development Indicators Project, Kiev, March 1994, p. 1.

living standards of the majority of the population, a survey in late 1992 found that availability of basic food had become the most important concern of people, whereas previously availability of housing had been the main concern.[28] Others have also highlighted the growing average food share of total consumption expenditure, from 39% of the total in 1989 to 45.6% in 1992.[29] This is often taken as a proxy index of impoverishment.

At the end of 1993, following Parliamentary decisions in November, the official poverty level of income per person was set at 197,000 karbovanets per month, the official minimum wage was raised to 60,000 karbovanets per month and the minimum pension was raised to 120,000 karbovanets per month. At the same time, according to the main trade unions, the actual poverty line was 340,000 karbovanets in Kiev and 293,000 karbovanets for the country overall. The unions also estimated, on the basis of surveys (of unknown methodology) that for a minimum living standard for an average household an income of 1,117,000 karbovanets per month was required, and on that measure about 85% of the population were in poverty. By contrast, in 1990 it was estimated that 77.7% of the population had per capita incomes within the range of one to three times the minimum consumption budget (MCB). Even allowing for possible methodological and measurement changes, these figures highlight a remarkable transformation and process of impoverishment.

The figures should not be interpreted too literally or rigorously. Besides indicating the growth in poverty, they highlight the rudimentary nature of official and unofficial statistics on poverty in the country.[30] In a hyperinflationary situation, with a new currency that has never had time to acquire a stable or meaningful value, the numbers that emerge are likely to err rather considerably. There is also a hidden component in the productive and consumption system, due to the own-account production on the land and in the 'informal economy'. Critics of the official data have been quick to point out that there is little evidence of mass starvation or acute malnutrition, which one would anticipate if the above poverty statistics were accurate reflections of reality. Nevertheless, one should certainly not

---

[28] Institute of Sociology, Academy of Science, Socioeconomic and Political Situation in Ukraine's Regions, Kiev, mimeo, 1994, p. 4.

[29] UNICEF, *Public Policy and Social Conditions: Central and Eastern Europe in Transition*, Florence, November 1993, p. 10. The authors noted that these figures probably understate the averages, because the surveys on which they are based tended to omit more of the poorest, who spend the highest share of their income on food.

[30] One prominent person in Ukraine described the country as belonging to what should be described as the LICs (least informed countries), in that due to past practices there is relatively little reliable data on issues of importance. The Ministry of Statistics and others have been making important efforts to rectify that situation, and deserve further support.

be complacent, since the demographic as well as the income statistics tell a chilling story.[31]

Another indicator of the growing difficulty being faced by those on incomes that were relatively fixed or low is that, according to the only available data, the cost of living for the average citizen rose drastically during 1993. Based on a very basic basket of consumer goods and services, the average cost of living rose from 54,701 karbovanets in July 1993 to 856,492 karbovanets in December 1993.[32]

At independence, as far as social protection is concerned, Ukraine had a very extensive set of social policies, centrally regulated and largely based on provision through enterprises of employment. For 1992, according to some estimates, social protection policies accounted for about 44% of GDP, and more than half the population received cash benefits of some kind. The social policy's share of GNP, which continued to rise in 1993, had risen sharply from the level of the previous few years, largely because social policies had represented a relatively fixed set of commitments at a time of rapidly falling national income.[33]

Up to 1994, the social protection system has continued to be what could be described as essentially universalistic, in that it has provided a wide range of benefits as basic social rights and has relied relatively little on means-testing, or social assistance-type targeting of benefits. This orientation has been criticised by the IMF and World Bank, among others.[34] Feasible and desirable reorientations of social protection policies are considered in Chapter 7.

Finally, in considering the scope for reform of social protection policy, three characteristics should be kept in mind:

- First, it is important to appreciate the role of consumer subsidies as a means of providing social protection in the old system, and to recognise that in the early period there has been a relative shift from producer to consumer subsidies as the Government has tried to cut subsidies in general.
- Second, formally at least, the minimum wage has continued to be an anchor of the wage system and of the social protection system, as

---

[31] One additional set of figures to prompt serious concern relate to fertility. In 1993, the live fertility rate was under 2, and has fallen in recent years, whereas there are about 50% more abortions than live births.

[32] M. Zienchuk, 1994, op. cit., p. 44.

[33] The World Bank estimated that social policies took about 25% of GNP in 1990 and 'over 40%' in 1992. *Ukraine: The Social Sectors during Transition*, The World Bank, Washington D.C., 1993, p. 1. ILO-CEET investigations suggest that the 1992 figure was somewhat lower. UNICEF gives a figure of 18.2% as the 'public social expenditure as percent of GDP' for 1992. UNICEF, 1993, op. cit., Table D3, p. 76.

[34] See, for example, *Intelnews*, Vol. IV, No. 56, February 26, 1994, p. 3. There were some reports that in 1992–93 the number of people entitled to social benefits fell by huge numbers.

discussed in later chapters. Yet Ukraine in 1994 had the dubious honour of having the lowest statutory minimum wage in the world, as expressed in international currency terms (less than US$ 1.4 per month in mid-1994) and in relation to the estimated subsistence income, or the official minimum consumption budget, which as of mid-1994 was about $17.5 per month. Put more mundanely, in 1994 the minimum monthly wage was just sufficient to enable someone to purchase a loaf of bread each day of the month.

• Third, in composing a picture of the system of social protection, it is important to recognise the specific role of local government, which has been a major source of subsidies for basic consumer goods, and thus for regional variations in the extent of state assistance. Subsidies of this sort are blunt instruments of social policy, since by reducing the scope for freedom of choice they impose a welfare loss compared with direct income transfers designed to prevent poverty. The substantial role of local government is unlikely to subside in the wake of the 1994 elections, and any proposed reforms should take that into account rather than presume that all policy will be determined in Kiev.

6. The Emerging Labour Market

The structure of the employed labour force at the beginning of the reform process was heavily skewed to heavy industry, notably the military-industrial complex, which perhaps accounted for 40% of the labour force in industry, half directly, half indirectly, and to agriculture, which accounted for nearly a quarter of the labour force.

The outstanding feature of the labour market at independence was the absence of recognised unemployment. This reflected the legacy of many decades of full employment, in the sense that unemployment had been banned as a parasitic activity in the command economy until the 1991 *Employment Act*, passed when the country was part of the Soviet Union. This Law legitimised unemployment for the first time.

The Employment Act of 1991 was a radical break with the previous labour regime, and although it had some contradictions and limitations, it was undoubtedly a major initiative to create a more open labour market.[35] Besides legitimising and conceptualising unemployment, it did a number of other things, including banning forced labour (article 1, para 2), allowing for freedom of choice on type of work (article 4, para 1), providing for

---

[35] For a discussion of the rationale and limitations, see G. Standing (ed.), *In Search of Flexibility: The New Soviet Labour Market*, Geneva, 1991. The Ukraine Act was modelled on the Act of the USSR.

financial and labour market assistance to socially vulnerable groups, such as the disabled, and introducing unemployment benefits. Labour market policy was to be financed from the Employment Fund, founded in June 1991, and in turn that was to be financed by a 3% tax on enterprise wage funds, as well as by small contributions from the state and local budgets and from revenue received from the state Employment Service.

It was expected that in the wake of the early stages of reform, with the cut in consumer and producer subsidies, as well as the intended conversion of military industrial enterprises and the intended stabilisation policy, considerable open unemployment would emerge. Accordingly, the Council of Ministers in January 1991 created the State Employment Service, under the Ministry of Labour, and made it responsible for dealing with the registration of the unemployed and of job vacancies and practical measures to assist the unemployed to find jobs.

Since 1991, a network of employment exchanges has been built up, totalling 668 as of early 1994, consisting of a national centre in Kiev, one Republican office in Crimea, 24 oblast offices, one office for Kiev City and one for Sevastopol City, overseeing 523 district offices, coupled with 125 city offices. Those offices have been responsible for placing job-seekers in jobs, for paying unemployment benefits and for sending unemployed job-seekers for training or to so-called public works, which have scarcely existed. The capacities and experience of the Employment Service will be considered in Chapter 3.

For various reasons, in 1991–1993 registered unemployment did not rise to anything like the levels anticipated by policymakers. At the end of 1991, there were about 7,000 registered unemployed; a year later the figure was 70,500, although a further 70,000 were registered job-seekers without being counted as unemployed for benefit entitlement purposes. During 1993 and into 1994, as Chapter 2 shows, the numbers remained low, rising to a little over 100,000 by the middle of 1994. Undoubtedly, those figures did not reflect anything like the real numbers of unemployed. According to trade union leaders in Kiev, by July 1994 there were 400,000 unemployed in Kiev alone, although at the time there were only about 3,000 registered unemployed.[36] One should be sceptical about the higher figure, as well as the lower, yet the claim itself reflected the sense of alarm about the state of the labour market.

Among the reasons for doubting the official unemployment figures is that various estimates have suggested that employment has fallen quite sharply, and even if one made optimistic assumptions about unrecorded private sector employment growth, the process of employment restructuring itself

---

[36] *Intelnews*, July 8, 1994, p. 5.

would imply a much higher level of unemployment. One factor in the underrecording of unemployment is that few of those losing jobs have been going to the Employment Service. The Ministry of Statistics estimated that in 1993 only a minority of workers released from work went to employment offices, and not all of those would have registered. Many of those who became unemployed in the period would not have been released, and there are reasons for believing that those becoming unemployed by other routes would have had an even lower propensity to register and be counted as unemployed under the 1991 Act.

Another factor discouraging registration, as discussed in Chapter 2, has been the nature of the unemployment benefit system. Securing entitlement to benefits seems difficult, and for those who succeed, the level of unemployment benefits typically has been meagre, averaging 198,000 karbovanets, or the equivalent of about US$ 5, per month in mid-1994.

More significantly, all observers agree that there has been massive surplus labour, or hidden unemployment, within enterprises, whether formally at work or on administrative leave, without pay or with only partial pay. According to the Ministry of Labour, its own investigations in 1993 led them to conclude that between 18% and 25% of workers in enterprises were really in hidden unemployment.[37] There is a strong prospect that, unless there are fundamental labour market and managerial policy reforms, there will continue to be a widespread phenomenon of 'growthless jobs', as Stephen Browne, the United Nations' Resident Representative in Kiev has described the situation in which an increasing number of people are nominally employed yet merely occupying their time unproductively. The issues of rising open and hidden unemployment and the process of employment restructuring are considered in Chapter 2, and in an accompanying analysis of the Ukraine Labour Flexibility Survey. The existing labour market and employment policies intended to deal with these challenges are assessed in Chapter 3.

Similarly, wage policy in Ukraine should be regarded as a priority area for reform. The system has remained essentially similar to that inherited from the 1980s, that is, based on the wage tariff system, with differentials being built as multiples of the statutory minimum wage. In Ukraine, as in all parts of the former Soviet system, money wages were low and were only a modest part of total production costs, being under 21% in industry in 1991, as discussed in Chapter 4. In principle, real wages will have to rise and be linked more closely to productivity and economic performance. The wage system should involve a higher share of money wages to non-cash benefits and services.

[37] Interviews with ILO-CEET, October 1993.

As of April 1994, the average monthly wage in Ukraine was about 880,000 karbovanets, or about US$ 19 at the prevailing exchange rate. As discussed in Chapter 4 and elsewhere, that is dysfunctionally low and out of step with measures of subsistence income. This has been recognised in the course of the protracted negotiations on the General Tariff Agreement. The tariff rate and related issues will continue to be sources of concern. Yet it is encouraging that, slowly and hesitantly, a negotiated incomes policy has been taking shape, through negotiations between the Government and the trade unions. Representatives of independent employers will have to be incorporated into this process, and those representatives will have to take up an independent position. However, it should be regarded as a positive sign that the 1993 General Tariff Agreement was settled and extended in mid-1994, and that it was agreed that negotiations would take place in October 1994 on the 1994 Agreement.

As employment restructuring and job shedding have started, so wage differentials and income inequality have become much greater than was the case in the 1980s. The latter was brought out in a report by UNICEF in 1993.[38] As discussed in Chapter 4, this set of issues represents an important challenge for labour market and social policy in the next few years, since while income incentives and wage differentiation are necessary for an efficient labour market, the risk of growing socio-economic fragmentation should be averted if possible.

Labour legislation has been evolving slowly, and probably all observers would agree that there is a long way to go to establish a sound basis for an efficient and equitably regulated labour market. Sorting out and implementing labour legislation should be regarded as having high priority in the new Government. This should involve a thorough revision of the Labour Code, and formulation of stronger occupational health and safety regulations. The latter is a considerable source of concern, most particularly in the coal mines. There are credible reports that, stimulated by low real wages and an outmoded piece-rate system, there has been a dangerous disregard of safety regulations in mining areas.[39] In the labour market sphere, there can surely be no higher priority in Ukraine than reform of occupational health and safety procedures and practices.

So far, industrial relations have been developing at a slow pace. In 1994, as discussed in Chapters 5 and 6, the trade unions were still in the process of adapting to changed circumstances, without a clear basis of independent representation of workers. Although there have been a growing number of trade unions, many seem too small to be viable as effective instruments of

[38] UNICEF, 1993, op. cit., pp. 34–5.
[39] J. MacNeil, Waiting for Change: Notes from the Underground, *Intelnews*, June 26, 1994, pp. 4–6.

worker representation. Meanwhile, employers had yet to establish them-selves as a single or united body, and thus the fledgling tripartite council, the National Council for Social Partnership, had yet to establish an autonomous existence or play a needed role in formulating, legitimising and implementing social and labour policy.

7. Concluding Points

> 'We have had so many Programmes already;
>
> I don't even want to talk about mine. Now is the time to do it.' — President Leonid Kuchma, July 17, 1994.

Ukraine has moved from the difficulties of achieving independence through an extraordinary period of stagflation to what seemed to be a period in which substantive reforms could be introduced more effectively and more willingly. Despite the worst forebodings, Ukraine has come through its ini-tial crisis period democratically and intact. As the international community has turned its attention to the country more constructively and with more resources, the time has surely come to establish more effective institutional mechanisms for labour market and employment restructuring, for respond-ing more meaningfully to mass unemployment that will surely come out into the open, for establishing more efficient and equitable social protec-tion systems, and for creating a properly regulated yet flexible labour mar-ket in which there is respect for labour law and a spirit of constructive compromise in negotiations on production and work organisation between genuinely independent employers and workers.

The following chapters review the labour market developments since independence, the limited evolution of labour market policy, the need for wage reform, the changing pattern of industrial relations, including the changing roles of the trade unions and employer organisations, and the emergence of the basic ingredients of a modern, integrated social protec-tion system. In all those spheres of social and labour policy, 1995 will pre-sent a massive opportunity to extend and implement substantial reforms.

2

Labour Market Developments in Ukraine

1. Introduction

There is a basic paradox in the Ukrainian labour market. In spite of huge declines in output and massive inflation, there has been little overt evidence of the mass unemployment that would be a normal outcome of such a configuration of economic misery indicators.

We believe that the answer to this paradox is largely statistical and the result of administrative procedures, although it is also partly political and partly the result of the inertia that has gripped Ukraine since its formal independence. The paradox can be seen in another way. The basic labour market issue is whether the former illusion of full employment, the pervasive pattern of labour market distortions and the restricted forms of labour mobility that characterised the Ukrainian labour market in the 1980s have changed in the wake of the massive economic decline and the structural pressures exerted on the whole population.

As this Chapter will suggest, considerable change has occurred. Yet there can be no doubt that in the next decade a formidable process of labour market restructuring will be required if Ukraine is to be merged satisfactorily into the mainstream of European society. The following analysis will attempt to identify the main changes needed, and will try to give a coherent response to the paradox that is at least consistent with the inadequate data currently available.

2. Pre-Independence Labour Market Distortions

The Ukrainian labour market has many features common to other command economies of central and southern Europe, but retains characteristics typical only of former Soviet republics. Historically, an embryonic labour market only emerged in the late 1950s, after the introduction of passports for farmers (who had previously not been allowed to leave villages without permission) and abolition of the prohibition on workers and employees to quit their jobs. Yet the directive character of the labour market persisted until the late 1980s.

2.1. Labour Force Participation Rate

Full employment was an obligation both for the state administration and the population. As a result, many investments were devoted to the creation of jobs in selected regions where there was perceived to be a labour surplus, regardless of the economic value of the jobs being created.

As for income, apart from social benefits for people with disabilities, work-related earnings were considered the only legal source of income for the working-age population once they had completed their schooling and vocational training. Wage policy, educational policy and social policy were set to preserve a stable labour force in which manual labour was given a relatively high status as epitomising productive labour.

As a result of this system, in the 1980s there was a combination of a very high labour force participation rate and unsatisfied demand for labour.[1] Officially, the participation rate was 83.7% for women aged 15 to 55 and 86.3% for men aged 15 to 59 in 1989, and for the whole population it was 50.4%.[2] As a matter of routine, pensioners and students were encouraged to accept paid jobs.

Since the retirement age was low – 60 years for men and 55 years for women – and since the very low old-age pensions meant sharp cuts in incomes in comparison with previous earnings, it became the social norm to continue to work for at least five more years. The state supported their work by allowing – and even presuming – the coexistence of pensions and earnings, without lowering the pension. In the 1980s, the share of pensioners in the employed labour force was between 6% and 7%.

Meanwhile, the vast majority of women were in employment. This reflected their rising level of education, the opportunity for prolonged maternity leave, availability of child care facilities and the low level of wages of men. Women also worked longer after retirement age. That is probably why the share of women in the labour force exceeded that of men

---

[1] The high adult participation rate is overestimated, since pensioners are included in the figures for employment and are excluded in the age-specific population figures, i.e., included in the numerator and excluded in the denominator. With the official data, it is not possible to correct this distortion. Many publications have ignored the effect in presenting the statistics.

[2] These figures were estimated by V. Steshenko, from the Institute of Economics of the Ukrainian Academy of Sciences, using unpublished material from the 1989 Census.

[3] Ministry of Statistics, *Statistical Yearbook of Ukraine, 1990*, Kiev, 1991. This was the only published figure for women's share of employment and refers to their share of workers and employees in the state sector. According to the 1989 Population Census, women accounted for 49.2% of the total labour force, including unpaid family workers.

in the early 1970s, remaining stable at about 52% of total employment after 1975.[3] Although indication of their integration into employment, this latter pattern is not quite accurate, since the way of measuring inflated the participation rate, because post-retirement-age women and men in employment were included as employed in the numerator, whereas the denominator was only the working-age population. Those on maternity or parental leave were also included as economically active. Their number was considerable because the leave was usually for two years (and was subsequently prolonged to three). Despite these caveats, the integration of women into the labour force was extensive.

In terms of the age pattern of labour supply, youth participation in the labour force was limited, although students were encouraged to take paid jobs while studying. The number of years spent in schooling and vocational training was prolonged. Compulsory school attendance was 10 or 11 years, from age 7, and in the 1980s only about a third of teenagers went directly to paid employment after school, and many of those studied at evening schools or extra-murally, while the remainder went on to higher secondary vocational or general schools and to university. As a result, in 1989 only 3.7% of the labour force was below 20 years of age.[4]

2.2. Level of Education

The level of education was high by international standards. According to the population census of 1989, 11.9% of the adult population had university education including incomplete, 49.1% had upper secondary schooling, 18.4% lower or incomplete secondary schooling and only 13.8% primary school.

There was a remarkable gender difference in the level of education. A much larger share of women had only primary and secondary education. On the secondary level, they tended to have more vocational training *(Table 2.1)*.

Among the working population, the average level of schooling was higher than for the overall population, primarily due to the fact that younger cohorts were better educated than those in retirement *(Figure 2.1)*. Although analysts may have reservations about the quality of education in certain spheres, it seems widely agreed that both the average level of education and training in natural sciences and technical skills were good by international standards, even by comparison with industrialised countries.

---

[4] Ministry of Statistics, *Demographic Yearbook of Ukraine, 1992*, Kiev, 1993.

Table 2.1 *Population over 15 by Education and Gender, Ukraine, 1989 (%)*

Level of education	Men	Women	Total
University (including incomplete)	12.9	11.3	11.9
Secondary vocational	16.5	19.2	18.0
Secondary general	36.5	26.8	31.1
Lower or incomplete secondary	19.7	17.3	18.4
Basic and lower education	14.4	25.4	20.6

Source: Ministry of Statistics, *Demographic Yearbook of Ukraine*, Kiev, 1993.

2.3. Mobility of Labour

In the 1970s and 1980s, occupational and territorial mobility of labour was low. Territorial mobility was impeded by administrative barriers, notably by the requirement that a person wishing to move to another district needed a permit from the authorities in that district (so-called propiska), which was partially dependent on the availability of accommodation. In practice, because of the housing shortage, mobility was controlled by state interests and investment priorities rather than by personal wishes.

Data on internal migration are scarce. According to the available literature, for some decades the main migration flow was from villages to towns, but in the 1980s this internal movement slowed.[5] The evacuation of 100,000 people from the contaminated 30 km circle around Chernobyl after the nuclear catastrophe was exceptional, and concealed the rigid distribution of the population.

Emigration was also administratively restricted, since only a limited number of citizens was given passports and it was extremely difficult to obtain permission to leave the country legally (practically the only way to do so being by marriage) or to obtain a visa to emigrate outside the Soviet Union. Between 1979 and 1988, the average net annual emigration was 16,000 people. Since 1989, emigration has increased substantially, amounting to almost 300,000 people in 1992.

Overall, mobility of labour was rather high but declined during the 1980s. In 1980, 16.3% of all workers left their enterprise, including those dismissed due to misconduct, whereas in 1985 it was 12.4% and in 1990 11.9%.[6] However, this mobility mainly took the form of a shift from one

[5] E. Libanova, *Ukrainskiy rinok truda: problemy i perspektivy* (*The Ukrainian Labour Market: Problems and Perspectives*), International Institute of Market Relations and Entrepreneurship, Kiev, 1993.

[6] Ministry of Statistics, *Pracya v narodnomu gospodarstvi Ukraini* (*Labour in the Ukrainian National Economy*), Kiev, 1991.

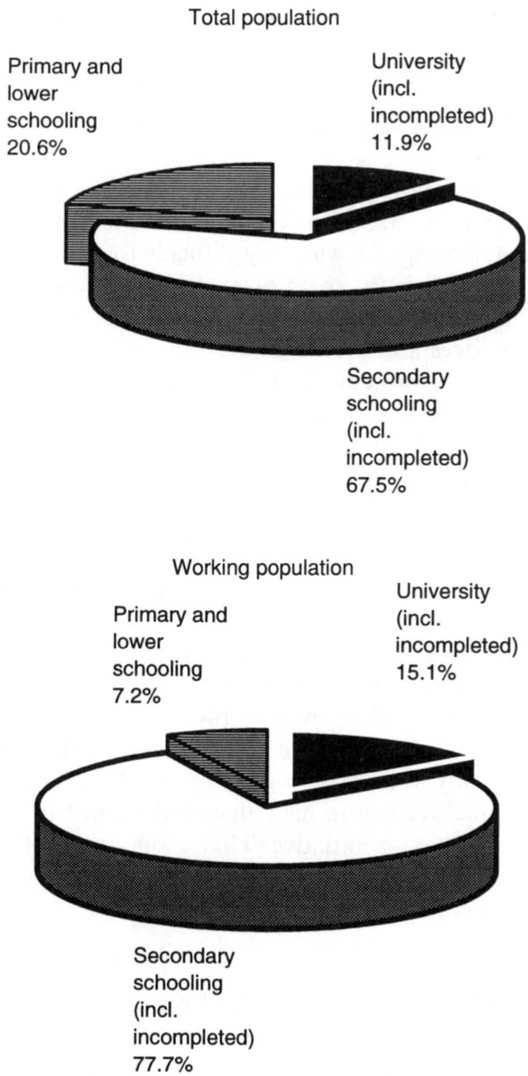

Total population

Primary and
lower
schooling
20.6%

University
(incl.
incompleted)
11.9%

Secondary
schooling
(incl.
incompleted)
67.5%

Working population

Primary and
lower
schooling
7.2%

University
(incl.
incompleted)
15.1%

Secondary
schooling
(incl.
incompleted)
77.7%

Figure 2.1 *Education of Total Population over 15 and Working Population,
Ukraine, 1989*

Source: Ministry of Statistics, *Demographic Yearbook of Ukraine*, Kiev 1993.

enterprise to another within the same occupation and region, while both occupational and territorial mobility were very low.

There seem to have been three reasons for the low mobility.

• Schooling and vocational training were so specialised that it was difficult to change occupation.
• To obtain a job in another region was tied to gaining a residence permit dependent among others, on available accommodation there. Due to a severe housing shortage, it was very difficult to obtain a flat, especially in big cities, which was the main obstacle for territorial mobility.
• The only promising way of improving wages was by changing a job. As many social services and privileges were provided by the enterprise and their quality varied from one enterprise to another, this was another reason why workers wanted to change a job. This concerned more blue-collar workers, whereas possibilities for white-collar workers were more restricted. However, job changes involving a change of enterprise were considered economically costly, both for the enterprise and for the national economy, and were thus condemned by the authorities.

In short, long-term or life-long employment with one enterprise or institution was supported as a social norm. When upgrading was dependent more on political decisions than on competence, such life-long attachment to one enterprise, and in most cases to one type of work, discouraged individual effort to achieve higher levels of productivity.

Usually, workers were not given the chance to take responsibility for their careers or to adjust to changing labour market conditions, while psychological barriers also seem to have operated against the development of personal responsibility and initiative. That is one reason for believing that labour market restructuring in Ukraine will be more difficult and last longer than elsewhere in central and eastern Europe.

3. Pre-Independence Employment Structure

The evolution of the labour force before independence was dictated in part by the Ukrainian resource base and in part by the Soviet industrialisation strategy and the role given to Ukraine in the USSR's division of production. By 1990, the structure of employment had evolved in a different way than in market based economies. It is worth reflecting on that structure to highlight the type and extent of employment restructuring required in the 1990s.

With its highly fertile soil, Ukraine was traditionally a large exporter of agricultural products, first to other European countries, and then within the USSR, even if the collectivisation of family farms in the 1930s destroyed much of its agricultural power. At the beginning of the 1960s, almost half the labour force was still in agriculture. That share of total employment fell and by 1989 it accounted for 21%. However, even this is high by international standards, especially when many people with their main jobs in other sectors also produced agricultural products for their needs as their second, informal activity.[7] Thus, actual employment in agriculture has long been much higher than implied by national statistics. A basic problem was that labour productivity in agriculture was very low and that by the 1980s, Ukraine had lost much of its exporting capacity through years of low investment and lack of technological advance.

The share of industry and construction in total employment was already almost 30% in 1960 and increased to 40.1% in 1990, with 30.7% in industry and 9.4% in construction. In 1990, 43.1% of the industrial labour force worked in machine-building and electrotechnics, and no less than 39% of the industrial workforce was employed in the military industry.[8] Over the previous three decades, an increasing share of Ukraine's labour force had been concentrated in heavy industry. By 1990, only 10.6% of industrial workers were in light industry. In contrast, the share in food processing had risen slightly, reaching 9.6% in 1990.

By then, heavy industry and engineering accounted for 71% of total industrial employment. During the 1970s and 1980s, Ukraine had become the main source of iron ore for Russian industry and for the industry of other parts of COMECON, so that once that system was disrupted, Ukraine's industrial base and employment structure were bound to be severely affected.

Meanwhile, the tertiary sector increased its share of employment, in effect receiving labour from agriculture. In 1960, its share of total employment was 24.4%, and in 1990, 40.2%. The main increase was in social services – education, culture, health and social care and research. Their employment share almost doubled, from 9.5% in 1960 to 17.7% in 1990. For other services, the relative change did not exceed two percentage points over those thirty years. By international standards, the share of trade, public catering, household services and banking and insurance remained remarkably small, leaving no doubt about the character and priorities of the Ukrainian

[7] The number of private plots possessed by urban residents (35.4 million people) was 6.8 million in 1993. This was the outcome of the policy in the 1970s and 1980s of distributing such plots, the size of which were about 600 square metres on average. In effect, every second family was growing fruit, vegetables and potatoes for its own consumption, and in many cases was also supplying relatives. See also V. Yatsenko, Employment Policy in Ukraine in 1991–1994, paper presented at ILO conference on Employment Policy and Programmes, Budapest, June 2–3, 1994.

[8] The Economist Intelligence Unit, *Ukraine, Belarus, Moldova: Country Profiles*, London, 1994.

economy. Financial flows played a mere accounting role without any impact on the domestic economy, and consumer services outside enterprises were almost considered an anachronism. In effect, it was not the overall share of services in total employment that was the distortion in international terms, but the distribution within services, with the share in education and health being well above what it was in industrialised market economies.

Another factor that gave the impression that services were under-represented in the official statistics was that, as many services were provided within and by enterprises, those working in service functions there were included under the main industrial activity of the enterprise. This also concerned many production services, such as repair and maintenance of machines and equipment, computer operations and research, many of which are externalised in other countries where vertical and horizontal integration within giant enterprises is less common. In spite of this bias, aggregate employment in services probably remained low, simply because many kinds of service did not exist or were rudimentary, most notably financial and marketing services.

Beside the industrial pattern of employment, a pervasive form of labour market distortion was the pattern of labour utilisation throughout the economy in the pre-independence era. Although no research seems to have been done on the subject, labour hoarding was almost certainly very widespread in Ukraine. According to official statistics, loss of working hours due to absenteeism was less than one per cent. However, if workers were present at their workplaces and utilised only part of their working hours that was not considered as lost time.

Labour hoarding took six forms:

- Loss of working hours due to material and energy shortages.
- Loss of working time due to low work discipline.
- Deliberate overmanning, to ensure a labour reserve in case of any increase in production plan targets by the centre.
- Overmanning to cover for low labour intensity and the poor level of work organisation.
- Excess labour due to the production of unneeded goods and services.
- Social employment, particularly of elderly workers and workers with disabilities, kept in employment because of low pensions.

In other command economies, labour hoarding or surplus was estimated to have been about 15% of total employment, although in some estimations the figure was higher.[9] In Ukraine, there is anecdotal evidence that it was

[9] See, for instance, M. Rutkowski, *Labour Hoarding and Future Open Unemployment in Eastern Europe: The Case of Polish industry*, London School of Economics, Centre for Economic Performance, Discussion Paper No. 6, London, July 1990.

higher. Most observers claim that labour hoarding was particularly high in agriculture, industry and construction, and, it has been suggested that it extended to education and the health services. Thus, including students in evening and extra-mural courses, there were 12.8 students per teacher in primary and secondary schools and 4.8 students per teacher in universities. Similarly, the number of physicians and para-medical staff per thousand population was high by international standards.[10] These statistics do not necessarily indicate overmanning, yet they do raise questions about the desirable or optimal levels.[11]

For employment restructuring, it is useful to know the age structure in individual economic sectors. According to the population census of 1989, in information and computer services more than one third of all workers were below 30 years of age and only 10% above 50. Relatively young age structures were also found in educational and cultural services, construction, trade and industry. By contrast, agriculture and forestry, transport, health and social care, and research retained older age structures, and in the case of agriculture 29% of workers were older than fifty.

As for the employment structure by property form of enterprise, in 1990, 78.3% of employment was in state-owned enterprises or institutions, 18.6% in cooperatives, of which 13.4% in agricultural cooperatives, 2.8% in enterprises owned by consumer cooperatives and 2.4% in new production cooperatives in 1990. The so-called individual sector (i.e., family farms, working in helping family members on small private plots and self-employment) accounted for only 3%. Although small-scale private business was finally legalised in the late 1980s, the share of the private sector in total employment was still negligible in 1990, although even there was a secondary informal economy, in which workers compensated for low wages by small-scale, own account activities.

In sum, the picture of the Ukrainian labour market, before the break-up of the Soviet Union and the attempted introduction of reforms designed to restructure the economy and pattern of employment, had the following characteristics:

• Relatively high shares of employment in agriculture and manufacturing by international standards.
• Low share of employment in services, although not as low as some have suggested.
• Pervasive distortions due to labour hoarding.
• Concentration of employment in state-owned enterprises.

[10] The World Bank, *Ukraine: Employment, Social Protection and Social Spending in the Transition to a Market Economy*, Washington D.C., November 1992.
[11] Some external analysts have claimed that the ratio of teachers to students in Ukraine should be cut to a level.

Above all, there was very little change in the employment structure during the 1970s and 1980s, which created a huge backlog of essential restructuring, much of which has yet to be addressed.

4. Employment Restructuring

4.1. Labour Force and Employment

With the accelerating decline in production after 1990, the level and structure of employment could have been expected to show corresponding changes, albeit with a lag.[12] In fact, according to the official data, there was a decline in employment of 1.5 million people, i.e. 5.8%, between 1990 and 1993 *(Table 2.2)*. Although the decline was much less than what might have been expected on the basis of the catastrophic decline in economic output, it was substantial.

The demographic shift was puzzling. While the working age population was almost constant, the number of pensioners in employment increased by 138,300. So, the employment fall hit predominantly working-age employees. The number of high school and university students also declined in this period.[13]

Table 2.2 *Able-Bodied Working-Age Population, Labour Resources and Labour Force in Ukraine, 1985–1992 (thousand)*

Year	Working-age population	Labour force	Employment
1985	27,884	29,542	25,600
1990	28,023	29,688	25,419
1992	27,989	29,524	24,505
1993	28,015	29,743	23,945

Source: Ministry of Statistics, *Demographic Yearbook of Ukraine, 1992*, Kiev, 1993; Libanova, 1993, op. cit.; for 1993 not yet published materials of the Ministry of Statistics.

[12] Elsewhere, we have postulated a three phase process of employment decline, beginning with a period of high labour turnover without much replacement, followed by a drying up of vacancies and a growth of individual redundancies and then by a phase of mass redundancies and bankruptcies.

[13] Between 1990 and 1993, the number of students in vocational training fell by 14,000, in technical secondary schools by 76,300 and in universities by over 50,000, according to the Ministry of Statistics, *Statistical Yearbook of Ukraine*, Kiev 1993 and not yet published statistics for 1993.

These facts imply that, since 1990, a growing proportion of working age people

- have been unemployed,
- have left the labour market,
- have been operating in the informal economy,
- have been working abroad, or
- have been passively unemployed, discouraged from looking for work by the poor prospects of finding any.

In 1994, it was unclear which of these tendencies had been the most substantial, although there was evidence that all had grown, as we will see.

4.2. Employment in Different Sectors

Employment restructuring began to accelerate after 1991, with some shift from industry and construction towards services, while the share of agriculture has been constant or may have increased slightly *(Table 2.3)*. By 1993, services were the largest source of jobs *(Figure 2.2)*.

However, in 1991–1993, apart from the employment cuts in construction and industry, the changes in relative shares were modest and primarily the result of different rates of employment decline, reflecting the fact that Ukraine had prevaricated on major restructuring. Economic and property restructuring were insufficient to have much impact on employment restructuring, so that the shifts in the industrial structure primarily reflected the economic demand and supply shocks in 1991–1993.

By comparison with central European countries undergoing restructuring, Ukraine had a roughly similar structure of employment, although it seems to have a relatively small proportion in trade and catering services

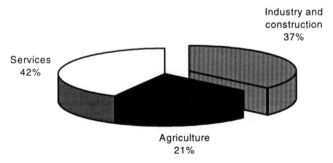

Figure 2.2 *Services, Agriculture, Industry and Construction as a Percentage of Total Employment, Ukraine, 1993*

Source: Not yet published figures of the Ministry of Statistics.

Table 2.3 *Employment Structure by Sector, Ukraine, 1985–1993*

Branch	1985	1990	1992	1993	1992	
Employment in the national economy (million)	25.6	25.4	24.5	23.9	Hungary	Poland
National economy (%)	100	100	100	100	100	100
Agriculture	20.9	19.5	20.5	20.8	10.0	27.6
Mining, manufacturing, gas, electricity and water supply	31.4	30.8	30.9	30.0	32.0	26.0
Construction	7.7	9.5	8.0	7.6	4.7	7.1
Transport and communications	8.3	7.0	6.8	6.9	8.8	6.5
Trade and public catering	7.7	7.5	7.3	7.3	11.0[a]	11.2
Housing and household services	3.6	3.9	3.7	3.6	3.4[b]	–
Health and social care, sport	5.3	5.9	6.3	6.5	8.4[c]	12.7[f]
Education, culture, arts, science and research	11.2	11.8	11.9	11.7	9.5[d]	–
Banking and insurance	0.5	0.5	0.6	0.7	1.8	2.6
State administration, political and social organisations	1.7	1.9	2.3	2.7	7.7[e]	1.5[g]
Other branches	1.7	1.7	1.7	2.2	2.7	4.8
Non-specified activities	0.0	0.0	0.5	0.5	–	–

[a] Including repair and maintenance of motor vehicles, personal and household goods.
[b] Real estate, renting and business activities.
[c] Health and social care.
[d] Education.
[e] Public administration, defence, compulsory social security.
[f] Health and social care and education.
[g] Public administration.
Hungary: all figures concern employment in enterprises with over 20 employees, excluding employees in military service.
Poland: the civilian labour force.

Source: Ministry of Statistics, *Statistical Yearbook of Ukraine*, 1992; *Statistical Yearbook of Hungary*, 1993; *Employment Observatory, Central and Eastern Europe*, No. 5, December 1993.

and in banking and insurance, whereas it has had a relatively large proportion in education, culture and scientific research.

However it is important to mention that in Ukraine many services were and still are provided by agricultural farms and industrial enterprises, and also farms are engaged with industrial production and construction. All those non-agricultural or non-industrial activities are not separated in production and labour statistics and the share of industry and especially agriculture in employment and production is thus overestimated. Unfortunately, no estimations of this statistical bias are available.

By contrast with western European countries, the biggest restructuring still seems likely to involve a major shift out of agriculture, probably involving a transfer of up to four million workers.[14] Given the tendency for agriculture to be a source of labour absorption in the current period of stagflation, the long-term restructuring challenge is, in a sense, being accentuated by the short-term response to the shocks.

4.3. Employment within Industry

As for inter-industry shifts, the share of primary industries – coal mining, gas, electricity, metallurgy and oil-processing – in industrial employment increased relative to light industry, mechanical and electrical engineering *(Figure 2.3 and Table 2.4)*.

Food processing's share of total employment increased in 1990–1993. Apparently, Ukraine moved further towards the position of a resource-

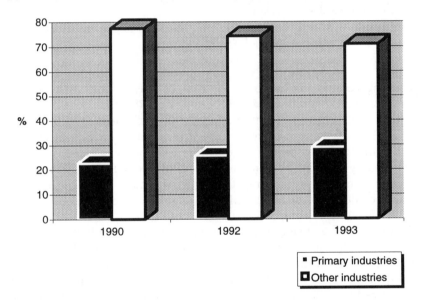

- Primary industries
- Other industries

The share of primary industries has grown

Figure 2.3   *Primary Industries' Share of All Industries, Ukraine, 1990–1993*
Source: Ministry of Statistics of Ukraine, *Pracya v narodnomu gospodarstvi Ukrainy (Labour in the National Economy of Ukraine)*, Kiev, 1991 and 1993.

---

[14] By contrast with the fact that 21% of Ukraine's employment was in agriculture in 1993, in France the figure was 6.6%, in the United Kingdom 2.3% and in the United States of America 2.9%. Much of this transfer, however, will be in the form of externalization of production of non-agricultural goods and services.

Table 2.4 *Employment* Restructuring within Industry, Ukraine, 1985–1993 (%)*

Industry	1985	1990	1992	1993
Mining	9.2	9.2	10.6	11.4
Electricity	1.7	1.9	2.6	2.8
Metallurgy	7.3	6.9	7.8	8.2
Mechanical and				
electrical engineering, metal processing	42.7	43.1	41.0	40.4
Chemicals	4.6	4.6	4.8	4.9
Wood and paper products	4.2	4.2	4.2	4.2
Construction materials	5.9	5.6	5.8	5.8
Light industry**	11.2	10.6	9.4	8.0
Food processing	9.2	9.6	9.8	10.4
Other industries	4.0	4.3	4.1	3.9
Total	100	100	100	100

*Employment refers to the industrial-productive personnel.
**Textile, clothing and leather industries.

Source: Ministry of Statistics of Ukraine, *Pracya v narodnomu gospodarstvi Ukrainy (Labour in the National Economy of Ukraine)*, Kiev, 1991, 1993.

processing country, as has been the case of Russia since 1990. In both countries, one explanation that has been advanced is that this reflected the fact that those sectors were internationally relatively price competitive, due to low labour costs – including very low expenditure on occupational safety and health – and low energy prices. More technology-intensive industries, most notably machine-building and other engineering, as well as most of the light industry were uncompetitive internationally and were hit by the collapse of domestic demand and were unable to expand exports or prevent or substitute for imports.

However, the relative changes in employment were not highly correlated with output changes in real terms. For instance, between 1990 and 1993, output in real terms in the fuel and energy sector declined by 41.6%, while employment rose by 4.9%. By contrast, in so-called light industry real output declined by 12.9%, while employment declined by 36.4%, and by 21.8% in 1993 alone.[15] In effect, the elasticity of employment with respect to output was considerably greater in light industry, in which productivity must have improved.

How could enterprises in heavy industry afford to recruit additional workers while those in light industry were forced to reduce the workforce? The explanation is probably that because of their monopoly position, then access to hard currency markets, and receipt of subsidies, enterprises in

[15] V. Yatsenko, 1994, op. cit, p. 17.

heavy industry were able to increase their prices disproportionately. From December 1991 to December 1992, wholesale prices in coal mining increased 237 times, in chemical industry 72 times, in metallurgy and oil-processing 55 times, and in electricity production 52 times, while in light industry they rose only 20 times, in wood and paper production 31 times, food processing 11–30 times and engineering 32 times. Through price rises, monopolistic enterprises of heavy industry obtained funds to pay workers. Moreover, enterprises in light industry and engineering were confronted with increasing sales difficulties and insolvency of their trading partners, so stocks of unsold production probably rose tremendously.

4.4. Property Form Restructuring

As for property form restructuring, the main shift occurred between the cooperative and private sectors, while the share of the state sector was unchanged in 1990–1992 and declined slightly in 1993 (Table 2.5). By early 1994, the size of the overt private sector was still too modest to have much economic impact, although many changes had taken place in the preceding three years. First, many small enterprises (with fewer than 25 workers) of all forms of ownership had emerged, the registered number jumping from 19,600 in 1991 to 50,500 at the end of 1992, during which time the total workforce in such enterprises increased by about 50%.[16]

Most small firms operated in trade and catering – in which the registered number of firms increased by six times within a year – construction and household and personal services. Many small firms also emerged in industry, which by 1993 accounted for one-fifth of their total number and almost one-quarter of the number of workers in small private enterprises.

Yet the situation is complicated. A substantial proportion of those working in small-scale enterprises were doing so as a second job. In other words,

Table 2.5 *Employment Structure by Form of Ownership, Ukraine, 1990–1993*

Sector	1990	1992	1993
State	78.4	78.5	77.9
Cooperative	18.5	17.9	16.8
Private*	3.1	3.6	5.3
Total	100	100	100

*Including mixed enterprises.

[16] Ministry of Statistics, *Statistical Yearbook of Ukraine*, Kiev 1991, 1992.

the expansion of such enterprises was not necessarily absorbing large numbers of those displaced from regular wage employment. Another peculiarity was that as of 1993, 12.3% of the total number of 1,038,227 persons working in small enterprises worked in small state-owned enterprises, 42.1% in collectively owned enterprises, while only 40.8% in small private firms, the rest being in enterprises of mixed ownership.[17]

A related aspect of initial restructuring was the widespread leasing of state enterprises by collectives of workers. This type of privatisation was the one preferred by the Government in 1992–1993. *Figure 2.4* shows leaseholdings' share of employment and *Figure 2.5* their share of production in household services, trade and public catering, construction and industry.

No official information is available on what types of enterprises were leased. Apparently such enterprises were smaller and belonged to non-prosperous industries, such as light industry.[18] As a whole, in 1993 they recorded worse economic results than other enterprises – while industrial production on average fell by 8%, output of leased enterprises fell by 10.4%

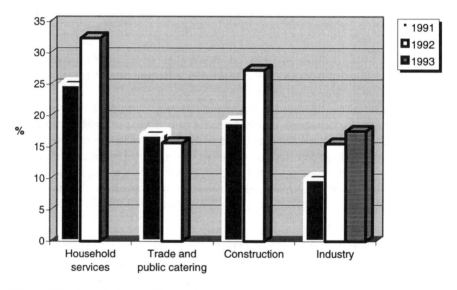

Figure 2.4 *Leaseholdings' Share of Employment in Different Sectors, Ukraine, 1991–1993*

Source: Ministry of Statistics, *Statistical Yearbook of Ukraine 1991 and 1992. Statistichniy byuleten* (Statistical Bulletin), May 1994, No. 2.

[17] Ministry of Statistics, *Statistichniy byuleten* (Statistical Bulletin), Kiev, March 1994.
[18] According to the ILO's NLFs, capacity utilisation level in early 1994 was lowest in leaseholders' establishments.

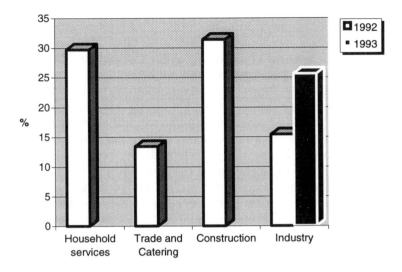

Figure 2.5 *Leaseholdings' Share of Production in Different Sectors, Ukraine, 1992–1993*

Source: Ministry of Statistics, *Statistical Yearbook of Ukraine 1991 and 1992* and *Statistichniy byuleten* (Statistical Bulletin), May 1994, No. 2.

on average. There were greater regional differences in economic performance of leased enterprises than for total industry.

4.5. Occupational Restructuring

As for occupational restructuring, some basic official data are available only from the population census of 1989. At that time, 69% of the labour force were manual or blue-collar workers. Among white-collar workers (so-called employees) constituting 31% of the labour force, 8.3% were classified as managers and administrators and 20.9% were specialists with secondary and university education. 18.6% of university graduates and workers with secondary vocational education were employed as blue-collar workers. The remaining 2.1% were not specified. Since 1989, this latter group has probably grown, since highly educated specialists have been facing labour market problems, and remuneration of specialists is often lower than of blue-collar skilled workers. The Ukraine Labour Flexibility Survey (ULFS) indicates that in 1993–1994 manual work employment in manufacturing declined by more than average, so there has been some occupational restructuring by default.

One key aspect of employment restructuring is the shift into the informal economy and the black economy. The former is not illegal, and has been particularly prominent in terms of secondary, agricultural activity. It is usually defined in terms of being unregistered and not contributing tax and social security contributions by virtue of the status according to the work. Black labour is illegal economic activity. When not overtly criminal, it has been a means of evading taxes and coverage by protective and other regulations.

In the past, black labour was apparently continental mainly to the spa region in southern Ukraine. Since independence, so-called economic tourism involving trips to neighbouring countries and the subsequent sale of goods in shortage, has become one of the most profitable activities in Ukraine in connection with the partial opening of borders, the deterioration of supply in the domestic market and the first half-hearted steps in economic reform. Apart from trade, anecdotal evidence suggests that black labour is concentrated in public catering, household services, agriculture, medical services and education (private lessons for preparation of students for entrance exams to prestigious schools).

Some might believe that the majority of 1.6 million workers 'missing' in the labour market in 1993 in comparison with 1990 were in the informal economy and that many others were working in it as a secondary economic activity. Informal activities were probably widespread among school leavers, not only because there were insufficient job vacancies for them, but because their ambitions would have been at variance with available jobs.

According to estimates of the National Employment Service, in bigger cities and border regions up to 40% of youths have been active in the informal economy.[19] Most of those probably never worked in the state sector. Yet too many have been a source of labour for the black economy, bearing in mind that the net outflow of workers leaving the state sector was much higher than the flow of workers into the private and other property sectors. In trade and public catering, it was more than twice as high in 1992, in industry almost three times as high.

In sum, some employment restructuring had taken place by 1994, although a great deal more will be required in the near future if the employment structure is to resemble a modern market-oriented economy capable of being integrated into western Europe.

5. Labour Hoarding: The Crisis of Hidden Unemployment

Before turning to the question of open unemployment, it is important to stress that there seems to have been a large increase in labour hoarding,

---

[19] E. Libanova, 1993, op. cit.

reflected in the fall in productivity. This has taken the form partly of cuts in working hours and partly in an enormous growth of unpaid administrative leave whereby workers have been told to stay away from work. Published statistical data give only loss of working days due to shortage of raw materials, energy and components and due to unauthorised absenteeism. According to those data, this increased from an average of less than one day per worker in 1990 to 10 days per worker in 1993. As an average figure, this is a very substantial change.

Among individual sectors, above average losses were recorded in industry, transport and construction. Apparently, in most cases (85%) the losses were due primarily to shortage of energy and raw materials and to sales problems. How quickly this practice has spread can be estimated from the fact that between 1992 and 1993, lost working days grew by almost 50%.

Even from the underestimated data, it is clear which industrial branches were those most hit by the economic slump. The electrical energy and oil industries lost slightly more than one working day on average per worker, and coal mining about five days in 1993. Metallurgy, glass and china production and printing also recorded relatively small losses of working time, each below ten days per worker in 1993. Meanwhile, chemicals, textiles, leather and footwear, paper and pulp, and machine-building industries each lost more than 20 days per worker, and in the case of light industry, the figure was twice the overall average for all industry in 1993. Actual labour utilisation in terms of hours of work was almost certainly even lower, as information on intra-shift losses was not collected.

After 1990, full-time employment on permanent contract in the state sector started to fall. Even though published data exist only for 1992 and 1993 and even though the levels of non-regular forms of employment are still tiny by international standards, the beginning of a change is clear. In December 1992, 1.3% of workers were on fixed-term contracts and 1.6% were part-time workers in the state sector, whereas their shares in December 1993 were 1.9% and 4.2% respectively. Of the share of part-time workers, in December 1993, 73% (i.e., 3.1% of all workers) had been forced to shift to work part-time because of the economic problems of their enterprise. Only three months later, on March 31, 1994, the share of workers on forced short-time had doubled to 6.1% of the total workforce in the state sector.[20]

In December 1993, the highest shares of part-time workers were in telecommunications (12.2%), industry (7.4%) and research (5.5%), while typical sectors for part-time work like trade or services had only small numbers of them (3.6% and 0.9% respectively). Also, the number of multiple job-holders in the state sector has fallen from 2.4% to 1.7%.

[20] These data come from Ministry of Statistics, *Statistichniy byuleten* (Statistical Bulletin), various numbers.

Working conditions in the emerging private sector and in mixed enterprises are likely to become more flexible, and become more like those found in western European economies. Legislative regulations and labour market policies will have to adopt to those trends.

Yet part-time working is not the same as involuntary short-time working. The number of enterprises resorting to short-time working has increased since 1991, and both the Ministry of Labour and the National Employment Centre have conducted sample surveys to find out the share of employees hit by these forms of work. According to a survey organised by the National Employment Centre in 330 industrial enterprises in February 1992, one quarter of all employees were on unpaid leave at that time.

Since the beginning of 1993, the National Employment Centre has been conducting quarterly sample surveys of enterprises to assess working time in state enterprises. This has covered between 6,000 and 8,500 enterprises, employing between 4 and 4.6 million workers, and according to the Centre, short-time working and unpaid leave grew steadily during 1993. In the first quarter of 1993, 14.6% of all workers were on unpaid leave, two-thirds of them for at least two weeks, and a further 6.2% were working shorter hours. In the last quarter of 1993, unpaid leave accounted for 23.6% of all workers – 12.5% for up to two weeks, 6.8% for between two and four weeks, and 4.3% for more than a month – while 15.7% were working shorter hours.[21]

The Ministry of Statistics started to collect data on short-time work and unpaid leave in January 1994. Their findings are not so striking. At the end of March 1994, 4.2% of all workers in the state sector were on shorter working hours, and during the first three months of 1994, 13% of workers were on unpaid leave.[22]

Finally, the ULFS, carried out as part of ILO-CEET's work programme in Ukraine, and covering 348 industrial enterprises in six major industrial regions of the country, suggested that in March 1994 over two in every five factories had workers on unpaid administrative leave, or on lay-offs.[23]

This extraordinary incidence of short-time work and administrative leave, or lay-offs, suggests how the growing problem of labour surplus has been handled in Ukraine. Whatever has happened to the levels of employment and unemployment, there has been new or more intensified forms of

[21] V. Yatsenko, 1994, op. cit. We have attempted to obtain more information on this survey, notably on its methodology, without success. It would be useful to explain the differences between these data and the more modest estimates of the Ministry of Statistics.

[22] These data are from unpublished material kindly supplied by the Ministry of Statistics.

[23] For more details on the survey, see ILO-CEET, *Labour Market Dynamics in Ukrainian Industry: Results from the Ukrainian Labour Flexibility Survey*, ILO-CEET Paper No. 9, Budapest, 1994.

labour hoarding and labour market distortion. There are various reasons for this pattern.

First, managers, particularly in state enterprises, have preferred to keep redundant workers and have been supported by the Government that has been afraid of possible social conflict caused by mass lay-offs. It has been cheaper to put workers on unpaid leave than to release them, because in case of release the employers have to pay severance pay for three months, as discussed later, whereas it is free to send workers on unpaid leave. For the workers directly affected, it has seemed better to stay in the enterprise and continue to have access to the social amenities of an enterprise, rather than to be sent to an employment exchange.

Second, both the Government and banks have been willing to support enterprises directly through subsidies, or indirectly through low-interest credit, so as to limit labour shedding. Powerful enterprises – particularly in coal mining, metallurgy and heavy and military industry – have frequently used that willingness in bargaining for subsidies or cheap credits, or for bribing the Government. Because of different bargaining power and new regulations concerning foreign trade, enterprises producing consumer goods and services have often ended up in economic difficulties while enterprises of heavy and military industries, who have long enjoyed privileges, have continued to be able to benefit from them even if deeply in debt.

In 1993, this kind of hidden unemployment was presumed to account for 25–30% of the employed.[24] According to an estimate of the State Employment Service, it reached 40%.[25]

In spite of the apparent inertia in cutting employment, labour turnover increased sharply after 1990. In 1992, according to official data, 23.3% of all workers in the state sector changed or left their jobs, of whom 14.5% did so voluntarily. In that year, the number of recruited workers was 3,453,013 (19.1% of all workers) i.e., 770,000 less than the number of those who left their jobs.[26] The highest labour turnover in 1992 was recorded in household services (72% of all workers), information-computing services (50%), and catering, construction, trade and research (over 30%) while education, culture, financial services, health care and agriculture remained lower and similar to what had been the case in 1990.

The 1993 data suggested that labour turnover had stabilised, at 23.1% for the whole economy and 17.8% for industry. Recruitment in state enterprises and institutions declined to 18% of total employment, reflecting the

---

[24] E. Libanova, 1993, op. cit.

[25] Ministry of Labour and State Employment Service, *Pro vikonanya Derzhavnoy programi zaynyatosti naselenija na 1993 rik (On Execution of the State Programme of Population Employment in 1993)*, Kiev, December 1993.

[26] Ministry of Statistics, *Pracya v narodnomu gospodarstvi Ukraini (Labour in the Ukrainian National Economy)*, Ministry of Statistics, Kiev, 1993.

falling level of total employment.[27] Still, it has been reported that 16.6% of all workers and 17% of workers in industry quit their jobs, while only 1.0% and 1.2% respectively were released for economic reasons. In other words, of 4,000,000 workers having left their enterprise in the state sector, and 1,600,000 workers in industry, 72% and 64% respectively apparently did so voluntarily, while only 4.3% and 4.6% respectively were made redundant.

These data are significant, for they show that employment has not been characterised by rigidity. Some observers have claimed that enterprises have held on to their workers and so impeded employment restructuring and the growth of unemployment. This interpretation is incompatible with the high and rising levels of labour turnover.

However, one worrying development has been the high level of so-called voluntary quits. Because of the nature of severance pay, whereby the worker receives such pay if and only if released from employment, enterprises have a vested interest in inducing workers to quit, and if someone is put on long-term (or uncertain) unpaid leave, he/she is relatively likely to quit in discouragement or to seek another job. Thus, the figures on voluntary quits should be interpreted sceptically. The distinction between voluntary and involuntary is at best an arbitrary or subjective one.

In sum, labour surplus conditions had become chronic by 1994 and there was a growing degree of employment flexibility manifesting itself in high labour turnover. This trend does not match with the rigid adherence to the notion of full employment that prevailed in the command economy model.

6. The Enigma of Unemployment

By early 1994, registered unemployment stood at less than 100,000. Yet the official unemployment rate is far from the actual one. Most fundamentally, the 1991 *Employment Act,* as amended in November 1992 has resulted in systematic under-recording of unemployment, particularly all unemployment due to redundancies. Unemployment started to be registered in July 1991, following the approval of the Supreme Council in March 1991, which was modelled closely on the USSR's *Employment Law*, which was also introduced in early 1991. The Law recognised the legitimacy of unemployment for the first time since the 1920s, and stipulated a series of conditions that had to be met for someone to be registered at employment exchanges as unemployed.

In July 1991, the first month of registration, the number of registered jobseekers was 1,400. By December 1992, the number of registered

---

[27] Ministry of Statistics, *Statistichniy byuleten* (Statistical Bulletin), No. 2, May 1994.

unemployed had reached 6,800, i.e. 0.02% of the labour force. A year later it had increased to 70,500, corresponding to an unemployment rate of 0.3%. After that, registered unemployment increased slightly to 0.4% in March 1994, or 98,600 persons *(Table 2.6)*.

Bearing in mind that economic output had slumped by about 40%, that inflation had been over 10,000% during 1993 and that Ukraine has been suffering from one of the most severe cases of stagflation known, these figures are remarkably low. What could be the explanation for this paradox? There are three possible explanations:

• Rigid labour market, in which inertia prevented mass employment cuts.
• Structural mismatches leading to departures from the labour market.
• Statistical-administrative procedures leading to a chronic understatement of real unemployment.

We will consider each of these alternatives in turn.

Table 2.6 *Registered Unemployment in Ukraine, 1991–1994*

Indicator	July 1991	Dec. 1991	June 1992	Dec. 1992	June 1993	Dec. 1993	April 1994
Registered unemployed (thousand)	1.4	6.8	35.6	70.5	73.3	83.9	102.6
Unemployment rate (%)	0.0	0.02	0.1	0.3	0.3	0.3	0.4
Benefit recipients as a % of registered unemployed	51.7	79.9	76.3	74.4	56.7	47.6	47.5
Vacancies (thousand)	–	277.8	150.9	129.1	192.9	131.6	113.2
Unemployed/vacancies	–	0.02	0.24	0.55	0.38	0.64	0.91

Source: State Employment Service, 1994.

6.1. Rigid Labour Market

The first explanation is that there has been an increase in labour hoarding and that rigidities have prevented or discouraged enterprises from releasing large numbers of workers. The evidence to support this view is that labour hoarding has increased, as noted earlier, and the number of registered vacancies in December 1993 (131,600) was only a quarter lower than the number of released workers (165,100) over the whole year 1993.

Some observers have suggested that managers of state enterprises have been reluctant to release redundant workers for the following reasons:

• Managers of state enterprises have had a sense of social responsibility, since they did not see any possibility of placements in other enterprises.

- Managers of state enterprises have been under pressure from the state administration, which prefers giving subsidies or short-term loans to prevent social unrest which might come from mass lay-offs.
- Labour costs have become such a small part of production costs that retaining surplus workers is a relatively low-cost option, especially when putting them on unpaid leave or shorter working hours. Redundancies were costly for enterprises, since severance pay had to be paid for three months regardless of the enterprise's capacity to pay.
- Managers have retained a belief in recovery of production and demand and have wanted to retain experienced workers.
- It could be that the widespread resort to enterprise leasing by work collectives had created a type of enterprise in which worker solidarity prevented redundancies.

There is no direct evidence on such claims. Some analysts have suggested that the low level of redundancies supports this interpretation of the low unemployment. Thus, in 1992, 4,225,000 workers left their jobs but only 315,000 workers were actually made redundant.[28] Thus, interpreted literally, only one of every thirteen workers who left their jobs in 1992 was forced to do so for organisational or economic reasons. Almost two-thirds apparently left their job voluntarily. And in spite of expectations of a worsening labour market in 1993, the situation seemed to improve. Of 3,999,000 workers who left their jobs in 1993, the number released for organisational reasons fell to 173,000, almost half the level of 1992. The share of quits was almost three-quarters of all job departures.

This composite explanation seems most unconvincing. Employment did fall quite substantially after 1990. Certainly, it was not so much due to economic decline as might have been expected, yet the net decline of employment was about 15 times the number of registered unemployed. Moreover, the decline took place at the same time as the employment of pensioners was rising, which means that the employment decline among the working-age population was even greater.

Further, strong evidence against the rigidity thesis is that the labour turnover has been very high in recent years, as shown earlier. The fact that actual releases were apparently quite limited is not relevant, since if turnover was high there was little need to resort to releases. Moreover, one should be extremely cautious about the statistics suggesting that a low ratio of redundancies was due to voluntary departures from employment, for reasons mentioned earlier. Induced quitting is likely to have been widespread.

---

[28] Data are available only for the state sector.

6.2. Structural Mismatch

The high ratio of registered job vacancies to registered unemployed *(Table 2.6)* means that overall, there is a labour market problem of structural mismatch. At least through 1992, registered vacancies exceeded the number of registered unemployed. This cannot indicate only the low official unemployment rate, because any bias in the unemployment statistics would be matched by a same type of bias in registered vacancies. Only a small proportion of vacancies is registered at employment exchanges. Until the beginning of 1994, the number of registered vacancies was higher than the number of jobseekers with the status of unemployment, but even higher than registered unemployment. This, according to the second explanation of low unemployment, partly reflected structural problems arising from the following:

• Skill supply did not meet skill requirements.
• Demanded skills were not present in the right place.
• Jobseekers were not interested in vacancies due to their low remuneration.
• Geographical mobility was restricted by regulatory procedures.

This behavioural aspects of labour mobility deserve more attention from policymakers than they have received, although once again there is no direct evidence that they explain the low level of registered unemployment. Territorial mobility was undoubtedly limited by administrative restrictions. For instance, in Kiev, enterprises asked the city administration for 'propiska' for 4,200 workers with special skills in 1992 and 3,900 in 1993, apparently on the grounds that they were unable to find specialists in the city. However, the city administration granted 'propiska' only to 650 workers in 1992 and 950 a year later.[29] It seemed easier to obtain permits for blue-collar workers than for white-collar employees.

One suggestion is that enterprises have been holding onto manual workers. If enterprises did shed labour, they tended to release administrative workers and unskilled workers. According to the official statistics, the share of white-collar workers in redundancies (37%) was greater than their share in total employment (31%). The share of white-collar workers was even greater in industry and construction and the pattern of redundancies may have reflected the persistence of the old way of thinking that manual workers created the wealth while other groups were non-productive.

Figures on labour shedding are available only for the state sector. So the number of redundancies is underestimated. First, they exclude agriculture,

[29] V. Shamota, An Analysis of the Ukrainian Labour Market and Efficiency of the State Employment Policy, paper prepared for the ILO-CEET, Kiev, 1994.

in which cooperative farms are the most common form of enterprise. Second, privatised enterprises were expected to reduce labour hoarding most. However, their share in total employment was still very small, so underestimates due to their omission could not have been large, and the main forms of property restructuring in 1992–1993 involved a shift to lease-holdings and closed joint-stock companies, in which the workers' employment interest could be expected to be relatively strong. Bearing in mind these two sources of underestimate, industry was responsible for 42.1% of labour shedding in 1993, followed by trade and catering (14.6%), construction (9%), transport (8.6%), research (3.2%) and education (3.8%).

The number of vacancies reported to employment exchanges by enterprises fell substantially in 1993, and at the end of the year it was less than half the level of a year earlier. Of all registered vacancies, 38.8% were in industry, 19.1% in construction, 9.1% in agriculture, 7.7% in transport and communications, and 6.0% in housing and household services.[30] If we compare all redundancies in 1993 with vacancies reported in December 1993 in trade, public administration, research, education and other social services, the relation between labour shedding and demand for labour was much less favourable than in agriculture, construction and even industry. This was contrary to the expected employment shift from primary and secondary sectors towards the services sector.

The occupational structure of labour demand revealed a similar inconsistency. 62.4% of vacancies were for manual workers, only 37.1% for employees (i.e. white-collar workers in the Ukrainian labour terminology), and 0.5% were for agricultural workers. It seemed that by 1993, the Ukrainian labour market was saturated with so-called specialists, and that schooling had lost some of its social prestige. However, this should be only a temporary feature of the emerging labour market, and is a phenomenon found in all countries of central and eastern Europe in the early stages of their reforms.

In other countries, after a brief period, demand for labour has shifted to educated specialists and selected groups of skilled workers, while the unskilled and other groups of skilled workers could not be placed without retraining or assistance from other labour market schemes. In those countries, most vacancies are now in the private sector, especially in services and construction. As the private sector is still weak in Ukraine, this explains why labour demand comes mostly from the state sector and is still distorted in favour of sectors that were regarded as productive.

---

[30] Ministry of Statistics, *Statistichniy byuleten* (Statistical Bulletin), No. 2, Kiev, 1994.

6.3. Administrative and Statistical Factors

Under the 1991 Employment Law, as amended in November 1992, persons could be counted as unemployed if they

- were of working age,
- were able-bodied,
- were out of employment for reasons that did not depend on them,
- had no paid employment or self-employment providing them with an income greater than the minimum wage,
- were looking for paid employment,
- were available to start employment within two weeks, and
- were registered at a local employment exchange.

Under the Employment Law, unemployment status established eligibility to unemployment benefits, whereas entitlement to participation in labour market schemes (as described in the next Chapter) was made conditional on registration, regardless of whether or not the person was eligible for unemployment benefits.

6.3.1. Counting Unemployment by Registration

The administrative and recording procedures have resulted in a chronic underestimate of actual unemployment. Only those registered at a local employment exchange can be called unemployed, as long as they also satisfy other conditions. International experience has shown that counting unemployment by registration in itself results in lower estimates of actual unemployment than measurement based on household or labour force surveys.

In Ukraine, that procedure is particularly likely to result in a severe undercount, since the probability to register is likely to be low. There is a social stigma for the unemployed to overcome and it appeared that most registered vacancies are low-status jobs. Among employers, there is a corresponding reluctance to recruit through employment exchanges, since people seeking a job in this way are often considered less capable and disciplined. The low use by employers was in the ILO-CEET's ULFS, which showed that most enterprises in industry bypassed the employment service in recruiting workers.

To be registered as unemployed, a person must have a complete work history book and other documents in good order, including a residence permit ('propiska'). How many workers fail to have such documents is a matter of speculation, but it is likely to be a substantial number.

To remain in the register, an unemployed jobseeker must report to the employment exchange once a month. Given relatively high transport fares and low prospects of receiving a well-paid job offer, in many rural areas in particular, the incentive to go to an exchange once a month is not high, especially if the person is only entitled to a minimum wage level of unemployment benefits, or none at all.

6.3.2. Excluding the Disabled and Persons on Severance Pay

Under the Employment Law, those formally released from employment can not obtain unemployment benefits for three months, unless they wish to lose their severance pay, to which they are entitled for those three months. To earn entitlement to unemployment benefits higher than for other categories of jobseekers, they must register ten days before the end of the three months, implying that financially they have no incentive to register for over two and a half months.

As a person is not counted as unemployed for the first ten days after registration, this means that for the first three months of unemployment, a released worker is not counted as unemployed. With labour shedding accounting for a growing share of entrants into the labour market, a growing proportion of the short-term and medium-term unemployed will thus be excluded from statistical unemployment. This practice should be discontinued, so that a more realistic picture of unemployment can be seen and so that employment exchanges can assist such workers in their jobseeking.

According to the official statistics, the status of unemployment was only given to those regarded as able-bodied. Those with certified disabilities receive disability pensions but not unemployment benefits. Yet it is clear that a very large proportion of the disabled lost their jobs in 1991–1993, and the vast majority of those have not been included in the total unemployment figure.[31]

6.3.3. Low Level of Unemployment Benefit

A third factor reducing observed unemployment is that the level of unemployment benefits has been very low, even though they are nominally earnings-related and indexed to price inflation. As described in Chapter 3, they are calculated as a certain percentage of his or her average earnings in the last three months of the last job before unemployment, unless the worker was earning less than the minimum wage, in which case he or she receives the minimum wage.

If they were on partially paid or unpaid leave before becoming unemployed, they could receive the minimum wage amount, which would mean, in effect, considerably less than an income level required for minimal

---

[31] T. Berezanetz, Disabled Workers in Ukraine, paper prepared for ILO-CEET, Budapest, October 1993.

subsistence. In any case, the average unemployment benefits have constituted only a small fraction of the national average wage and the official subsistence minimum (see Chapter 3) and do not encourage people to register with employment exchanges.

6.3.4. Very Low Retirement Age

Fourth, to be counted as unemployed a woman must be between 15 and 54 years old and men between 15 and 59. Thus, women aged 55 or older and men aged 60 or older are not counted as unemployed, even if satisfying the conditions of being available for work, needing work, wanting work and seeking paid employment, unless they have no entitlement to a pension. Although persons over the official working ages are usually not registered in western countries either, the upper age limits in Ukraine are very low by international standards. Moreover, another 34,000 workers accepted early retirement only in 1993.

The effect on measured unemployment was strengthened by the fact that if a pensioner was in employment, he or she was counted as employed and thus was included in the denominator for estimates of the unemployment rate, while being excluded from the numerator.

In sum, there have been numerous factors tending to conceal the real extent of unemployment. The figures given earlier in *Table 2.6* surely seriously underestimate the actual level of unemployment, given that they cover only jobseekers who gained the status of unemployment.

6.4. Indicators of Unemployment

The Employment Service provides two other indicators of unemployment, neither of which is anything close to ideal.

First, it provides statistics on the total number of persons who turned to employment exchanges to look for a job regardless of work status. This figure includes those in employment who want to change their job or seek a secondary job, students looking for a part-time job and those looking for placement in public works. Second, it gives data on the number of registered jobless, including those who had not yet gained unemployment status or were not eligible for it. This second figure may be considered a marginally better indicator of unemployment than the registered unemployment figure, and has been higher (*Table 2.7*).

While the number of registered persons with unemployment status increased over the period, registered non-employment actually started to fall in March 1993. The ratio of registered non-employment to registered unemployment decreased from two in December 1992 to 1.4 in April 1994. This reflected the effect of changes in entitlement to unemployment

Table 2.7 *Registered Jobseekers, Ukraine, 1992–1994*

Indicator	Dec. 1992	June 1993	Dec. 1993	April 1994
Non-employed (thousand)	141.1	121.6	123.4	145.5
Non-employment/Unemployment	2.0	1.66	1.47	1.42
Benefit recipients as a % of the non-employed	38.6	34.1	32.4	33.5

Source: State Employment Service, 1994.

benefits, as discussed in Chapter 3, and the fact that more people were losing their jobs because of redundancy, while the share of those supposedly quitting their jobs was decreasing.

Another feature of the unemployment is the decreasing proportion of unemployment benefit recipients among the registered unemployed. As shown in *Table 2.6,* in 1992 three out of every four registrants were receiving benefits, but by the end of 1993 less than one out of every two was receiving them. Although we do not have figures on duration of unemployment (data on that are available only for those placed by the Employment Service), the decline in benefit-receiving might be an evidence of growing long-term unemployment.[32]

The share of benefit recipients deteriorated sharply after the beginning of 1993, suggesting that a growing number had become long-term unemployed or that more of the registered unemployed were losing, or not gaining, entitlement to unemployment benefits for other reasons. An additional cause for the decline may have been the increasing share of school-leavers among the unemployed whose benefits expire quickly because they do not fulfil the condition of having working experience necessary for longer payment of benefits.

Examination of the flow data on unemployment also shows that a high and growing number of registered unemployed have been leaving the register for reasons other than job placement. Thus, over the period 1991–1993, the number of jobseekers registered with employment exchanges increased from 532,000 to 584,000, but the placement rate fell sharply. In 1991, 54.4% of registered jobseekers were placed in jobs; in 1993 this had declined to 35.8%. In the first four months of 1994, the placement rate fell to 20.8%.

[32] In 1993, according to Employment Service data, 18% of the placed registered jobseekers were placed within a month of registration. About 28% were placed within one and three months, another 28% between 4 and 9 months, 17.4% between 9 and 12 months, and 3.1% after more than 12 months.

Table 2.8 *Registered Unemployment Flows*, Ukraine, 1993 (thousand)*

	January 1993	June 1993	December 1993	April 1994
New registrants	35.0	33.7	35.2	36.5
Unemployed placed in jobs	13.0	17.3	15.8	15.7
Unemployed placed in employment schemes**	1.9	3.8	2.3	4.0
Unemployed deregistered	18.8	20.0	23.4	34.6

*All registered jobseekers regardless of work status.
**These cover so-called public works, labour market training and placement in additional jobs. See Chapter 3 for details.

Source: State Employment Service, 1994.

Unemployment flows in 1993 are given in *Table 2.8*. While the number of newly registered jobseekers with employment exchanges was fairly constant, with only seasonal fluctuations (typically, the number of jobseekers falls in spring due to seasonal job openings and rises sharply between July and September due to the labour market entry of school-leavers, with another peak in December), total outflows from the register have been on an upward trend since the beginning of 1993.

Most significantly, the number of unemployed deregistering for reasons other than employment has increased more than job placements and participation in employment schemes. Deregistration for reasons other than employment became especially widespread in early 1994. Among deregistrations, early retirements also rose sharply. During 1993, their number tripled, almost certainly reflecting a growing inability of older workers to find jobs once they were laid off.

When restricted to jobseekers with the recognised status of unemployment, the placement rate was most unfavourable and declining. Among this group, during 1993 only 24.6% of all registered jobseekers with the unemployment status were placed in job, and in the first four months of 1994 this dropped further to 9.6%. As unemployment status was more often granted to workers released for economic reasons, those evidently had more difficulty in finding new jobs. Finally, according to official sources, unemployed workers looking for jobs through the Employment Service accounted for only 13–20% of all jobseekers in 1993.[33] One suspects that many more who should be counted as unemployed simply did not meet the conditions specified. So, all we can say with confidence is that by early

[33] V. Shamota, 1994, op. cit.

1994, the real level of unemployment was substantially higher than the official statistics suggested.

7. The Incidence of Unemployment: Incipient Labour Force Fragmentation?

It is difficult to discern a clear picture of the incidence, or distribution, of unemployment in the context of the widespread unrecorded unemployment, which has been accompanied by pervasive informal and black economic activities, widespread discouragement from labour force participation and extraordinarily high levels of what in labour economics is called visible underemployment. It is always a concern that, with rising unemployment and a period of economic and employment restructuring, certain social groups will be hit disproportionately hard, and that this could lead to what is commonly described as labour market segmentation and stratification. *Table 2.9* presents the structure of registered unemployment by gender, age, occupation and level of education.

In Ukraine, it is particularly difficult to discern whether certain social

Table 2.9 *Unemployment Structure by Gender, Age, Occupation and Level of Education, Ukraine, 1991–1994*

Indicator	December 1991	December 1992	December 1993	April 1994
Women as a % of the registered unemployed	84.1	79.2	74.7	72.4
Manual workers	–	31.6	42.8	49.4
Other employees	–	68.4	57.2	50.6
Age: below 20 years	11.7[c]	8.5	13.9	–
between 21–30 years	21.2[d]	32.3	34.6	39.9[e]
pre-retirement[a]	–	2.1	1.6	–
University degree[b]	48.9	34.3	32.3	–
Secondary vocational	35.5	35.6	30.7	–
Secondary general	13.0	26.8	33.7	–
Below secondary	2.6	3.3	3.3	2.9

[a]Less than 2 years before retirement age.
[b]Including incomplete university education.
[c]18–22 years of age.
[d]23–29 years of age.
[e]Below 28 years of age.

Source: Ministry of Statistics, *Pracya v narodnomu gospodarstvi Ukraini (Labour in the National Economy of Ukraine)*, Kiev, 1993; State Employment Service, *Annual Report 1993* and *Report of the State Employment Service*, Kiev, April 1994.

groups have been disadvantaged by the labour market changes that have been taking place. A conventional view is that older workers, women, school-leavers, those with disabilities and ethnic minorities would be relatively disadvantaged. Yet, experience in other countries undergoing somewhat comparable economic changes should make us cautious about presuming such outcomes. Analysis is not helped by the lack of reliable information. With those caveats, the impact of labour market restructuring on groups usually regarded as socially vulnerable should be monitored.

7.1. Women

For what they are worth, the registered unemployment statistics suggest that women have been disproportionately hit by unemployment, accounting for nearly three-quarters of all unemployed in early 1994. Although their share had fallen slightly by April 1994, they still accounted for three-quarters of all registered jobseekers with the status of unemployment *(Figure 2.6)*.

Women's much larger share of jobseekers could have one or more of the following explanations.

* Most workers becoming unemployed are women.
* Most of the unemployed who register as such are women.

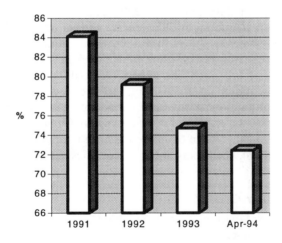

Figure 2.6   *Women as a Percentage of Registered Unemployed, Ukraine, 1991–1994*

Source: Ministry of Statistics, *Pracya v narodnomu gospodarstvi Ukraini (Labour in the National Economy of Ukraine)*, Kiev, 1993; State Employment Service, *Annual Report 1993* and *Report of the State Employment Service*, Kiev, April 1994.

- The placement rate of women is much lower, so that most unemployed who stay as unemployed are women.

The evidence is too patchy to reach definitive conclusions. Yet, let us consider each of these hypotheses in turn.

7.1.1. Women among Workers Becoming Unemployed

Industries most hit by economic contraction were those with high shares of women workers, notably light industry, which did not receive large-scale subsidies or low interest loans from the state to the extent received by heavy industry. However, women comprise a high share of the workforce in food processing, which increased its share of total industrial employment, and the industrial shift in itself did not necessarily result in disproportionate cuts in women's employment.

It seems that, at least in the period 1990–1992, the overall share of women in employment may have fallen. In the recorded state sector (including leaseholding enterprises), their overall share declined from 53% to 51%. Women's relative employment declined most in sectors in which women traditionally predominated.

While in some industrial branches (industry, construction, transport) the proportion of women increased by one or two percentage points, in most services (mainly trade, public catering, housing administration, household services, education, culture and state administration), the share of women fell by 10 or more percentage points in 1990–1992.

Services have been stagnating in Ukraine (or at least their official part), and international experience shows that women take a disproportionately large share of service sector jobs. If there were a tendency to replace women by men in services, there might be a process of discrimination against women in recruiting and/or dismissals that needs to be addressed.

Yet the picture of employment change cannot explain the high proportion of women among the registered unemployed, and it was clear from the ILO's ULFS that women's share of employment in manufacturing actually increased in 1993–1994, increasing most in factories where total employment fell.

7.1.2. Women's Propensity to Register as Unemployed

A second possible explanation for women's high registered unemployment is that they have a much higher propensity to register as unemployed. There is evidence that this has been the case in Russia, where somewhat similar procedures have been applied.[34] A reason for this is that women are

---

[34] G. Standing, *Developing a Labour Market Information System for the Russian Federation,* ILO-CEET, Budapest, 1993.

more used to collect benefits and have greater pressure to register and less sense of stigma in doing so. They may also have less propensity to enter the black economy or informal economy. Such issues deserve research, but a much higher propensity to register cannot be dismissed as a possible explanation.

A related explanation of differential unemployment rates by gender may be that men are more frequently engaged in nonregistered economic activities. This is evident when arriving in Ukraine. People selling goods in street stalls, people involved in business tourism and illegal money exchange, illegal taxi drivers, etc., are predominantly men. Because of the lack of corresponding job opportunities (and often because of their dangerous character), perhaps women are more often obliged to register at the employment service when seeking a job.

7.1.3. Placement of Women by Employment Service

Once registered as jobseekers, men may be seen as the main bread-winners in the family. If so, the exchanges might tend to place men first, although they might not admit it. Another possible explanation is that once unemployed women face greater barriers to placement in new jobs. There has been a suggestion that employers prefer men to women because the costs of running child care facilities generate additional labour costs for them.[35] Women also stay more often at home with their sick children or relatives. This discrimination against women might be more probable in the case of private firms.

Once registered as jobseekers, men may be seen as the main bread-winners in the family, and they may also have more bargaining power in negotiations with predominantly female employees in employment centres.

The evidence on this hypothesis is unclear. In 1991, among all jobseekers placed by the Employment Service, 47.3% were women. In 1992, only 45% of all unemployed workers placed in jobs were women. In 1993, the share rose to 48.5%. These figures are low, if one considers that about three-quarters of the registrants were women.

As only 24% of all job vacancies registered by enterprises were explicitly specified for women, the placement of the double percentage of women in jobs might be interpreted as a success by employment exchanges. However, once again, one could be misled by the nature of the statistics. Many jobs registered have been regarded as suitable for either men or women. And, of course, the very notion of jobs suitable for either men or women should be unacceptable.

---

[35] World Bank, 1992, op. cit., p. 29.

7.2. Older Workers

As for the age pattern of unemployment, the official statistics cannot be used to indicate anything. If accepted as reliable, the registration statistics would imply that older workers had a relatively low unemployment rate. Once again, this could be the reality, or the result of administrative-statistical practices.

Some observers claim that enterprises have been reluctant to release older workers out of a sense of social responsibility, in part because of the low level of pensions, in part due to personal relations as enterprise managers are mostly people in their late forties, fifties and even older. This may or may not be true as a widespread phenomenon.

Another explanation for their low official unemployment might be a lack of structural changes at the enterprise level. In such an environment, older workers with long work experience and better working discipline (as many managers claim) may be more appreciated than young workers, and thus be rarely laid off.

Perhaps most importantly, unemployed older people are recorded as such only if they have less than two years until retirement age. And as employment offices are under instruction to offer older unemployed workers early retirement, their share in registered unemployment is likely to be negligible. So, all one can conclude with confidence is that, based on experience elsewhere, with an acceleration of structural change and an increasing inability to maintain a low retirement age, older workers' share of real unemployment will surely increase.

7.3. Youth

As for youth unemployment, in Ukraine school-leavers could be expected to have a particularly low propensity to register at employment exchanges as unemployed, since they can not receive proper unemployment benefits, and by all accounts have a low probability of being offered a job vacancy if they do register.

Nevertheless, teenagers have experienced the highest rate of registered unemployment and their share in total unemployment increased in 1993–1994. Those between age 21 and 30 years have constituted the largest group of jobseekers, and their share of the total has also increased since 1990. The two age groups accounted for almost half of total registered unemployment in 1993.

There is also anecdotal evidence that many youths have been discouraged from legal labour force activity. As mentioned earlier, according to estimates of the State Employment Service, up to 40% of youths in large cities and border regions work regularly or occasionally in the informal economy. Total unemployment of young people may thus be much higher than official figures.

School-leavers have had increasing difficulties in finding regular jobs, perhaps because enterprises have not been interested in employing those without work experience. Even when young people have gained experience, it is likely that they have been among the first to be made redundant because of the tendency to apply the LIFO (last in, first out) rule.[36]

7.4. Education

One group that seems to have been hit disproportionately hard by unemployment consists of the educated white-collar workers, so-called employees. This may seem strange to those used to international patterns of employment and unemployment. According to the Ministry of Statistics, in December 1992, they constituted 33% of total employment in the state sector, whereas they accounted for two-thirds of all registered unemployed. By April 1994, their situation had improved, but they still constituted 50.6% of total registered unemployment *(Figure 2.7)*.

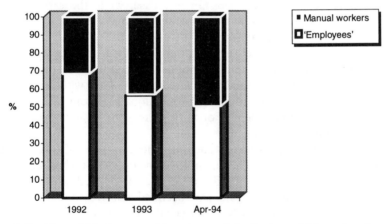

Figure 2.7 *Manual Workers as a Percentage of the Registered Unemployed, Ukraine, 1992–1994*

Source:Ministry of Statistics, *Pracya v narodnomu gospodarstvi Ukraini (Labour in the National Economy of Ukraine)*, Kiev, 1993; State Employment Service, *Annual Report 1993 and Report of the State Employment Service*, Kiev, April 1994

[36] This latter tendency has been reported in official reports. See, for instance, Ministry of Labour, *Osnovni konceptualni polozhenya rozrobki proyektu derzhavnoy programi sprianya molodi na 1994–1995 roki (Basic Conceptual Issues of Elaboration of the State Programme of Youth Employment for the Years 1994–95)*, Kiev, August 1993.

Again, this could reflect a pattern of job shedding, a pattern of recruitment or a pattern of registration. In terms of relative job-shedding, it seems as if Ukraine has been repeating the tendency found in other countries of central and eastern Europe. Enterprises in economic difficulties seem to have tried first to shed administrative workers and specialists. Also state administration employment was cut.[37] While the demand for skilled workers has recovered in central Europe as restructuring has gathered pace, this process had not started in Ukraine by early 1994.

The declining share of white-collar workers in unemployment might be due to an exhaustion of white-collar labour reserves rather than to substantial enterprise restructuring of employment. That is why the ratio of white-collar and blue-collar workers in unemployment has changed in favour of the former. In 1991, they comprised 61% of the total, in 1993 only 37.5%. However, employment prospects of white-collar workers released or endangered by dismissal are unfavourable, judging from the structure of vacancies. In 1993, only 13.5% of all registered vacancies were for white-collar workers. Although this was higher than the 4% in 1991 and 8.6% in 1992, the improvement still left them in a small minority. Their situation seemed slightly better if measured in terms of the total number of job placements by the employment service. In 1993, 22.4% of those placed in jobs were in white-collar jobs. In any case, while the ratio of placed workers to dismissed workers due to economic reasons was 1.57 for blue-collar ones, for white-collar workers it was only 0.77.

A form of labour force segmentation expected to develop with the growth of unemployment and economic restructuring is precisely that based on education. It is usual to postulate that those with relatively low levels of schooling would suffer disproportionately from disemployment and persistent unemployment. For various reasons, that is not what has happened in Ukraine, so far.

The composition of registered unemployment by level of formal schooling is shown in *Figure 2.8*. The unemployment rate was highest among university graduates, who comprised a third of all registered jobseekers at the end of 1993, although the rate had declined relative to those with less schooling. Jobseekers with secondary vocational schooling had the second highest rate, and their share had declined to 31% of total unemployment.

---

[37] There is an opinion that the centrally planned system demanded too many administrative workers. That was partly an illusion due to the fact that the structure of administrative and professional workers was different. While more workers were engaged with central planning and statistics, work on supplying raw-materials, accounting and finance as well as sales were partly taken away from enterprises and centralised, so that there were relatively few workers dealing with these operations in enterprises. That is one reason for the share of white-collar workers in the enterprise sector being lower in comparison with enterprises operating in the market system.

The rate of unemployed with secondary general schooling had risen, being the highest in 1993, while those with less than secondary schooling constituted a negligible share of unemployment.

Again, one could interpret this pattern in a number of ways. It could be that the relatively educated were disproportionately affected by redundancies, since administrative and specialist employees have been displaced by the break-down of the administrative-command economic system. It could be that they have had a relatively high propensity to register as unemployed if they have lost jobs, perhaps because they have more knowledge or fewer

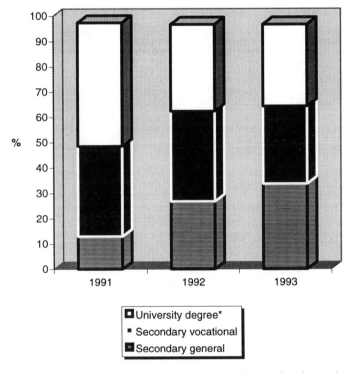

□ University degree*
■ Secondary vocational
■ Secondary general

Unemployed with the lowest secondary schooling have replaced university graduates as the largest group

Figure 2.8 *Education Levels as Percentages of Registered Unemployment, Ukraine, 1991–1993*

*Including incomplete university education. The remainder to 100% is for jobseekers with education below secondary.

Source: Ministry of Statistics, *Pracya v narodnomu gospodarstvi Ukraini (Labour in the National Economy of Ukraine)*, Kiev, 1993; State Employment Service, *Annual Report 1993* and *Report of the State Employment Service*, Kiev, April 1994.

fears of employment offices, or perhaps because they have been concentrated in urban-industrial areas with proximity to local employment exchanges. It could be due in part to a cohort effect, in which successive age groups have higher levels of education on average, so that the relative unemployment rates reflect the higher levels of youth unemployment.

Finally, it is apparent that Ukraine has had a relatively educated population for its level of industrial development, so that many workers with upper secondary or tertiary schooling would have been in jobs that did not require that level. If labour market policy is to develop sensibly, the authorities should be able to explain the pattern of unemployment, and work the available data.

In sum, while the relatively educated comprise a higher share of the registered unemployed than of employed, the explanation is unlikely to be a simple one, and all that can be concluded is that unemployment is not attributable to a lack of general schooling. Unless claims are correct that the standard and quality of education have been lower than they seem, this pattern certainly augurs well for the capacity of the Ukrainian labour force to adapt to restructuring pressures.

7.5. Workers with Disabilities

In Ukraine, workers with disabilities have been hit severely by labour market restructuring. This is by no means a small group. According to official statistics, at the beginning of 1994, there were 2,105,000 people registered as having disabilities; 101,600 of them were children. The total were divide into three categories *(Table 2.10)*.

We have reservations about such classifications, for reasons elaborated elsewhere.[38] Yet it seems clear that workers with disabilities represent a large share of the working age population.

According to Ukrainian labour legislation, those with disabilities who receive a disability pension, which means Groups I and II, or any other benefits higher than the minimum wage, cannot receive unemployment benefits and, as noted earlier, cannot be classified as unemployed, even if seeking employment. Consistent with that perspective, the Employment Law does not identify workers with disabilities as a special group deserving of, or eligible for, more intensive assistance from the employment services. As a result, employment offices have not paid special attention to the placement of workers with disabilities or to their involvement in labour market policy schemes, and have accepted only jobseekers from Group III. This represents severe institutional discrimination.

---

[38] ILO-CEET, *Policy Manual for Disabled Workers*, Budapest, April 1994.

Table 2.10 *Classification of Disabilities among Adult Population, Ukraine, April 1994*

Category	Definition	Number of people
Group I	No working capacity	276,600
Group II	Much reduced working capacity	1,233,500
Group III	Limited reduction in working capacity	490,300

Source: Ministry of Statistics, *Statistichniy byuleten* (Statistical Bulletin), No. 2, May 1994.

On January 1, 1993, the total employment of workers with disabilities, as officially recognised, was 332,850. The Ministry of Social Protection estimated at the time that another 479,600 people with disabilities wanted paid employment. According to the Law on Principles of Social Protection of the Disabled in Ukraine, state enterprises are obliged to fill 5% of all jobs with workers with disabilities, which as of January 1993, would have been 471,000 jobs. Given the deterioration in the labour market, it is unlikely that many of the disabled obtained jobs during 1993. And because of the administrative procedures they did not appear in the unemployment statistics either. The number involved was many times the level of registered unemployment, and their exclusion represents a severe labour market distortion and a major factor in the undercounting of real unemployment.

In principle, according to the 5% quota system, an enterprise refusing to recruit an available worker with a disability is liable to pay a levy, or fine, equal to the annual average wage of workers in the enterprise into a special Fund for the Social Protection of Disabled Workers. Unfortunately, very little of that Fund seems to have gone to create jobs for workers with disabilities.[39]

In sum, the disabled are the group most hard hit by the early phase of employment and labour market restructuring.

8. Regional Dimension of Unemployment

Finally, and perhaps most importantly for the emerging pattern of unemployment and economic restructuring, regional disparities in unemployment are likely to develop in Ukraine, given its distorted industrial structure, huge size and restrictions on geographical mobility.

[39] According to an information from officials of that Fund, in 1992, the Fund received more than 310 million karbovanets from the levy and from other sources. Yet only 59 million karbovanets were used to provide credit for job placements of disabled workers, creating a mere 247 jobs.

For what the data are worth, at the end of 1993, the rate of registered unemployment ranged from an incredible 0.1% in the Kharkiv oblast (region) to 1.1% in the Ivano-Frankivsk oblast, while the average national rate was only 0.3% *(Table 2.11)*.

Western Ukraine had higher registered unemployment than other parts of the country. To the extent that the statistics reflect real differences, this may reflect inherited structural factors. However, one would expect that western Ukraine would have a relatively low unemployment rate, because of its long tradition of small-scale private farming, trade and handicrafts. This region with its ethnically mixed population and close to central Europe could be expected to have a more favourable environment for small-scale business development and self-employment. So far, the difference in this respect seem rather negligible and newly established private firms, joint ventures with foreign partners or foreign firms are still rare. Cross-border commuting for work is restricted, since the neighbouring regions in Hungary, Slovakia and Poland are hit by economic recession as well. The most prosperous regional activity involving substantial numbers of people is thus so-called economic tourism.

The lowest registered unemployment has been in eastern Ukraine and in regions in the southern part of the country. As a rule, the more industrialised the region the better its labour market situation. Also, enterprises located in regions bordering with Russia have benefited from the former cooperation and trade contacts with Russian enterprises. Many Ukrainians from that region commute officially or unofficially to work in Russia, made easier by the common language. Similarly, southern Ukraine uses its proximity to the Black Sea to generate jobs in trade, transport, and tourism and recreation.

The reported level of registered unemployment does not, however, correspond to the pattern of labour turnover by region. Regions with lower unemployment rates tend to have much higher labour turnover, apparently due to many more vacancies on offer in comparison with regions more hit by unemployment. Due to this fact, frictional unemployment should be much higher than reported. Moreover, the same regions tend to have higher difference between hirings and departures. As at the same time the rate of registered unemployment is very low, this phenomenon can be explained partly by larger non-registered economic activity, partly by higher involvement in the non-state sector, in that the concentration of people in these regions generates demand for such legal and illegal activities. The same large difference between hirings and departures can also be found in the Transcarpathian region, where many workers commute to neighbouring countries or are engaged in economic tourism.

At the same time, regions of low registered unemployment have had

Table 2.11 *Labour Turnover, Redundancies, Unemployment and Vacancies by Region, Ukraine, 1993*

Region	Labour Turnover*		Redundancy Rate (%)**	Unemployment Rate (%)***	Unemployment/Vacancy Ratio
	hiring	departures			December 1993
Ukraine	18.0	23.1	1.0	0.3	0.64
Crimea	21.7	27.7	1.1	0.1	0.33
Vinnitsa	15.4	18.9	0.8	0.2	0.49
Volyn	14.6	18.7	1.3	0.9	13.00
Dnipropetrovsk	19.8	25.3	0.5	0.1	0.11
Donetsk	20.3	25.5	0.5	0.2	0.34
Zhitomir	16.5	20.6	0.9	0.7	3.38
Transcarpatian	11.5	17.8	1.0	0.5	3.20
Zaporizhie	20.5	26.7	1.0	0.2	0.15
Ivano-Frankivsk	13.8	16.1	0.9	1.1	16.60
Kiev region, excl. Kiev City	18.0	20.9	1.1	0.4	1.89
Kiev City	18.2	24.5	1.3	0.1	0.08
Kirovograd	18.8	24.3	1.2	0.4	1.09
Lugansk	21.0	27.0	0.8	0.1	0.16
Lviv	13.4	16.8	1.1	0.7	3.59
Mykolaiv	18.8	22.7	1.1	0.2	0.30
Odessa	19.2	23.6	1.2	0.2	0.61
Poltava	18.4	21.5	0.9	0.3	1.04
Rivne	14.0	16.5	1.2	0.8	3.50
Sumy	15.9	20.4	0.6	0.3	0.33
Ternopil	10.8	14.7	1.0	0.9	3.18
Kharkiv	20.1	29.3	0.9	0.1	0.08
Kherson	19.8	23.7	1.1	0.3	1.00
Khmelnitskiy	14.3	18.9	1.4	0.5	2.22
Cherkasy	16.2	21.2	1.2	0.1	0.27
Chernivtsi	15.4	20.2	0.9	0.4	2.11
Chernigiv	14.5	18.9	1.6	0.4	2.00

*Labour turnover in 1993, the figures are shares of hirings and departures to total average staff in state enterprises. Under 'departures', all forms of dismissals, releases, voluntary leaves, etc. are understood.
**Ratio of the number of dismissals to the labour force in the state sector.
***Ratio of unemployed persons in December 1993 to total labour force in 1992.

Source: Ministry of Statistics, *Statistichniy byuleten* (Statistical Bulletin), No. 2, November 1993, February 1994, May 1994; Ministry of Statistics, *Pracya v narodnomu gospodarstvi Ukraini* (*Labour in the Ukrainian Economy*), Kiev, 1993.

relatively high rates of recorded redundancy due to economic reasons. Even though all recorded regional redundancy rates are incredibly low, it seems as if structural changes and job generation have advanced more rapidly in more industrialised regions. In those regions, the registered number of vacancies has continued to exceed the number of registered unemployed – in the Kharkiv, Vinnitsa, Cherkasy, Lugansk, Zaporizhie, Donetsk, Dnipropetrovsk, Mykolaiv oblasts, the city of Kiev and Crimea – for every registered jobseeker there were between three and ten vacancies. In western Ukraine, the situation is the opposite – a shortage of job vacancies is becoming a worrying feature of the regional labour markets. In the Volyn oblast, there were 13 registered jobseekers for each vacancy, and in Ivano-Frankivsk the number was about 17 for every vacancy.

Not too much should be made of these regional data. In spite of Government efforts to stimulate job creation in less developed regions, as described in Chapter 3, regional disparities in employment and unemployment can be expected to increase in the near future. And the authorities should ensure that the developments are monitored more adequately than was possible in early 1994.

9. Concluding Remarks

In Ukraine, so far labour market restructuring has been limited. Although there has been some diversification of employment forms, with an apparently flourishing private informal economy, regular employment has declined and much of the change in the structure of employment could be characterised as restructuring by downsizing. At the same time, education and training have deteriorated, so that the potential for positive restructuring may have been reduced, supported by opinion poll evidence that many students intend to do other forms of work than those for which they have been trained.

Among officials, job losses and unemployment are still observed in a political rather than in an economic context as by-product of necessary structural changes in the national economy. The Ukrainian labour market has been characterised by very extensive labour hoarding and misleadingly low visible, or registered, unemployment. That has not reflected rigidities, for there has been substantial labour market turmoil, with high labour turnover and vast employment decline. Some observers have suggested that the registered unemployment rate, which is well below the actual unemployment rate, could exceed 15% in 1993 if the government ceases to pump money into the economy. This implies that over four million workers would be unemployed, with particularly high rates of unemployment in regions in eastern Ukraine, areas of heavy industry and arms production. They believe that, for social and political reasons, such high unemployment is improbable, and a more realistic prognosis in their opinion stands at 6.5–7% by the end of 1995.[40] Given the economic realities of stagflation, then the more pessimistic scenario is more likely to be closer to the actual outcome.

Ironically, the sort of economic and employment restructuring required to bring Ukraine into line with comparable countries would mean that, given the demographic developments in the country, there would be little need for massive redundancies, although such redundancies will come from the results of stagflation and the efforts to stabilise the economy. We agree with those who have claimed that restructuring per se need not be a socially disruptive process, although the longer it is postponed the more painful the labour market consequences are likely to be.

Each year the labour force could be expected to gain 2% from new labour force entrants, plus a further 1% or so from re-entrants, and would lose about 2% due to exits into retirement.[41] So, over half a million would enter, and half a million would leave the labour force each year. This implies that, hypothetically, mobility into service sector employment to the point where services comprised about the same share of employment as in other comparable countries (i.e. about 60%) would take 8–9 years, assuming nobody actually would change their jobs. Of course, it would not happen that way. Yet this indicates, that there is no necessity for employment and production restructuring to involve prolonged mass unemployment. Unfortunately, the type of labour market and employment policies and flexible labour markets required to make anything like such smooth restructuring a reality are extremely unlikely in Ukraine.

In 1994, labour surplus has taken the form of more intensified lay offs and non-recorded unemployment. Formally, officially recognised part-time employment is minimal, in absolute terms and by the standards of western European and North American economies. We recommend that the authorities and management explore ways of creating proper part-time jobs as part of a strategy for employment restructuring.

In terms of analysis, the most urgent need is to acquire knowledge of what has been happening to those displaced from regular employment and those not having entered it at all. In terms of policies for employment and labour market restructuring, it would be valuable to ascertain to what extent those have been in informal forms of work, in the black economy, in unemployment, in labour migration or discouraged from labour force activity of any sort. The distribution of those people has implications for

[40] World Bank, 1992, op. cit.; V. Shamota, 1994, op. cit.
[41] World Bank, 1992, op. cit., p. 25.

the direction of fiscal, regulatory and labour market policy. Finally, there is an urgent need to determine why a declining proportion of the registered unemployed have been receiving unemployment benefits. This could be the source of considerable and growing labour market hardship and deserves a full-scale enquiry before the level of unemployment rises much further.

Whether or not unemployment continues to be concealed by statistics and administrative procedures, the Ukrainian labour market for the foreseeable future looks likely to be characterised by very high and rising levels of unemployment. There are few signs that the social and labour market policies required to respond to that outcome are in place or are emerging.

3

Creating Labour Market Policies

1. Introduction

Ukraine has no tradition or experience of labour market policies, and this fact is crucial to any assessment of its existing role and of its potential in the near future. In abstract terms, labour market policies encompass a wide array of mechanisms, the main ingredients being:

- Employment services for jobseekers, with the underlying objective of reducing the level of unemployment, including
  - vocational guidance and
  - job placement activities.
- Labour market training.
- So-called public works.
- Wage or other financial subsidies to promote employment or to limit dis-employment.
- Various schemes to promote self-employment and small-scale businesses.

Conceptually, labour market policies have various objectives, which are not always consistent.[1] The main objectives are

- to reduce frictional unemployment.
- to limit unemployment in cyclical downturns.
- to assist in employment restructuring.
- to raise labour productivity.
- to reduce labour force fragmentation and segmentation.

[1] Originally, in the 1950s in the 'Swedish model' (or Rein-Meidner model), the term 'active labour market policy' was used to imply that investment in and coverage of labour market policies were increased as the economy went into recession and were cut back in periods of cyclical upturn, thus maintaining a low degree of labour market slack to allow for flexibility and the avoidance of potentially inflationary bottlenecks. The term 'active labour market policy' has been distorted in recent years, and has been juxtaposed with passive policy, where the latter has been used to describe the provision of unemployment and related financial benefits. This is triply unfortunate. First, it leads thinking away from the useful original terms; second, it implies that there is a direct competition for resources between two types of activity when there is no need for such a dichotomy; third, it conveys a pejorative meaning to income protection, for few could be in favour of passive over active policy.

It is important to recognise that labour market policies should have distributional or equity objectives as well as efficiency, flexibility and restructuring objectives, particularly in a country like Ukraine where the policies are just emerging. At this stage, our assessment must be oriented primarily to consideration of whether they are tending to reduce or to accentuate the distortions that have characterised the Ukrainian labour market.

The former economic system put emphasis on guaranteeing employment to all able-bodied working-age persons and disabled persons assessed by a medical commission as able to work. In the USSR, the duty to work existed until 1989. One of the main responsibilities of labour departments of local authorities (soviets, in Ukrainian radas) was to check whether working-age citizens were employed and, if not, whether they had a legitimate reason, such as school attendance, training, military service or child care. Children and youths were educated for employment, while economic inactivity (even child care) was considered inferior. Job changes uninitiated by state authorities were considered economically detrimental, and long-term employment with a firm was taken as a social norm.

No wonder that psychological barriers worked against labour mobility and flexibility. Psychological factors influenced not only the behaviour of workers but the attitude of employers and state authorities as well, producing a paternalistic approach to employment and labour market problems. This is why, in spite of progress in labour market institutions and legal labour rules since 1990, changes in the labour market have been small. The anticipated increase in redundancies in the near future should be met by an improvement in labour market institutions as well as by an employment strategy and labour market policies.

This Chapter reviews the development of labour market institutions and policies in Ukraine since 1990. It assesses their effectiveness in the light of actual and expected labour market needs, and provides recommendations on how to increase their effectiveness for improving labour market flexibility and reducing unemployment.

2. The Law on Employment of the Population

As mentioned in Chapter 2, the Ukrainian labour market since independence has been taking shape under the influence of the Law on Employment that came into effect in July 1991. This law, together with the amended Labour Code and laws on social security, established a legal framework for the Ukrainian labour market.[2] According to the Law's pre-

---

[2] Until 1994, the old Soviet Labour Code was still operating, with minor amendments. More substantial amendments to bring it into line with other new legislation had been prepared and at the time of writing they were under review by the Ukrainian Supreme Council.

amble, it sets out 'the legal, economic and organisational foundations of employment of the Ukrainian population and its protection against unemployment, and provides social guarantees for citizens in carrying out their right to work by the state.'[3] The law was substantially amended in November 1992, but adhered to its original perspective.

2.1. Labour Force Concepts

The first part of the Law specified basic concepts such as employment, unemployment and suitable jobs for jobseekers, and set out basic principles of the state employment policy. It also allowed for free choice of work activity, which was a significant change in 1991, and it provided a formal guarantee of free assistance to those seeking jobs and to those wishing to change jobs or occupation. This too was a major change. Under the previous system, employment was guaranteed to all working age citizens, which in practice had meant that labour rights had been transformed into the duty to labour. Labour departments of local authorities had the delegated responsibility to ensure that all working age citizens were employed, or had an administratively acceptable reason for not being in employment, such as school attendance, training, military service, child care, disability or retirement.

So, for the first time in modern Ukrainian history, the Law on Employment stipulated the voluntary character of economic activity and put all types of activity, including entrepreneurial and self-employment, on the same legal level. It banned all forms of work enforcement, and as such it stipulated that unemployment could not be the subject of administrative or criminal punishment.[4]

According to the Law (Article 1, para 3(e)), the employed not only include employees in firms of all types of ownership, self-employed, freelance workers, farmers, their helping family members, soldiers and policemen, but also all those undergoing training or retraining in training facilities, apprentices and students over the age of 15 in secondary general schools and universities.[5]

As discussed in the preceding Chapter, the status of unemployed was given only to working-age, able-bodied persons involuntarily without jobs,

---

[3] *Chelovek i Rabota, Zakon Ukrainy o zanyatosti naselenia* (*Law of Ukraine on Employment of the Population*), Kiev, February 1993.

[4] Under the old regime, unemployment was regarded as social parasitism. This perspective survives in the public consciousness. We were told by labour office staff that they were often asked to combat black labour and economic inactivity, particularly of young people, as if it were their responsibility to ensure utilisation of labour resources.

[5] However, regular labour statistics exclude students, apprentices and trainees from employment.

who did not have earned income equal to or greater than the minimum wage, who were looking for a job, were ready, and able to accept one and were registered with a local employment exchange, and who satisfied certain other conditions mentioned earlier. The unemployed may only register where they had a residence permit (propiska). The status of unemployed was denied to jobseekers without work experience and without vocational qualifications, if they refused an offer of vocational training or a job, even a temporary one.

Until the amendments of November 1992, all school leavers without work and seeking it were also entitled to unemployment status. Since then, those under 16 without employment may obtain unemployment status only if they have worked and have been released from jobs for organisational reasons. Those jobseekers beyond the standard retirement age can only be classified as unemployed if they have no right to a pension.

All able-bodied working-age jobseekers are guaranteed free assistance in jobseeking from the employment service. According to the Employment Law, persons with unemployment status may be provided with free training and a stipend during it. Those with unemployment status not undergoing training are, subject to various conditions, entitled to unemployment benefits and social assistance for their dependants. Such jobseekers are also entitled to compensation for costs connected with job placement in another part of the country, if they choose to move in response to a job offer, and if the employment exchange accepts. Workers losing permanent jobs are eligible for severance pay, which in the Law is specified as 'equal to their last average wage over the period of job placement, in accordance with labour legislation.'[6]

Under the Law, an unemployed worker should be directed by the employment service to a 'suitable job', and should normally accept such a job, although he or she is not obliged to do so. If a person refuses to accept two vacancies deemed suitable by the local employment office then unemployment status should be suspended for three months. A job is deemed suitable if, according to its description, it corresponds to the jobseeker's schooling, occupation (specialisation) and qualifications, and does not involve moving from his or her place of residence. To be suitable, remuneration should not be lower than the average wage earned in the last three months of the previous job, as long as that does not exceed the average wage in the industry in which the worker was previously employed. Other

---

[6] Article 4, para.1(d). This Article is unclear. It evidently refers to the three months of severance pay (which is equal to the average wage in the three months prior to lay-off), which an enterprise is obliged to pay workers released for organisational reasons. However, this rule does not fully cover 'the period of their placement in a new job', as stated in the Law, but just three months.

criteria, such as age, duration of past employment in determining what is a suitable job. Jobseekers without work experience or vocational education, and long-term unemployed may be offered jobs combined with training, or if that were not possible, a part-time job. A jobseeker exhausting entitlement to unemployment benefits without finding a job may be offered a different type of job requiring retraining.

Beside its emphasis on the voluntary nature of labour force participation, the Employment Law (Article 5) provided supplementary guarantees of employment for the following groups deemed vulnerable in the labour market:

- Women with children under the age of 6.
- Single mothers with children under the age of 14.
- 15 year old youngsters entering the labour market with the approval of one of their parents.
- Workers within two years of pensionable retirement.
- Those who had been unemployed for more than a year.
- School leavers from secondary general school or vocational educational facilities who have not been placed in jobs.
- Other young people below 21.
- People released from prison.

Local authorities were requested to keep 5% of all jobs in enterprises and organisations for those belonging to these groups. If an enterprise does not meet this quota and refuses to employ such persons sent by the employment service, it is obliged to pay a penalty equal to the average annual wage in the enterprise. The Law does not specify what is meant by the average annual wage, but in subsequent practice it seems to be interpreted as the average monthly wage at the time of the incurred penalty multiplied by 12.

Somewhat surprisingly, workers with disabilities are not mentioned in the Law on Employment as among vulnerable groups. Their employment is meant to be promoted by the Law on Principles of Social Protection of Disabled People in Ukraine, passed in March 1991, which stipulates that they should obtain a quota of 5% of all jobs in enterprises with more than 20 workers, and also legitimises other measures for workers with disabilities, such as sheltered jobs and vocational rehabilitation.[7]

2.2. State Obligations under the Employment Law

The Employment Law specifies ways of regulating and stimulating employment. The state employment policy is expected to promote employment

---

[7] According to employment service officials, although these have 5% quota rules for disabled persons and another 5% quota rules for other vulnerable groups they only take notice of the latter one because it is in the Employment Law.

and combat unemployment. Employment measures should be coordinated with other economic and social policies on the basis of national and regional employment schemes. Labour market institutions are supposed to cooperate with trade unions and employer organisations in designing and implementing such schemes. The Government is committed by the Law to respect employment goals in its economic policy, including investment and tax regulations, and to protect the domestic labour market.

Central, regional and local government authorities are obliged by the Law to prepare annual and long-term national and regional employment programmes. Their objectives are to promote economic development and employment restructuring, prevent large-scale unemployment, promote job creation and provide social protection for the unemployed and their families. In the case of structural shifts and/or mass unemployment in particular regions, the Government may issue a Decree declaring such regions as having priority development status. These regions should then be given preference in development policies, which should be designed to promote employment growth, redeployment of workers, development of small businesses, and so on. If appropriate, a coordination committee may be created consisting of representatives of trade unions, employers and the state administration.

The Law specifies tasks and responsibilities of the State Employment Service, which is supervised by the Ministry of Labour and regional/local authorities. The Employment Service is responsible for the following tasks:

- Assisting jobseekers in job placement.
- Assisting employers to look for workers with required skills.
- Collecting information on labour supply and demand.
- Registering jobseekers.
- Providing income support to the unemployed and their families.
- Implementing labour market schemes.

It is also expected to conduct analyses and forecasts of labour market developments, and on the basis of those it is expected to cooperate with the Ministry of Labour in the design and refinement of labour market schemes.

2.3. Enterprise-Employer Obligations

As for enterprises, under the Law they are obliged every month to inform the local Employment Service of job vacancies and of all hired workers. In the case of redundancies due to enterprise restructuring or production change, they are obliged to inform the Employment Service of the reasons for release, the composition of released workers by occupation, specialisation, skill and wage level, two months prior to redundancy. If they do not do so, they are liable to be penalised by paying the equivalent of the annual wage for each released worker into the Employment Fund.

If the enterprise provides redundant workers with retraining, the costs may be deducted from taxable gross profits. However, the enterprise is obliged to bear retraining costs if the redundant worker was not retrained in the two years prior to his release. When recruiting workers or providing them with retraining, the enterprise can ask the Employment Service for 50% compensation of the retraining costs.

2.4. Labour Market Measures

The Employment Law envisaged five types of labour market measures:

a) Training and retraining of unemployed, if they cannot obtain a suitable job or are unlikely to be able to use their skills in a job.
b) Social (public) works, organised by regional or local authorities and the state administration, in cooperation with labour offices in selected enterprises or institutions. The organisers conclude a temporary contract with the unemployed, with a possibility of extending it until his/her placement in a job. The unemployed retains entitlement to unemployment benefit, after the period in public works, and in that work the unemployed cannot be remunerated below the minimum wage.
c) Measures to ensure job quotas are met for vulnerable groups, as specified above. Quotas are supposed to be proposed by regional labour offices and approved by regional authorities according to the needs of individual regions.
d) Subsidised job creation measures. Enterprises or institutions creating so-called additional regular jobs or jobs under public works' schemes, or jobs for vulnerable groups above the quota determined by the Employment Service, are entitled to partial or full compensation of costs in the form of reduced tax or other payments into the state budget.[8] The extent of compensation is determined by regional/local authorities, and agreed with local coordinating committees.
e) Interest-free loans, provided to those unemployed starting their own business.

The costs of labour market services and policies are covered from the State Fund of Employment. According to the Law, this Fund can finance the following expenditure:

---

[8] The Law does not mention any possibility of providing credit or grants or payment of interest on loans for job creation by the State Employment Service. That is why job creation projects launched by the employment service may be questioned from a legal point of view.

- Labour market training of laid-off and unemployed workers.
- Unemployment benefits.
- Financial support for the families of the unemployed.
- Interest-free loans to those unemployed starting their own business.
- Financial and wage costs of the National Employment Service.
- Costs of creating so-called additional jobs.
- Costs associated with organisation of social works (leaving material and wage costs of social works to be covered from the budget of regional authorities).

The State Fund of Employment is financed mostly by contributions from employers, at a level fixed by the Supreme Council, which was 3% of the enterprise wage fund, as of early 1994. The Supreme Council may also determine transfers from state and regional budgets. Other sources may be voluntary contributions of non-government organisations, citizens, foreign firms, earnings of the Employment Service from paid services, etc. Although the Employment Service is the only user of this fund, its distribution must be approved by the Cabinet of Ministers.

The contributions from enterprises are collected by the local employment offices, which send them to the regional centres, which in turn retain 80%, sending the remainder to the national centre. The regional centres use part of the money to pay for training centres and part is distributed to the local employment offices to pay unemployment benefits and expenses connected with labour market schemes.

Until 1993, the national state budget covered salaries and operational costs of regional employment offices. Budgetary difficulties led the authorities to make regional authorities responsible for those expenses. When the regional authorities objected that they wished to supervise employment offices, which was opposed by the national government, the delegation of financial responsibility was annulled. As a result, the salaries of all employees of the State Employment Service, plus the costs of training employment office officials, administration and research, are covered by the 20% of contributions transferred to the national centre. This situation may create distributional difficulties if and when registered unemployment rises to 5% or more, when certain regions will face increasingly severe financial difficulties due to much higher rates of unemployment and dwindling contributions.

2.5. Unemployment Benefits

Unemployment insurance is compulsory in Ukraine for all forms of enterprise. There are essentially four forms of benefit for those who lose jobs, to which individual workers may or may not be entitled:

- Severance pay.
- Stipends or scholarships for retraining.
- Unemployment benefits.
- Dependants' allowances and social assistance.

Entitlement to unemployment benefit arises when a jobless person is registered with the Employment Service, cooperates with it according to existing rules, has unemployment status, and does not have any other income exceeding the minimum wage. The benefit is paid from the eleventh day after the date of registration. Duration of benefits is limited to 12 months, or to 18 months in the case of workers having less than two years to retirement age, and – except for workers released due to organisational reasons (i.e., made redundant) – that period of benefit is spread over three years, with a maximum of six months in the first year after becoming unemployed, and a maximum of three months in each of the second and third years.

School leavers from vocational schooling facilities, university graduates and persons leaving military service (or alternative non-military service) are eligible for unemployment benefits after a three months' waiting period, or after one month in the case of school leavers and university graduates, if they register at a local employment exchange. As of early 1994, the unemployment benefit scheme, entitlement conditions and level of benefits are as summarised in *Table 3.1*.

Workers made redundant due to changes in production or labour organisation or if losing a job due to a work accident or occupational disease are granted certain privileges. They must register with the Employment Service only 10 days before expiry of their severance pay, as the combination of severance pay and unemployment benefits is not permitted.

The maximum level of unemployment benefits is the average wage of the region (oblast), and the benefit cannot fall below the minimum wage. If placed in a job or undergoing off-the-job vocational retraining, a worker cannot obtain a wage or stipend lower than his/her previous wage. If the worker has less than one and a half years until retirement age, he/she may be provided with a regular old-age pension instead of unemployment benefits.

All other workers losing their job may be registered with the Employment Service as jobseekers, and if attending training or retraining courses, are eligible for a stipend at the level of 75% of their previous wage if they have family dependants, or 50% of it if not. The stipend may be between the minimum wage and the average wage of the corresponding industry. In the case of trainees who have not yet worked or who were dismissed for disciplinary reasons or who have been jobless for a long time, the stipend cannot fall below what they would receive in unemployment benefits.

Table 3.1 *Unemployment Benefit Scheme, Ukraine, 1994*

Category of unemployed	Maximum duration of benefit payment	Level of benefit
Workers released for organisational reasons.	12 months, or 18 months in the case of workers with less than 2 years before their retirement age.	First 3 months: • no unemployment benefit; • severance pay: average wage of past three months (paid by enterprise).* Second 3 months: • 75% of their average wage in past three months.* Following 6 months or 12 months for workers with less than 2 years before their retirement age: • 50% of their average wage in past three months.*
Workers having worked for at least 12 weeks in the last 12 months.	12 months:** • 6 months in first year, • 3 months in second year and • 3 months in third year.	50% of their average wage in past three months.*

*As long as their past wage was above the minimum wage, otherwise the minimum wage. Maximum level is the average wage in the region.
** According to the Law on Employment, workers with less than 2 years before their retirement age, belonging to this category, are also eligible for 18 months of benefit payment. However, as the 6 more months can be utilised only in the third year, this rule is in conflict with the right to benefits applicable only to persons in working age having no entitlement to pension. An unemployed in a training scheme receives a stipend, not unemployment benefits.

Source: The Law on Employment of the Population, November 1992.

Unemployment benefits are indexed for price inflation and are earnings-related in a fairly complex way. Benefits are terminated in the case of job placement, retraining, criminal conviction or receipt of a pension. Their payment may be postponed for three months, if the person is receiving severance pay from the enterprise, or if the person does not cooperate with the labour office, or if he left the previous job voluntarily, or if he was released due to misconduct.[9] It may be interrupted for three months (and the eligi-

[9] Whether or not the person left the job voluntarily is determined by the enterprise and is recorded in the worker's work history book. This raises questions about fairness and the ability of workers to challenge judgments affecting their future.

Table 3.2 *Average Monthly Unemployment Benefits, Ukraine, 1993–1994*

	Average monthly unemployment benefit (karbovanets)	Unemployment benefit as a percentage of		
		Average wage	Minimum wage	Minimum consumption budget
1993				
January	3,292	21.7	71.6	21.1
February	4,849	25.2	105.4	24.1
March	5,363	23.2	116.6	21.8
April	5,331	20.8	115.9	17.4
May	5,856	19.3	127.3	15.1
June	11,760	20.2	170.4	17.4
July	14,170	19.7	205.5	15.5
August	14,199	17.6	205.8	12.7
September	35,155	17.8	175.8	17.5
October	44,371	18.5	221.9	13.1
November	50,570	16.5	252.9	10.5
December	99,974	12.6	166.6	10.8
1994				
January	127,550	16.7	212.5	11.6
February	147,834	19.4	246.4	11.9
March	169,066	20.0	281.8	12.9

Source: V. Yatsenko, Employment Policy in Ukraine in 1991–1994, paper prepared for ILO conference, Employment Policy and Programmes, Budapest, June 2–3, 1994.

bility period reduced for that period) in the case of two refusals of a suitable job, or if the person refuses a job deemed suitable after retraining, interrupting a retraining course without serious reason, or if the person stays away from his normal residence for more than a month.

All family dependants of an unemployed person are entitled to social assistance, paid at the level of 50% of the minimum wage if their income per head falls below the subsistence minimum. The same means-tested assistance is paid to an unemployed person whose period of benefit payment has expired. This assistance is usually paid once or twice a year according to the financial situation of the local employment centre and its practice. If an unemployed person dies, his/her family is eligible for a one-time payment equal to two months of unemployment benefit, which must be equal to at least five minimum wages.

What is most clear about the operation of the unemployment benefits is that they have been inadequate. As can be seen from *Table 3.2*, the average monthly benefit was a small and declining percentage of the average wage and the official subsistence income, even though it has fluctuated between one and three times the minimum wage, which in turn has been detached from any semblance of a minimum acceptable wage, as Chapter 4 indicates.

2.6. Desirable Reforms of the Employment Law

Although the unemployment benefits have been inadequate, the Law on Employment represented a major step forward in the regulation of the Ukrainian labour market, in the promotion of structural change in employment and in providing income protection for those in unemployment. Some changes should be regarded as having high priority.

First, the double supervision of the State Employment Service and its network of regional labour offices by the Ministry of Labour and by regional authorities is likely to cause complications. The Government's intention behind this rule was to control employment services in order to link labour market policies with macro-economic development and general economic policy, while taking into account regional economic and labour market needs. This might work if there were no differences in economic and employment interests between Kiev and the regions; otherwise a conflict of interest could paralyse the activity of employment offices.

Another problem could arise if the Ministry of Labour established labour market policies without having the knowledge of regional labour market needs possessed by employment exchanges, or if the Employment Service as the body responsible for their implementation differed in its opinion on what policies were most appropriate.

All costs of the State Employment Service and expenditure on labour market policies are covered from the Employment Fund, which is financed mostly by employers, with the state budget only providing supplements. So, control of the activities and expenses of employment services solely by central government officials is likely to be inefficient and inadequate. It is recommended that the Employment Service should become independent (preferably as a juridical body) managed by a tripartite body representing the state, trade unions and employers at the national and regional levels, according to the ILO Convention No. 88.

Although the Law specified five labour market policies, they may not be the most relevant for Ukraine, as discussed later in this Chapter. For example, rigidity of the production and employment structure of enterprises represents a major impediment to economic reform in Ukraine. Yet none of the specified labour market policies aims to promote employment restructuring and labour productivity in enterprises. If an employment exchange sees a need to focus on such goals, it apparently has to hide its intervention measures under other policies, such as creation of additional jobs.[10]

---

[10] Personal communication from employment service officials.

Even then, it has to balance between legality and illegality in financing such measures from the Employment Fund, to the detriment of solutions of the most urgent problems in the labour market. Both the labour market policies and the permitted expenditure of the Employment Fund should be formulated more broadly, or the approach to employment promotion changed to ensure they address the main priorities.

The unemployment benefit scheme should be modified, so that while stimulating the search for employment, it provides income protection for more of the unemployed, perhaps including those on long-term unpaid leave and those enforced to work short-time. First, it is not sensible to pay released workers from the enterprise wage fund for three months only if they do not accept a job during that period, as this discourages them from searching for a job earlier. As in other countries, while the unemployed should be encouraged to find jobs as soon as possible, severance pay should be paid as a lump-sum to compensate for hardships associated with loss of employment and to facilitate their reemployment, while discouraging enterprises from making workers redundant unnecessarily.

The duration of employment required for eligibility for unemployment benefits should be reconsidered. The required period of only three months of employment (or more precisely 12 weeks, except in the case of redundancy, when there is no time condition) in the last 12 months might encourage some groups of workers to accept short-term, seasonal jobs (or to operate in the informal economy while being out of employment and collecting unemployment benefit), and employers to create temporary jobs instead of permanent ones. As unemployment increases, this will put a strain on the Employment Fund and will not promote permanent employment. The required period should be prolonged. Otherwise it is unjust for workers with longer period of work and may occur too costly in a situation of high unemployment and high share of short-term contracts.

The reason for distributing unemployment benefits over three years is not clear. Unemployment benefits should not be discontinued for someone out of work for six or more months. It is also essential to provide financial support for the unemployed after termination of normal unemployment benefits if this person is unable to find a job or he/she participates in a labour market programme.

3. Revising the Labour Code

Before turning to the institutional framework being developed for implementation of labour market policies, it is appropriate to emphasise that the old Labour Code of the USSR, modified by the Supreme Council of

Ukraine in 1991 and 1992, needs further amendments to facilitate labour market policies.

The Labour Code does not correspond with the Employment Law in some respects, and still refers to old institutions. In early 1994, the Cabinet of Ministers submitted to Parliament a draft bill entitled 'On Submission of Alterations and Amendments to the Labour Code of Ukraine'. Much of the reform refers to issues covered in other Chapters. The Labour Code would still have a very broad coverage and in principle would retain a tightly regulated labour market. In practice, the Ukrainian labour market has been less regulated than it might appear, since the capacity to monitor the regulations has probably not been what the authorities might have wished.

The old Labour Code states in Article 1, that it regulates labour relations with the intention of ensuring that labour should be a fundamental necessity for all individuals able to work. The 1994 amendments would remove that objective, on the grounds that it could contradict the individual right to choose between types of activity. We strongly support the proposed amendment. A related amendment would bring the Code into line with other legislation in guaranteeing the same rights to all those involved in all forms of work activity, regardless of ownership or management form. This should also be supported.

Chapter III of the Code specifies permissible forms and duration of labour contracts, which may be without limit of time or be on a fixed-term basis, or be for specific jobs. It allows for probationary periods of employment of up to one month for manual workers and of up to three months for others, although in the latter case, up to six months is allowed exceptionally. Probation cannot be applied for workers under the age of 18, university graduates, those leaving vocational schooling, persons leaving the army, workers with disabilities (if placed in jobs according to a medical recommendation), migrants from other regions or workers transferred from another enterprise. The regulation is thus very selective. It protects the groups just mentioned from early dismissal. Yet it may result in discrimination against them in recruitment and promotion in employment, and can penalise enterprises if they find that a worker from one of the groups does not perform adequately.

The old Code allows for workers to be transferred to another type of work, enterprise or region only with their prior approval. Such approval is not needed if the transfer is for a job demanding the same skills or specialisation, or if it is made to satisfy production needs, or for lack of work in the normal job if the period of transfer does not exceed one month, and as long as the tasks in the temporary job correspond to those of the worker, so that skilled workers could not be transferred to carry out unskilled jobs.

A requested period of notice is two weeks on the worker's side if the labour contract is of unlimited duration. A contract can be terminated immediately on the employer's side if there are disciplinary grounds. If a worker changes his mind and wishes to remain in a job after the end of a notice period, the enterprise may still require him to leave if it has already recruited a replacement worker. The two weeks notice period does seem to be very short, particularly for skilled labour, as the enterprise may not be able to find adequate replacement in such a short time. We recommend to prolong the notice period to one month.

The Labour Code, in Article 40, legitimises the following reasons for termination of a labour contract by the enterprise:

a) Changes in production and employment structure, including employment reduction.
b) When an employee reaches the normal retirement age and is eligible for an old-age pension.
c) Employees' inability to perform the work to normal levels due to ill-health or lack of qualifications.
d) Return to the job by the worker who had been performing it earlier.
e) Repeated non-performance of work in compliance with the labour contract without serious reasons.
f) Unauthorised absence from work for more than three hours in a working day.
g) Absence from work, including temporary disability, for longer than four months, except for pregnancy or maternity leave or occupational disease or injury – in these cases the job must be preserved until the worker returns to work after maternity leave or after attaining rehabilitation, or gains disability status.
h) Serious misconduct, notably drunkenness at work, theft and sabotage.

Workers whose contracts are terminated for any of the reasons **b, c** or **d** are entitled to one month of severance pay equal to their monthly wage. Under the Employment Act, severance pay must be paid for three months in the case of workers whose contracts are terminated for the reason **a**.

This regulation raises problems. The Code does not stipulate the required notice period for contract termination by the employer, except in the case of workers being made redundant due to changes in production (i.e., category **a**), which Article 49 fixes as two months. This implies that workers are less protected than enterprises. The situation is particularly unsatisfactory for workers affected by ill-health, since it could lead to discrimination. It might seem that this is safeguarded by the condition that contracts can be terminated only with the approval of the trade union (if the redundant worker is a member of the trade union), except in the case of an enterprise's or establishment's closure. However, private firms in particular may not have a trade union, and thus many workers may not have that residual protection in the future.

Finally, condition **d** on returning workers is not clear, and any interpretation might be misleading, or the condition might be misused. In short, we recommend that Article 40 on employment contract termination should be reassessed and revised.

Under the Draft Bill Amending the Labour Code, Chapter III(a) – entitled 'Ensuring Employment for Released Workers' – is set to be revised as the 'Provision of Employment and Guarantee of the Right to Work'. The proposed amendment would require enterprises to notify workers that they were to be released two months beforehand and to offer them a similar job within the enterprise, if possible. If no such job were available, the firm would be obliged to inform the local employment service of the occupation, skills and wage of the worker to be released, and then pay the worker three months of severance pay. The rights of such workers and the obligations on the employment service would be as determined in the *Employment Act*. No extra provisions are proposed for mass lay-offs. Since we anticipate that mass lay-offs will become widespread and represent a serious labour market challenge in 1995, we recommend that attention be given to legislative provision for mass lay-offs.

The Labour Code also has regulations on the following subjects:

- Working time.
- Rest during work.
- Leave for various categories of workers.
- Work norms.
- Guarantees and compensation for workers moving to work in another region.
- Training and retraining.
- Health care.
- Guarantees for workers bearing financial responsibility for damages in enterprises caused by breaking working rules.

The existing regulations are complex and may need to be revised to allow more scope for collective bargaining.

In the Code, there are regulations on the work of women and youths. These could influence their employment and unemployment. For women, night work, work in harmful conditions and work underground is forbidden, except in health care and certain other services. The latter exceptions do not apply to pregnant women and mothers of children under the age of three. These two groups cannot be required to work overtime, or during holidays, or be sent on business trips. On medical recommendation, they should be transferred to easier work, or they should have their work norms

reduced, without that involving any wage reduction. If a woman is await-
ing a medical examination to determine whether she should be transferred,
she may stay away from work on full pay.

Under the Code, mothers on maternity leave and others on so-called
parental leave, that is, fathers, grandparents or other relatives caring for a
child under the age of three or, in special cases, under the age of six, are
allowed to work part-time without that resulting in a reduction in maternity or parental allowance (such persons remain in employment for statistical reasons). In effect, this allows them to complement what have been
meagre social allowances.

Pregnant women, women with children under the age of three (or six, in
special cases), and single mothers or fathers with children under the age of
14, or with children with disabilities, may be released by employers only if
the enterprise is closing, and they have to be offered another suitable job.
If they have fixed-term (temporary) employment contracts, they have to be
offered a new job after its termination and are entitled to severance pay for
three months. Employers are also obliged to pay for stays in sanatoria and
access to recreational facilities by pregnant women and women with children under the age of 14, or with children with disabilities. Enterprises
employing large numbers of women are obliged to open child care facilities, although the Code specifies neither the size of enterprise, nor what
'large number of women' actually means.

All these protective regulations have become controversial in some countries, on the grounds that while protecting women is desirable, they may
lead to discrimination in recruitment, promotion or retention. Without pre-
judging the outcome, we recommend that an analysis of these regulations
be conducted to determine whether they operate effectively and fairly.

As for youths, under the Labour Code they may be employed from age
16, or in special cases, with the approval of at least one parent, from age
15. Those aged 14 may do part-time work in their leisure time if that is
approved by one parent (Article 188). Workers below the age of 18 should
work fewer hours per week and have lower work norms than older workers, although they should be paid a wage equal to a full-time adult worker
doing similar type of work. Enterprises and organisations are obliged to
reserve vacancies and vocational training places for school leavers who
have completed general secondary schools or vocational training centre
courses, and also for other workers below the age of 18. Unless this
reserved quota is filled, they cannot refuse to employ a youth who applies
for a vacancy, if other qualifications are fulfilled. Also, jobs are reserved
for school leavers from vocational training centres, vocational secondary
schools and universities according to their qualifications and specialisation.
Moreover, under Article 196 of the Code, regional and city councils are

obliged to draw up employment plans for general secondary school leavers and are expected to ensure their implementation.

In the draft Bill to amend the Code, the reservation of vacancies would be replaced by a quota fixed and controlled by local authorities, a change that would correspond to the Employment Law. Also, Article 197 of the Code – ensuring employment for school leavers from vocational training and secondary vocational schools and universities – would be modified. The amendment would guarantee able-bodied citizens of Ukraine aged between 15 and 28 initial employment for two years after finishing or dropping-out of vocational training, secondary school, university or military or alternative non-military service. School leavers previously assigned to jobs by an enterprise would be entitled to at least a three-year employment contract in a suitable job.

Again, this regulatory approach may have adverse as well as beneficial effects on the employment of young workers. The amendments, on their own terms, do not specify in sufficient detail what sort of work would be suitable. More generally, international experience shows that such quotas can be, and often are, avoided or evaded by employers, especially if they are not combined with advantages for the firm, or if the penalty for noncompliance is minor.

A related part of the Labour Code (Chapter 14) deals with privileges for workers undergoing on-the-job training. They are granted a reduction in working time or a paid study leave. Thus, workers who are also studying at secondary general school or receiving vocational training are eligible for 50% of their wage for the days or hours off the job. Perhaps oddly, the Code does not mention the need for an employer to agree to such training or studying. That omission is appropriate in the case of compulsory schooling (supposing that to be incomplete for some reason), but perhaps not in other cases, since it would seem onerous on the enterprise to pay for training or studying on issues not relevant to the enterprise.

Clearly, the Labour Code has provided an extensive array of protective regulations for young workers. Are they appropriate for a more open, flexible labour market? We recommend that the regulations for youth workers should be reassessed to determine whether they promote their productive employment and provide them with appropriate avenues of labour market entry and assimilation.

4. Institutional Framework

As of early 1994, the institutional structure for regulating the Ukrainian labour market consisted of the Ministry of Labour and the State

Employment Service, which was affiliated to the Ministry, under which there was a national centre and a network of republican (Crimea), regional and local employment centres.

In the former USSR, Moscow controlled labour markets in all the republics, so that autonomy in labour market regulation was illusory. The main task of republican ministries of labour was to make so-called balances of labour resources, that is, estimating available labour supply and its sectoral and territorial distribution in order to secure full employment at the national and regional levels.

In case of an imbalance between the number of workers to be placed and the number of vacancies, it was the joint task of the State Planning Committee and sectoral ministries to invest in the relevant region. These investments were made mainly by allotting funds to regional enterprises or opening subsidiaries of other enterprises, in order to create jobs, in most cases regardless of the efficiency of such investment. The second main task was to control fulfilment of labour regulations in enterprises and institutions and to establish and modify wage tariff rates for individual industries.

After Ukraine became independent, the Ministry of Labour had to reformulate its tasks to reflect the changing character of the labour market. The new tasks were rather difficult, since ministerial officials had limited experience of independent work and no experience of market-consistent measures promoting labour flexibility and employment. So, their working methods were rudimentary.

The Ministry still bases its work on the notion of balances of current and future labour supply and demand at the national and regional levels. The balances are based on information from regions that summarise expected employment changes in enterprises and anticipated migration. Labour supply is specified as the sum of school leavers, men returning from military service, planned redundancies by enterprises, and estimates of the number of quits and labour force entrants. Labour demand is determined as the number of reported vacancies multiplied by the average number of daily shifts per worker plus vacancies due to retirement, maternity leave, etc. The Ministry also considers possible increases in the average number of daily shifts, creation of jobs from various resources, etc.

The Ministry of Labour establishes an annual national employment programme on the basis of the forecast labour market balance, regional employment programmes (prepared by local employment offices in collaboration with regional authorities) as well as development objectives of branch ministries. It is subject to approval by the Cabinet of Ministers, and then becomes the state norm. In the case of revealed imbalances in regional labour markets, special programmes and measures may be launched.

The Ministry of Labour is responsible for the design, planning, organisation and financing of all large-scale programmes designed to combat unemployment, such as the Programme of Social (Public) Works announced in 1993 and the Concept of the Programme Promoting Employment of Young People, approved in January 1994. It also determines how labour market policies should be implemented, as well as their funding. Other tasks of the Ministry include the preparation of labour legislation, the practical regulation of labour migration and the design of the wage system.

The national centre of the State Employment Service operates like a ministerial department and controls a network of employment offices, consisting of one republican centre for Crimea, 24 regional centres (plus two city centres in Kiev and Sevastopol with similar functions), and 648 local employment centres (125 town and 523 district centres). At the end of 1993, the national centre employed about 100 specialists (plus a few supplementary workers), while regional centres operated with over 1,300 employees, and local centres with about 7,800.[11] Of the 9,049 employees of the State Employment Service, 7,860 were managers and specialists, 362 other white-collar employees and 827 were manual workers. This implies one employment specialist per every ten jobseekers with unemployment status, or 18 jobseekers regardless of status, which in principle means conditions for high quality services.

A local employment centre usually consists of five departments. The largest in terms of number of employees is the job placement department, which provides the unemployed with job counselling, assistance in applying for suitable jobs, if available, or an opportunity to participate in a labour market scheme, in which case they are sent to the relevant department.

If not interested in participating in any scheme, the person is registered as a jobseeker and after ten days starts to receive unemployment benefit, if eligible. Enterprises are obliged to report to this department all employment changes in the past month until the twentieth day of the following month – how many workers were recruited and released or quit, and what is their present level of employment. They are also expected to inform the local employment office of intended redundancies two months before they are due to occur to give the employment office a chance to prepare. In return, personnel departments in enterprises receive information from the local employment centre about all vacancies in the region. Should an enterprise experience temporary economic problems, the employment office may

---

[11] National Centre of the State Employment Service, *Zvit pro pracevlashtuvannya i zaynyatist naselenya, yake zvernulosya do sluzhbi zaynyatisti Ukraini* (*Report on Job Placement and Employment of the Population Turning to the Employment Service of Ukraine*), Form No. 2-PN, Annual Report for 1993, Kiev, January 1994.

assist it to find short-term employment for otherwise redundant workers, thus preventing their unemployment.

The financial department is the second largest department. It collects contributions from enterprises for the Employment Fund and turns them over to the regional employment centre. Then it supplies to the regional centre funds necessary to cover unemployment benefits and labour market programmes. It is responsible for paying unemployment benefits to the unemployed, who collect cheques, which are payable from the account of the employment centre in the State savings bank. It finances the costs of labour market programmes and does all the office's accounting.

The other three departments are the labour market programmes' department, mainly responsible for training and retraining, the statistics' department, and the social works department, which may also be responsible for organising subsidies for the creation of additional jobs in enterprises. Besides these departments, each employment centre has a reception area; a receptionist is the first person the jobseeker meets and the receptionist sends them to the relevant department.

The potential of a local employment centre to promote employment or to combat unemployment in its district is limited. According to official estimates, less than one-third of jobseekers come to the employment service; the remainder try to find a job on their own. Others have estimated that less than 20% of the unemployed go to register.[12] Bearing that in mind, the rate of job placement by employment centres is still relatively high in comparison with what is usual in other countries. In 1993, of 584,000 registering jobseekers, 558,000 of them being jobless, 36% were placed in a job.[13] But considering the low propensity to register among jobseekers in Ukraine, the performance of employment centres should not be overestimated.

Apart from job placements, a local employment centre may arrange training courses according to labour and skill demand of enterprises. In the case of public works, it concludes contracts with enterprises. The condition is that enterprises and regional authorities have to finance them, as the Employment Fund can cover only organisational costs. As for the generation of additional jobs, all subsidies higher than 5 million karbovanets (about US$ 100 in May 1994) have to be agreed with Kiev. Since the internal regulation of the Ministry fixes a 3% unemployment rate as the threshold for implementing special measures, such as more generous subsidies for job creation, and since the registered unemployment rate in most regions has been well below that, the regulation has actually meant that there has

[12] V. Shamota, An Analysis of the Ukrainian Labour Market and Efficiency of the State Employment Policy, background paper prepared for ILO-CEET, 1994.
[13] State Employment Service, Annual Report for 1993, op. cit.

been no possibility for opening additional jobs in the regions. Generation of additional jobs is thus directly controlled from the centre and mostly limited to those regions designated as deserving preferential development. A few local employment centres have succeeded in establishing and funding small enterprises, which provide employment for those difficult to place in regular jobs. But the number is tiny. In 1993, 31 such enterprises gave jobs to 479 people.[14]

The State Employment Service also includes a network of regional centres for vocational guidance, training and retraining (in five regions they have merged into one centre), providing technical assistance and other services to local employment centres. These 48 centres (including one in Crimea, and two in the cities of Kiev and Sevastopol) employed 1,048 employees, as of December 31, 1993.

According to the State Employment Service, its biggest problems have been insufficient equipment, in the form of computers and so on, and unsuitable premises for employment centres in many of the regions. By the end of 1993, only one-fifth of the network of employment centres was equipped with computers.[15] Because of the limited number of registered unemployed, it was still possible to operate sufficiently well to provide jobseekers with up-to-date information on vacancies. However, even exchange of information between neighbouring employment centres on registered jobseekers or on vacancies demanding certain skills has been impractical without a computerised information network, and that in itself impeded geographical and other labour mobility. With the anticipated growth in unemployment, the quality of services to jobseekers and to employers will deteriorate without a computerised information system.

Also, deteriorating transport and the high fares for such transport make it difficult for many of the unemployed to have access to employment services, especially in agricultural regions. Improvements in this regard are being made. In 1993, the Employment Service opened five new employment centres and started to construct 60 new subsidiaries. And considerable financial resources were devoted to the reconstruction and extension of existing premises. In 1994–1995, the main goal should be to develop an effective network of labour market institutions, which would provide both the unemployed and employers with properly structured information on labour supply and demand, promote flexible adjustment of the labour force to changing skill and territorial requirements, and stimulate labour productivity and competitiveness.

---

[14] State Employment Service, Annual Report 1993, op. cit., p. 26; and ILO-CEET calculations.

[15] Ministry of Labour, *Pro vikonannya* . . ., 1993, op. cit., p. 5.

5. Labour Market Policies

5.1. Employment Programme for 1993

The Ministry of Labour's *State Employment Programme for 1993* – which was the second annual programme of this type – envisaged a rapid increase in open unemployment, due to problems in agriculture, conversion of military production, closure of unprofitable coal mines in Donbas and economic pressure in enterprises forcing them to shed redundant workers.[16] The Programme presented two scenarios of future labour market developments.

5.1.1. Scenarios about Labour Market Developments

According to a first scenario of the Ministry of Labour and regional authorities, in 1993, unemployment was expected to reach the level of 1,540,000 (i.e., 5.5% of the labour force). In the case of an unexpectedly deep fall in production, which was not defined in the programme, the rate of open unemployment was expected by the second scenario to rise to 9%, although the timing was not specified.

In the Programme, the Ministry of Labour also anticipated a second outline, with much slower developments in the labour market in 1993. Under this, total labour supply was expected to reach 1,540,000 persons, of which only a third was expected to be due to redundancies, the remainder being school leavers and other labour force entrants. Total labour demand should have reached 990,000, which represented a level of unemployment equal to 550,000 persons and an 1.8% rate of unemployment. These considerations assumed neither a falling participation rate, which has been typical of other central and eastern European countries, nor any substantial increase in part-time work and other flexible forms of work, nor any radical changes in the employment structure. Almost two-thirds of the expected additions to the labour force were expected to fill existing vacancies or vacancies freed by retiring workers. Only a third were expected to enter new jobs created by state or private investment or subsidised from the Employment Fund.

These forecasts of the State Employment Service led it to focus on job placement and job creation. New jobs were expected to be financed from the state budget, enterprise investments, private investment, or partly subsidised from the Employment Fund. The Employment Programme further calculated on placing 106,300 unemployed in social (public) works and it expected regional authorities to ensure that occurred. Social works should

[16] Ministry of Labour, *Derzhavna programa zaynyatosti naselenya na 1993 rik* (*State Programme of Employment for 1993*), Kiev, 1993.

have promoted regional development and stabilised agricultural production, as well as food processing. Social works combined with vocational training were scheduled for young unemployed lacking such training.

5.1.2. Territories of Preferential Development

According to the Employment Programme, special attention should be devoted to job generation in so-called territories of preferential development, which comprise sub-regions facing problems due to excess labour supply, high structural unemployment or the envisaged closure of enterprises, notably major regional employers such as coal mines. It was expected that schemes would be set up by combining public, enterprise and private funds, including the Employment Fund.

For 1993, the number of socially vulnerable persons requiring job placement with the help of employment exchanges was estimated at 346,000. It was expected that they would be placed in jobs primarily via the obligatory 5% quota of jobs determined for them in all larger enterprises. That should have covered almost 90% of the required number of jobs. Some 54,000 additional jobs should have been generated through subsidies from the Employment Fund.

Among labour market policies, the Programme designers preferred to put emphasis on training and retraining. The Employment Programme envisaged participation of 137,000 persons in such training, to be funded from the Employment Fund and from other sources. Vocational retraining was also scheduled to be the main measure for soldiers released from the army, which was to be reduced by an estimated 33,000 in 1993, or 46,000 if their families are included. The Ministry intended to open special readaptation centres for them in places of large-scale lay-offs and a special retraining centre in Kiev to facilitate their labour market entry. Also, some subsidised additional jobs should have been generated for them, financed from the Employment Fund.

It was stipulated that special regional employment policy should focus on sub-regions foreseen to face difficulties in the labour market in connection with restructuring. Sub-regions gaining the status of territories of preferential development thereby gain access to extra funds for job creation, training and retraining, etc. In the period 1993–1995, the Programme intended to assist in creating 174,000 jobs. The form of assistance should be mainly organisational, but if necessary the Programme allowed for provision of financial resources for the creation of additional jobs.

Territories of preferential development included five types of sub-regions:

a) Rural and mountainous sub-regions (51 districts, 'rayons', mainly in western and south-western Ukraine) where labour supply exceeded demand. According to estimations from these sub-regions, 113,000 new jobseekers should enter the labour market between 1993–1995, for whom about 80,300 new vacancies should be created. Also, unemployed people from these sub-regions should be assisted in securing work in such activities as private family farming, in agricultural cooperatives including non-agricultural activities of those cooperatives, in doing seasonal jobs in other regions facing labour shortage.[17]

b) Sub-regions expecting production cuts due to exhaustion of natural resources, closure of big enterprises or structural changes in production. There are 14 subregions in this category, mainly located in central and eastern Ukraine. The Programme envisaged 53,000 jobseekers entering the labour market due to these reasons and the creation of 24,000 vacancies in 1993–1995. Among the expected jobseekers were the 3,000 coal miners estimated to be made redundant in 1993, with more to follow in 1994–1995.

The conversion of military production was another source of structural change. The total number of redundant workers forecast for 1993 was 43,000. The conversion programme was supposed to contain proposals to provide employment and social protection for released workers. They were supposed to be offered training and retraining or additional jobs funded from the Employment Fund. But only sub-regions in which over 20% of the released workers were laid off as a result of military conversion were granted the status of territory of preferential development, a status that gave them special possibilities for development promotion. So, the number of jobseekers and vacancies mentioned in the previous paragraph refer only to those districts.

c) The third type comprises 36 sub-regions with what are perceived as structural distortions in the labour market. These are mainly coal-mining sub-regions of eastern Ukraine and a few in western Ukraine with very limited job opportunities for women. Until 1995, in these sub-regions about 104,000 such jobseekers were expected to enter the labour market, for whom 37,000 new jobs should be created.

d) The fourth type comprises 13 sub-regions where workers have been released in connection with the gradual closure of the Chernobyl nuclear power station. Members of nations deported from their Ukrainian settlements under Stalin's regime and now returning, should be settled in those areas, mainly in Crimea, and to a small extent in central and

---

[17] These activities should however, be supported only by regional and local administrations, not by the Employment Service which does not want to take over any responsibility for promoting employment in agriculture because agricultural enterprises do not pay contributions to the Employment Fund.

eastern Ukraine. This should bring 32,000 new jobseekers into these districts, where 22,000 new vacancies should be generated.

e) The fifth type of territory of preferential development consists of four districts particularly hit by cuts in the size of the army, mainly located in central Ukraine. The Programme planned the creation of 9,000 vacancies for about 16,000 jobseekers emerging due to the cuts.

Apart from additional jobs, other policies to be applied in these special territories should be training and retraining, social (public) works and organisational assistance in creating jobs from other resources.

The Employment Programme also committed the Ministry of Labour to work out a proposal to promote job creation in small businesses and to organise training and retraining in enterprises, at the enterprises' expense.

5.1.3. Experiences from the Employment Programme

Realisation of the 1993 Employment Programme was complicated by developments in the labour market which were quite unlike the Programme's assumptions. Although production fell even more than expected, few large structural changes seemed to occur in production or employment.

In 1993, only 165,000 workers were formally released from employment, or less than a third of the expected figure. The registered number of jobless was 123,000, or only slightly more than a sixth of the assumed figure. The number released due to military conversion was only 788, compared with an assumed 43,000, of which 1,289 soldiers left the army, compared with the 33,000 that the Programme had anticipated. As observed in Chapter 2, the increasing labour surplus was solved by putting workers on unpaid administrative leave although there was also a considerable cut in employment. The fact is that the labour market changes did not show up in the registered unemployment, which the Programme took as its guide to labour market policy.

In spite of increasing hidden unemployment, the Employment Service reported that the number of newly created vacancies was 114,100, or 97.1% of the figure planned in the Employment Programme.

However, all labour market schemes were carried out on a much more modest scale than envisaged in the Programme. The State Employment Service subsidised the creation of 5,600 additional jobs determined for socially vulnerable persons in 460 enterprises, instead of the 50,000 jobs it had announced. Also, in 1993 only 13,100 persons (2.2% of all jobseekers) participated in so-called social works (of whom 12,261 persons started in 1993), instead of the planned 106,300. The largest number was in agriculture (36.6% of the total), with 16% in industry.

The main reasons for the small number of participants in social works seem to have been the absence of revealed pressure in the labour market and the unattractiveness of vacancies, which mostly required low skills and were low paid. In many regions, social works were not launched, due to a lack of resources in regional budgets. Originally, participation in social works was limited to two months for each participant, but the Employment Service removed this condition. Workers put on unpaid leave were also allowed to participate in social works, if the number of unemployed applicants was insufficient.

The unemployed were allowed to collect unemployment benefits as well as a wage while working on social works, but only a tiny fraction of the registered unemployed (0.6%) had participated in social works as of December 31, 1993.[18] The income from such work was more attractive for those not eligible for unemployment benefits. Most participants in social work schemes were women, youths without work experience and workers who have been made redundant. The costs of social works were borne mainly by enterprises (81%), supplemented by small subsidies from municipal budgets (4.6%), the Employment Fund (6.1%) and other sources (8.3%).

Only 14% of the obligatory quota of jobs set aside for vulnerable social groups was met; some 44,000 persons belonging to these groups were placed in such jobs, and another 18,500 were placed in regular jobs.

During 1993, 32,400 jobseekers underwent training or retraining. This was less than a quarter of the planned number of 137,100, and only 5.8% of all those registering with the employment service. Of the total number starting training courses, only 45% subsequently found a new job. This efficiency indicator is distorted by drop-outs, and taking into account only those who completed training courses, the job placement rate was about 50%. In any case, our impression is that training and retraining has not yet much affected the Ukrainian labour market, reflecting the lack of substantial structural change. Moreover, retraining is offered for skills that are well represented in the pool of jobseekers, in preparation for such jobs as car and bus driver, shop assistant, secretary, PC operator, seamstress and nurse.

In July 1993, a new measure was adopted offering interest-free loans to any unemployed intending to start their own business, or to small firms creating vacancies for registered unemployed persons. The maximum amount of the loan was limited to thirty minimum monthly wages for individuals or 50 minimum wages for firms. The loan was limited to one year, and

---

[18] The notion of public works or social works is unclear in Ukraine since it is likely that many jobs of this type are merely subsidised jobs in enterprises. As such they may involve serious limitations. The concept is discussed later.

given only for production, not for other activities such as services. Since the amount was too small as seed capital for commodity production, few seem to have been seriously interested in it, while employment offices seem to have hesitated to give it to firms because there was no guarantee of repayment if they went bankrupt.[19]

Another, rather informal labour market policy applied by employment centres in 1993 was to arrange for the temporary 'lending' of workers by one enterprise to another one if the former could not pay their wages. In the past, such workers would have received 50% of their wage in the temporary job. This limit has recently been cancelled. It is not clear how many workers were involved in this practice.

Finally, the employment service practised the policy of reducing labour supply as a response to unemployment. Older unemployed workers with eighteen months or less to retirement age and fulfilling the condition of 30 years of employment for men and 25 years for women were put on old-age pension prematurely. In 1993, 34,000 persons were put on early pension in this way.[20]

The numbers of participants in all the labour market schemes in 1993 are given in *Table 3.3*. In 1993, the State Employment Service was able to place in jobs or to place in schemes or to put into early retirement 45.1% of all persons registering at employment offices, which was 47.3% of all non-employed jobseekers. The majority were placed in jobs (35.8%). However, job placement was much more difficult for those with the unemployment status than for others, only 24.8% of whom were placed in jobs. Among older jobseekers, the most common outcome was early retirement. As for labour market policies, they had very modest results – 5.8% of all non-employed jobseekers participated in vocational training and retraining courses, 2.2% in social works and 1.1% were placed in additional jobs.

The first quarter of 1994 showed a substantial deterioration in employment prospects for jobseekers registering with the State Employment Service. Of 273,342 jobseekers registered in this period (47.7% with unemployment status), only 20.8% were placed in a job (9.6% of those with unemployment status), 6.9% were put into early retirement, 10% underwent training or retraining and only 1.4% participated in public works.

Correspondingly, expenditure on labour market policies has been modest so far. The total income and expenditure of the Employment Promotion

---

[19] The Ministry of Labour reported that in 1993 they gave the highest priority to the support of small-scale firms, which created 7,400 new jobs. *Derzhavna programa . . .*, 1993, op. cit., p. 2.

[20] National Centre of the State Employment Service, *Zvit pro pracevlashtuvannya . . .*, 1994 op. cit.

Table 3.3 *Participation in Labour Market Schemes, Ukraine, 1993*

Persons seeking assistance from Employment Service	Thousand
All unemployed persons	557,512
– Jobseekers with unemployment status	180,898
Employed persons	52,921
Total	583,433
Average monthly number of benefit recipients	43,742
All persons placed in a job	199,538
Registered jobseekers placed in a job	44,433
Persons placed in a job under the 5% quota	44,000
Persons placed in newly created additional jobs	5,600
Persons placed in early retirement	33,746
Persons placed in retraining courses	32,408
Persons placed in social works	12,261

Source: *Report of the State Employment Service on the Implementation of the State Employment Programme for 1993*, Kiev, December 1993.

Fund for 1992–93 are given in *Table 3.4*. In 1992, the Employment Fund was financed almost wholly from enterprise contributions.[21]

Their share was 95.1%, while the state budget contributed with 2.7% and the rest was from other sources. In 1993, the Government originally committed itself to give 5 billion karbovanets to the Fund. This was later reduced to 700 million karbovanets, which were given but later taken back due to budget deficit problems. Thus, in 1993, 91.1% of the Employment Fund's income was raised from enterprises, 8.6% from the Employment Service's own means or reserves, and 0.3% from other sources.

As can be seen in *Table 3.3*, in 1992 expenditure from the Employment Fund comprised only 21% of available income, and in 1993 the figure was only 37.6%, which meant that a large part of the income was effectively idle and losing value, given the hyperinflation.[22] An explanation may be the much lower registered open unemployment than expected, which reduced the cost of providing income protection and the funds needed to cover employment promotion measures. Another reason was the strict regulation of resources available for regional and local employment centres on job creation policies above the level specified in the regional programme.

[21] The following enterprises and institutions do not have to pay contributions to the Employment Fund: agricultural farms if engaged only in agricultural production, enterprises of disabled persons and pensioners, and non-profit organisations. Enterprises engaged only partly in commercial activity are obliged to pay contributions from the commercialised share of production.

[22] Until the end of 1993, funds of the Employment Fund were deposited in an interest-free account of the State Bank of Ukraine. Since then, they have been deposited in interest-bearing accounts in commercial banks.

Table 3.4 *Income and Expenditure of the Employment Promotion Fund, Ukraine, 1992–1993 (million karbovanets)*

Indicator	1992		1993	
	Million	%	Million	%
Total income	28,285.3		608,477.7	
Items of expenditure				
Creation of new jobs	211.4	3.6	45,318.3	19.9
Training and retraining	78.7	1.3	8,670.7	3.8
Social works	2.1	0.0	58.1	0.0
Operational costs of employment centres	851.0	14.6	52,338.1	23.0
Transfers to the centralised part of EF	4,063.6	69.5	64,538.1	28.3
Improvement of the information network and operational costs of the network of regional centres of vocational guidance and training	145.7	2.5	44,325.2	19.5
Unemployment benefits and social assistance	419.8	7.2	11,322.8	5.0
Other	74.5	1.3	1,095.8	0.5
Total	5,846.8	100	227,667.1	100
Reserves	22,428.5	20.9*	380,810.6	37.6*

*Percentage of the total income.

Source: V. Yatsenko, Employment Policy in Ukraine in 1991–1994, paper prepared for ILO conference Employment Policy and Programmes, Budapest, June 2–3, 1994, State Employment Service, 1994.

Although the National Employment Centre was responsible for approval of large-scale job creation projects, it found it difficult to justify supporting projects outside territories of preferential development, especially given its lack of experience in such ventures. So, it preferred to avoid such projects, however important they were perceived to be for the regional economy and labour market. Some progress was achieved in implementation of job creation policy in 1992 and 1993, which became the most used measure.

However, the main part of expenditure from the Employment Fund was devoted to expansion of the State Employment Service, improvement of its equipment, premises and computers, staff training, development of its information system and coverage of operational costs. Over the next few years, the priorities will have to change quite radically.

5.2. Employment Programme for 1994

5.2.1. Scenarios about Labour Market Developments

Perhaps reflecting its experience with forecasts for 1993, the Ministry of Labour and the National Employment Service foresaw no radical changes in the labour market for 1994.[23] As in the previous year, the Ministry of Labour made two scenarios for its Employment Programme for 1994. Under its optimistic variant, the anticipated number of workers entering the labour market would be 1.2 million, of whom 340,000 would be redundancies. Of the total, almost 650,000 were expected to be placed either in existing vacancies or in newly created jobs, 220,000 were expected to find jobs themselves or withdraw from the labour force, and 300,000 were expected to remain jobless at the end of 1994, which would mean an unemployment rate of 1.3%. This variant, derived from expected labour market developments and regional employment programmes, was used as a basis for the Employment Programme. The Programme stipulated individual labour market policies, numbers of participants (or created jobs) and expenditure from the Employment Fund and other resources.

The other variant was based on the assumption of a crisis in the labour market. It assumes higher joblessness, mainly due to more redundancies (840,000 workers), fewer quits and higher demand for jobs from the economically inactive population. According to this estimate there would be 840,000 unemployed and the unemployment rate would be 3.5% at the end of the year.

Both variants still considered that only a small fraction of hidden unemployment would be transformed into open unemployment and that the absorptive capacity of the Ukrainian economy was still high. The hidden assumption behind both variants was the continuation of slow structural change. A more radical economic programme of a new Government intent on promoting economic growth would undermine these sanguine expectations.

5.2.2. Promoting Small Businesses and Self-Employment

To some extent, a more radical economic programme was taken into account by the Employment Programme, which foresaw measures stimulating structural change and development of small businesses and self-employment. It stated that the former should be done by selective temporary support to enterprises with good economic prospects rather than by more widely dispersed short-term loans and subsidies. The Programme

[23] Ministry of Labour, *Derzhavna programa zaynyatosti naselennya na 1994 rik* (*State Programme of Employment in 1994*), approved by the Cabinet of Ministers, Kiev, February 23, 1994.

stated that unprofitable enterprises should be assisted in regulating redundancies. Assessment of enterprises' financial situation and economic prospects, and proposals for assistance from the Employment Fund and other sources, should be the responsibility of newly created expert councils affiliated to regional authorities. The relevant ministries and regional authorities would have the right to correct and approve specific programmes. Enterprises forced to reduce working time would be able to obtain technical, organisational and financial assistance from the Employment Promotion Fund, at least according to the 1994 Programme.[24]

The Programme also considered new forms of self-employment and small business promotion for the unemployed. Apart from the interest-free start-up loan scheme, introduced on a small scale in 1993, a new scheme was envisaged whereby an unemployed worker could receive a lump-sum equivalent of the amount of unemployment benefits for the maximum period for which the person is eligible to receive such benefits, to start a business or self-employment, or to invest in a cooperative when entering one. Financial and other assistance should be concentrated on small-scale enterprises producing goods and processing domestic raw-materials, and on enterprises employing highly qualified workers released from machine-building and military industry.

Unfortunately, all the schemes in the 1994 Programme were formulated very generally, without indicating necessary financial backstopping, and their scope was limited. For instance, the Programme envisaged provision of interest-free loans to only 3,600 unemployed workers.[25]

5.2.3. Territories of Preferential Development

The Ministry of Labour estimated that about 100,000 new jobs would be generated from various resources and another 40,000 additional jobs would be created from the Employment Fund, mainly in territories of preferential development (27,000 jobs) and for socially vulnerable jobseekers in 1994. Apart from that, 40% of the unemployed should be placed in existing vacancies.

In the 1994 Programme, the number of territories of preferential development was increased and the schedule of job creation was made more precise:

a) The number of rural and mountainous sub-regions was increased to 65 newly covering also some districts in central and southern Ukraine. Of the 90,000 vacancies planned to be created there in 1994–95, 6,000 additional jobs were to be funded from the Employment Fund in 1994.

[24] Ministry of Labour, 1994, op. cit., p. 10.
[25] Ministry of Labour, 1994, op. cit., p. 10.

b) As far as sub-regions suffering from production cuts are concerned, two more were added in comparison with the 1993 Programme, and altogether 29,000 jobs were to be generated in the 1994–1995 period. The Programme planned to subsidise creation of more than 3,000 vacancies in 1994.

c) The number of sub-regions with structural mismatches in the labour market was increased substantially, to 46. Altogether 41,000 jobs, including 8,000 additional jobs in 1994, were to be generated in these sub-regions in the two-year period. Additional jobs should be financed from the Employment Fund.

d) The fourth type of sub-region where people from the Chernobyl area and of formerly deported nations should be settled included 20 sub-regions needing 25,000 new vacancies in 1994–95, more than 9,000 of them funded from the Employment Fund in 1994.

e) Eight sub-regions hit by cuts in the size of the army needed 12,000 more vacancies in 1994–95, according to the Employment Programme, of which 500 would be additional jobs in 1994.

5.2.4. Social Works, Training and Labour Market Institutions

The 1994 Programme stated that social (public) works should be used for those unemployed unable to find regular jobs, and that public works would be improved under a new Programme on Social Works. It estimated that about 95,000 workers would participate in social works in 1994.[26] This represented a major increase over the actual experience in 1993. There is no evidence that any monitoring or evaluation of that experience had been carried out before the expansion was decided.

The Programme committed the Government to strengthening training and retraining, which were to be oriented towards released workers, women and those with unemployment status. A goal for 1994 was to offer retraining to 91,000 people (51,000 of whom should be women). It stated that programmes would be prepared for employment promotion and social protection for soldiers released from the army, enterprises producing armaments, machine-building enterprises and coal mines and that such schemes should specify how many people would be affected and the costs of their reemployment in those regions or elsewhere.

The Employment Programme expected improvement of the network of labour market institutions, periodical training of their staff and progress in creating a uniform computerised labour market information system. In labour and social legislation, it stated that the Government intended to complete the reform of social insurance in the case of employment

---

[26] Ministry of Labour, 1994, op. cit., Annex 2.

loss and to consider ratification of ILO Conventions No. 89, 132, 135 and 168.

Although the 1994 Programme seemed to strengthen labour market policies, it is questionable whether the declared goals could be achieved when only small changes in institutional and financial support were made. This applies most to mechanisms of assistance to enterprises, including legal aspects. Similarly, no measures were set up to demonstrate support for small businesses, since the funds available through both schemes were insufficient to start a firm, particularly in production.

Social works could not be launched on the planned scale, due to a lack of resources in the regions, since the Employment Fund could not be used for that purpose. Regional policies were thus restricted to the creation of additional jobs in territories of preferential development, while instruments actually supporting regional restructuring and economic development were not established. Ultimately, the 1994 Programme was more a declaration than a programme designed to achieve employment restructuring.

5.3. The Concept of the State Programme of Youth Employment Promotion for 1994–1995

On August 6, 1993, the Government approved a 'Concept', or conceptual plan, intended to improve the position of young people in the Ukrainian labour market.[27] Although there were only 35,000 jobseekers registered at employment exchanges under the age of 30 at the end of 1993, it has been widely accepted that the actual number of unemployed youth is much greater, perhaps rising to nearly one million.[28] In the near future, their situation will deteriorate as overall labour supply will grow, due to demographic factors and the reduction of the army.

Demand for young workers was expected to decline as a result of the economic crisis, a mismatch between the qualifications of school leavers and apprentices and the availability of jobs because of the nature of the educational system, and obstacles to labour migration (high transport costs and reduction in housing construction), and a lack of demand in the emerging private sector.

According to the outline plan, the main measures for promoting employment of young people would be oriented towards increasing their labour market competitiveness and facilitating their job placement. More attention

---

[27] Ministry of Labour, *Osnovni konceptualni polozhennya rozrobki proektu cilovoy derzhavnoy programi spriami spriannya zaynyatosti molodi na 1994–1995 roki* (*Basic Conceptual Principles of Project Elaboration of the State Programme for Youth Employment Promotion in 1994–1995*), Kiev, August 1993.

[28] Ministry of Labour, August 1993, op. cit.

was to be paid to vocational guidance according to their abilities and employment prospects. According to the Concept, the system of schooling and training would be restructured to correspond to market needs. After completing education, young people would have guaranteed jobs according to the Law on Promotion of Social Adaptation and Development of Youth in Ukraine.

Unemployed young people would be offered training and retraining, support in self-employment or starting of small business, or participation in special public work schemes taking into consideration their social needs. Emigration in order to find work and informal economic activity by youth would be regulated. Assistance would be given to disadvantaged young people, such as those with disabilities and ex-prisoners. Labour market programmes would be accompanied by appropriate financial assistance to young jobseekers and their families. Both regional employment programmes and the State Employment Programme would incorporate these goals and measures and the State Employment Service would guarantee their implementation.

The Concept addressed important aspects of employment promotion of young people. Yet they were formulated generally, and were supposed to be elaborated in the National Employment Programme and regional programmes. Unfortunately, the 1994 Programme did not include any measure targeted at young people, and the constraints of existing policies mentioned earlier did not suggest that the hopes of the Concept would be realised.

5.4. The Concept of the State System of Vocational Guidance

On January 27, 1994, another 'Concept' was approved by the Government.[29] It set out to elaborate ideas from the Concept on youth employment to extend them to other groups. Its main goal underlying this very ambitious Concept is the creation of a network of institutions providing vocational guidance for the population to facilitate structural change in the economy by minimising mobility costs and adverse social consequences. These institutions would be established or extended within the educational system, youth institutions, the State Employment Service, large-scale enterprises and social security departments affiliated to regional and local authorities.

These institutions would have access to a data bank containing information on labour market developments, demand for labour, structured by skills and occupation, and supply of skilled labour force at the national and regional levels. They should also be informed about educational and

[29] Ministry of Labour, *Koncepcia derzhavnoy sistemi profesiynoy orientacii naselennya (Concept of the State System of Professional Orientation of Population)*, Kiev, January 1994.

training possibilities. Their staff would include psychologists, sociologists, labour specialists and medical doctors for those with disabilities. Their task would be to make individual assessments of abilities, skills, wishes, health and personal preferences, and – on the basis of labour market forecasts – give advice on which profession to choose for schooling or retraining. Although the basic network would be state-funded, services associated with professional guidance would also be provided by non-governmental organisations, including private firms. Higher educational institutions and vocational training centres would also be obliged to open specialised departments providing vocational education and training to people with certain disabilities.

This Concept of vocational assessment and guidance for young people and workers made redundant due to production and technological change would require a sophisticated information network and extensive staff training, probably with international technical assistance, since there is only limited experience with such services in Ukraine.

5.5. National Programme of Social (Public) Works

The Government has introduced a social works scheme that seems to provide for two types of social works.[30] The first consists of traditional activities such as cleaning of public areas, social care, seasonal jobs in agriculture, and construction and maintenance of roads. These are performed within enterprises or institutions engaged in such activities and financed from regional and local budgets, so that regional employment centres bear only organisational costs.

The second type involves large-scale investment in national or regional projects, which are supposed to be funded from the state budget or from a combination of state and regional resources.

The programme was determined for 1994–1995 and indicated that public works would be carried out on such projects as the construction of railways connecting Kiev with Lviv, Krakow with Berlin, Kiev with Crimea and Kharkiv with Crimea, construction and reconstruction of highways connecting northern Ukraine with Poland and central Russia, and central Ukraine with central Europe and the Near East, reconstruction of both Kiev airports and construction of factories producing tiles from the waste of coalmining.

The Programme also proposed to combine public works with the continuation or completion of large state investment projects that had been started and temporarily interrupted or slowed down because of financial

---

[30] Ministry of Labour, *Nacionalna programa gromadskikh robit* (*National Programme of Social Works*), Kiev, November 1993.

tensions in the state budget. The Appendix of the Programme gave a comprehensive list of such projects, ranging from the construction of oil and gas pipelines and water-supplies in eastern Ukraine, to railways, roads and electrical lines in agricultural regions, land improvement systems for agriculture, water channels, underground railways in Kiev, Dnipropetrovsk, Donetsk, etc. As most of these projects are constructional, the Employment Service was expected to organise training for participants, especially the unemployed.

For 1994, the Programme of Social Works planned to create 119,400 jobs for 132,700 workers. The costs of the planned social works (estimated at 52.7 billion karbovanets in January 1994) were to be shared between enterprises or institutions organising them (42%), regional and local budgets (16%), the Employment Fund (17%) and the state budget (20%). It is not clear from the Programme why this division of financial responsibility was made.

Social works are carried out mainly in the May–September period, so it is difficult to discern the recent trend. However, the actual number of those involved in the first quarter of 1994 showed a slight decrease over the previous year, even though workers on unpaid leave and shorter working time were allowed to take part without reduction in their income from their main job.[31] The reasons seem to have been financial. The government lacked funds, which was why the second type of public works was not implemented at all, and regional and enterprise budgets for traditional activities of the first type were stretched.

Municipalities and employment centres were not pressed by their local populations to organise such projects and workers did not seem to be interested, either due to the very low earnings or the unattractive character of such jobs, according to employment exchange officials.

6. Assessment of Labour Market Policies and Recommendations for Improvement

These are early days in the development of Ukraine's labour market policies. At one level, one might conclude that it is a positive feature that the Government has made employment one of the pillars of its macroeconomic and social policy and considers reforms from the point of view of their possible effect on employment. The goals and measures of the

---

[31] See the quarterly report of the State Employment Service for the first quarter of 1994. In this period, the number of participants in public works was 3,966, or 1.4% of all jobseekers. Among those with unemployment status, the share participating in public works was practically the same, 1.5% (1,987 persons).

annual Employment Programme are specified after taking into account the consequences of reforms at the macroeconomic level, in economic sectors and regions and after considering regional economic and labour market trends.

Unfortunately, this approach also has negative drawbacks. First, anticipated adverse employment and social effects impede implementation of more radical reform, which is unavoidable for macro-economic stabilisation and economic growth. The aim of maintaining full employment is transformed in reality into the creation of barriers to structural change in production and employment. The price of this cautious policy is high inflation, sustained in part by short-term credits to enterprises and big loans to agriculture, deteriorating real incomes, rising poverty, massive hidden unemployment and sharpening social and political tensions.

Second, regional employment programmes prepared jointly by regional authorities and employment offices are usually passive in their goals in respect of economic development and employment restructuring. This may be due to inexperience of regional political and state administration representatives with the functioning of a market economy and the ways of influencing regional development, and to limited financial resources. The central authorities do not leave much independence to regional bodies in economic decision-making, for fear of political decentralisation and claims of autonomy. This is why no influential economic policy measures are delegated to regional authorities. Also, the aggregation of regional employment programmes, with small corrections in the centre regarding demographic and some regional labour market mismatches, tends to produce inertia and does not stimulate employment restructuring.

To begin to tackle the accumulated labour market problems, it is necessary to create a macro-economic environment promoting enterprise restructuring and shifts in employment. The 1994 Employment Programme was a step in the right direction, even if it failed to show how the proposals could be translated into reality. Above all, while the labour market situation is dependent largely on economic development and economic policy, it is important to recognise that labour market policies in the narrow sense can have only minor effects.

6.1. Promoting the Development of Small Firms and Self-Employment

Initially, an employment-promotion strategy should be based on promoting the development of small firms, networks of such firms and self-employment, since they could absorb part of the labour released from large-scale enterprises. As this is dependent on the availability of premises and access to bank credit or other financial resources for entrepreneurs, the

Government should accelerate a programme of privatisation of small-scale enterprises and encourage the restructuring of large-scale enterprises into smaller units – a process that has started according to findings from the ILO's Ukraine Labour Flexibility Survey (ULFS).[32] Experience of central and southern European countries shows that the process of small privatisation can create a good base for private sector development. Although public auctions as the main form of privatisation seem to be the best method, lack of capital in the hands of the population, the underdeveloped banking sector and possibly unfair practices excluding large strata of the population from participation and raising social tensions may be solved by using non-traditional methods.

The following procedure is already partially implemented and can be improved. Traditional auctions should be used as one method of privatisation for small units. In the case of larger units, special regional privatisation commissions under public control should evaluate submitted privatisation plans. These commissions should choose the best plans from the point of view of their feasibility, development prospects, skills and appropriate experience of submitters, etc.

Privatisation plans should comprise the way of covering the price of privatised unit (in cash, by bank credit with special guarantees paid from future revenue, i.e. by mortgage credit, or privatisation vouchers), business plan, personnel plan and guarantees for their implementation. The possibility of preferential sale to the workers' collective if they are interested may also be considered, on the condition that it submits a viable business plan.

The Government should extend policies to promote small businesses, such as tax holidays, subsidies and preferential loans. These measures may be differentiated according to national goals, regional needs, field of activity and so on. The right to make such differentiation should be given to regional authorities. To facilitate access of small entrepreneurs to loans, a special state (or state-supported) bank should be set up to concentrate exclusively on small-scale businesses and provide them with preferential loans or state guarantees to loans from commercial banks. Credit should be given on a competitive basis after assessment of business plans.

6.2. Improvement of Human Resources and Technical Conditions

Apart from creating conditions for small business, it is important to promote improvement of human resources and technical conditions for sustainable business development. Seven decades of state rule has distorted

---

[32] This showed that in 1993–1994 about 10% of industrial establishments had divested, by detaching production units.

entrepreneurial spirit and business skills. Past education and recent experience with the informal economy have created an atmosphere of suspicion and animosity against private business. It will take time to rectify those failings.

Entrepreneurial skills – such as how to choose the type of activity, work out a business plan, find collaborators and staff, run a firm and market products and services – have to be learnt. A network of business incubators and business innovation and promotion centres should be created, which would provide training for potential businessmen, assist them in running their firms, and facilitate access to financial resources and technologies. Education in managerial and business skills should also be included in the educational system.

6.3. Achieving Regional Economic Autonomy

In a country as vast as Ukraine, regional development initiatives may prove to be vital for national regeneration. Regions should be enabled to formulate long-term development strategies. These should be based on comprehensive analyses of the economic and social potential of specific regions, including the skills and capacities of the population.

Regional development strategies should assess the anticipated employment effects of the intended restructuring that will be involved, with the aim of optimally utilising human resources.

The leading role should be played by regional authorities, who should initiate partnerships with state administrations, employment offices, enterprises, regional employer organisations, trade unions, other non-governmental organisations, educational and research institutions and others interested in formulating and implementing the strategy and schedule.

This call for higher economic autonomy of regions is not in conflict with the political goals of national sovereignty, cohesion and stability. Economically strong regions are more likely to be politically stable and constitute a stabilising element for the country. Regionalisation of large complex economies such as Ukraine is consistent with establishment of networks of industrial enterprises, with the sharing of technology, and with more coordinated labour market and human resource policies and with more meaningful democratisation. A balance of central and regional interests, rights, responsibilities and constraints should be established through regional strategies. While prosperous regions should be given reasonable economic independence, the more economically depressed could be supported from the centre.

If such an economic and employment strategy existed, regional economic and labour market policies could be coordinated with it. Regional authorities could encourage business projects for the production of goods or services in demand and stimulate development of other economic activities. This support could be given in the form of extra tax holidays, special grants, subsidised credits and provision of premises, depending on regional financial possibilities.

6.4. Close Contacts with Enterprises

Regional authorities and employment offices should be in close contact with all enterprises in the region. In the case of enterprises with economic problems, regional authorities should decide (after assessment of the financial situation and prospects of these enterprises by expert councils, as proposed in the 1994 Employment Programme) together with enterprise owners and managers how to solve this situation with respect to the labour force. If the enterprise were viable and temporary assistance could help to prevent large-scale redundancies, the regional authorities in cooperation with employment offices could conclude agreement with the enterprise specifying type of assistance, conditions for it, time schedule and sanctions if the Programme were not fulfilled.

Because of the risk of strengthening inefficient structures, assistance should be made dependant on the submission of realistic production, sales and personnel development plans by the enterprise, including restructuring and the scale of lay-offs or redeployment and retraining needs. Assistance may include credit for restructuring, temporary wage subsidies for shorter working time and assistance in staff retraining.

If a large-scale enterprise is undergoing restructuring and mass redundancies are inevitable, formal procedures should be established and followed. The enterprise should cooperate with regional authorities and employment centres in assisting workers made redundant to find jobs or to start businesses. Enterprise management should prepare, jointly with the trade union, a list of workers to be laid off. This should be done in consultation with regional authorities and employment centres in order to identify re-employment opportunities, and the enterprise should pay for the retraining of redundant workers, if needed.

Workers interested in starting their own business could be offered assistance by the enterprise in the form of loans, premises, or cheap sale of equipment, if their business plans were feasible. The enterprise could also commission services or production of spare parts for them. Another option is for firms retrenching workers to offer support to other firms (premises, equipment, orders, etc.) if they accepted redundant workers. If no possibility of placement existed, laid-off workers should be offered assistance of employment offices and labour market schemes.

Enterprises should cooperate with regional educational facilities.

Vocational schools and training centres should be informed of their actual and future demand for skills, so as to be able to adjust their curricula accordingly. One form of partnership could be participation of enterprise specialists in training of students and apprentices, and vice versa teachers to be trained in enterprise operations.

6.5. Creation of Technology Parks

Schools could also offer retraining courses for workers of enterprises undergoing restructuring, or do research and development activity for such enterprises. Universities, special schools and research centres should work with regional authorities and enterprises, with support from the state, to create technology parks, which could stimulate application of results of research and development in production and dissemination of technologies among enterprises.

Although large-scale enterprises may also benefit, small ones can benefit most from technology parks, since new technologies are often unaffordable for them. Such centres usually attract foreign capital, due to the concentration of specialists and good technological base.

In cooperation with the state administration, regional authorities could also create favourable conditions in duty free zones, to increase the attraction of these technology centres, which could become development foci for surrounding areas. Ukraine has advantageous conditions for such technology parks, especially in areas where industrial conversion from military to civilian production is taking place, since there is a high concentration of skilled and low-cost labour in such areas.

6.6. Economic Approach to Employment

As for labour market policies in the narrow sense, they should be improved and oriented to support an economic approach to employment. Their aim should be to promote labour flexibility and effective utilisation of human resources, and prevent labour market marginalisation of various social groups.

It is important to adjust legal rules to enable and facilitate implementation of more effective labour market policies. More decision-making and responsibility for employment should be delegated to regional authorities and regional employment centres, which should be overseen by regional tripartite bodies.

The State Employment Service should thus become an independent juridical body supervised by a national tripartite council, and by those regional tripartite bodies. Regional employment centres should also be responsible for expenditure from the Employment Fund at their disposal under broader rules for spending, in accordance with basic aims of the regional employment programmes and national labour market policies. In such cases regional centres would be able to use as much money as possible in a rational way for unemployment benefits and other financial assistance, employment services and labour market programmes, and no money would remain in the Fund.

The situation of workers put on unpaid leave or reduced working time must be addressed as a matter of urgency. If an enterprise is considered viable when undergoing restructuring and receives credit or subsidies from an employment office or other source, it should be obliged to support workers financially until its recovery and return to regular wages (or such support may be paid by the employment centre as part of a consolidation assistance package). If the enterprise is not considered viable, workers should be encouraged to use the employment service to find another job. If workers quit in such circumstances, they should be treated as normal jobseekers with the right to severance pay and unemployment benefits.

While support to small-scale business and self-employment should be given through a large-scale economic programme, any unemployed willing to start business should be given additional assistance covered from the Employment Fund. If their business plan is approved by an expert committee, they should receive their accumulated unemployment benefits as seed capital and be covered for interest on their credit and training costs, for up to one year.

Subsidised job creation schemes could be expanded, depending on the ability of the authorities to manage them effectively. Where they should be located should be determined on a competitive basis, depending on assessments by a tripartite committee working with local employment offices. The selection criteria should include the firm's situation, the existence of a well-prepared viable development project, assured recruitment of workers from the pool of unemployed and planned duration of their jobs. Employment offices might conclude contracts with selected firms, stipulating forms of assistance, conditions, obligations and guarantees.

Support might be in the form of preferential credit, payment of interest on commercial loans or grants. These might be equal to the sum of unemployment benefits for the recruited workers for the period of employment or be negotiated according to the expected cost of job creation and regional priorities. Such job creation should be coordinated with the economic and employment development strategy of the region.

Although international experience shows that there is likely to be a substantial 'dead-weight effect' (i.e., such jobs would have been created in any case, so that the money was wasted), in transition economies such policies can be useful for promoting employment restructuring and small businesses.[33] As long as too much is not expected of such initiatives, they should be regarded as valuable component in the employment-based strategy.

6.7. Linking Public Works with Public Investments

Public works schemes are usually used for disadvantaged groups, notably the low-skilled and long-term unemployed. So far, in Ukraine they have not been attractive for jobseekers because they involve low-skilled, low-status jobs. The national scheme stipulates the possibility of linking social works with public investment in infrastructure and other nationally important projects.

However, such projects have not yet been launched, for financial reasons. Such projects could provide higher-skilled, better-paid jobs and, through a multiplier effect, promote more employment. Public orders should be linked to the condition to employ registered jobseekers with the required skills or who would be retrained at the cost of employment centres. Smaller projects at the regional level could follow this principle and provide jobs that are more attractive for skilled jobseekers. For social works concentrated on cleaning of public areas, social care and so on, participants should be offered training to enable them to increase skills and broaden their subsequent employment prospects, or their temporary job could be changed into a permanent job.

Labour market training seems promising for combating unemployment. However, international experience shows that expectations are usually inflated. There is either little difference in job placement between those unemployed who complete a training course and those without it, or there are substantial dead-weight and substitution effects.[34] Training is also rather costly.

---

[33] In the Czech Republic, a large job creation scheme combined with promotion of private business and self-employment was launched at the start of economic reform. In a situation of scarce capital and limited access to commercial loans, it provided entrepreneurs with capital, provided many jobs in small firms of all forms of ownership (though most were private) and facilitated redeployment of redundant workers to firms utilising labour resources more effectively. The employment restructuring and small business promotion had a demonstrative effect and moderated tensions in the labour market. V. Uldrichova and Z. Karpisek, *Labour Market Policy in the Former Czech and Slovak Federal Republic*, and A. Nesporova, *Comments*, in OECD-CEET, *Unemployment in Transition Countries: Transient or Persistent?*, Paris, 1994.

[34] Substitution effects arise from a trainee merely displacing someone who was doing or could do a job as adequately.

6.8. More Responsibility for the Quality of Training and Education

Often, training courses do not correspond to actual or prospective demand for skills, or involve poor quality training, or are not trusted by employers or by those who participate in them. That is why it is essential to implement them carefully. Once credibility has been lost, it is hard to regain respect for such courses. For numerous reasons, it is important to investigate actual and potential needs of enterprises and fit training to them. In some countries, good results have been achieved through contracts between employers, training facilities, trainees and employment offices, by which a training centre tailors courses to the needs of the worker and the firm, the employment centre selects suitable candidates and covers training costs and the employer is obliged to provide the trainee with a job for at least certain period, subject to certain reasonable conditions.

Employment offices may also partially or fully cover training costs in enterprises undergoing restructuring, if the enterprise's prospects are promising and if that seems likely to prevent large-scale redundancies. Training should be provided for skills of which there is a shortage or which correspond to a regional development strategy. Some fields are national – such as foreign languages, financial operations, accounting, marketing, human relations and foreign trade; others are specific to individual regions.

This issue goes back to the concept of the educational system, which should be responsive to the changing labour market requirements for skills. Vocational training facilities and universities should be given more responsibility for the quality of education and training. Vocational schooling in secondary schools and training centres should be transformed and the narrow specialisations that have long characterised the Ukrainian system should be consolidated.

After the general part of higher education, vocational education should be more flexible upon individual request and vocational assessment and orientation, combining several disciplines according to emerging skill demands. The last stage could be designed in cooperation with a future employer. Such skills can be easily upgraded or broadened later, if needed. Adjusting school curricula to changing requirements of employers should be done in partnerships of educational facilities with enterprises in the region.

Labour market schemes targeted at young people should provide incentives for employers to recruit youths to enable them to gain working experience. This practice was used in the Czech Republic, in the form of a one-year wage subsidy for every school leaver, which facilitated the initial employment of secondary and university graduates.[35] The drawback of this

---

[35] V. Uldrichova and Z. Karpisek, op. cit.

sort of scheme is that it tends to favour groups with higher education, since less educated youths typically have the highest unemployment rates. Another scheme, with similar advantages and disadvantages, would be bilateral agreements with other countries, by which young people could receive training and working practice abroad.

For workers with disabilities, good education (complemented by temporary assistance from specialised institutions) is the key to their competitiveness in the labour market. Labour market schemes targeted at those with disabilities should combine vocational assessment (evaluating skills, capabilities, working habits and health constraints and needs for workplace adjustment and technical aids), rehabilitation and training with incentives for employers (wage subsidies, compensation of workplace adjustment costs, etc.), and social and on-the-job assistance, if necessary. Possibly, quotas for workers with disabilities in large-scale enterprises may ensure that a sufficient number of jobs are allocated for workers with disabilies.[36] They should be supplemented with more substantial levies than currently exist, with effective penalties for non-compliance, which could raise resources for generating jobs through the Social Protection Fund of Disabled People in Ukraine.

Effective utilisation of such resources needs a good executive mechanism, which is not yet in place. In 1992, only 34% of all the Fund's income was used for subsidies or credit for organisations employing disabled workers.[37]

The State Employment Service should be made responsible for the placement of the longer-term unemployed, who usually lose self-confidence. It is important to organise courses on how to apply for jobs and on how to regain normal work habits and attitudes. It might be useful for local employment offices to organise training courses focused on such issues. For the long-term unemployed, 'jobclubs' would be useful; these would help in restarting their regular employment, provide them with psychological counselling and more informal vocational assessment than in regular employment centres.

6.9. Policies for Disabled Workers

For workers with disabilities, good education complemented by temporary assistance from specialised institutions is the key to their competitiveness with other workers and placement, preferably in regular jobs. We strongly recommend that employment services should endeavour to ensure that workers with disabilities are placed in regular jobs – a policy known internationally as mainstreaming. Labour market schemes targeted at those

---

[36] ILO-CEET, *Policy Manual for Disabled Workers*, Budapest, 1994, Chapter 7.
[37] T. Berezanetz, 1993, op. cit.

with disabilities should combine vocational assessment (evaluating skills, capabilities, working habits and health constraints and needs for workplace adjustment and technical aids), rehabilitation and training with incentives for employers (wage subsidies, compensation of workplace adjustment costs, etc.), and social and on-the-job assistance, if necessary. Job quotas for workers with disabilities in large-scale enterprises can be useful, although they are too easily evaded. Sheltered jobs in normal enterprises or in sheltered workshops subsidised by the state should be created for those with more severe impairments, if they cannot be placed in normal jobs.

We recommend that more attention should be paid to this issue, since it is apparent that the marginalisation of workers with disabilities in Ukraine has been extensive.

6.10. Improving the Employment Service's Information Base

The State Employment Service and its network of regional and local employment centres need to improve their information base, technical equipment, organisational structure and methods of work. Employment centres should be linked through a uniform computerised information network giving them a picture of available jobseekers and vacancies throughout Ukraine, facilitating cooperation and promoting labour mobility. Employees in employment centres should undergo periodic training that provides up-to-date skills in employment counselling, effective work with enterprises and municipalities, available labour market schemes, analysis and prognosis of regional labour market developments, selective approach to different vulnerable social groups to encourage them in job search and participation in labour market schemes.

A similar need for periodical training and knowledge of international experience exists in the case of senior officials of the Ministry of Labour. They need to participate more in international seminars devoted to labour market analyses and forecasts, labour market policies, problems of migration and labour legislation. They need more frequent opportunities to discuss problems and investigate other countries' approaches during stays in ministries of labour of other European countries. This could also be facilitated through technical assistance from international organisations, such as the ILO, the UNDP (United Nations Development Programme) or the European Union (EU), through its Programme for Technical Assistance to the Commonwealth of Independent States (TACIS) programmes designed for countries of eastern Europe.

Employment promotion and regulation of labour market developments are dependent on reliable statistics. Although much progress has been made in redesigning labour statistics, there are still many issues to be resolved. Most importantly, there is a need to measure the number of unemployed and the incidence, or pattern, of unemployment. The registration data are inadequate.

At the end of 1993, a pilot labour force survey was conducted which could give some answers to these questions. At the time of writing, no results had been published, so evaluation of the methodology, underlying concepts, sample and survey design and quality of analysis would be premature. Since January 1994, the Ministry of Statistics has started to collect periodically data on workers on unpaid leave and enforced short-time working hours in state enterprises and institutions. This should be extended to agricultural cooperatives, since underemployment may be especially widespread in agriculture.

More information is also needed on the officially economically inactive part of the population. How many are potential jobseekers, how many are discouraged jobseekers, how many are regularly or occasionally engaged in the informal economy? Research would also be useful for the refinement of labour market policies, notably on the situation of jobseekers, and the reasons for many not receiving unemployment benefits, those who were discharged from the register and remained jobless, their attitude to work and experience with job search, experience of social groups and the recruitment practices of employers.

7. Multilateral and Bilateral Technical Assistance in Labour Market Policies

So far, technical assistance in labour market problems provided by international organisations and foreign governments to Ukraine has been extremely limited, especially in comparison with other central and eastern European countries. The need for such assistance is probably as great as anywhere, and much greater than in most countries. The following are some of the main forms of technical assistance provided in the sphere of labour market policies.

7.1. Multilateral Assistance

The European Union's programme TACIS-92 is funding a project entitled 'Human Resources – the Employment Service'.[38] This project, to be exe-

---

[38] This information comes in part from discussion with J.-M. Mouette, resident coordinator of the project in Kiev, who is responsible for preparing its terms of reference.

cuted by a French consultancy firm, was approved under the EC's 1992 Programme, although it actually started in March 1994.

The duration of the project should be 18 months, with the possibility of being extended for another 6 months. It has six components.

- Labour legislation.
- Labour statistics – collection and processing of data.
- Structure and operation of local employment centres, staff training.
- Work psychology and vocational guidance.
- Training methods for vocational training.
- Labour sociology and employment security schemes.

So far, three pilot regions have been selected – Kiev, Rivne (western Ukraine) and Dnipropetrovsk (eastern Ukraine), representing three regions with different development problems. The project should provide technical assistance to local employment offices, to improve their structure and methods of work and to offer better services to jobseekers, including psychological help, vocational guidance and training and information on the means of income protection.

That TACIS project seems to be the largest of the multilateral programmes, although the World Bank is planning to step up its human resource activities and the UNDP has been working on an ambitious Human Resource Development Report.

Apart from the ILO-CEET's work, there is another project being executed by the ILO, funded by the UNDP. This is a two-year Local Economic Development Project for Central and Eastern Europe and CIS, covering a number of countries including Ukraine. Its main goal is to promote economic and employment development at the local level. Selected pilot localities (1–2 per country) will receive assistance from a team of ILO consultants on how to develop local employment and economic development strategies, and on how to work out and finance feasible development scenarios. At the time of writing this report, the project was still in its initial phase of collecting information and negotiating with governments. The ILO has also been working with the Ministry of Statistics on a labour force and establishment survey, the latest activities being the ILO-CEET Ukraine Labour Flexibility Survey conducted in 1994 and the international conference on reforming labour statistics, held in Minsk at the end of August 1994.

7.2. Bilateral Assistance

Bilateral agreements on labour market policy issues have been concluded with the governments, or related agencies, of France, Germany, Hungary and the United Kingdom.

With France, a bilateral agreement in operation since 1992 has concentrated on regional labour market and employment policies and the vocational training of jobseekers. The form of assistance is based essentially on first-hand experience in France. Every year, several groups of Ukrainian employment office employees are invited for short-term stays in France, and French specialists also visit Kiev to train Ukrainian Labour Ministry officials in seminars.

Germany has established and equipped a model local employment centre in Kiev. It was scheduled for opening in 1994, and German specialists were scheduled to provide local staff with on-the-job training, and they had already undergone extensive preparatory training in Germany. Since 1993, the German Federal Employment Service has also organised seminars on labour market measures, the system of operation of employment services and assistance to jobseekers, and invited several groups of the Ukrainian Employment Service specialists to Germany.

Hungary invited 25 employment services specialists for a short-term stay with the National Labour Market Centre in Budapest in 1993. Also, in 1994 a seminar on employment services for Ukrainian specialists was organised in Uzhgorod.

The United Kingdom established a three-year programme for 1992–1994 to provide training for Ukrainian Employment Service officials in the UK on how to open and run jobcentres and create other labour market schemes for the long-term unemployed and workers with disabilities. It has also organised training in regular employment services for State Employment Service staff. Under this programme, two groups of senior Ukrainian officials also went on short-term study visits to the UK, and a seminar was organised in Kiev in 1993. Similar events were planned for 1994.

Apart from it, in 1992 the UK's Employment Service, in cooperation with the UK's Ministry of Defence, provided counselling to the Ukrainian Ministry of Labour on how to develop a programme for employment promotion of persons discharged from the army. In 1992–1993, the Donetsk Regional Council received advice from the UK's Employment Department on mass lay-offs, skill audit and retraining.

The technical assistance from these countries has surely been valuable and valued. Surely, the amount and breadth of it should be much greater.

8. Concluding Points

In Ukraine, labour market policies have a long way to go to reach international standards and have been hampered by a chronic lack of personnel experienced enough to develop them. They have also been hampered by a lack of information and by inadequate information, most notably on unemployment. Until the perception of the seriousness of the labour market is modified, it is unlikely that labour market policies will receive the attention and priority that we believe are required.

Labour market policy development has also been hampered by the lack of international technical and financial assistance, which perhaps reflects a view that the authorities are not yet interested enough to make substantial progress in designing or implementing effective policies. Certainly, the needs are enormous. First and foremost, assistance should be provided in the sphere of public administration, to help in the development of institutions to design and implement labour market policies.

It is recommended that, in formulating an Employment Programme for 1995, the authorities should evaluate the experience of the 1993 and 1994 Programmes, and link the proposed schemes and activities realistically to the actual availability of resources. Above all, it is essential to recognise that labour market policies must evolve strongly and not be launched with massive expectations. They can and should be helpful in the process of labour market restructuring, yet they are not a panacea for mass unemployment and they must be complemented by an effective system of social protection.

4

Reforming Wage Policy in a Hyper-Inflationary Context

1. Introduction

Under the planned economy, almost all sources of income were determined by the Government, including the basic wage and additional sources of earned income, such as incentives and bonuses. Wage rates were applied by enterprises according to a centralised tariff system which provided wage coefficients for different grades, and supplements for time worked and conditions of work. Tariff rates were differentiated by branches depending on the complexity and character of the work. Manuals were distributed to all enterprises, providing for a list of possible grades, determined according to the workers' qualifications, education, and job content. Total expenditure for labour were also controlled centrally, through the so-called 'wage norms' directly linked by the government to planned volume of production.

This system combined low wages with small money wage differentials between branches, regions and categories of workers, in order to pursue the principle of equal pay for equal work in all spheres of activity. While the starting tariff wage for unskilled workers was 1, the tariff coefficient for the highest grade never exceeded 2. This 'egalitarian principle' limited differences in remuneration between occupations and qualification groups,

Table 4.1 *Growth of Production Volume by Industry, Ukraine, 1986–1990 (1985 = 100)*

	1986	1987	1988	1989	1990
Total Industry	104	108	113	116	116
Electricity industry	100	105	110	109	110
Fuel industry	102	101	103	100	95
Metallurgy industry	104	105	108	107	103
Machinery industry	108	114	121	126	128
Chemical industry	105	111	115	117	116
Light industry	101	103	107	110	110
Food industry	98	106	104	112	112

Source: Ministry of Statistics, 1994.

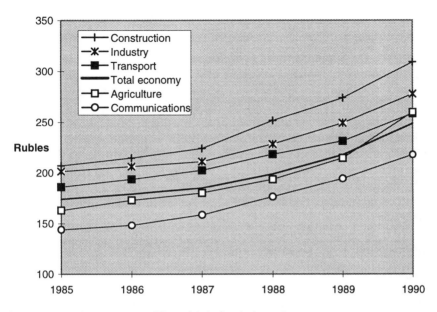

Low wages and narrow wage differentials before independence

Figure 4.1   *Average Monthly Wages by Sector, Ukraine, 1985–1990*
Source: Ministry of Statistics, 1994.

thus de-linking wages from productivity and undermining workers' motivation, even though wage and earnings differentials did persist throughout the Soviet era.

Figure 4.1, and *Table A4.1* in Annex present data on average wages by branches for the period 1985–1990 showing small wage increases between 1985 and 1990 and limited wage differences between branches. The slow rate of wage rise reflected the restrictions on annual wage increases to 3%. Strict wage limitations, low wages and the effort to maintain employment regardless of productivity implied labour hoarding, a lack of incentives for labour mobility and insufficient emphasis on technological change.

Enterprises continuously increased production (*Table 4.1*) in order to have access to greater wage funds, without any consideration for production costs, and in particular their expenditure on energy and raw materials. They also increased their labour-intensive products, with no attempts to adapt production to a changing demand, shifting towards more capital and higher value-added products.

2. Changes in the Wage Determination System

Since 1991, the Supreme Parliament (Supreme Soviet) and the Government of Ukraine have adopted a series of measures to regulate wage-fixing. In connection with the incorporation of amendments into wage legislation, the Supreme Parliament also introduced amendments into the Labour Code of Ukraine. In 1991–1993, the Government switched between two incomes policies. From April 1991 to November 1992, it promoted a very decentralised system, which gave some independence to enterprises to determine wage increases and payment systems. Partially due to enterprises' monopolistic behaviour, the government decided in December 1992 to reintroduce centralised control over wage increases and to suppress wage indexation.

Reforms of the Wage Determination Process

1991	1992	1993
March 1st • Law on Employment of Population	April 29th • Resolution on Social Guarantees for Population	July 1st • Law on Collective Agreements
March 27th • Law on Enterprises in Ukraine	November 21st • Law on State Assistance for Families with Children	December 16th • Law on Civil Service
July 3rd • Law on Indexation of Money Incomes of Population	December 9th • Law on Indexation suspended in accordance with Decree on Temporary Suspension of Indexation of Money Incomes of Population	
	December 31st • Decree on Wages	

2.1. Decentralisation of Wage Bargaining

After the political changes of early 1991 and the decision of independent Ukraine to move towards a market economy, democratisation was extended in all spheres of activity. The centralised system of wage determination was abolished and a new wage bargaining system was introduced by the Law on Enterprises in Ukraine in April 1991. Enterprises – 92% of them still being state-owned – were given autonomy to determine wage levels and payment systems. The only obligation (according to Article 19 of this Law) was to use the tariff system as a bench-mark to ensure wage differentials between workers according to their occupation, skill, complexity and conditions of work.

This general law promoted wage bargaining between trade unions and employers. Although the unions welcomed this democratisation of wage policy, managers were unprepared to implement decentralised payment systems. The absence of competition and the lack of a law limiting monopolistic behaviour allowed most of them to increase their prices in order to pay higher wages, without taking into account workers' productivity or the enterprise's productive performance. The resultant uncontrolled growth of wages (*Figure 4.2*) contributed to the spectacular inflation, which then implied a rapid fall of real wages and living standards. It also contributed to wider income differentials, which did not reflect differences in skill or quality of work, or differences of performance between sectors or enterprises.

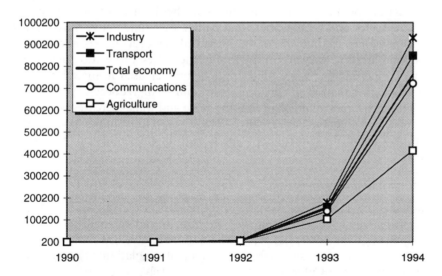

High nominal wages and wider wage differentials since independence

Figure 4.2   *Average Monthly Wages by Sector, Ukraine, 1990–1994 (rubles, coupons, karbovanets)*

Source: Ministry of Statistics, 1994.

2.2. The Return to a Restrictive Incomes Policy

In December 1992, during the period of its extraordinary powers, the Government suspended Article 9 of the Law on Enterprises in Ukraine and put into force a Decree of the Cabinet of Ministers on Wages, which reintroduced a centralised system of wage regulation.

Since then, the wage system has been controlled by the Cabinet of Ministers. The first decision of the Government was to suspend the Law on Indexation of Wages. Indexation was replaced by a fixed compensation of 43,000 karbovanets per worker for price increases of basic food products, which was distributed to enterprises to be allocated to employees.

Besides that, three main instruments have been used by the government to control wages.

a) The wage fund limits for enterprises in the budget sector.
b) The tariff system.
c) Minimum wage regulations.

2.2.1. The Tax-Based Incomes Policy

Despite opposition from Parliament and industrialists, the Government introduced a tax-based incomes policy at the end of 1992. Under this policy, it set national norms for wage funds in the 'budget sector' enterprises (i.e. state sector only). Enterprises that paid a wage fund above those norms had to pay a progressive tax. In 1993, the Cabinet of Ministers allowed the wage fund limits to vary according to the enterprises' production in volume terms, the permissible wage fund limits being increased if annual production was higher than in the previous year, and being reduced if production fell. This measure was aimed at limiting price and wage increases which did not reflect production performance. These wage fund limits became the main instrument for controlling wage growth in enterprises of the budget sector.

2.2.2. The Wage-Tariff System

Following the Decree on Wages at the end of 1992, a General Tariff Agreement was concluded, followed by branch and regional agreements and applied at the enterprise level. The national agreement, whose provisions were binding at all levels of contractual regulation of wages, was agreed between the Cabinet of Ministers and twelve associations of trade unions. It set wage coefficients for different categories of workers and branches of industry on the basis of the minimum wage, which thus continued to play a key role in the entire wage structure.

The first aim of this amended tariff system was to limit wage-inflation by controlling the growth of wages above the tariff wage; the second aim was to limit wage differentials between enterprises and sectors of the economy, since according to the Cabinet of Ministers, wage differentials in Ukraine were too large compared to those existing in other countries.

Within the tariff-system, there are six grades in all sectors of the economy, except in the machine-building industry where eight grades prevail. Managers of state enterprises are directly paid by the state according to their (individualised) labour contracts. The base of the tariff system is calculated on the basis of the minimum wage. In 1993, it was equivalent to the minimum wage multiplied by the coefficient 1.02. In June 1993, the minimum tariff rate for unskilled workers was fixed at the level of two minimum wages. Consequently, the minimum monthly rate for unskilled workers in December 1993 was 120,000 karbovanets, plus a fixed compensation from the state of 43,000 karbovanets for price increases of bread and other basic food products. To put that into perspective, this minimum rate constituted 13.9% of the minimum subsistence level in late 1993. Legislation allowed some non-profitable enterprises to pay workers less than this minimum rate, but only for a maximum period of six months, on condition that they did not pay below the national minimum wage. This is the case in less profitable sectors, such as construction and agriculture.

2.2.3. Minimum Wage Regulations

In Ukraine, the procedure for fixing the statutory minimum wage was not established by legislation. The Decree of the Cabinet of Ministers of Ukraine on Wages established that the minimum wage must be regulated by the State taking into account economic development, labour productivity, average wages and the cost of the minimum consumption basket (MCB). This Law also stipulates that the minimum wage must be determined according to the prices of 70 basic goods needed for subsistence and should not fall below that subsistence level. The Decree was introduced in January 1993.

Since December 1992, changes in the minimum wage level have been decided by the Cabinet of Ministers before being submitted to the Supreme Parliament. Today, there is no regular negotiation between unions and employers to adjust the minimum wage and thereby the base of the tariff system.

The level of the minimum wage between 1989 and 1994 seems to have been changed only in response to pressure from the workers and trade unions. In June 1993, for instance, miners' strikes obliged the Government – through a Decree from the Cabinet of Ministers – to increase the national minimum wage from 6,900 to 20,000 karbovanets and to increase the coefficient linking the base of the tariff system to the minimum wage, from 1.02

to 2.04 times the minimum wage. The coefficient for miners was fixed at 3.2 the minimum wage.

In this new context of no relation with the subsistence minimum, no indexation and a lack of negotiations, the national minimum wage, to which all wages of the tariff system were connected, became the major mechanism for controlling wage growth. It thus lost its primary function, that of protecting the incomes of low-paid workers.

3. Social Aspects: Drastic Fall of Purchasing Power and Growing Poverty

While the Government thus tried to cure inflation by controlling wages and by implementing a restrictive incomes policy, inflation continued to increase, so that real wages and real minimum wages fell dramatically in 1993 and 1994, to well below the subsistence minimum.

3.1. The Free Fall of Real Wages

Average real wages started to fall rapidly when wage indexation was abolished in December 1992. Although nominal wages in 1994 were 3,078 times higher than in 1990, that rise lagged well behind the rise in the consumer price index. In 1993, real wages fell by more than 80%, due to an inflation rate of over 10,000%. As a result of this hyper-inflation, real wages fell by nearly 70% between 1990 and 1993 (*Figure 4.3* and *Table A4.2* in *Annex*).

Average wages also fell below the official subsistence minimum (*Figure 4.4* and *Table A4.3* in *Annex*). While average wages increased in proportion to the subsistence level up to late 1991, when they had reached three times the subsistence level, they decreased continuously from late 1992 when indexation was stopped. By early 1994, they had fallen more than 40% below the minimum subsistance level. According to the trade unions, when the production decreases by 1%, wages decline by 3%.

By early 1994, wages of most Ukrainian workers were well below the subsistence minimum, a situation which contrasted with the period before 1991 when the planned system at least guaranteed a subsistence minimum to the workers. In 1990, minimum wages amounted to 80 rubles a month, i.e. 73% of the subsistence minimum at the time (110 rubles). A combination of state transfers and services provided by the enterprise through its wage fund complemented this monetary income: free housing, education medical care, subsidised food for workers in canteens etc. The average wage (248 rubles) in 1990 was 2.3 times the subsistence minimum. The contrast with what has happened since 1991 may explain why many Ukrainians

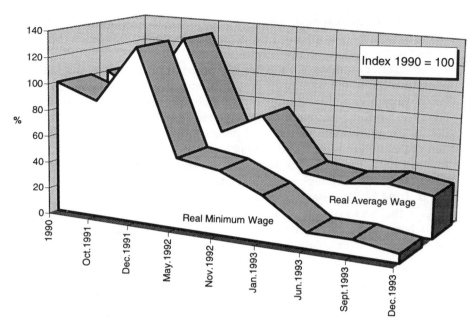

Real wages started to fall rapidly in 1992

Figure 4.3   *Real Average Wage and Real Minimum Wage, Ukraine, 1990–1993*
Source: Ministry of Statistics, 1994.

have become disillusioned with the current economic and political reforms, and perhaps even nostalgic for the previous centralised system.

In some sectors, the fall of real wages seemed to contribute to massive labour mobility. For instance, many miners left for Russia, where their average wage was more than six times the average wage in Ukraine. This was particularly important among engineers and highly skilled workers. According to the trade unions, all power stations today are losing their best specialists because of low wages.

3.2. Downward Pressure on the Minimum Wage

The real value of the minimum wage in late 1993 was 14.3 times lower than in 1990 (*Figure 4.3* and *Table A4.2* in the *Annex*). The minimum wage also fell in proportion to the average wage. The minimum wage was 7.8% of the average wage in January 1994, compared to 53% in 1991. This ratio was even smaller in some industries such as in the fuel (2.9%) and the coal

(2.8%) industries. Although higher in engineering (8.7%) and microbiological industry (9%) for instance, the ratio remained very low, below 10%, in all sectors.

The statutory minimum wage has continued to be used as an instrument to control the whole wage tariff system. Between 1990 and 1992, the minimum wage increased in relation to the subsistence minimum. In early 1992, however, when the minimum wage had nearly reached the subsistence level (94%), the government decided to abolish the wage indexation system so that the minimum wage started to fall again to well below the poverty line. In early 1994, the minimum wage was less than 7% of the official subsistence minimum, although wage regulations still stipulated that it should not be fixed below the subsistence minimum.

As if that was not bad enough, the trade unions have complained that many basic food items have not been included in the basket of goods taken into account in calculating the subsistence minimum. They have also

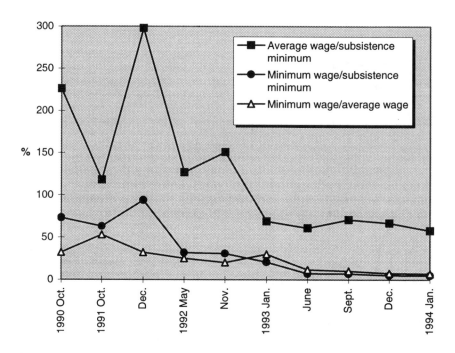

Minimum and average wages have fallen below the subsistence minimum since 1992

Figure 4.4 *Average Wage and Minimum Wage Compared to Subsistence Minimum, Ukraine, 1991–1994*

Source: Ministry of Statistics, 1994.

requested that the minimum subsistence level should be determined jointly with the unions and employers through a tripartite negotiation process, with the help of independent researchers.

It might be suggested that this issue is not important because too few workers receive the minimum wage to make it a major issue. In April 1993, when the minimum wage was 4,600 karbovanets, merely 1.5% of workers received less than that level, 0.9% received between 4,600 and 5,000 karbovanets, and 6.9% had a wage between 5,000 and 8,000 karbovanets. However, there are reasons for thinking that these rates are underestimated. Although a majority of employers introduced rates above the minimum, other would still pay wages even lower than the minimum wage despite the law. This hidden phenomenon is difficult to estimate but appeared to be widespread in some enterprises we visited, for instance in the regions of Kiev, Zhitomyr and Lviv.

Moreover, the decline in the minimum wage compared to subsistence minimum not only influenced workers at the bottom of the wage tariff system but all other categories of workers, whose tariff wage is determined on the basis of the minimum wage. And, because certain social benefits are linked to the minimum wage, its decline has wider ramifications, leading to an erosion of unemployment benefits and some other social transfers.

In 1993, the fall in the real average wage and the real minimum wage, combined with growing unemployment, led to a sharp increase in strikes. The first major strike occurred in June 1993, launched by coal-miners. After several days, and in spite of government threats to import coal in order to break the strike, the President decided to concede wage increases. The minimum wage was also increased substantially. This highlighted a risk of using the minimum wage as a mechanism for macro-economic stabilisation policy, and gave trade unions a sense of purpose in the emerging labour market.

3.3. Disruption of the Income Structure

The erosion of real average wages and minimum wages has contributed to a recomposition of the income structure, in which there has been a trend toward non-monetary sources of income. As shown in *Figure 4.5* and *Table A4.4* in the *Annex*, the wage share of total income fell between 1990 and 1993, the fall being greatest in 1993, after implementation of new wage regulations. Between 1992 and 1993, the wage share of total national income fell from 93.6% to 85.8%.

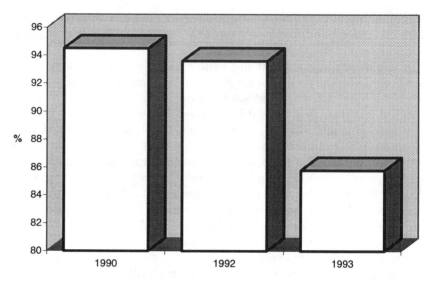

Under the new wage regulations the share of wages in total income has decreased

Figure 4.5 *Share of Average Wage in Total Income, Ukraine, 1990–1993**

*The share for 1990 has been calculated from data of the Ministry of Statistics published in *Pravda Ukrainy*, July 2, 1993. The shares for 1992 and 1993 have been calculated from data of the Ministry of Statistics for the first nine months of 1993.

Source: Ministry of Statistics, 1994.

4. Economic Aspects: High Inflation and Low Productivity

4.1. Limitations of a Restrictive Wage Policy for Controlling Hyper-Inflation

Several indicators suggest that wages have not constituted a basic factor of hyper-inflation in Ukraine. The fact that nominal wage growth lagged well behind inflation (*Figure 4.6*) is a first sign that wages were not the main source of inflation. With an inflation rate of more than 10,000% in 1993, it is difficult to imagine that inflation would have been much worse if wage controls were removed.

The wage share of total production costs was less than 10% in 1993 (*Figure 4.7* and *Table A4.5* in *Annex*). Being a minor share of production costs, wages could have only had a minimal impact on product prices. However, the increase of the wage share in the coal industry, from 25% to 35% in 1993, may have been a cause of inflation and should lead the government to take measures to control wages in such monopolistic sectors rather than in the whole economy.

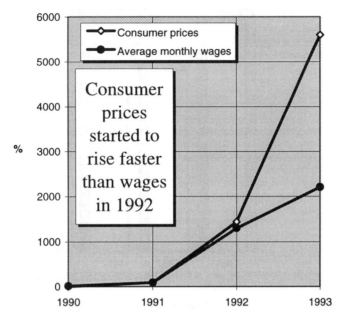

Figure 4.6 *Change in Average Monthly Wages and Consumer Prices, Ukraine, 1990–1993*
Source: Ministry of Statistics, 1994 and The Economist Intelligence Unit, 1994.

The low share of wages in production costs and falling real wages raise questions about attributing much of the inflation to wage changes and using that to justify a tax-based incomes policy. According to estimates of the Institute of Economics, wages in 1993 accounted for 15–20% of the increased inflation, the remainder being due to rising prices of raw materials and energy, due in turn to their shortage. According to the trade unions, wages only accounted for 5–6% of inflation.

It seems likely that the partial price liberalisation of energy and raw materials was the main cause of inflation. As an example, in December 1992, while average industrial prices increased by 42 times, prices grew by 72 times in the chemical industry and by 237 times in the fuel industry.[1] In late 1993, there was a new jump in inflation following the government's decision to increase the price of coal by six times.[2] Wages played no part in that.

---

[1] Ministry of Statistics, *Narodne gospodarstvo Ukrainy u 1992 rotsi*, Statistical Year Book, Kiev, 1993, p. 279.
[2] Ekonomika Ukrainy u 1993 rotsi, *Uriadovyi Kurier*, No. 14, January 25, 1994, p. 6.

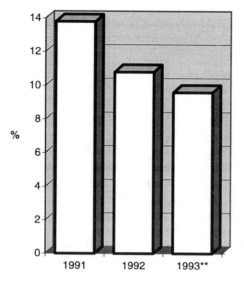

Wages fell as share of production costs

Figure 4.7 *Wage Share of Total Production Costs in Industry, Ukraine, 1991 –1993**

*From 1993, in accordance with the new wage Decree, only basic wages were included in wage costs, additional payments such as individual and profit-sharing bonuses being excluded. In order to have a comparative picture, the Ministry of Statistics calculated for 1993 the share of the wage fund – which includes additional payments – in total production costs.
**First nine months of 1993.

Source: Ministry of Statistics, 1994.

Since most industrial sectors use these inputs (fuel, coal, electricity, etc.), they passed on the increases in the price of their products in order to main- tain profitability, thus leading to a vicious circle of growing inflation. In a context in which prices of energy and raw materials were out of control, a restrictive incomes policy in itself could have little positive effect and was merely likely to lower the incomes of those groups and sectors with the weakest bargaining power. It lowered the purchasing power of workers, leading to further demotivation and lower productivity, and leading monopolistic enterprises to compensate for falling sales by raising prices.

The behaviour of enterprises in a monopolistic position also explains the hyper–inflation during 1993. Despite the general decline in production, most monopolistic enterprises increased prices in order to increase profits and to pay higher money wages. Production fell in quantitative terms but not in value, due to price increases. A more restrictive law against monop- olies would be more effective in limiting inflation. At the moment, non-profitable enterprises can also pay higher wages through bank credits, a possibility which should also be reduced in order to limit inflationary pressures.

Apart from increasingly costly raw materials and monopolistic prices, other factors explaining inflation seem to have been high interest rates for bank credit, exchange rate policy, indirect taxes and high public expenditure. The monetary policy followed by the government also contributed. New money put into circulation by the Central Bank increased by 42 times in 1992 compared to 1991, and by 25 times in 1993 compared to 1992, reaching 12.3 billion karbovanets in 1993. Compared with 1992, cash payments increased by 28 times in 1993. Inflation fell in April 1994, after the government operated a tight monetary policy.

Ukraine shows the ineffectiveness of using wages to control inflation if other elements are not kept under control, such as the price of raw materials, or if other policies are not simultaneously carried out (anti-monopolistic policy, restrictive monetary policy, restrictive budget policy, etc.), particularly if wages are not the main source of inflation. There is no evidence that the adoption of wage bargaining in 1991–1992 caused inflation. Indeed, Ukraine could probably move to free wage bargaining, as long as those other economic policy elements were kept under control.

4.2. The Fall in Workers' Motivation and Productivity

According to estimates of the Ministry of Labour, productivity fell by more than 40% between 1990 and 1993. Factors contributing to this included: scarcity of resources, increasing prices of energy and raw materials, obsolete technologies and workers' demotivation. The last should not be underestimated. The centralised wage system has been demotivating for workers, mainly because it has not guaranteed a subsistence minimum for all workers, and led to the drastic fall of real wages. But also because the wage tariff system combined with a restrictive tax-based incomes policy does not leave much room for linking wages more closely to education and skills or to individual and collective performance. Although labour productivity in industry was virtually unchanged in 1992–1993 the real wage decline was more than three times as large in 1993 as in 1992 (*Table 4.2*). Thus, real wage dynamics seem to be unconnected to productivity.

Industrial differentials in real wages were much greater in 1992 than in earlier years, the real wage decline having been very strong in some sectors, such as in the microbiological industry and printing industry, and less pronounced in sectors such as the fuel and coal industries. Although some sectors, such as electricity, non-ferrous metallurgy, engineering, metal, food processing, flour-grinding and compound feed industries, registered a

Table 4.2 *Production, Labour Productivity and Decline in Real Wages (%) in Industry, Ukraine, 1992–1993**

	Production		Labour productivity		Decline in real wages	
	1992	1993	1992	1993	1992	1993
Total industry	93.6	91.0	96.0	96.7	−27.7	−82.6
Electric power generation industry	93.6	95.4	87.3	94.9	−35.6	−83.1
Fuel industry	85.5	76.9	82.9	76.8	−2.8	−83.7
Coal industry	95.3	83.5	92.2	83.3	−3.5	−83.2
Ferrous metallurgy industry	90.3	78.6	86.5	80.9	−5.9	−85.6
Non-ferrous metal industry	83.7	89.5	82.7	92.3	−11.0	−85.5
Chemical industry	87.3	76.3	87.3	81.9	−24.9	−85.5
Engineering and metal working industry	96.4	104.3	103.4	115.0	−40.9	−81.9
Timber, wood, pulp and paper industries	101.3	97.5	105.5	101.6	−36.6	−81.7
Building materials industry	96.3	81.1	94.8	88.1	−35.0	−83.7
Glass industry	108.9	95.4	107.2	101.4	−39.2	−82.1
Light industry	105.4	84.8	108.1	89.6	−34.3	−81.0
Food industry	85.5	88.5	86.5	90.1	−31.9	−82.1
Microbiological industry	73.9	68.6	76.3	84.9	−51.5	−84.1
Flour-grinding, cereals, compound feed industry	79.0	90.9	82.6	92.8	−23.4	−82.4
Medical industry	90.4	99.3	91.5	–	−45.1	−80.3
Printing industry	152.3	158.8	148.6	–	−46.3	−80.2

*Production and productivity are indexes as percent of the previous year. Productivity index is calculated by dividing total production by the number of workers. Real wages are calculated by dividing monthly average nominal wages by annual inflation rates (2,094.5% in 1992 and 12,375.9% in 1993) and multiplying by 100%. The figures are official, although we tend to think that the figures on the fall of labour productivity for 1993 are underestimated, especially for the engineering sector.

Source: Ministry of Statistics., 1994.

growth of production and productivity in 1993, those sectors continued to experience a fall of real wages well above the national average (*Table 4.2*). Better performance did not lead to higher nominal wage increases. This might be due to the fact that some non-profitable sectors, which experienced sharp declines in production and productivity in 1993, continued to pay wages above the national average.

This was the case in fuel and coal industries and in ferrous metallurgy, which experienced higher increases in nominal and real wages in 1992–1993, despite falls in production and productivity. In many sectors, the fall of production was caused by higher prices, which reduced demand.

Lower purchasing power due to the inflation may have lowered the already low motivation and productivity of workers.

4.3. Monopolistic Behaviour and Growing Wage Differentials

In 1992 and 1993, wage differentials widened considerably. Although this could be partially explained by free wage bargaining in 1991 and 1992, growing wage differentials in 1993 and 1994 seem to have been caused by monopolistic pricing and wage setting in some enterprises.

The tendency to raise wages seems to have been stronger in energy sectors, a phenomenon which is explained by several factors which may have been inter-related: first, the lack of competitiveness in these sectors, where only a few large enterprises prevail, allowed them to increase prices and wages without any fear of losing part of their market.

Second, the fact that they are capital intensive enterprises, where labour costs constitute only a minor part of their production costs, reinforced their freedom to increase wages. External shocks, especially the jump of prices of Russian energy, contributed to push up prices in these sectors, and to create an inflationary spiral in the whole economy. Finally, high trade union bargaining position in these sectors and enterprises may have helped workers to get higher wage increases.

These various factors seem to have contributed to increase inter-sectoral wage differentials. According to the Ministry of Statistics, in December 1993, 7.7% of the working population (4% in industry) was paid less than three times the minimum wage (180,000 karbovanets), while 40% (60% in industry) was paid more than 10 minimum wages (600,000 karbovanets). Average wages were much higher in the banking sector (*Table A4.6 in Annex*).

In January 1994, the average wage in banking was more than 2 million karbovanets, compared to an average for the whole economy of 763,396 karbovanets. Average monthly wages of some managers of Commercial Banks amounted to 150–170 million karbovanets at the end of 1993, that is to say about 200 times more than the average wage.[3]

Inter-sectoral wage differentials also increased in 1993–1994. The highest wages were paid in the energy sectors (fuel, coal, electric power generation), the lowest in timber, wood, pulp and paper industries, microbiological industry, engineering and metal industry. The growing wage differentials did not reflect relative economic performance. Higher wages in energy sectors did not reflect higher productivity or higher volume of production, but were due again to their monopolistic position. In 1993, 90%

---

[3] G. Kulikov, *Remuneration System: Reforms and Needs*, Report for ILO-CEET, Budapest, April 1994.

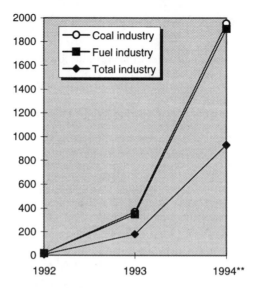

In monopolistic industries nominal wages increased much more than in total industry

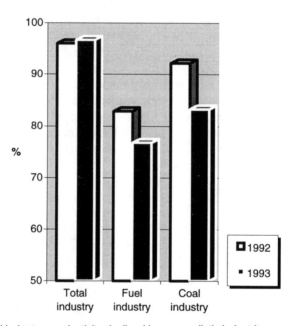

Contrary to total industry, productivity declined in monopolistic industries

Figure 4.8 *Average Monthly Wages (thousand karbovanets) and Productivity* in Energy Compared to Total Industry, Ukraine, 1992–1994*

*Productivity is an index as a percent of the previous year.
**January 1994.

Source: Ministry of Statistics, 1994.

of workers in the energy sectors were paid more than ten times the minimum wage (*Figure 4.8*).

In contrast, wages were much lower in industries where production and productivity were growing, such as in non-ferrous metallurgy, engineering and metal working and food processing industries (*Table A4.7 in Annex*).

At the regional level, the highest wages were paid in the regions of Donetsk, Lugansk and Dnipropetrovsk, the lowest in the Transcarpatian and Volyn regions. Three regions were most affected by wage decline in early 1994: Chernivtsi, Lviv and Volyn. The highest wage increases in 1994 were in Poltava, Kherson and Cherniguiv (*Table A4.8 in Annex*). Regional differentials may reflect industrial restructuring, yet should be monitored because of the political and social consequences of excessive disparities between the regions of the country.

4.4. The Wage Structure and New Payment Systems

Figure 4.9 and *Table A4.9* in *Annex* present the share of basic wages in total wage fund. Because of the restrictive incomes policy, the share of the basic wage in total remuneration, which is determined by the tariff system, decreased compared to other additional forms of payment, such as individual incentives or profit-sharing. The share of the basic wage in the total wage fund was 56.2% in 1993 compared to 70.6% in 1992. In contrast, *Figure 4.9* shows an increase in additional payments based on enterprise results, which increased from 6.8% of the total wage fund in 1992 to 27.9% in 1993.[4] The growth of these incentive systems was particularly strong in electric power generation, ferrous metallurgy, chemical, glass and food processing industries (*Figure 4.10*).

The payment system thus seems to lead to a decrease in the guaranteed part of wages and a growth of the variable part. This trend is confirmed by statistics on the tariff part of total wage, which has experienced a steady decline since 1990, from 61.5% of wages in 1990 to 52% in 1992 (*Figure 4.11* and *Table A4.10* in *Annex*).

The fall of tariff wages was greater in ferrous metallurgy, glass, medical, fuel, and flour-grinding and compound feed industries (by 12.0 to 18.9 percentage points). The share of the tariff wage remains the most important in building materials, timber, wood and pulp and paper industries, as well as in food and printing industries, from 64.6% to 58.8% (*Table A4.10* in *Annex*).

Among the non-tariff components, there are discretionary production

---

[4] According to the Ministry of Statistics, these additional payments, which are called 'monetary payments and incentives', include bonuses linked to enterprise (annual) results, individual premiums, and other cash incentives.

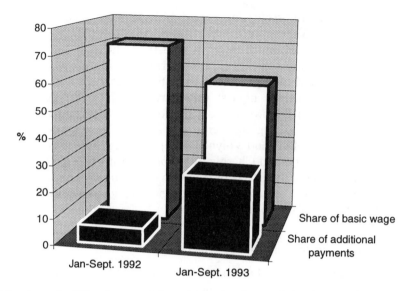

The share of additional payments based on enterprise results has increased

Figure 4.9   *Wage Fund Structure in Industry, Ukraine, 1992–1993**

*The sum of basic wage and additional payments is less than 100% because of other wage fund components, such as share of dividends, etc.

Source: Ministry of Statistics, 1994.

incentives – which are the most widespread – as well as annual bonuses ostensibly based on enterprise results, and other forms of payment by collective or individual results. All these are more common for production workers in industry and less developed for non-production workers and in other sectors.[5]

Decentralisation of wage bargaining in 1992 may have contributed to this movement towards payment systems being more linked to individual and enterprise performance. The restrictive incomes policy followed by the government since 1993 did not stop the development of additional variable payments in favour of tariff wage. Paradoxically, it may have reinforced this trend.

Figure 4.9 shows that enterprises continued to develop these decentralised payment systems. Payment systems linked to enterprise performance have been promoted in most cases to pay higher wages to the workers despite central regulations over wage funds. This is probably also the reason for these additional payments being distributed on a discre-

[5] G. Kulikov, 1994, op. cit.

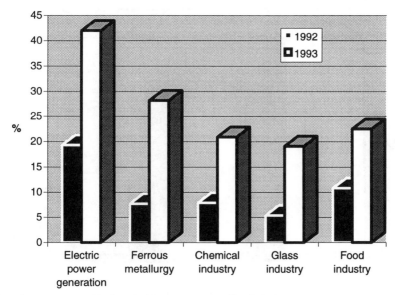

Growth was strongest in the electric power generation industry

Figure 4.10   *Share of Additional Payments by Industry, Ukraine, 1992–1993*
Source: Ministry of Statistics, 1994.

tionary basis, without reflecting productivity or other enterprise performance (*Table 4.2*). This shows the ineffectiveness of central wage regulations when an economy is moving towards a market system, which requires
more flexible and motivating payment systems. These regulations led to
decentralised payment systems unconnected to economic performance.

4.5. Adverse Effects on Consumption

Most consumer goods became inaccessible for most people. For instance,
the price of furniture often exceeded the average monthly wage by more
than 100 times. According to the household surveys conducted by the
Ministry of Statistics, in 1990–1992, Ukrainian households spent 30.2 to
37.2% of their budget to buy food and 34.3 to 34.7% to buy other goods.
Early 1994, 80 to 90% of household budget was spent on food items.

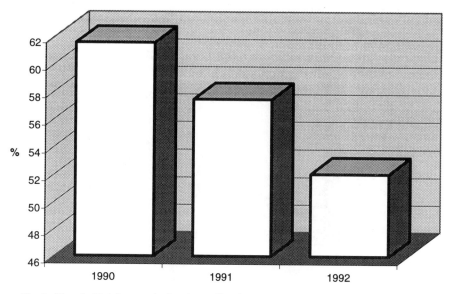

The tariff part of total wage declined steadily after 1990

Figure 4.11   *Share of Tariff Wage in Earnings, Ukraine, 1990–1992**
*Statistics for 1993 were not available. It seems that the tariff part continued to decline in 1993.
Source: Ministry of Statistics, 1994

5. Government Wage Policy: Towards a More Restrictive Policy?

In early 1994, the Cabinet of Ministers revised the Draft Law on Wages, which it intended to present in the second half of 1994. The objective of the new law was to provide more restrictive wage regulations.

As regards the minimum wage, the government decided to increase the minimum wage to the poverty line. However, the minimum wage in June 1994 was still fixed at 60,000 karbovanets, while the subsistence minimum was more than 1,000,000 karbovanets. Although tripartite negotiations to substantially increase the minimum wage were pursued in 1994, no changes had been introduced yet in October 1994, and the minimum wage has continued to fall in real terms. The wage system will continue to be based on wage tariffs to be applied by all enterprises regardless of their property form. Besides, the Cabinet of Ministers also decided to continue to apply wage funds controls, although this measure has been criticised by most employers and political leaders, and has not been very effective. According to the Ministry of Labour, this system was not applied by most enterprises. In 1993, only 6 billion karbovanets were collected in wage fund taxes, while inspection services uncovered tax evasions of more than 4 billion karbovanets. Moreover, some sectors, such as the mining industry, seem to have been exempted from these regulations.

To improve worker motivation, which the Government regarded as having high priority, the Cabinet of Ministers would like to develop a comprehensive set of payment mechanisms linked to economic performance: individual incentives related to individual output and performance; collective incentives such as profit-sharing schemes, related to profits or enterprise performance.[6] The Cabinet of Ministers would also like to relate wages to national macro-economic performances. We saw, however, that a restrictive policy helps limit the development of payment systems linked to economic performance, and declining real average wages and minimum wages lead to falls of productivity and consumption.

The Government also prepared a package of wage regulations in case of extraordinary conditions, to be applied if a new national currency were introduced or if 1993 levels of hyper-inflation were reached in 1994. Most officials responsible for wage policy at the Ministry of Economy, Ministry of Labour and Cabinet of Ministers, have indicated that they were in favour of the immediate introduction of a wage freeze in early 1994. They also emphasised that this would be a temporary measure to control inflation and that a more decentralised wage fixing system should prevail in the long run.

6. Policy Recommendations and Scope for International Assistance

6.1. Against a Wage Freeze

It would be misleading to think that a wage freeze, even if accompanied by a price freeze, would solve current economic problems. This would stop the move of Ukraine towards a decentralised free market economy, delaying the transformation of its economy. A wage freeze might just accelerate social conflict and lead to extreme situations of social exclusion and poverty, especially if this decision does not help to control inflation, which seems to be due mainly to higher prices of energy and raw materials rather than to high labour costs. On the economic side, this policy might also aggravate the fall of worker motivation and productivity, lead to even lower consumption and contribute to the growth of the informal economy.

[6] V. Timofeev, *Formation of a New System of Work Motivation in Ukraine*, Report for the ILO-CEET, Budapest, May 1994.

The need to control wages is dictated by the need to control inflation, although wages do not seem to be the main source of inflation. Moreover, it is questionable whether a process of national negotiations between unions and employers over wage increases, with collective agreements at more decentralised levels, could not be more appropriate for fixing wages according to economic conditions. An incomes policy carried out through consultation between unions and employer representatives at the national level, followed by collective agreement at the branch level, linking wages to economic performance, would be a more efficient way of controlling wage growth.

International technical assistance on procedures of tripartite consultations on incomes policy would be useful in this regard, and Ukraine could benefit from the experiences of some other countries, specifically from those that have implemented a consistent incomes policy through a consultation process between the government, the employer representatives and the trade unions, such as the Scandinavian countries. Ukraine could also benefit from the experience of some other Central and Eastern European countries which have already abandoned a tax-based incomes policy to implement a more decentralised wage bargaining process.

The challenge for Ukraine is to be able to decentralise wage bargaining despite growing economic and financial problems. Many questions are raised. At the macro-economic level, the primary one is how to increase the purchasing power of the population while limiting wage increases in order to reduce inflation. At the micro-economic level, the main challenge is to find ways of paying workers higher wages when most enterprises have financial and economic difficulties in paying the current level of wages.

6.2. Protecting Low Wages from Inflation

It is crucial to protect low wages from inflation. For this, it is essential to increase the minimum wage at least to the level of the subsistence minimum or poverty line, so that it recovers its function of social protection and minimum guarantee for all workers. Today, many enterprises pay well below the minimum wage. In a context of hyper-inflation, the only way to have the minimum wage following price increases would be to establish some minimum wage indexation formula. The fall of average real wages started to accelerate when the indexation system was dropped. The minimum wage and average real wages fell below the poverty line, a trend which should be reversed if social conflict is to be avoided.

6.3. Disconnecting Average Wages and Social Benefits from the Minimum Wage

To the extent that the minimum wage determines all wage levels and the level of social benefits, the Cabinet of Ministers has been reluctant to raise the minimum wage because of its direct financial implications. As in Poland, it will become possible to increase the minimum wage only after disconnecting wage tariffs and social benefits from the minimum wage. While allowing the minimum wage to follow the inflation rate, it would prevent the government from cutting social benefits and controlling the whole wage system through minimum wage regulations.

The centralised system of automatic coefficients between the minimum wage and tariff wages fixed by the government might be replaced by collective bargaining between employers' and workers' representatives at the branch level. While allowing the minimum wage to continue to act as the base for the whole wage fixing system, this would ensure that the minimum wage and wages of other grades within the tariff system would be adapted to economic and social conditions of the various branches of the economy.

6.4. A Flexible Indexation System

It is also important to stop the fall of real average wages, which fell by more than 80% in 1993. Real wages should not be allowed to fall any further. A system of partial wage indexation should be re-introduced. In the context of hyper-inflation, even if wages are not the main source of inflation, a 100% wage indexation is not advisable. With full price indexation, wages might become a growing source of inflation, accelerating economic problems and social tensions instead of reducing them.

A partial indexation mechanism, by which the minimum wage would be adjusted by 60% of any inflation rate, and complemented by free bargaining between unions and employers to negotiate wage increases linked to economic performance, might guarantee minimal living standards for all workers while not overburdening enterprises confronted with serious financial and economic problems. A partial wage indexation might be adapted to changing economic and social conditions by tripartite consultations between the Government and employers' and workers' representatives. If inflation were lowered, the part of wages being indexed to inflation could be reduced and the part linked to economic performance increased. Such a policy could help the government to control wages in order to reduce inflation. At the same time, partial indexation could help workers to obtain wages more in line with price increases, complemented by a flexible part linked to the performance of their enterprises and industries.

Workers in declining enterprises could be disadvantaged by this system, due to an absence of profits impeding that prevents employers from increasing wages. In order to avoid a continuing decline of real wages in the least profitable sectors, enterprises in these sectors should be allowed to distribute fringe benefits or payments in kind to workers to stabilise their living standards. These benefits or payments could be agreed on at the establishment level by trade unions. Such agreements might also be promoted at the branch level between employers' and workers' representatives. However, restructuring should be accelerated in enterprises with financial problems.

6.5. Countering Monopolistic Behaviour

At the same time, it is important to control wage increases in the sectors where a few large enterprises are still in a monopolistic position. In particular, as was stated earlier, the main source of inflation in 1993 was the shortage of energy and raw materials, which led to a spectacular growth of their prices, which employers of those monopolistic enterprises partly transferred into higher wages. In those sectors, the fall of real wages in 1992 was much lower than the national average. Such inflationary sources could be limited through comprehensive anti-monopoly laws, and the attempt by the government to adjust the wages of those sectors to the national average, for instance by differentiating the indexation system by economic sectors, as it was done in Romania in 1992 and 1993.

6.6. Linking Wages to Productivity and Economic Performance

Wages should be allowed to rise in most profitable sectors and enterprises. We have described a development of additional payment systems, with a reduction of the basic wage as a share of total remuneration. Paradoxically, these additional payments have been developed mainly during the second phase of government wage policy, during its restrictive tax-based incomes policy phase, rather than during its first phase (1991–1992), characterised by greater reliance on wage bargaining. The disconnection between wages and productivity also shows that these additional payments have not been effective either in linking wages more closely to productivity, or in ensuring a subsistence minimum for all workers. In this respect, government action will be crucial to promote decentralised payment systems that would reflect industry or enterprise performance.

A formula determined by Law that would automatically link part of wages to productivity or profits or other enterprise performance, and being adapted at the firm or establishment level by employers and unions might be more efficient than additional payments decided on a discretionary basis by the employer. The Government could study the possibility of legislation in this field. At the same time, the government must ensure that this trend is not contradictory to the guarantee of a basic wage that would not fall below the subsistence minimum for all workers.

Throughout the world, there has been a trend towards more decentralised and flexible forms of payments. In that context, there has been a growing interest in profit-sharing schemes, which imply regular cash distribution to the workers of part of the enterprise profits. These schemes have a significant and positive effect on productivity.[7] For employers, these more flexible forms have the potential advantage of being more oriented to work efficiency and productivity and can be adjusted easily in response to fluctuations in demand. For workers, they are motivational schemes, although they provide a more uncertain level of income. This trend is observed not only in the West,[8] but also in Russia where bonuses and surplus-sharing payments comprise a large part of total earnings.[9]

6.7. Promoting Workers' Share-ownership in the Privatisation Process

The distribution of shares to the workers – for free or at preferential conditions – in the privatisation process would also help to give the workers a complementary source of income, while being an incentive to increase workers' motivation and productivity and to involve them in the transition process. These different schemes proved to enhance workers' motivation and productivity in the USA and Japan[10] but also had positive motivational effects in some Central and Eastern European countries.[11]

Although the development of employee share-ownership schemes is at a preliminary stage in Ukraine, the government decided to encourage these schemes, and some enterprises already successfully implemented workers' share-ownership schemes in the privatisation process: labour management buy-outs, in particular, seem to develop in Ukraine, especially in small enterprises. These experiences show that these schemes, by rendering

---

[7] M.L. Weitzman and D.L. Kruse, Profit-sharing and Productivity, in Alan Blinder (ed.), *Paying for Productivity – A Look at the Evidence*, Brookings Institution, Washington, D.C., 1990.

[8] D. Vaughan-Whitehead, Workers' Financial Participation: An East–west Comparative Perspective, *Economic and Industrial Democracy*, Vol. 14, No. 2, May 1993, pp. 195–215.

[9] G. Standing, Industrial Wages, Payment Systems and Benefits, Conference on Employment Restructuring in Russian Industry, Moscow and St. Petersburg, October 1992.

[10] For the USA. see M. Conte and J. Svejnar, The Performance Effects of Employee Ownership Plans, in Blinder, 1990, op. cit. For Japan, see D. Jones and T. Kato, The Productivity Effects of Employee Stock Ownership Plans and Bonuses: Evidence from Japanese Panel Data, *Industrial and Labour Relations Review*, 1993.

[11] Vaughan-Whitehead, 1993, op. cit.

labour costs more flexible, or by motivating workers to temporarily accept wage cuts, might help avoid lay-offs, despite a situation of mass unemployment.[12] This greater employment stability could increase human capital and enhance workers' motivation. The entrepreneur might, by sharing the risks with the workers, be in a better position to promote innovation and investment while stabilising employment.

In some regions facing a lack of local as well as foreign capital, as in the Lviv region, this is also the only way to achieve privatisation. However, the workers, who are sometimes not paid for several months, may not have the money to buy those shares. The State would need to develop different instruments for helping the workers to acquire more shares. In this respect, the privatisation coupons might become a good instrument for developing worker share-ownership schemes.

In the current corporatisation process, shares can be bought by the workers through the system of vouchers, or property certificates directly placed on bank accounts for all Ukrainian citizens. 4,000 coupons were distributed in 1991, and 30,000 in 1993. These amounts are marginal, however, compared to the inflation rate and to average wage. Moreover, the amount of vouchers that can be converted into workers' shares can only represent 5% of enterprise capital. Even if workers complement these initial shares by those bought by their friends or family, their total share cannot exceed 8% of the capital of their enterprise. Vouchers are thus insufficient for having Ukrainian citizens or workers applying Western types of investment funds, and for leading to substantial worker share-ownership schemes.

The Government could study the possibility of promoting employee share-ownership in the privatisation process, and to combine it as often as possible with other property forms. The combination of workers' share-ownership with foreign investment seems to be particularly effective for providing new technologies and increasing worker motivation. Trade unions and employers should develop their analysis of these schemes that involve employees in their enterprise profits and capital.

Presentations of experiences of profit-sharing as well as share-ownership schemes followed in the West and in other central and eastern European countries would be useful to Ukrainian unions and employers and a conference could be organised and funded by donors on this issue.

---

[12] Such effects were also observed in some enterprises in the USA and in France. For the USA see D. Kruse: Profit-sharing and Employment Variability, Microeconomic Evidence on the Weitzman Theory, *Industrial and Labor Relations Review*, 44, April 1991. For France see D. Vaughan-Whitehead, Intéressement Participation Actionnariat – Impacts economiques dans l'entreprise, *Economica*, Paris 1992.

Cooperation with international experts in these fields would enhance the debate on alternative payment systems and contribute to their development in Ukraine.

Annex

Table A4.1 *Average Monthly Wages by Sector, Ukraine, 1985–1990 (rubles)*

	1985	1986	1987	1988	1989	1990
Total economy	173.9	179.0	185.0	199.8	217.7	248.4
Industry	201.5	206.2	211.0	228.2	249.1	277.7
Agriculture	162.8	172.8	180.0	193.5	214.5	259.6
Construction	207.1	214.6	224.0	251.4	273.7	308.9
Transport	186.1	193.7	202.3	218.3	231.1	258.2
Communications	143.9	148.2	158.5	176.3	194.2	217.8

Source: Ministry of Statistics, 1994.

Table A4.2 *Nominal Wage and Minimum Wage, Ukraine, 1990–1993 (1990 = 100)*

	Growth of nominal wage	Growth of minimum wage	Real average wage	Real minimum wage
1990	100	100	100	100
October 1991	210	231	80	89
December 1991	499	500	131	132
May 1992	1,440	1,125	61	53
November 1992	4,562	2,875	77	48
January 1993	6,119	5,750	37	34
June 1993	23,494	8,625	33	12
September 1993	79,422	25,000	37	12
December 1993	319,676	75,000	32	7

Source: Ministry of Statistics, 1994.

Table A4.3 *Average and Minimum Wages Relative to the Subsistence Minimum Income, Ukraine, 1991–1993 (rubles, coupons, karbovanets)*

	Minimum wage (MW)*	Average wage (AW)*	Subsistence minimum (SM)*	MW/SM %	AW/SM %	MW/AW %
December 1972	70	–	–	–	–	–
October 1990	80	248.4	110	73	226	32.3
October 1991	185	349	296	63	118	53
December 1991	400	1,237	428	94	289	32.3
May 1992	900	3,572	2,823	32	127	25.2
November 1992	2,300	11,314	7,483	31	151	20.3
January 1993	4,600	15,175	22,000	21	69	30.3
June 1993	6,900	58,266	94,846	7.3	61	11.8
September 1993	20,000	196,966	278,332	7.0	71	10.2
December 1993	60,000	792,797	1,176,160	5.1	67	7.6
January 1994	60,000	763,396	1,307,000	5	58	7

Source: Ministry of Statistics, 1994.

Table A4.4 *Relative Share of Average Wage in Total Income by Industry, Ukraine, 1990–1992 (%)*

	1990	September 1992	September 1993
Total industry	95.8	93.6	85.0
Electric power generation	87.0	93.8	64.9
Fuel industry	98.5	98.0	85.0
Coal industry	98.7	97.8	86.1
Ferrous metallurgy	93.7	85.1	78.7
Non-ferrous metallurgy	96.0	97.1	92.3
Chemical industry	92.1	84.9	85.3
Engineering and metal working industry	95.9	92.3	89.9
Timber, wood, pulp and paper industries	94.0	89.6	87.7
Building materials industry	92.8	92.2	86.2
Glass industry	93.3	94.8	82.5
Light industry	89.9	81.7	85.8
Food industry	91.7	87.8	82.3
Microbiological industry	85.3	95.1	91.4
Flour-grinding, cereals, compound feed industry	91.1	81.6	81.2
Medical industry	91.0	92.6	89.7
Printing industry	92.8	90.1	87.6

*The share for 1990 has been calculated from data of the Ministry of Statistics published in *Pravda Ukraini*, July 2, 1993. The shares for 1992 and 1993 have been calculating from data of the Ministry of Statistics.

Source: Ministry of Statistics, 1994.

Table A4.5 *Share of Wages in Total Production Costs, Ukraine, 1991–1993 (%)**

	1991	1992	1993
Total industry	13.8	10.7	6.7
Electricity industry	8.5	4.2	1.6
Fuel industry	29.6	16.9	15.4
Coal mining industry	29.1	25.0	23.4
Ferrous metallurgy industry	11.1	4.5	2.6
Non-ferrous metal industry	11.2	5.9	3.1
Chemical industry	11.7	8.7	3.6
Engineering and metal working industry	20.9	18.0	12.5
Timber, wood, pulp and paper industry	20.9	17.0	10.5
Building materials industry	22.7	16.2	8.9
Glass, china and ceramic industry	30.0	22.0	11.4
Light industry	10.1	11.5	8.6
Food industry	5.0	6.4	3.0
Microbiological industry	12.3	8.9	6.1
Flour-grinding, cereals, compound feed industry	3.2	3.2	1.6
Medical products industry	12.5	21.4	13.0

*From 1993, in accordance to a new Decree, only basic wages were included in wage costs, additional payments such as individual and profit-sharing bonuses being excluded.

Source: Ministry of Statistics, 1994.

Table A4.6 *Average Monthly Wage by Sector, Ukraine, 1990–1994 (rubles, coupons, karbovanets)*

	1990	1991	1992	1993	January 1994
Total economy	248	474	6,650	155,400	763,396
Industry	278	548	8,297	185,617	931,711
Agriculture	260	436	4,992	108,863	416,072
Transport	258	507	7,052	160,812	936,127
Communications	218	479	5,001	139,324	763,726
Trade	225	409	5,334	120,828	561,311
Catering	182	320	3,286	91,959	384,572
Information and computation services	223	399	4,269	124,705	691,328
Housing	159	335	4,628	114,869	587,192
Municipal economy	212	422	5,898	147,372	782,059
Personal and household services	160	252	1,952	68,165	362,128
Health care	164	346	5,397	111,242	523,619
Social welfare	143	275	3,612	93,115	433,811
Education	176	349	4,986	111,309	513,542
Culture	143	298	3,978	95,066	433,255
Arts	177	352	3,741	93,624	443,799
Science	314	469	5,656	142,409	643,071
Finance, banking and Insurance	366	756	11,035	453,418	2,019,754
State administration, non-governmental organisations	305	455	5,345	189,796	891,878

Source: Ministry of Statistics, 1994.

Table A4.7 *Average Monthly Wage by Industry, Ukraine, 1990-1994 (rubles, coupons, karbovanets)*

	1990	1991	1992	1993	January 1994
Total industry	278	548	8,297	185,617	931,711
Electric power generation industry	317	826	11,138	244,868	1,431,621
Fuel industry	407	856	17,418	396,034	1,907,856
Coal industry	414	870	17,769	404,636	1,954,310
Ferrous metallurgy industry	311	666	13,132	247,687	1,199,296
Non-ferrous metal industry	306	562	10,473	208,181	810,165
Chemical industry	264	519	8,162	139,099	737,815
Engineering and metal working industry	277	492	6,094	140,036	681,608
Timber, wood, pulp and papers industries	240	457	6,072	140,523	671,733
Building materials industry	257	528	7,188	152,703	776,110
Glass, china and ceramic industry	250	509	6,482	143,563	800,837
Light industry	220	463	6,368	152,386	712,922
Food industry	234	533	7,608	168,131	831,738
Microbiological industry	286	621	6,294	129,137	678,102
Flour-grinding, cereals, compound feed industry	248	510	8,184	159,278	950,638
Medical industry	264	485	5,580	136,837	858,874
Printing industry	253	479	5,390	137,968	729,097

Source: Ministry of Statistics, 1994.

Table A4.8 *Average Monthly Wage in Industry by Region, Ukraine, 1993–1994 (karbovanets)*

	January 1994	January 1994 as % of December 1993
Total economy	931,711	97.1
Crimea	758,816	98.2
Vinnitsa	622,742	87.7
Volyn	596,946	83.1
Dnipropetrovsk	1,043,153	97.1
Donetsk	1,384,414	96.5
Zhitomyr	668,357	92.7
Transcarpatian	477,642	101.7
Zaporizhie	926,972	100.3
Ivano-Frankivsk	590,812	86.0
Kiev region, excl. Kiev	869,763	91.5
Kirovograd	653,952	98.9
Lviv	694,601	80.7
Lugansk	1,308,397	97.7
Mykolaiv	829,889	96.5
Odessa	757,002	102.3
Poltava	967,485	120.2
Rivne	676,232	88.0
Sumy	706,186	96.4
Ternopil	666,870	97.9
Kharkiv	774,410	98.5
Kherson	749,422	108.0
Khemlnytskyi	660,641	89.6
Cherkasy	677,437	101.8
Chernivtsi	600,346	80.4
Cherniguiv	734,665	105.9
The city of Kiev	839,599	91.7

Source: Ministry of Statistics, 1994.

Table A4.9 *Wage Fund Structure by Industry, Ukraine, 1992–1993**

	Share of basic wage in wage fund, (%)		Share of additional payments in wage fund, (%)	
	1992**	1993	1992**	1993
Total industry	70.6	56.2	6.8	27.9
Electric power generation industry	55.5	35.1	19.3	36.2
Fuel industry	70.4	66.4	2.0	26.1
Coal industry	70.7	67.7	1.7	25.5
Ferrous metallurgy industry	61.4	38.3	7.7	42.4
Non-ferrous metals industry	66.9	45.6	5.9	43.2
Chemical industry	69.4	51.7	7.9	30.6
Engineering and metal working industry	74.9	64.9	5.0	20.8
Timber, wood, pulp and papers industries	74.3	58.6	7.3	23.7
Building materials industry	76.4	49.8	8.4	20.2
Glass, china and ceramic industry	71.3	54.0	5.4	29.9
Light industry	71.3	57.0	14.4	29.9
Food industry	74.1	45.2	10.8	34.9
Microbiological industry	63.6	51.0	5.2	18.5
Flour-grinding, cereals, compound feed industry	63.8	58.1	15.0	21.1
Medical industry	76.7	59.2	8.0	23.4
Printing industry	72.6	56.0	11.0	27.6

*The sum of basic wage and additional payments is less than 100% because of other wage fund components, such as dividends.
**In 1992, basic wage was not separated from non-tariff wage within the wage fund.

Source: Ministry of Statistics, 1994.

Table A4.10 *Relative Share of Tariff Wages in Earnings of Blue Collar Workers by Industry, Ukraine, 1990–1992* (%)*

	1990	1991	1992
Total industry	61.5	57.4	52.0
Electric power generation industry	48.7	45.4	41.2
Fuel industry	53.5	51.1	42.6
Coal industry	53.3	50.9	42.3
Ferrous metallurgy industry	56.9	54.1	44.8
Non-ferrous metals industry	57.3	54.3	57.8
Chemical industry	61.2	58.0	52.8
Engineering and metal working industry	63.4	59.2	57.8
Timber, wood, pulp and papers industries	68.9	65.8	62.8
Building materials industry	70.6	67.1	64.6
Glass, china and ceramic industry	66.3	60.1	57.0
Light industry	63.7	55.9	55.1
Food industry	66.3	62.2	58.9
Microbiological industry	56.6	50.6	48.3
Flour-grinding, cereals, compound feed industry	67.6	62.9	48.7
Medical industry	63.1	60.7	54.1
Printing industry	60.8	59.1	58.8

*Statistics for 1993 were not available. According to preliminary information, the tariff part continued to decline in 1993.

Source: Ministry of Statistics, 1992.

5

Emergence of Industrial Relations

1. Introduction

To assess the progress made in Ukraine towards a mature and democratic system of industrial relations it is important to appreciate the basic characteristics of the system prior to the introduction of political reforms. Under the Communist system, the concept of industrial relations was not consistent with prevailing ideology. Many commentators have noted that there was no proper expression for this concept in the Russian language, and to the extent that terminology did exist, the meaning or interpretation was vastly different from that applied elsewhere.[1]

1.1. Relationship of Unions to the Communist Party

Under the former concept of industrial relations, the State (the Party and government), enterprise managers and trade unions were supposed to act in full harmony. The Communist Party and government worked out the one best way for social action within the framework of a centrally planned system and then supervised the achievement of targets thus established. Accordingly, neither trade unions nor employers could be identified as autonomous actors in the industrial relations system. Managers were bureaucrats taking care of state property on the basis of rigid instructions. For their part, trade unions were organised on strict hierarchical lines, according to principles of democratic centralism, which meant that once a decision had been passed it was obligatory to implement it without expressing opposing opinions.

The unions were subordinated to the Communist Party at every level and performed the role of a 'transmission belt', in the sense that they handed down the central will and decisions to the workers. An aspect of this involved attempts to stimulate productivity through, for example, organising production conferences and socialist competition, usually without much

---

[1] D. Gregory and L. Hethy, Trade Union Policy, *On Business and Work*, ILO, 1993, p. 181.

success.[2] Another primary role was the distribution of social and welfare benefits, including the allocation of places at holiday resorts and sanatoria, kindergartens and housing, as well as the administration of most components of the state social security system.

1.2. Role of Unions in Workplace Relationships

Workplace relations were handled not through trade unions, but by management structures. In theory, wages and conditions of work were determined centrally, but in practice, line managers and foremen had considerable discretion over such matters. This was utilised to negotiate informally with workers in their section to ensure they met their component of the plan target.

These informal negotiations were never conducted on a collective basis but in a personal and individual manner. In fact, collective labour disputes and conflicts were regarded as non-existent, while strikes were seen as actions by workers against their own interests. Consequently, legislation in Ukraine (Chapter 15 of the Labour Code) only provided procedures for consideration of individual labour disputes, that is, disputes between individual workers and management of an enterprise over the application, or failure to implement, norms established in legislation. Article 242 of the Labour Code stipulated that such disputes should be considered and resolved by management and the enterprise level trade union committee. If they failed to resolve the matter it could be referred to higher level trade union and ministerial bodies.

This did not mean that workplace relationships were tranquil. On the contrary, disputes would often occur about the calculation of wages and bonuses, the allocation of work, and the distribution of social and welfare benefits. These disputes would sometimes lead to short work stoppages, but usually only involving a small number of workers. On the rare occasions where a stoppage might involve the entire plant, senior managers and party officials would intervene immediately to reassure the workers and meet their demands. This might be followed by victimisation later.[3]

1.3. Collective Agreements and the Labour Code

Although collective agreements did exist, often at both enterprise and branch levels, their content differed dramatically from that in industrialised market economies. In the USSR, collective agreements often included

---

[2] S. Clarke, Trade Unions, Industrial Relations and Politics in Russia, *The Journal of Communist Studies*, Vol 9, No. 4, December 1994, p. 134.
[3] S. Clarke, 1994, p. 135, op. cit.

disciplinary measures to be taken by the workers' collective to punish any member who stepped out of line. The precise contents of collective agreements were specified in the Labour Code, and no flexibility existed to consider other issues. Given these conditions, collective agreements could not be regarded as the result of a bargaining process between two independent and autonomous partners representing diverse interests.

There were attempts in the late 1980s to make progress towards freedom of association and free collective bargaining or at least to loosen the tight grip of the state. For example, the Law of the USSR on State Enterprises in 1987 and the Law of the USSR on Enterprises of 1990 made some concessions. A major step was the USSR Law on Trade Unions, their Rights and Safeguards for their Activities of December 1990.[4] Further significant reforms of labour legislation and attempts to establish institutional arrangements that are required to underpin a mature and democratic industrial relations system have occurred since 1991. These legislative and institutional developments are the focus of this Chapter. One of the main objectives of these reforms should be to establish an environment that promotes free collective bargaining, that is, an 'even playing field' for negotiations between independent and representative worker and employer organisations.

1.4. Industrial Relations in an Economic and Political Context

However, before turning to those issues it must be emphasised that industrial relations can not be examined in a vacuum. The development of a well functioning industrial relations system is dependent on many factors in the economic and political field. Chapter 1 emphasised the lack of progress made with economic reforms in Ukraine. This has implications for industrial relations. For example, the progress with privatisation means that there is no wide class of independent employers motivated by the desire to maximise profits.

Some private entrepreneurs are emerging but they still do not constitute a suitable counterpart for an independent trade union movement. In their defence one notes that managers of state enterprises may often have legitimate grievances with the policies being pursued by the Government, and many managers have maintained a paternalistic manner towards their employees despite severe economic difficulties within their enterprises. Yet, it is also being argued that many state enterprise managers still have a mentality more akin to industrial ministry officials than independent employ-

---

[4] ILO, *Labour Law Documents*, January 1991, p. 117–122.

ers. This can manifest itself as opposition to the basic principles of industrial relations reform and obstinate defence of the status quo, including suppression of new forms of independent worker representation.

Debate about whether or not any independent trade union movement exists in the Ukraine remains moot. At least, it might be argued that there exist significant sections of the trade union movement devoted to preserving the powers and privileges they possessed in the past.

If doubts exist about the employers' and trade unions' independence and legitimacy, one might be tempted to argue that there is little point in reforming the legislative framework for collective bargaining or establishing institutional arrangements for tripartite consultations. What is the purpose of trying to create an 'even playing field' for industrial relations, if you do not have two or more independent and competitive teams to take advantage of these conditions? Of course the objective of the legislative and institutional changes should be to prepare the 'players as well as the pitch', that is, to facilitate trade union pluralism and the independence of the social partners from both the State and each other.

However, while legislative changes are a necessary prerequisite for such reforms they are unlikely to constitute a sufficient guarantee for success. The risk therefore exists that international observers might gain the mistaken impression that fundamental industrial relations reforms have been implemented just because basic components of the legislation have been changed, or a highly visible tripartite institution has been established, while the impact of these macro industrial relations changes may be minimal at the micro level or enterprise level.

It is debatable if Ukraine has even reached this stage. Because key groups have a vested interest in preserving the status quo, and often the political clout to control the legislative agenda, the civil servants and politicians who wish to push through changes in the industrial relations legislation have experienced considerable opposition. The climate for change is less than propitious.

In any country the political environment exercises a pervasive influence over industrial relations. In Ukraine, certain basic ingredients of a new political system – such as a multiparty system, democratic elections and a free press – have been established. The ILO is not in a position to pass judgement on these reforms, although they affect the industrial relations system and recommendations on future technical assistance. For the purpose of this review, other political problems deserve to be highlighted. In Chapter 1, reference was made to unresolved struggles between elements of the administration. The result of this lack of good 'governance' can be political paralysis. The publicised disputes about responsibilities and powers between the previous President and the Parliament in Ukraine are the most obvious symptom of this. Such disputes can have significant implications for industrial relations.

Commentators have suggested that in Ukraine and other countries of the Commonwealth of Independent States (CIS) there is a lack of political sophistication in the political parties and groups in Parliament and that none can formulate a coherent policy on industrial relations. As a result, discussions of social-labour issues are interpreted in narrow political parameters.[5] This will have a detrimental effect on other aspects of industrial relations. For example, there is no certainty that Government Ministers have the authority to ensure that undertakings they give to employers or trade unions will be honoured and reflected in legislation or policy. Then regardless of the formal structures created to facilitate tripartite dialogue, these discussions are going to be hollow and perhaps ultimately counterproductive.

However, political fighting is also entrenched at much lower levels in the bureaucracy that affect industrial relations and the development of a tripartite system that can underpin and sustain democratic political reforms. For example, as in many other countries, the Labour Ministry has a relatively low status in the Government. Moreover, the staff of the Ministry is inexperienced in the development and implementation of industrial relations policy. Because of this, the role of the Ministry seems peripheral, such that responsibility for industrial relations policy is concentrated to a small group of relatively young, dynamic and reform-minded advisors within the Cabinet of Ministers.

2. Labour Legislation Reforms: Freedom of Association

Throughout its 75 year history the ILO has argued that a fundamental characteristic for successful industrial relations is acceptance of democratic pluralism, in which autonomous interest groups operate within a sovereign State, governed by democratically elected representatives. Groups with divergent interests recognise each other's existence while promoting their views.

A premise for the successful operation of this system is freedom of association of workers and employers to form any organisations they prefer to represent their interest. It is in this context that freedom of association and protection of the right to unionism and collective bargaining become significant as essential elements of basic human rights. The two basic ILO Conventions 87 and 98, adopted by the ILO on these matters some 45 years

---

[5] M. Baglai, The Creation of a New System of Labour Relations in Russia, *Problems of Economic Transition*, Moscow, September 1992.

> *The freedom, de facto and de jure, to establish organisations is the foremost among trade union rights and is the essential prerequisite without which the other guarantees enunciated in Conventions Nos. 87 and 98 would remain a dead letter'.*[6] — The ILO Committee of Experts

ago, continue to provide the premise for a valid and enduring industrial relations system.

2.1. Freedom of Association

The Convention No. 87 on Freedom of Association and Protection of the Right to Organise lays down principles for guaranteeing to workers and employers the free exercise of the right to get organised in relation to public authorities.

The ILO Committee of Experts has argued that three conditions are necessary to exercise this right:

- The absence of any distinction, in law and in practice, among those entitled to the right of association.
- The absence of the need for previous authorisation to establish organisations.
- The freedom of choice with regard to membership of such organisations.

Convention No. 87 specifies four basic guarantees.

- Workers and employers have the right to unionise freely and without previous authorisation. This guarantee takes into account the above mentioned conditions.
- Trade union organisations and employer's organisations have the right to draw up their rules, to elect their representatives, to organise their administration and activities, and to formulate their programmes.
- The organisations have the right to establish federations and confederations.
- The organisations have the right to affiliate with international organisations of workers and employers.[7]

---

[6] ILO, *Freedom of Association and Collective Bargaining*, Report of the Committee of Experts on the Application of Conventions and Recommendations, International Labour Conference, 81st session, 1994, p. 23.

[7] Ukraine ratified Convention No. 87 in September 1956.

2.2. Drafts of the New Constitution

We will now describe some of the legislative changes implemented over the last few years, or are anticipated in the near future, to reflect the rights and obligations established by this aspect of Convention 87. However, there is no attempt in this review to in any way pass judgement on whether or not law and practice in Ukraine meet the requirements of this convention. The ILO has a well developed system of supervisory bodies, both expert and tripartite, within which deviations from these obligations, or violations thereof, are debated and determined. Comments made in this Chapter are therefore without prejudice to any observations that may be made by the ILO's supervisory bodies.

Despite the political reforms in Ukraine in recent years, a new national Constitution has not yet been adopted. Apparently, several slightly different drafts have been prepared and debated by various groups within the country. There are conflicting views on when a new Constitution will finally be adopted. The ILO has been unofficially informed that some versions of the draft Constitution embody the principles of freedom of association and the right to strike, while other versions remain silent on these issues.

Some organisations in Ukraine have expressed concern that the Constitution which is finally adopted may ignore these important principles. However, Section 6 of the existing Constitution – which had set out the leading role of the Communist Party over mass organisations, including trade unions – was repealed in 1990 and Section 7 of the existing text, as amended, enshrines the principle of political pluralism.

Consistent with this amendment to the Constitution, the Federation of Trade Unions of Ukraine (FPU) adopted a Charter recognising the principle of independence of trade unions from state and political authorities during its first Congress. The FPU was created in October 1990. As explained in more detail in Chapter 6, this Organisation is the historical successor of the trade union movement which existed under the former system. Its Charter also recognised that union membership is voluntary and that individual unions in the Ukraine were free to leave or join the FPU as they wished.

2.3. Draft Law on Trade Unions

In many, but not all, countries a number of the rights and obligations of workers and employers' organisations provided for in Convention 87 are guaranteed under separate legislation. They include rights to draw up their own rules and procedures for electing representatives and for other administrative matters referred to above. As noted above, the USSR adopted a new Trade Union Law in December 1990. Perhaps in response to this text, in early 1991, the FPU – utilising its powers of legislative initiative which still existed at that time – submitted to the Supreme Soviet of Ukraine a draft Law on Trade Unions. In October 1991, there was a first reading of the draft and many aspects received broad support.

However, four critical articles were set aside for further examination by the Commission of the Supreme Soviet on Social Policies and Labour. These articles guarantee the trade unions following rights:

- The right to legislative initiative (this had been withdrawn after the law was submitted in June 1991).
- The right to manage social security funds.
- The right to full-time trade union representatives.
- The right to property.

The FPU claims that the draft law was blocked by members of the Supreme Soviet who were also fulfilling the functions of state enterprise directors and therefore had a private interest in preventing legitimate trade union activities being placed on a firm legal footing.

Revised drafts of this law were prepared by the FPU and submitted in April 1992 and again in June 1993, but were rejected on both occasions. In mid 1994, a stalemate existed on this legislation. Yet some components of the draft do raise questions about the functions and authority that FPU envisages a trade union should possess. This in turn may raise questions about the extent of real reform within the trade union movement.

'Trade unions – All Ukrainian (national) associations – have the right of legislative initiative. They can make propositions to the Supreme Soviet of Ukraine about the adoption or change of a law, and also can prepare laws on labour and other social and economic problems.

Laws introduced for consideration of the Supreme Soviet by State Bodies . . . must be sent to trade unions not less than one month before consideration. State bodies should consider the comments and proposals of trade unions and ensure their participation in the discussion of those comments.'[8] — Article 19 of the latest draft of the Law on Trade Unions.

For example, the FPU remains adamant that trade unions should have the right to initiate legislation and participate in the development of legislation. The arguments they mount in defence of this proposal are

[8] Based on a English translation of the Draft Law of the Ukraine on Trade Unions, provided to the ILO by the FPU, see Article 19, p. 5.

potentially counterproductive. For example, they have explained to representatives of the ILO that without the right to legislative initiative they face a situation where their proposals might be rejected. It is legitimate to expect a government to consult representative elements of civil society, including trade unions, over potential or pending legislation. In many democratic countries, tripartite councils or ad hoc committees are established for such consultations.

However, tripartite bodies normally advise parliaments, or a government administration, which is free to accept or reject the advice. If the intent of the draft legislative provision is to provide a particular trade union, or trade unions, with authority over legislation equivalent to that normally reserved for Members of Parliament or Government Ministers, then it may be considered inconsistent with accepted practice in a democratic market economy. Moreover, the pursuit of such powers by a trade union may merely provide fertile ground for those who wish to challenge the legitimacy and independence of the organisation.

Another potentially controversial aspect of the Draft Law on Trade Unions is Article 32, which gives trade unions far-reaching rights to economic and commercial activities.

> *'trade unions and their associations can carry out necessary economic and other commercial activity, create commercial firms, carry out foreign trade activity, create trade union banks, insurance and joint-stock companies . . .'* — Article 32 of the latest draft of the Law on Trade Unions.

Article 43 lends credence to claims that the FPU envisages that the unions should maintain many of their 'transmission belt' functions. This section of the draft provides for, inter alia, the following trade union functions at the enterprise level.

- Distribution of funds for social, cultural and housing activities provided by the enterprise.
- Allocation of bonuses to workers.
- Determination of reductions in bonuses for managers who violate labour legislation or collective agreements.
- Management of state social insurance of workers, preparation of documentation necessary for workers to receive pensions, and determination of access to sanatoriums and other medical services.
- Control over access to medical services of retired and disabled workers.
- Determination of the conditions for hiring of the general manager together with the body authorised by the owner.

The arguments mounted by the FPU for retaining control of the social security functions may be more plausible than those concerning their right to legislative initiative. It argues that in a situation where the fiscal deficit is enormous, and the potential for effective governance of any state institution is minimal, destruction of the existing social security managerial system would leave a vacuum and the funds would be siphoned off for other purposes at the expense of the workers and their families.

On the other hand, representatives of the Cabinet of Ministers dealing with industrial relations see the removal of this function as a strategic measure to promote trade union pluralism. They argue that many workers remain members of the FPU merely because they fear that access to social security and other social provisions would be denied if they withdrew from the organisation.

2.4. Law on Citizens' Organisations

It would appear that the attempt by the FPU to implement this Law on Trade Unions had broader industrial relations repercussions. It was at least partly – and perhaps predominantly – the reason behind the development of other legislation subsequently passed by the Government. For example, the first substantive step in the reform process, after the original Draft Law on Trade Unions had been considered, was enactment of a Law on Citizens' Organisations, passed by the Supreme Soviet of Ukraine in June 1992.

The law stipulates that Citizens' Organisations are based on the following principles.

- Membership is voluntary.
- Members have equal rights.
- Organisations have the right to govern their own affairs.
- Organisations will respect all Ukrainian legislation.
- Organisations are free to choose their own policies and programmes.

Moreover, non-interference in the activities of citizens' organisations by public authorities and officials is guaranteed by the law, as is the right of these organisations to establish and join federations, and to affiliate with international organisations on a voluntary basis.

According to the FPU, in introducing the Law on Citizens' Organisations the Government had foreshadowed that further specific legislation on trade unions would be adopted. There appears to be a degree of uncertainty within the Government and the relevant Ministries about whether or not to proceed with this undertaking. Some representatives of the Government indicated in early 1994 to the ILO that a decision had been taken at a political level not to press ahead with this legislation. This has not been publicly confirmed. Nevertheless, those advocating this course point out that many countries do not have specific legislation on trade unions. It is plausible that the real reason for procrastination is that the Government considers that the draft law prepared by the FPU was designed to restore much of the power trade unions had prior to 1990. It is therefore politically more opportune – for the Government – simply to ignore this draft law rather than re-enter a debate about amendments to the text.

To fill the legislative vacuum on trade unions, the Government is considering an amendment to the Law on Citizens' Organisations to indicate that this law applies to trade unions. Moreover, the Cabinet of Ministers submitted to the Supreme Soviet on 29 December 1993 a package of amendments to the existing Labour Code.[9]

In a cover letter, the Prime Minister stated that these changes were necessary to bring the Labour Code into conformity with conditions necessary for transition to a market economy, as well as with the Law on Citizens Organisations and ILO Convention No. 135 on Workers' Representatives and Convention No. 154 on Collective Bargaining, which the Government intended to ratify.[10] The proposed amendments to the Labour Code that are related to the matters discussed above include a substantive change to Article 244 on the Rights of Trade Unions. This would eliminate the role and existing rights of trade unions in the following areas: participation in elaboration of central plans; organisation of socialist competitions; promotion of productivity and enforcement of labour discipline; management of state social insurance, sanatoriums, cultural facilities, tourist and sport facilities.

The Government has also revised aspects of the Labour Code concerning the procedure for termination of employment at the initiative of the employer.[11] This alteration only applies to certain managerial positions such as the director and deputy director of an enterprise, the chief accountant and senior officials of certain state bodies like the customs office and the tax office. The amendments also provide for dismissal of an employee, without the prior consent of the trade union, in cases were the employee has been found guilty of stealing from the enterprise by a court of law.[12]

As many of these legislative changes and proposals for change are contrary to the FPU Draft Law on Trade Unions, it is hardly surprising that it has opposed these amendments. However, the Government claims that the new independent trade unions recognise that the FPU is merely

---

[9] Cabinet of Ministers of Ukraine, Draft Law on Submission of Alterations and Amendments into the Labour Code of Ukraine, December 31, 1993, No. 26–2799/4.
[10] Ukraine ratified ILO Convention No. 154 on Collective Bargaining, May 16, 1994.
[11] Chapter XII Articles 43–1 and 232 of the Labour Code were revised, November 19, 1993.
[12] Chapter XII Article 43 revised, December 16, 1993.

attempting to preserve its monopolistic position and basically support the above mentioned changes to the Labour Code. In fact, the Cabinet of Ministers indicated to the ILO in mid-1994, that in their opinion the Ukrainian trade union movement has developed into a very heterogeneous force which is torn apart by competing interests and opposite political sympathies. They argue that the most progressive trade unions may criticise legislative reforms because they do not conform with ILO principles or standards, while the motivating force behind criticism from the most conservative trade unions are less objective.

The relationship between the trade union federations and an examination of the factors motivating their actions are considered in the next Chapter. However, it is worth noting that in support of the claims referred to above, the Cabinet of Ministers has cited a series of public attacks mounted by the FPU on individual Government officials. For example, apparently in 1992 officials from the Ministries of Labour, Justice and Finance along with representatives of the National Bank commented on what they considered to be the unlawful practice of deducting trade union membership fees from wages ('check-off' system) without workers' consent.

The Government officials conducted inquiries at a number of enterprises in response to complaints by certain new independent trade unions. They found evidence that supported the claims and subsequently indicated through the media that they considered such practices violated legislation in Ukraine. The Government officials also argued that such practices were contrary to ILO Convention 87, since they impeded the independent decision making of the workers about which trade union to join. It has been claimed that in response, the FPU organised a campaign of intimidation and public criticism against the Government officials involved, and sought their dismissal. The association Solidarity and the All-Ukrainian Association of Solidarity of Workers condemned the actions of the FPU in this matter.

In defence of their stance on this issue the FPU has argued that the investigations undertaken by the Ministries mentioned above, were inconclusive, yet they issued a general statement condemning the existing check-off system. The FPU also claim that enterprise directors responded positively to the statements issued by the Ministries and stopped forthwith the deduction of union fees from wages.

2.5. Amendments to Labour Code and Law on the Procedures for Resolving Collective Labour Disputes

It was noted earlier that prior to political reforms in the USSR only individual labour disputes were legal. In February 1992, the Ukrainian

Government introduced amendments to the Labour Code that revised procedures for resolving individual labour disputes.[13]

Considerable attention has also been given to legislation governing collective disputes. From the start of political and economic reforms in the USSR collective labour disputes rapidly became more politically acceptable than had been the case. In recognition of this, the Law of the USSR on the 'Procedures for Resolving Collective Labour Disputes' was adopted in May 1991. This law remains in force in the Ukraine today.[14] Certain aspects of it might be considered excessively restrictive. The requirements for a termination of work are set out in Article 12 and the requirements for a legal strike in Article 7.

Article 3 of the law makes provision for a compulsory procedure for conciliation over labour disputes, and if this fails, compulsory labour arbitration is supposed to be utilised.

Although the above mentioned USSR law remains in force, work began on a Ukrainian Law on the Procedures for Resolving Collective Labour Disputes in 1991. However, after three years no law has yet been adopted. Although the draft Ukrainian law was prepared by the Government with the participation of consultants from trade unions, major disputes between the FPU and the Government have not been resolved. Whether or not this draft law will be finally adopted remains unclear.

Certain aspects of the draft law might be considered preferable to the USSR law from a freedom of association perspective. For example, the provision dealing with the right to strike in essential services (Article 22 of the draft Ukrainian law) might be considered an improvement on the existing USSR law, which outlaws strikes in a whole range of industries. In Ukraine, negotiations between the Government and the FPU resulted in agreement on a list of industries that could be considered essential services, and the draft law allows for strikes in these industries on condition that a minimum level of service is maintained. Unfortunately, the two sides have not been able to reach agreement on what should constitute a minimal level of service in the event of a strike in such industries. Nor does the current text make provision for case-by-case negotiation at the time of a strike about what should be considered a minimal service.

This remains a matter of dispute but a more significant schism centres on the provisions in the draft law concerning the right of employers to 'lock-out' their employees. This aspect of the legislation is vehemently opposed by the FPU and consequently is a politically sensitive issue.

[13] Chapter XII Articles 43, 133, 134, 142 and 147 plus Chapter XV, Articles 221–242 were revised, February 18, 1992.

[14] In accordance with the legislation of Ukraine, prior to adoption of national legislation by the Government of Ukraine, legislation of the former Soviet Union, providing it does not contradict legislation of Ukraine, remains in force.

*'The decision to strike must be taken at a meeting of the labour col-
lective or trade union by secret ballot and will be considered adopted
if at least 2/3 of the members voted for it. The Administration must
be notified in writing concerning the starting date of the strike, and
its possible duration, at least two weeks in advance.'* — Article 7 of
the Law on the Procedure for Resolving Collective Labour
Disputes

*'Termination of work, as a method of resolution of collective labour
dispute (conflict) is not allowed, if it creates threat to the life and
health of people, as well as if it is done at enterprises and in organisations of railway and municipal public transportation (including
metro), civil aviation, communications, power generation, defence
industries (in departments which are directly involved in military production), bodies of the state power, at enterprises and in organisations responsible for ensuring the defence capacity of the state, law
enforcement and national security, at non-stop types of production,
stoppage which may lead to serious and dangerous consequences'.* —
Article 12 of the Law on the Procedure for Resolving Collective
Labour Disputes

The proposed law has been redrafted several times and the ILO has been
supplied with a translated version of the draft dated July 30, 1993.[15] Article
7 of that draft defines a strike in fairly conventional terms as 'a temporary
collective stop of work by the employees'. From this definition it is reasonably clear that the effect of a strike on the contract of employment is
one of suspension rather than a complete cessation of the contract.
However, Article 8 defines a lock-out in the following way: 'a full or partial closure of an enterprise followed by dismissal of its employees'. This
reference to the dismissal of employees would appear to be inappropriate
since the normal effect of a lock-out, like a strike, is to suspend rather than
terminate the contract of employment. There seems to be considerable confusion in Ukraine about the concept of lock-out.

The same Article of the draft law states that lock-out can only be used
by an employer as a last resort to defend the interest of the enterprise in a
situation where the trade union (or labour collective) has already taken the

---

[15] The ILO has supplied comments to the Government of the Ukraine on two previous
drafts of this law. These comments were made without prejudice to any observations that may
be made on the text, if it becomes law, by the ILO Committee of Experts on the application
of Conventions and Recommendations.

decision to strike, and where conceding to the union demands 'could lead to the possible bankruptcy of the enterprise'.

Article 28 of the draft requires the employer to obtain an independent audit or a decision by the (yet to be established) National Mediation and Reconciliation Service, which would have to confirm the threat of bankruptcy. Officials from the FPU are concerned about these provisions. They argue that the intention of the Government is to outlaw strikes and/or provide legal grounds for employers to implement mass redundancies in unprofitable enterprises. As the provision stands, these arguments seem plausible.

Given the definition currently proposed, employers would have the right to implement a lock-out in any enterprise where trade union demands may lead to the threat of bankruptcy and this would effectively result in the dismissal of all workers involved in a strike or threatening to strike. This provision is particularly dangerous given the prevailing economic conditions and the state of Ukrainian industry. At present there would be very few enterprises in the country that would not meet the bankruptcy criteria.

That being said, the Government naturally has the right, and even an obligation, to provide a legal framework for dealing with the dismissal of employees in enterprises that are bankrupt. However, legislation over such matters should be considered independently of laws relating to the settlement of industrial disputes. The attempt in the current draft to link these two issues is confusing and counterproductive.

An earlier version of the draft law was submitted to the Supreme Soviet of Ukraine in June 1992, and in October the same year it was voted on, article by article. Most of the draft was approved, including the basic provisions on lock-out. But because three Articles, concerning procedural matters, were not passed, adoption of the law was postponed. Debate on the draft law in the Parliament occurred concurrently with the increase of strikes and social tension in the Donbas region. According to the Government, this contributed to the creation of favourable conditions for a trade union campaign against the draft law and particularly the lock-out provisions. Certain forces in the Parliament, supportive of the trade union position, were prepared to use procedural tactics to postpone passage of the law. Since then more revisions have been made to the draft and it has been resubmitted to the Parliament for a third reading, but as of mid-1994, this had not taken place.

Officials in the Government responsible for drafting the law remain adamant about the importance of the provision on lock-out. They argue that access to lock-out should be on an equal basis with access to strike action. Yet as indicated above, given the definitions currently being applied to these two concepts, their impact would not be equivalent. Moreover, in many countries the legal limits on lock-outs are more stringent than those on strikes. For its part the FPU remains equally adamant that all references to lock-out should be removed from the draft law.

There are several other contentious issues in the draft law. First, it includes a new provision in Article 9 which concerns procedures for formulating trade union demands for a collective dispute. The new provision states that 'trade union demands must be based on social-economic grounds'. This is at best ambiguous since no definition of 'social-economic grounds' is provided. At worst, the provision could be used to discriminate against trade unions in comparison with other organisations, such as an informal strike committee which may wish to formulate demands and possibly lead a strike. This arises, because there is no corresponding 'social-economic grounds' requirement on the latter type of organisation even though the draft does envisage that such organisations will have the right to represent workers in collective negotiations.

The FPU is also opposed to the rigid procedures that the law envisages for the formulation of trade union demands and their consideration by management or the competent authorities. They argue that these procedures will drastically lengthen (by two to three times) the time taken to resolve the matter or allow a legal strike to take place. With hyperinflation, as experienced in Ukraine, a significant delay in considering and resolving the collective demands of a trade union could represent a substantial financial gain for the enterprise and a major disadvantage for the workers.

The FPU has raised a number of other objections to the draft law, some of which seem to have less validity. For example, Article 27 provides for penalties on workers who participate in strikes that are considered illegal, and the FPU has argued that this could result in the unfair prosecution of workers. It cites cases where organisers of a strike ignore certain procedural requirements to make a strike legal, where workers undertaking strike action are unaware of the correct procedures and/or when a breach of these regulations has occurred. The FPU argues that it would be unfair to penalise all strikers in a situation like this. It also disputes the provision in Article 35 which allows for dismissal of workers organising an illegal strike. The FPU is particularly concerned that the guarantees provided under the existing *Labour Code* – that the employer obtain the consent of the enterprise trade union committee before a worker can be dismissed – would not apply to workers organising an illegal strike.

3. Labour Legislation Reforms: Collective Bargaining

In the field of collective bargaining, ILO Convention 98 enjoins governments to ensure the following guarantees.

- Workers enjoy adequate protection against anti-union discrimination.
- Workers' and employers' organisations enjoy protection against acts of
  interference by each other.
- Voluntary collective bargaining shall be promoted between the parties.

Issues related to the first and second aspects of this convention are discussed in Chapter 6, while the third aspect is taken up below.
Promoting collective bargaining contains two essential elements.

- Action by public authorities to promote collective bargaining.
- The voluntary nature of negotiation, which implies autonomy of the parties.

3.1. Law on Collective Contracts and Agreements

One of the first significant legislative steps in promoting collective bargaining in Ukraine was abolition of Article 97 of the Labour Code in
January 1992. This Article enabled enterprises to use state tariff and salary
rates as bench marks for determining wages. The Government claimed it
removed this provision because it was committed to promoting free collective negotiations over wages, having already prepared a new draft of the
Law on Collective Contracts and Agreements. The Government foreshadowed the preparation of this new law during 1991 in response to a direct
request from the ILO Committee of Experts concerning Convention 98.
The Government indicated that this law would extend the legal guarantees
of labour organisations with regard to collective bargaining and strengthen
the level of autonomy of the negotiating parties from the government.[16]

A draft of the law was submitted to the Supreme Soviet of Ukraine in
1991 but was rejected on procedural grounds in early 1992. In December
1992, utilising its special powers that existed at that time, the Government
adopted a Decree on Wages, which had been prepared by the Cabinet of
Ministers. This Decree specified, for the first time, the spheres of state and
contractual regulation of remuneration at national, branch, territorial and
enterprise levels. It also established a strict procedure for regulating wage
adjustments that might be considered inconsistent with the spirit of the

---

[16] Comments made by the Committee of Experts on the Application of Conventions and
Recommendations. Convention No. 98, Direct request to the Government of the Ukraine,
1991.

Draft Law on Collective Contracts. These regulations were strongly opposed by both managers of state enterprises and trade unions.

The Government of Ukraine is certainly not the first government facing severe economic difficulties to grapple with the thorny issue of preventing or restricting the free fixing of wages by means of collective bargaining. In fact, the ILO Committee of Experts has been called upon to consider this issue on a number of occasions. The Committee has indicated that if, for imperative reasons of national economic interest, wage rates cannot be fixed freely by means of collective bargaining, these restrictions should be applied as an exceptional measure, should not exceed a reasonable period and should be accompanied by safeguards to protect those on low incomes.[17]

According to Government representatives the FPU continued to lobby for the adoption of a Law on Collective Contracts and Agreements with the expectation that this would override the Decree on Wages and undermine attempts by the Government to regulate wage adjustments. The FPU received support from the Independent Trade Union of Miners and the faction in the Parliament representing the interests of state enterprise managers. In the end, this combination of forces was successful in having a revised draft of the law adopted in July 1993.

Revisions to the draft law were prepared jointly by the FPU and a Commission on Social Policy and Labour within the Parliament. The FPU claims that it was responsible for 75% of the final draft and is satisfied with the law as adopted. By contrast, the Government may be more concerned about the economic impact of the legislation, since questions remain about the autonomy of trade unions and state managers and their willingness or ability to represent the divergent interests normally associated with free collective bargaining.

The law makes provision for collective bargaining in all sectors of the economy and at virtually all levels (i.e. national, branch, regional and enterprise). Section 3 defines the parties to a collective contract. On the worker side, this makes provision for 'one or more trade union or other bodies authorised by the work collective to represent it'. It should be noted here that the ILO Collective Bargaining Convention, 1981 (No. 154) does make provision for workers' representatives other than trade unions to participate in collective bargaining provided they are not used to undermine the position of the trade unions.[18]

In situations where there is more than one trade union, or other representative bodies of workers, the law provides for the establishment of a joint representative body for bargaining. If consensus is not reached within

---

[17] ILO, General Survey on Freedom of Association and Collective Bargaining, International Labour Conference, 81st Session, 1994.
[18] Article 3 of Convention No. 154.

this joint body, the legislation provides that the collective contract is valid providing it is signed by trade union(s) or other representative bodies that cover more than half of the workers in the entity concerned (i.e. enterprise, industrial branch, etc.).

Article 3 of ILO Recommendation No. 163, which provides for recognition of representative employer and employee organisations for the purpose of collective bargaining, might be germane to such situations. It refers to 'pre-established and objective criteria with regard to the organisations' representative character, established in consultation with representative employers' and workers' organisations'. It also notes that when workers are represented by trade unions, the 'other representative bodies' should not be allowed to enter into collective bargaining.

As is the case in some other countries, the Ukrainian legislation specifies the nature and scope of negotiable issues for collective bargaining at different levels. Sections 7 and 8 of the legislation prescribe the discussion of certain matters to ensure the parties reach a settlement on major problems affecting them. For example, the legislation states: 'The collective contract lays down the mutual obligations of the parties in regulating production, labour and socio-economic relations'. It then goes on to specify a number of areas in which this should apply, including topics like wage rates, working time, working conditions, non-wage benefits and guarantees for trade union activity. All this is consistent with international practice in industrialised market economies.

However, the legislation also specifies that collective contracts should cover the following subjects:

• Changes in the organisation of production and work.
• Provision of productive employment.
• Participation of the work collective in forming, distributing and using the profits of the enterprise (if provision is made for this in the staff regulations).

It might be argued that these later three issues have been defined too broadly and too vaguely.

3.1.1. First General Tariff Agreement

Consistent with the legislation, collective bargaining has been taking place on four levels; national, branch, regional and enterprise. At most levels, however, collective bargaining remains a process that only involves the Government, and the trade unions. For example, the first General Tariff Agreement was concluded in April 1993.[19] Negotiations took place, over

---

[19] General Tariff Agreement between the Cabinet of Ministers of Ukraine and Trade Unions of Ukraine, April 30, 1993.

the course of a year, between the Government and 12 unions without any employer involvement. The agreement is comprehensive. *Table 5.1* presents some of the major provisions.

Section 8 of the Law on Collective Contracts outlines issues that should be covered in a General Agreement and the above list exceeds those foreseen in the law. For example, the provisions on the environment, housing and health would seem beyond the scope of topics foreseen in the legislation. The ILO was informed that the FPU wanted even more issues to be included in the General Agreement and that the Government had attempted to restrict negotiations to the scope envisaged in the law. The final result was a compromise between these two positions.

The 1993 General Agreement also contained a section dealing with social partnership. Its provisions raise some connotations, and therefore concerns, relating to the role that trade unions played in the Communist system. For example, the Agreement states that 'Trade unions will assist work collectives of organisations, enterprises and institutions with their efforts to increase the volume of output and to improve labour discipline'.[20] It also contains what might be considered a 'peace clause', which states that trade unions will not organise strikes over issues covered by the agreement, provided the provisions of the Agreement are honoured.

The trade unions argue that many aspects of the Agreement were not fulfilled. The provision which provided for increases in the Consumption Fund to reflect past price increases and the introduction of legislation for overtime payments, as well as the provision which promised indexation of the minimum wage, pensions and other government benefits, were not implemented, they say.[21] Moreover, the FPU argues that of the 59 items in the Agreement only 20 had been completely implemented by early 1994, while a further 26 had been partly fulfilled.

In response, the trade unions organised protest actions in June and December of 1993, which was during the life of the Agreement. Later, in response to further price increases in December 1993, and the failure to implement the agreed indexation procedures, the FPU and other trade union confederations decided to terminate negotiations with the Government on a General Agreement for 1994.

During the first four months of 1994, the trade unions repeatedly called on the Government to convene a special meeting with the Cabinet of Ministers to discuss the outcome of the 1993 Agreement and to re-open negotiations about the unresolved issues and the contents of a new Agreement for 1994.[22] The trade unions claimed in May 1994 that this proposal was not taken seriously by the Government and was referred to

[20] General Tariff Agreement, 1993, op. cit., p 12.
[21] FPU, Resolution No. 11–12–1, Kiev, March 2, 1994, p. 3.

Table 5.1 *Provisions of the First General Tariff Agreement, Ukraine, 1993*

Item	Content
Remuneration	Adjustment of the Consumption Fund to reflect price increases between 1990 and May 1993.
	Introduction of penalty payments for overtime work equivalent to double the payment for standard hours of work (see Chapter 4 for further details).
Taxation	Tax free allowances.
	Items that would not incur VAT (i.e. baby foods, medicines, child care services, school text-books, housing construction and public transport).
Working hours and working conditions	Legislation increasing minimum annual leave to 24 days per year.
	Introduction of a 40 hour working week.
Labour relations	Limitations on individual contracts to managers of state enterprises.
	3 months notice of dismissal in enterprises undergoing structural changes.
Ratification of ILO Conventions	No. 144, No. 135 and No. 154.
	Examination with a view to ratification of Conventions No. 158 and No. 168.
Health and safety	Limitations on night work for women.
	Trade union participation in the establishment of a labour inspection system.
	Provision of basic safety equipment.
Guarantee of living standards	Establishment (by May 1993) of a minimum consumption budget to serve as a reference point for living standard assessments and socio-economic forecasting.
	Introduction of a system for indexation of minimum wages, pensions and government grants to the disabled and low income earners.
	Public transport subsidies for low income earners.
Employment promotion and protection of the unemployed	Research on the socio-economic impact of short-time working.
	Elaboration of youth employment programme.
	Other emergency employment programmes.
Social security	Development of proposals for a new social security system (by July 1993).
	Examination of why delays had occurred in payment of pensions and other social benefits.
Health care	Development of proposals for a new health care system.
	Maintenance of existing price controls on essential medicines and medical appliances.
	Preparation of a new Law on Ecologically Dangerous Areas.
	Programme for up to the year 2000 to mitigate consequences of the Chernobyl disaster.
	Upgrading technical facilities at certain sanatoriums.

Table 5.1 *continued*

Item	Content
Housing guarantees	Elaboration of principles for a new state housing policy. Maintenance of existing subsidies for housing repairs. Public utilities to remain effective throughout 1993.
Cultural environment	Introduction of regulations to control the operations of educational, cultural and sport institutions which are currently being restructured. Allocations from the state budget to subsidise trade union cultural and educational activities.

officials who, they believe, should be prosecuted for failing to implement the 1993 Agreement in the first place. In defence of its stance, the FPU claims that the Tripartite National Council of Social Partnership examined the steps taken to implement the 1993 Agreement and reached conclusions similar to the trade unions'.[23]

In April 1994, the trade unions took a decision to publicly condemn the Government officials they were negotiating with on these matters and pressed for their prosecution. They also decided to lodge a complaint with the ILO over the 1993 Agreement 'complaining the violation of international norms of social partnership and of workers' rights in the sphere of social and labour relations'.[24]

They also resolved to lobby the President of the Ukraine[25] and mount a press campaign against the Government on this matter. In response to this campaign, the Government admitted that some aspects of the 1993 Agreement were not fully implemented. However, it claims that the unions exaggerated the extent to which the Agreement was not implemented. For example, the Government claims that overtime penalty payments are being incorporated in collective agreements and that they did take into account price movements when adjusting the minimum salary and pensions during 1993. The Government points out that these minimum state guarantees were adjusted four times in 1993 and that the trade unions were consulted

[22] The trade union demands were addressed to the acting Prime Minister, Mr. Y. Zviahilskyi.
[23] Resolution of representatives of trade union associations authorised to review with the government the 1993 General Agreement and enter negotiations for a new General Agreement, April 4, 1994.
[24] Resolution of representatives of trade union associations authorised to review with the government the 1993 General Agreement and enter negotiations for a new General Agreement, April 4, 1994, p. 3.
[25] Open letter to the President of Ukraine, on behalf of the trade union associations, April 4, 1994.

on the methodology used to determine these adjustments. Nevertheless, it does acknowledge that exceptional economic circumstances prevented it from honouring certain aspects of the Agreement.

Shortly after the appointment of Vitalii Masol as Prime Minister in mid-1994 meetings took place with the FPU which resulted in a compromise solution to this dispute. At the FPU Congress on June 29, 1994 it was announced that the Government had agreed to double the base wage tariff as from July. The FPU had pressed for a more significant increase but eventually agreed to the Government offer and put aside the other issues outstanding from the 1993 Agreement. Negotiations for a new General Agreement are scheduled to commence in October 1994 and the expectation is that the parties will seek an agreement that covers more than a twelve month period.

3.1.2. Regional, Branch and Enterprise Level Collective Agreements

In 1993, there were 54 branch-level collective agreements and 10 regional agreements concluded and registered with the Ministry of Labour. The branch agreements are the result of negotiations between the Ministry responsible for each respective branch of industry and the branch union. In about half of these cases officials from the Ministry of Labour also participated in the negotiations, but the power on the Government side rests with the branch Ministry. The key component of these agreements are the wage coefficients for all occupations that exist within the branch (See Chapter 4). Branch agreements can also improve on minimum conditions of employment established in the national agreement.

The Law on Collective Contracts and Agreements states that agreements must be reached in all enterprises that use hired labour, regardless of their form of management or ownership. However, as these agreements are not being routinely registered by the Ministry of Labour, exact figures are not available on the coverage of agreements. Officials from the Ministry claim that most state enterprises had concluded agreements in 1993, although they had no information about agreements in the private sector or among cooperatives. Interestingly one survey, by the Institute of Labour, which covered 10 private enterprises, revealed that none of them had a collective contract.[26]

The Ministry of Labour conducted a survey of collective agreements in some state enterprises during 1993.[27] The survey indicated that in half of the enterprises, agreement was reached to prolong annual leave to 24 days as against the minimum standard of 18. In about 25% of enterprises, the collective agreement made provision for a reduction in standard working

---

[26] Unpublished survey prepared for the Ministry of Labour.

hours and to supply workers with special clothes, shoes and other protective equipment. In about a third of enterprises, the collective agreement contained commitments to reduce prices in the plant cafeteria, and in some enterprises commitments were made to establish farms that could supply produce to the workers.

The survey also revealed that about half the collective agreements stated that there would be an increase in efficiency, labour productivity and output in the enterprise during 1993. This was then used as justification for increases in wages beyond the amount fixed by national and branch level norms and to provide workers with additional benefits. Given the general economic decline and falling productivity in Ukraine, it would be reasonable to cast doubt on the ability of management and workers to fulfil these expectations. While there is considerable economic and industrial relations merit in encouraging productivity bargaining, and/or other remuneration systems where wage increases and other benefits are linked to some indicator of performance, these concepts must be implemented in an honest and rigorous manner. One suspects that there may be an element of 'bogus bargaining' taking place, with management and workers agreeing to distort the figures in order to justify wage increases above the accepted norm. Such practices run the risk of bringing the entire system of collective bargaining into disrepute.

A survey examining the implementation of collective agreements for 1992 conducted by the Labour Ministry, showed that industrial output had declined in more than half of the enterprises covered.[28] Consequently profits had declined, and various social programmes and other measures promised in the collective agreements had not been implemented. This survey indicated that in two-thirds of enterprises, the collective agreements were not fully implemented. If this trend continues, workers may legitimately view collective bargaining with similar contempt as they previously viewed the preparation and implementation of a central plan. The integrity of the whole collective bargaining process could be undermined even before the parties and parameters for free bargaining are established.

4. Strikes and Other Forms of Industrial Action

4.1. Disruption to Economic Activity

Table 5.2 presents data on strikes collected by the Ministry of Statistics. According to this source, there were a total of 465 enterprises where strikes

---

[27] Ministry of Labour, Survey of Collective Agreements and Bargains, Kiev, March 1993 (unpublished).
[28] Unpublished survey conducted by the Ministry of Labour.

took place in Ukraine in 1993, involving 260,000 workers. A total of 2,676,653 man-days were lost, either directly or indirectly, due to strikes.

This implies that the ratio of man-days lost to workers involved was about 10:1, which is very substantial by international standards *(Figure 5.1)*. This can probably be explained by the fact that the major dispute during 1993 was in the coal mining industry, which would have disrupted energy supplies and the operation of other industries.

If we use man-days lost as the best indicator of the disruption to economic activity caused by strikes, then 1993 stands out as a particularly disastrous year for economic activity with a three-fold increase of man-days lost over the previous year. Unfortunately there is no comprehensive breakdown of strike data by industrial sector, but the information that is available shows that in 1993, most strikes were in industrial enterprises (75%), which was similar to the situation in 1990 and 1991.

Table 5.2 *Establishments with Strikes, Workers Involved in Them and Lost Man-Days Due to Strikes, Ukraine, 1990–1993*

	Establishments	Workers	Lost man-days
Total			
1990	260	130,936	126,132
1991	239	175,936	1,873,142
1992	2,239	181,616	865,726
1993	462	260,332	2,676,653
Industry			
1990	198	119,323	114,468
1991	156	163,835	1,794,376
1992	26	9,926	34,956
1993	345	240,092	2,354,890
Construction			
1990	36	7,047	7,044
1991	22	3,766	67,152
1992	2	237	3,938
1993	64	10,147	104,713
Transport			
1990	17	2,790	2,785
1991	31	6,841	9,088
1992	127	36,495	119,302
1993	20	5,190	43,413
Other			
1990	9	1,776	1,835
1991	30	1,494	2,526
1992	2,084	134,958	707,521
1993	33	4,903	173,637

Source: The Ministry of Statistics, *Praciya v Narodnomu Gospodarstvi Ukrainie*, Kiev, 1993.

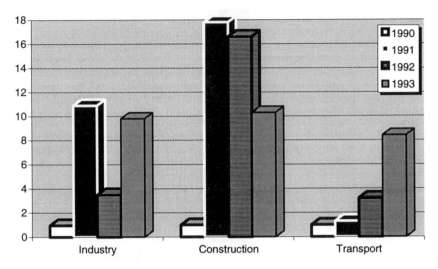

In construction the ratio has been the highest

Figure 5.1   *The Ratio of Man-Days Lost to Workers Involved in Strikes, Ukraine,*
1990–1993
Source: The Ministry of Statistics, *Praciya b Naro Dnomu Goopodarzstri Ukraini*, Kiev,
1993.

However, prima facie, 1992 presented a marked contrast to other recent
years for which data are available. In that year, there were over 2,000 enterprises where strikes occurred and 181,616 workers were involved in strikes,
but the total number of man-days lost was only 865,726. In other words,
it seems that in 1992 there was a dramatic increase in the number of short
protest type actions that only involved a relatively small number of workers *(Figure 5.2)*.

Many of these strikes were concentrated in the transport sector.
Compared with 1991, this sector experienced a four-fold increase in the
number of strikes, a five-fold increase in the number of workers involved
in strikes, and a thirteen-fold increase in working days lost due to strikes.
For example, there was a short two hour strike by flight personnel at
Donetsk Air Enterprise in June 1992, and a further short strike by air traffic controllers at the same enterprise in September. In both cases, the
unions demanded higher wages, which had been the main subject of protracted and unsuccessful negotiations, but the demands were rapidly met
once the strikes started. Other strikes in the same industry were connected
with the establishment and functioning of new small enterprises or joint
ventures.[29]

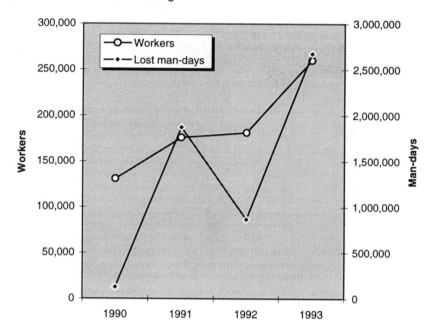

Number of striking workers increased but man-days lost due to strikes decreased in 1992

Figure 5.2 *Number of Workers on Strike and Working Days Lost in Strikes, Ukraine, 1990–1993*

Source: The Ministry of Statistics, *Praciya v Narodnomu Goopodarzstvi Ukraini*, Kiev, 1993.

4.2. Reasons for Strikes

The Ministry of Statistics does not publish data on the reasons for strikes, but industrial relations practitioners contacted by the ILO attributed most of the strikes in both 1992 and 1993 to declining real wages, the growth of part-time working and limitations placed on payments that state enterprises could make from their consumption funds. The single most important strike in 1993 from both a political and economic perspective was that by miners in June. This was organised by the Trade Union of Coal Industry Workers with participation of the Donetsk Permanent Strike Committee and the Independent Miners' Union. This strike lasted for 7 days and resulted in the establishment of a Commission from the Cabinet of Ministers to negotiate with the miners.

The Commission held negotiations with the representatives of the strik-

[29] Strikes over these issues took place at the Odessa and Borispol Air Enterprises during 1992.

ing miners, managers of enterprises, representatives of Dnipropetrovsk State Administration and the Krivoy Rog Executive Council. As a result of negotiations, the Commission prepared recommendations for the Government, most of which were adopted.The major demands of the miners are listed below.

- Upgrade wages of workers in agriculture and other branches of industry to bring them more into line with wages in the mining industry.
- Lift quotas, licensing and export duties on industrial products.
- Substantially increase minimum wages and pensions.
- Ensure agricultural products are supplied to industrial regions in proportion to the volume of industrial output from the latter regions.
- Proclaim Donbas an economic disaster area and provide compensations to people living in this region.
- Ensure that state orders from the coal mining industry are adequate to keep the industry operating at 70% capacity or higher. Any surplus output (exceeding the volume of state orders) should be sold independently including through exports.
- Provide for wage indexation.
- Provide strike pay to all workers participating in the strike.
- Restore economic, cultural and business relations with the countries of the CIS.

This is an extremely diverse and unusual set of demands from a trade union. While it is always desirable to observe trade union solidarity and to see that trade unions are concerned about the wider public interest rather than merely their own concerns, the list of demands could conceivably give rise to questions about the extent to which the strikers were acting in a independent fashion. It has been suggested that some strikes have been orchestrated by management of state enterprises and the demands being made largely reflect their concerns rather than those of the workers.

There have even been allegations that management of state enterprises have provided transport to Kiev for striking workers and meals for them while they were demonstrating there. It is difficult to substantiate such claims, but at least some of the concessions granted to the workers in the miners strike might be considered to add credence to assertions that the strike was at least partly about what might normally be considered problems for management rather than basic concerns of the workers.

The most important concessions granted by the Government are listed below.

- Abolition of limitations placed on the use of consumption funds in the coal industry.

- Creation of additional tax exemptions for the mining industry.
- Strike pay for the miners.
- Increased resources to purchase equipment and other materials required by the industry.

It would be inappropriate, however, to give the impression that all or most strikes in Ukraine are a management ploy. Another strike that received considerable attention in 1993 involved urban public transport drivers in Kiev.[30] This strike took place in February and involved the majority of the drivers. According to the union concerned, this action was extremely effective and virtually paralysed Kiev for several days. It appeared to be a spontaneous strike since the procedures required for a legal strike were not met. Moreover, it has been claimed by the independent trade union representing the transport drivers that the FPU was opposed to the strike and that the President of FPU intervened at the request of the Government to help to break the strike.

The major demands of the workers are listed below.

- An increase in wages for municipal bus drivers up to a level of not less than 10 minimum wages per month (an increase to 46,000 karbovanets from the existing average monthly wage for drivers of 25,400 karbovanets).
- The provision of apartments for workers in this industry.
- The establishment of a centralised fund to purchase spare parts for the buses.

To consider the workers' demands the Kiev City Administration established a reconciliation commission involving the Deputy Chief of the Transport Department and 15 representatives of the strike committee. The strike was settled at a meeting involving representatives of strike committee, the managers of the enterprise and the Minister for Transport. Issues concerning procurement of spare parts and the provision of housing for the workers were settled, but the wage demands were not met due to the enterprises financial difficulties. Surprisingly, the strike committee withdrew the wage demands and the drivers reported back to work.

In addition to strikes, there were other forms of industrial action by workers during 1993. For example, as indicated above, the FPU issued a pre-strike warning and organised a series of protests against the Government's economic/social policies, and the failure of the Government to honour undertakings in the General Agreement. The FPU claims that 11 million workers participated in the action organised in June 1993. In

---

[30] This strike took place at the Kiev Auto Transportation Enterprise 13034.

December 1993, the FPU organised a further series of demonstrations and pickets to protest against the Government's policies.

In the first two months of 1994 there were 8 reported strikes, involving 3,217 workers. This included a strike at the Nikitovsky Mercury Plant (January 1994) over wage arrears and strikes at 6 coal mines in the cities of Donetsk, Dmitrov and Shakhtersk. In a separate incident about 100 miners from the Independent Miners' Union went on a hunger strike protesting against delayed payment of wages. During February 1994, eight institutes, universities and technical colleges in Kiev held protest meetings at which workers demanded wage increases and increased budget allocations for education.

This description of recent developments understates the level of latent industrial relations tension in Ukraine. There has already been a considerable number of strikes and other forms of industrial disputation, and as earlier Chapters have made clear, the economic circumstances are ripe for cataclysm. The country is characterised by a breakdown of traditional economic linkages; a chronic lack of material and technical resources; and dramatic increases in income and employment insecurity.

This combination of problems understandably gives rise to a pervasive sense of nihilism about the economic future of the country and a sense of collapse and calamity. In the absence of the coercion that characterised labour relations under Communist system, the maintenance of industrial relations equanimity in these circumstances is impossible. Moreover, it is almost inevitable that many strikes and other forms of protest assume political overtones.

5. Industrial Relations Institutional Arrangements

5.1. Conciliation and Mediation Service

The draft Law on the Settlement of Collective Labour Disputes foreshadows the establishment of a National Service for Mediation and Reconciliation, which would be responsible for preventing collective disputes, providing forecasts on their development, assistance in the timely resolution of disputes and mediation of disputes.

However, virtually no progress has been made towards the establishment of this institution. Officials in both the Ministry of Labour and the Cabinet of Ministers appeared to be unsure about the structure or functions that this organisation would assume and they have little knowledge of the types of mediation or arbitration systems that operate in other countries. Despite the lack of clarity about the structure and functions of this Service, the

Government has estimated that about 200 employees will be needed to run it and that 90% of them will work from Regional offices. The FPU has suggested that Ukraine should establish a hybrid mediation system with both publicly funded and private arbitrators. It is unclear how this would operate and it is probable that the trade unions have not fully considered all implications of this proposal.

5.2. National Council for Social Partnership

5.2.1. Background

The National Council for Social Partnership (NCSP) was established in February 1993.[31] It is a tripartite organisation with 66 members, 22 from each side. A key step in the establishment of the NCSP was a round-table meeting between the President of Ukraine and representatives of all trade union organisations in June 1992.[32] In addition to the FPU, 12 other unions participated in this meeting. A communiqué issued at the conclusion called for the establishment of the Council. The meeting was convened in response to a crisis atmosphere after a series of strikes and protests directed against the Government over price increases and a perception that insufficient attention was being paid to social conditions. Another factor contributing to the decision to create the NCSP was that a tripartite structure had been established in Russia and, as with many other matters, the trade unions and employer associations may have felt they needed to replicate Russian institutions.

Other factors also played a role. There was a desire on the part of the Government to avoid involvement in internal disputes between competing trade union confederations. Following the advent of trade union pluralism, tensions and disputes between trade unions with different political sympathies emerged and the Government was increasingly called upon to arbitrate. It was felt that by establishing the NCSP the Government might be able to relinquish this responsibility and force the trade union side of the Council, and particularly the Workers' co-chairman, to fill the role of arbiter in inter-union disputes. The Government also claimed that creation of the NCSP was designed to encourage the establishment and better coordination of employer organisations, and to provide them with a more active role in resolving social and labour relations problems. The Government has argued that a strong and active employer organisation(s) would facilitate a more stable social balance within society.

[31] Decree of the President of Ukraine on the National Council for Social Partnership, No. 34/93, February 6, 1993.
[32] Communique adopted by members of the round table of the President of Ukraine and the representatives of trade union associations, June 5, 1992.

These are desirable objectives and the ILO congratulates the Government for espousing such principles. In some countries, however, a government may decide to establish a tripartite council like the NCSP merely for the sake of appearance and really have no intention of altering its policies, regardless of the advice forthcoming from the social partners. An even worse scenario would be where a government established a tripartite council because it considered this would enable it to exert control over the policies and public pronouncements of the social partners. If this were to be the case, tripartism may help to preserve the 'transmission belt' role that trade unions played prior to political reforms.

An alternative danger to be considered and carefully avoided is that a government may use the establishment of a tripartite forum to create disputes over representation among either the different unions or the competing employers' organisations. Such divide and rule strategies are not compatible with true tripartism. It is essential that such notions do not emerge in Ukraine.

5.2.2. Composition

The regulations governing the NCSP provide for each of the three parties to determine independently the procedure for selecting their representatives. It appears that the original proposal was for each of the three sides to have 15 members on the Council. But problems emerged, largely on the trade union side, with this arrangement. Initially the FPU insisted that it should obtain 75% of all seats, arguing that it represented the largest association.

The newly established trade unions did not agree with this proposition on the grounds that it was desirable that as many different points of view as possible should be represented in the NCSP. They claimed that the FPU proposal would not be compatible with this objective. The Government put forward a proposal which, after heated debates between the trade union representatives, was eventually accepted. This involved increasing the size of the Council to 22 members for each side. Among the trade unions, the FPU was allocated 10 seats and all the other 12 unions have one seat each.[33]

From the Government side all key ministries are represented, usually at Deputy Minister level, except for Labour, where both the Minister (who is co-chairman) and a Deputy are present. In addition, the following institutions are represented on the Government benches: State Property Fund,

---

[33] The FPU is represented by its Chairman and by representatives of the most active affiliates, this includes two representatives from territorial associations (Kiev City and Nikolayev Regional Councils) plus representatives from branch level associations (mining industry, agro-industrial complex, radioelectronic industry, education and science and coal industry).

National Bank, State Committee on Labour Safety Control, State Committee on Promotion on Small Businesses and Entrepreneurship, the Cabinet of Ministers of Ukraine and Council of Ministers of Crimea.

The composition of the employer side is less clear because of the complicated relationships that exist between various employer organisations. According to the Ministry of Labour, there are some 10 employer organisations and all are represented on the Council. However, the General Director of one of these (the Union of Leaseholders and Entrepreneurs) – who claims to have the only employers' organisation with members from the private sector – informed the ILO that the employer benches of the Council are dominated by direct and indirect representatives of the Ukrainian League of Industrialists and Entrepreneurs, which has 21 seats, while he occupies the only independent employer seat. Although there have been no formal changes in the composition of the NCSP since its establishment, the creation of a new organisation representing entrepreneurs, industrialists and agrarians has raised questions about composition on the employers' side, and as of mid-1994, there was a review underway.

5.2.3. Functions and Mode of Operation

The NCSP is an advisory body and reports directly to the President. The main objectives of the NCSP are listed below.

- Preparation of recommendations for the President of Ukraine on national social policies.
- Establishment of tripartite consensus on national economic and social issues with a view to preventing confrontation.
- Participation in preparation of draft laws, other legislative acts in the field of social and labour relations.
- Preparation of proposals concerning general and branch collective agreements, as well as analysis of measures taken to implement the General Agreement.
- Coordination of positions of the social partners concerning ratification or denunciation of ILO Conventions.
- Informing the public through the means of mass media on results of the Parties' agreements concerning labour and social relations.

The Council is supposed to meet at least quarterly but apparently does not have any fixed schedule for its meetings. There were four meetings in the first year of operation held at irregular intervals. The presence of a simple majority of members from each party is required for a quorum and decisions can be adopted if at least two-thirds of the members present support the proposal. All members have the right to submit proposals for the agenda, which is finalised by the three co-chairmen.

There is a small Secretariat which is supposed to undertake the following functions.

- Preparation of analytical, statistical and other informational material necessary for meetings.
- Preparation of summaries and analysis of positions adopted by the Parties on particular issues.
- Establishment of working groups from representatives of the Parties, as well as groups of experts, for consultations and negotiations on particular issues.

According to the Head of the Secretariat, who is a former senior official from the FPU, the Government has not actively opposed the operation of the NCSP, but it has not provided much material or political support for the institution either. For example, the Secretariat was promised premises and basic office facilities, but these had not eventuated. In 1993–1994, the Secretariat used offices and equipment belonging to the FPU. Meetings of the Council are held in different locations depending on what is available at the time. On most occasions they have used the FPU's conference facilities.

5.2.4. Activities and Assessment of Impact

Since it was established, the Council has held discussions on the following issues.

- Role and structure (membership) of the NCSP.
- The Labour Code of Ukraine.
- Legislation on collective agreements.
- Other legislation which has a direct impact on labour relations in industry.
- Possible methods for resolving industrial relations conflicts.
- Overall state of the Ukrainian national economy, including forecasts of economic growth, inflation, and unemployment.
- Governmental policies in the area of labour and employment.
- Professional training, executive development and other labour market programmes (National Programme of Public Works).
- Job creation in the public sector.
- Minimum wages and social security benefits.
- The content of, and procedures for negotiating, collective agreements.
- Ratification of ILO Conventions (including No. 2 on Unemployment, No. 144 on Tripartite Consultations, No. 154 on Collective Bargaining, No. 158 on Termination of Employment at the Initiative of the Employer).[34]
- The social and economic impact of decisions by the Government on price and tariffs regulations.

• Legislation on annual leave provisions.
• Progress achieved in developing the General Tariff Agreement.

Of all the issues listed, the general discussions about the Government's social and economic policies, and in particular the impact of changes in price and tariff regulations, have been extremely difficult and acrimonious. No consensus has emerged on these matters. Nevertheless, the Government claims that it is very interested in the opinion of trade unions and employers on policies in these areas and that the discussions in the NCSP have been largely constructive and fruitful. Representatives of the Government claim that these consultations have led to important negotiations and concessions on their behalf. In particular, they cite concessions made in regard to wages, and adjustments to the minimum wage as compensation for price increases. They also argue that concessions were made in regard to the fiscal budget, price increases, monetary policy and tax policies. The Government does concede that commitments in some other areas have not been fulfilled but attributes this to exceptional circumstances. They have argued that these promises will be met eventually.

In considering the impact of the NCSP, it is notable that it has not been able to resolve the controversy concerning the Law on Collective Dispute Settlements. Indeed, the Government has not even used this forum extensively for consideration of this matter. This may be indicative of the Government's real opinion about the potential of the Council. Moreover, it should be emphasised that the NCSP has not been given responsibility for determining alterations in the minimum wage.

The ILO questioned representatives from all sides on the impact of the Council. Both trade union and employer representatives were unimpressed by the operation of the Council and no one from these groups could name any issue on which it had significantly altered Government policy. It was felt that informal contacts between the union leaders, key managers of state enterprises, the President and particular groups within Parliament were much more important than formal discussions within the Council. Even the Government agrees that in cases where differences between the parties have been narrowed or resolved, this has resulted mainly from informal contacts outside the NCSP. However, the Government considers that this is because the NCSP is a new structure and, as yet, the parties have not become used to operating in such a forum.

---

[34] Following discussions in the NCSP the Supreme Soviet of Ukraine decided in February 1994 to ratify the following ILO Conventions: No. 2 of 1919, No. 144 of 1976, No. 154 of 1981 and No. 158 of 1982. These ratifications were registered by the ILO, May 26, 1994. Ukraine had already ratified Convention No. 147 on Merchant Shipping, March 17, 1994.

6. Conclusions and Recommendations

This Chapter commenced with a brief description of industrial relations in Ukraine under the former system. Since 1991 there have been some significant legislative and institutional changes designed to promote a mature industrial relations system compatible with a market or mixed economy. For example, attempts have been made to reflect basic principles like independence of trade unions from the State, promotion of trade union pluralism and support for bipartite collective bargaining in labour legislation. Positive developments include amendments to the Constitution, abolishing the leading role of the Communist Party over mass organisations, the introduction of a Law on Citizens' Organisations and, the introduction of a Law on Collective Contracts and Agreements. Undoubtedly, further steps in this direction are necessary.

6.1. Legislative Changes

If a new national Constitution is to be adopted, it should incorporate the principle of freedom of association as a basic human right.

Alterations to the Law on Citizens' Organisations to remove ambiguities about the application of principles of independence and pluralism to trade unions would also be appropriate. Further changes to the Labour Code and/or additional legislation on the rights and responsibilities of trade unions is probably necessary in a society where democratic practices and principles are still fragile and where people have traditionally placed a high priority on legislative solutions.

In that context the Draft Law on Trade Unions prepared by the FPU and amendments to the Labour Code proposed by the Cabinet of Ministers are relevant. Although we have commented on these proposals, the texts deserve further more detailed investigation. We recommend that the ILO be asked to assist the parties to reach a compromise solution between these two competing approaches by providing further technical advice to the Government, the employers and the trade unions on how their respective proposals could be made consistent with international principles and practice in industrialised market economy countries.

Policy makers responsible for drafting and debating labour legislation in Ukraine have limited expertise and experience with this topic in the context of a market economy. In fact, the current group of key industrial relations practitioners have never had the opportunity for training in either the theory or practice of industrial relations.

The German Government has apparently provided some technical assistance on some legislative issues but there is no significant or systematic programme of international assistance in this field. The lack of basic training for policy makers may have contributed to certain flaws with legislation that is currently being considered. For example, the ILO provided comments to the Government of Ukraine on the Draft Law on the Procedure for Resolving Collective Labour Disputes. The Government has been working on this draft for over three years and in that time many of the ILO comments were incorporated into the draft. However, particular points seem to have been misunderstood. As pointed out in this Chapter, the latest draft still makes provision for lock-out and equates this concept with a mass dismissal of employees, despite written advice from the ILO that a lock-out should only result in the suspension of an employment contract.

6.2. Industrial Relations

It is evident that confusion persists about this concept and other basic industrial relations ideas. At the very least, in the future, ILO experts providing comments on the Ukrainian Labour Code might present their comments in person, as well as in written form. This would help to ensure that such comments, and the basic underlying concepts, are clearly understood. An opportunity for such discussion will present itself in the near future as the Government has decided to formally ask for a further round of comments on the latest version of this draft law.

Government officials dealing with industrial relations and their counterparts in trade unions and employer organisations clearly require more training and exposure to western industrial relations. They might be given priority access to courses offered at the ILO Training Centre at Turin on collective bargaining and other courses on industrial relations subjects organised by the ILO. From the Government side, in the short term, it is probably a small group of advisers within the Cabinet of Ministers that offers the best possibility for promoting the development of industrial relations reform and they deserve high priority for ILO technical assistance. However, over the longer term, a priority must be to improve the quality of advice that the Ministry of Labour can provide.

6.3. Technical Assistance

Other more basic forms of technical assistance are required. For example, officials from the Cabinet of Ministers, Ministry of Labour and their counterparts in the trade unions and employer organisations should be urgently supplied with Russian translations of the Labour Codes from a wide range of countries. These people currently do not have access to very basic texts.

For example, academics from the Institute of State and Law within the Academy of Sciences have been requested to assist the Government in drafting various new labour laws and in revising the Labour Code, but they do not even have access to copies of ILO Conventions and Recommendations.

The immediate and widespread distribution of the Russian translation of this publication should be a priority. Until recently, officials within the Cabinet of Ministers had relied upon representatives from the international financial institutions for basic reading material on industrial relations. ILO-CEET has taken some steps to supply additional material. However, it would be desirable to have a separate budget to establish a library for basic industrial relations material in Kiev.

6.4. Industrial Disputes

Reference has been made to the increasing prevalence of strikes and other forms of industrial dispute. In a sense, this should be seen as a positive development after decades of coercion and suppression of the right to strike, yet the level of latent industrial tension is reaching extreme proportions. Moreover, most strikes and other forms of protest assume a political dimension. To some extent this is unavoidable in an economy that remains dominated by the public sector and the general population still expects politicians to produce some form of economic panacea for a plethora of economic problems.

However, Government officials and key politicians in Ukraine may be contributing to the political nature of strikes by personally intervening in the resolution of these disputes. In many cases ad hoc conciliation committees are established to consider strike demands, but these committees often include Government officials who have responsibility for drafting legislation and reforming the industrial relations system. It would be preferable if such officials could maintain a degree of independence and isolation from these strikes. If the government is constantly involved in day-to-day disputes with the trade unions and employers it will be difficult to establish the harmonious type of relationship necessary for achieving consensus on industrial relations reform.

It seems that the final decision about concessions to striking workers is often made at the highest political level. For example, it has been asserted that the previous President took the decision to concede to the demands made by the coal miners in mid-1993 despite strong opposition from the Cabinet of Ministers and former Prime Minister (and now President) Kuchma. It has been claimed that concessions made by the former President undermined the economic strategy being pursued by the

Government. Although it is unavoidable that governments and elected officials will become involved in the most protracted and politically damaging disputes, the establishment of independent procedures and institutions for the peaceful resolution of collective conflicts should be a priority.

The Government has indicated that it intended to establish a national Service for Mediation and Reconciliation, but so far has not put that into effect. Moreover, there exists a lack of clarity within the Government and among the unions and employers concerning the structure and functions of this institution. There is a pressing need for technical advice in this area. In the first instance, the Ukrainian authorities might be encouraged to study the ILO Voluntary Conciliation and Arbitration Recommendation, 1951 (No. 92), which outlines essential characteristics of conciliation and arbitration machinery: the joint nature of such machinery, voluntary recourse to procedures, which should be free of charge and expeditious.

However, the Ukrainian Government and the unions and employers will need technical assistance to implement these recommendations and assistance in training the staff to operate such an organisation. In the first instance, the ILO could conduct a tripartite seminar to discuss the various models for strike mediation that exist in western countries. Once there is consensus on the approach that would be most appropriate in Ukraine, the ILO could assist in developing a programme to implement this decision.

6.5. Collective Bargaining

Reference has been made to the growing incidence of collective bargaining and the settlement of collective contracts at national, regional, branch and enterprise level. It would appear that the nature of the bargaining process and the content of collective agreements have evolved since the Communist era. Serious reservations remain about certain aspects of this process. For example, collective bargaining remains in most instances a process that only involves the Government and the trade unions. Also it is evident that many collective agreements, including the General Tariff Agreement, have not been fully implemented. Perhaps one must accept that exceptional circumstances existed in 1993 preventing the full implementation of many agreements. However, any repetition of these events would undermine the integrity of the collective bargaining process. Perceptions already exist that a collective agreement is merely an ambitious 'wish list' and not a legally enforceable contract.

This raises connotations associated with the propaganda issued under the former system. If public confidence is to be created in a reformed industrial relations system a more responsible approach by all sides is necessary. The ILO could assist by conducting courses and seminars in collective bargaining techniques and by emphasising the importance of ensuring that provisions of a collective agreement are realistic and enforceable.

This Chapter has described the establishment, organisational structure and activities of the tripartite National Council for Social Partnership. Prima facie, this appears to be a valuable addition to the industrial relations institutional arrangements, which could help to maintain social peace and promote consensus on economic and social reforms. However, according to trade union and employer representatives, this forum has failed to fulfil their expectations. Both the employers and the trade unions see it merely as a 'talk shop', which has not been allowed to exert a substantial impact on Government policy. On the other hand, the Government cites a long and impressive list of issues that have been debated in the NCSP and concessions that they have made on policy issues in response to the arguments presented by the unions and employers.

In theory, one advantage that the trade union movement and employers' organisations might gain from the creation of the NCSP is an opportunity to improve their own image and demonstrate their relevance through a coherent contribution to the broader economic and social policy debate in the country. The key is to establish credibility which requires that trade unions and employers' organisations articulate constructive policy alternatives rather than merely complain about the impact of existing policies. The trade union and employer spokespersons must become active and not confine themselves to responding to government proposals. To be effective the message must be heard, and therefore a vehicle is necessary for transmitting proposals to the government and for publicising them more generally. The media can play a role in disseminating trade union and employers' views, but one can only expect the spotlight to focus on these proposals if they are well packaged and presented. One way of distinguishing the economic and social policies of a trade union or an employers' organisation from those of an academic institution or foreign consultant is to have them debated in a powerful tripartite forum. Viewed from this perspective, the NCSP might be seen as a publicity machine for trade unions and employers' organisations, and as one way of helping maintain and/or increase their membership.

Experience with tripartism in Western industrialised countries suggests that it is best to have trade union and employers' organisations that are both well resourced and evenly matched. In particular, if tripartite dialogue is to take place on social policy issues, employers' organisations and trade unions require the resources to analyse the complex economic and social implications of policy proposals. They also need competent researchers and advisors so they can develop their own independent policy proposals and are not always responding to government initiatives. The following

Chapter contains recommendations to help upgrade the technical capabilities of trade union and employer organisations.

We recommend that the ILO be invited to conduct a series of seminars in Ukraine about the functions and structures of tripartite councils in other European countries, as well as courses on technical issues that the NCSP needs to tackle.

One fundamental prerequisite for successful tripartite consultations is the existence of strong and independent trade unions and employers' organisations. It is equally important that these organisations be democratic. In the course of tripartite consultations or negotiations, interests are represented collectively by leaders designated from within the ranks of their groups. In turn, these groups are presumed to be free to defend the interests of their members by exercising the civil and political rights that underpin freedom of association, including the right to strike. The acknowledgement by the state of the legitimacy of trade unions and employers' organisations, their leaders and the important contribution they can make to policy-making is another necessary condition for successful consultations. The same preconditions apply for effective and free collective bargaining.

6

Trade Unions and Employers Searching for New Roles

1. Introduction

Without democratic, independent and representative organisations of employers and workers, the development of a well-functioning labour market is not possible. This we take as a basic premise of this chapter. Many of the policy issues discussed in other chapters need trade unions and employers' organisations for their effective implementation. In Ukraine in 1994, the most fundamental issues in that context for both workers and employers were whether or not the organisations established in their name were representative of their interests or becoming more representative, and whether they were recognised and given sufficient support to operate independently.

As of 1994, Ukraine possessed numerous organisations purporting to represent workers or employers. Their main forum for national negotiations should have been the tripartite arrangement, the National Council for Social Partnership. The trouble there has been that the tripartite Council has had only limited influence or real support, and its intended role has not been given much attention. The Council was set up mainly as a reaction to Russia setting up such an arrangement. It met irregularly through 1993, controversial issues were avoided, and it has made little impact on government policy and decisions. After December 1993, it lost momentum due to escalating internal tensions, and did not resume operations until the autumn of 1994, after all elections were completed.

Although the NCSP was operative in 1993, the prolonged election preparations caused tensions between the participating organisations and the government from late 1993, culminating in the disagreement on the implementation of the pioneering General Tariff Agreement, which caused the tripartite cooperation to collapse at the end of that year, as discussed in the previous chapter. Some branch-level collective agreements on wages were reached, however, and a few sectoral and local strikes were mediated through negotiations also in 1994.

This suggests that collective negotiations were after all emerging as the means of regulating the labour market. And private employers were emerging in the context of the slow but definite property restructuring of production and distribution. This tentative development of collective bargaining between organisations claiming to represent workers and employers took place even though labour legislation was limited, in spite of attempts to draft and implement new laws.

In short, the outward signs were that organisations of employers and trade unions were emerging as bargaining entities, although the legislative and institutional structures necessary for really effective developments were not yet in place.

In 1994, the institutional setup looked impressive enough, with over twenty trade unions, ten or more employer organisations and the tripartite National Council for Social Partnership reportedly assembling all these organisations.

However, there seems to be a lack of comprehension of the requirement for tripartism or the prerequisites for a market economy:

- The rule of law.
- Freedom of speech.
- Delegation of authority.
- Decentralisation and institutional pluralism.

The command structure may have been eroded since independence, at least at the national level. But the weakness of the central institutions of government made it easy for personalised networks to bypass laws and regulations. It is hard to envisage any rapid emergence of democratically representative bodies of workers and employers capable of replacing such traditional networks.

2. Emergence of Employers and Trade Unions in Ukraine

Before independence, as noted in Chapter 5, Ukrainian workers were organised as part of the traditional Soviet trade union system, which had well defined status and functions in society. By definition, no independent employers' organisations existed, but some functions normally attributable to such organisations were performed, under the leadership of the Central Committee of the Communist Party of the Soviet Union, by All-Union planning authorities, Ministries of Industry and Trade, Chambers of Commerce, etc., down through various subordinate structures.

After independence, the republic-level structures of the trade unions were reorganised into the Federation of Trade Unions of Ukraine (FPU).[1] By

---

[1] Throughout the text, we use this Ukrainian abbrevation rather than the English.

mid-1994 over twenty other national trade union organisations had emerged, separate from the FPU, and as we shall see these have been designated as free unions that is the term used by themselves as a distinction from FPU. The FPU has remained easily the most influential, as it took over much of the structure of the old union. Although it is being reformed in the process, there seems to be uncertainty in it and in other trade unions about what roles they ought to play and what roles they could play in the emerging labour market.

On the employers' side, the first organisation to emerge in Ukraine was the Business Union of Crimea, which was founded in February 1989, organising private businessmen and entrepreneurs but gradually also coming to represent industrial enterprises of this autonomous republic. At the national level, they soon became affiliated to the ULIE, the Ukrainian League of Industrialists and Entrepreneurs, which was founded later that year. Through the following three years, a surprising number of interest groups formed associations of various kinds throughout Ukraine – mostly at branch and regional levels – from seaports to municipal enterprises to economic funds and unions of economists and lawyers. Some of these were based on scientific and other societies that had been part of the previous infrastructure, but many emerged spontaneously.

An issue that remains sensitive is from where, and how, the impulses to these various initiatives originated – top-down, or 'democratically'. Clearly, in many cases it was a question of a quite democratic, spontaneous process, with interested parties forming an association by joining forces to protect their own interests, or those of their members. Yet as the state industries were organised, this was partly initiated from government circles rather than spontaneously by these companies and/or their managing directors, thus more top-down.

At the national level, most of the fifty-odd employer associations successively joined three major employer groups that have been formed – ULIE, which was founded in 1989/90; ULEU, the Union of Leaseholders and Entrepreneurs of Ukraine, founded in 1990; and UNAE, the Ukrainian National Assembly of Entrepreneurship, founded in 1993. Of these, ULIE has been dominated by the state-owned bulk of agriculture and industry. The existence of some other organisations has been reported, but their operations and/or affiliations are not yet clarified.

In the former model of industrial relations, there was a balance at enterprise level between the management, trade union committee and Communist Party committee. Each had the task of implementing policies of its hierarchically higher entities. In the case of disputes between the three elements, the party committee usually wielded decisive influence. The removal of the party presence from workplaces broke the balance. Since

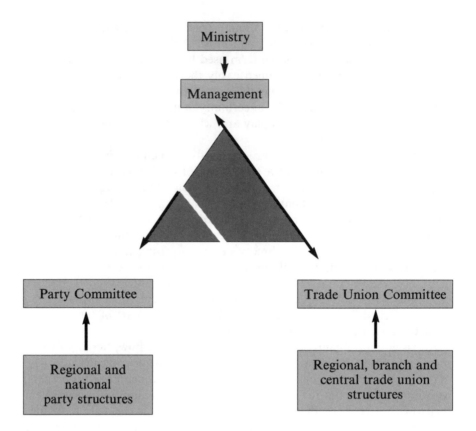

Figure 6.1   *The Structure of Industrial Relations in Soviet System*

then, the most important task in building and maintaining productive
industrial relations has been to find a new balance among management and
trade unions. This bipartite relationship in turn must have a functioning
connection to the public authorities, to facilitate the development of genuine tripartism (*Figure 6.1*).

The picture is further complicated because many forms of private enterprise are developing in Ukraine, some of which are anything but traditional. This has resulted in new organisations on both sides of the labour
market, which operate in unorthodox ways. They are as yet only marginal,
but they may take a more prominent role. One possible scenario is that
novel approaches will emerge as alternatives to the more conventional
organisations that in the main have been moving to represent the interests
of the larger, more established interest groups. The main issue is that as

more people fall out of the organised, structured labour market of full-time long-term employment, they may also fall out of the reach of traditional trade unions and employers' organisations and such social security arrangements as these agree between them.

3. Structures and Roles of Trade Unions

3.1. Effect of the Soviet Background

The challenges of Ukrainian trade unions are connected to the recent history of trade unionism in the Soviet Union and the collapse of the communist power structure.

In the Soviet Union, trade unions had a well defined status and functions in society. At the enterprise level, their main responsibility was to promote economic productivity through maintaining work discipline and solving workplace problems that would have threatened the operation of the enterprise. This task was promoted through large-scale schemes for socialist competition among workers in enterprises. The unions also had functions in the sphere of labour protection and were expected to guard the workers' rights against abuse from management, but those tasks did not interfere with the main objective. From an individual member's view, his trade union was the personnel department of the enterprise combined with a social and cultural services agency.

As with all other Soviet organisations, trade unions were structured on the basis of a strict centralised hierarchy. In accordance with the principle of democratic centralism, a lower unit had to obey instructions from a higher one. At the top of the pyramid was the Central Committee of the Communist Party. Its policies were implemented by the apparatus of the party, as well as the trade union (AUCCTU/VZSPS). The central trade union body in turn issued instructions to its subordinate structures, both in the branch or sectoral unions and in the regions. The Ukrainian trade union structure existed at the level of the republic, but was responsible primarily for the purpose of transmitting information between VZSPS and its Ukrainian constituents.

It is important to note the difference in the roles of regional and branch trade union structures. Regional bodies – such as the Centre for the Ukrainian Republic – were more involved in the politics of the Soviet society, whereas the branch unions concentrated on the productivity targets for their branch of the economy in the whole Soviet Union. A trade union committee in an enterprise was affiliated to both the regional and the branch structure. Whenever major production or organisation reviews were made, there was tension between the two. In sectors where the connection to their own centre in Moscow was strong, the regional structures would have less control. Prime examples were the union of atomic power workers, and some unions in the military industrial complex, including the military itself. They did not even belong to VZSPS, but subsequently they were to join the FPU in Ukraine.

Affiliates of VZSPS in the Russian Federation established their own organisation, the Federation of Independent Trade Unions of Russia (FITUR/FNPR) in 1990. The FNPR took possession of most of the staff and assets of VZSPS, which was transformed into an international organisation, the General Council of Trade Unions (GCTU/VKP), which concentrated its activities at the level of the Commonwealth of Independent States (CIS). Most, but not all successor organisations of the trade unions of former Soviet republics became members of the VKP. In Ukraine, FPU has maintained a cooperative relationship with the VKP and participates in many of its activities. Many of its affiliated branch unions belong to the branch structures of VKP, but these are no longer centres of power.

The disintegration of the Soviet trade union structures, in parallel with other power centres, has had a strong impact on the operating environment of trade unions. Since there was no longer a hierarchically higher body to instruct its subordinates, nor anyone to take responsibility for solving problems, at every level, organisations became less restrained in their actions. But they also received less support.

So, before independence, the trade union structure at the republican level in Ukraine was not designed to operate as a national trade union confederation. In that respect, when the FPU was established in 1990, it was a new organisation. Like the new alternative trade unions, it has had to learn to operate as a representative body for its members. That was a fundamentally new concept in Ukraine.

3.2. The Legislative Basis

The Ukrainian Constitution of 1978 is still the legal basis for trade union activities. The Law on Citizens' Organisations, passed in 1992, guaranteed non-interference by public authorities in the activities of citizens' organisations and the right of these organisations to establish and join federations, and to affiliate with international organisations on a voluntary basis. In 1993–1994, a Draft Law on Trade Unions was being debated. If that becomes law, it will affect the status and activities of trade unions. In principle, all workers and civil servants (including members of the armed forces) are free to form unions.

As described in Chapter 5, the law on labour conflict resolution guarantees the right to strike for most people, with the notable exceptions of the armed forces, civil and security services and employees of continuous process plants. Strikes based on political demands are illegal. This did not stop miners and transport workers from making political as well as economic demands during strikes in 1992–1993.

Although the issue of a new trade union law was debated intensely in 1993, interest waned in early 1994. One of the main problems was the issue of the 'right to legislative initiative', which VZSPS possessed in the Soviet Union, and which was used as part of the centralised development of Soviet society. After independence, that right was abolished in 1991. The need for direct access to the legislative process is seen by FPU as important, because of their distrust of parliamentary procedure and political parties.[2]

3.3. New Roles

Unlike some countries of the former Soviet Union, in Ukraine there has been regular cooperation between the various trade unions. In the period under review, all participated in the work of the tripartite body, and most of the time they advocated similar policy positions towards the government. An important aspect of the protracted negotiations over the 1993 General Tariff Agreement was that although the government tried to divide the unions in their negotiation positions, they remained united.

According to the Law on Enterprises, joint worker–management commissions should resolve issues concerning wages, working conditions and the rights and duties of management at the enterprise level, a system that is not clearly defined. Overlapping responsibility frequently impedes the collective bargaining process. Wages in each industrial sector are established by agreements between trade unions and the government. All unions are invited to participate in the negotiations. The Law on Labour Conflict Resolution introduced a National Mediation and Reconciliation Service, to mitigate labour-management disputes that could not be resolved at the enterprise level. The service was not functioning in early 1994.

Caring for working conditions is a new substantial area of responsibilities for trade unions. In the old system, unions had their own inspectors, who were effectively public authorities in implementing regulations. Now, that function is often not performed, and this is indicative of the need for unions to learn to represent their members' interests at enterprise level. Although the Constitution and other laws contain occupational safety and health standards, these are not implemented consistently, and the government machinery is insufficient.

There have been three major areas of working conditions and work-related hazards on which unions should concentrate:

[2] Interview with FPU President Stoyan in October 1993.

a) Coal mines: It is generally agreed that lax safety conditions were the principal causes of two serious mine accidents in June, 1992, which resulted in dozens of casualties, and in 1993–94, the miners' trade unions repeatedly demanded that the Government improve safety in the mines.
b) Chemicals: Ukraine has one of the largest chemical industries in the world; in October 1993, the Secretary of State of the Ministry of Industry estimated that the Ukrainian chemical industry had 1,500 production units using 250,000 chemicals, yet there was no integrated programme on prevention of accidents; about 83% of Ukraine's 52 million people are exposed to the potential effects of accidents in the chemical industry.
c) Energy: In early 1994, the Government decided to continue the use of two of the Chernobyl reactors, which has caused widespread international concern.

These three aspects of occupational safety and health deserve very high priority, and the trade unions seem likely to focus increasingly on that subject. Ultimately, of course, trade unions exist to protect and enhance the living standards of their members, and it is on this wider issue that the future role and strength of trade unionism in Ukraine will depend.

4. Trade Union Developments

Trade unions in Ukraine are faced by the extremely difficult challenge of responding effectively to hyper inflation and the problems of an economy that has been grinding to a halt. The main trade union is trying to establish a viable identity and some of the new unions are not representative, in terms of membership coverage, with the exception of a few specific sectors, such as the railways. The parliamentary elections occupied most effort and resources of most unions through early 1994, but in terms of labour market action their role has been limited by the virtual absence of a bargaining counterpart, since the government has not separated its roles as policy maker, legislator, owner and employer, while employers did not exist as a serious organised force in the private sector and nor do the unions.

As of mid-1994, there were four types of trade union organisation in Ukraine:

a) The Federation of Trade Unions of Ukraine (FPU), which is the inheritor of the Ukrainian structures of the VZSPS (English abbreviation AUCCTU, or the All Union Central Council of Trade Unions of the Soviet Union). Before Independence, the Ukrainian bodies were part of the Soviet organisations at both central, branch and regional level. In many practical ways, trade union committees in enterprises or institutes had more contact with their branch unions in Moscow than with the republic level bodies in Kiev. So, like the national government, FPU has had to try to build a new national organisation. The FPU (Deputy Chairman Grigory Ossovy) declared it had 21,215,000 members, as of January 1994. As with most other trade unions, there is no way of determining exact membership, but FPU has probably well over 95% of all trade union members in Ukraine.

b) New free unions that see themselves as alternatives to FPU. Most notable in this category is the Independent Miners' Union of Ukraine (NPGU), which emerged out of the 1989 strike committees. The Ukrainian miners were instrumental in creating the independent mineworkers' union of the Soviet Union (now NPG of Russia), but broke away from that union when Ukraine became independent. In 1992, the NPGU, together with the unions of airline pilots, civil air traffic controllers, locomotive engineers, and airline ground crews formed the Consultative Council of Free Trade Unions. In November 1993, eight alternative trade unions formed an association to act as a more structured channel for their joint representation. The association declares a membership of about 200,000.

c) Trade unions that had common structures within the Soviet Union, i.e. where there were no bodies at the level of the Ukrainian Republic (the Black Sea fleet, scientific workers of the Academy of Science, railway and railroad construction). These unions are between the two main groups, and are likely to join forces with one of the larger formations.

d) New unions that are oriented towards the policies of the government or FPU, but for formal or other reasons are not part of FPU. These include parts of the military and various police and security forces.

4.1. Federation of Trade Unions of Ukraine (FPU)

With independence, Ukrainian parts of the Soviet trade union structures were separated from the main bodies. Thus, FPU is a new organisation. Their second congress was held in August 1993, and it adopted a programme in favour of developing a market economy in Ukraine. The organisation seeks contacts with western trade unions, and according to its President wishes to approach the International Confederation of Free Trade Unions, with the objective of joining it.[3] Such contact would be instrumental in supporting its reform. The Federation is managed by the Council and its supreme authority is Congress; convened, according to the statutes, annually or more often, if necessary. The FPU's headquarters is

[3] Interview in October, 1993.

in the centre of Kiev. It also houses most of the headquarters of trade unions that belong to the FPU.

As of mid-1994, the FPU included 39 branch and 26 territorial trade union organisations (the number of regions plus Crimea). In early 1993 there were 19 branch trade unions. During 1993, more were established.

These developments suggest an increasing focus on the specific concerns and aspirations of different sectors and groups of workers. However, in discussions with leaders of FPU, their emphasis on political work became clear, and this was supported by the fact that before his election as FPU President, Alexander Stoyan served for eight months as President Leonid Kravchuk's adviser on union matters.

Within the FPU, the important relationship between sectoral and regional structures appears to lean in favour of sectors. Territorial and regional bodies are seldom more than meeting places for local leaders of different industries. This is partly due to the history of unions within Soviet Union. Branch unions were connected to the ministries in charge of the respective industries. For instance, about 20 representatives of industrial trade unions are members of the Collegia, the governing bodies of their industry's ministry.

In spite of, or perhaps because of the political emphasis of the FPU, during most of 1993 and 1994, the relationship between the government and FPU deteriorated. In June 1993, FPU reported that millions of its members participated in anti-government demonstrations. The poor relations

---

Bodies of the FPU Management

Member Organisation Contact Department;

Socio-economic Security Department;

Labour and Environment Protection department;

Health Protection and Elimination of Consequences of the Chernobyl Disaster Department;

Legal Department;

Information Centre;

Humanitarian Problems Department;

International Department;

Trade Union Property and Entrepreneurship Promotion Department;

Finance Department;

General Department;

Scientific and Analytical Centre;

Control and Revision Commission.

Independent Economic Entities Connected with the FPU

Trade Union House Management;

Union of Health and Recreation Facilities;

Union for Tourism;

'START' Union;

Academy of Labour and Social Relations;

Institute of Tourism;

Culture and Arts Centre;

Three Sport Societies (Ukraine, Spartak, Kolos);

Construction Complex;

Resort Project Department;

Printing House;

Trade union newspaper (Profsoyuznaya Gazeta).

Branch trade unions established in 1993

Trade Union of Ukrainian Machine Builders and Agricultural Machine Building;

Trade Union of Military and Specialised Construction Organisations;

Trade Union of the Gas Industry;

Trade Union of General Machine Building;

Trade Union of Innovation and Small Enterprises;

Trade Union of Machine and Tool Building;

Trade Union of Youth, Housing Complexes and Self-governance Committees;

Trade Union of Sea Transport.

---

reached a peak in December 1993 with the break-up of the negotiations on a new wage tariff agreement.

The disillusion was even stronger within branch unions affiliated to FPU. In particular, delays in paying wages in industry and public services caused tension, as did hidden unemployment (*Figure 6.2*).[4]

In discussions in May and June 1994, leaders of several branch unions estimated that hidden unemployment in mid-1994 accounted about 25–35% of

[4] A. Korol, President of the Road Transport Workers' Union, reported in May 1994 that from 1990 to 1993, there was a reduction of 62% in the volume of transport by trucks, 32% in bus traffic and 90% in taxi traffic. This union is convening discussions of all transport sector unions, regardless of their affiliation.

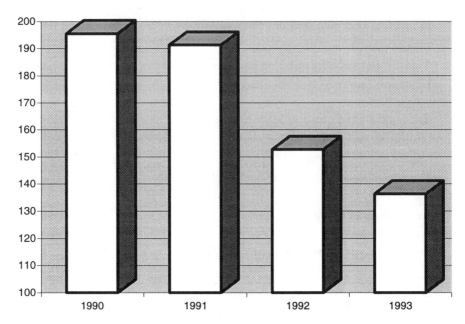

Figure 6.2 *Transport Workers' Actual Monthly Working Hours, Ukraine, 1990–1993*

Source: A. Korol, President of the Road Transport Workers' Union, 1994.

total employment. This concern was combined with difficulties in reaching collective agreements, and with difficulties in securing implementation of agreements that had been reached. They were concerned that privatisation was not advancing, that not enough investment was taking place, that many enterprises faced even more extensive falls in production or complete shut-down, that no one had the resources necessary for substantial conversion of the large military industry, and that only a few foreign enterprises have started production, often being discouraged by taxes and other barriers.

Bitterness was probably felt most by workers in the educational services. Their union is the second largest in FPU, affiliating 1.9 million members drawn from pre-school institutes up to universities. The Academy of Science staff are not members, although the large students' union with nearly half a million members is, because students used to be considered employees of the state, receiving grants and subsidies like wages. The Teachers' Union President says that its main concern is to save the educational system of Ukraine, which has been in a parlous state with budget allocations failing to match price increases, and with wages being lower than elsewhere in the economy and often not paid on time. In 1993, over one hundred new private education institutes were founded, and they were charging high fees, for teaching languages, computer skills and other marketable skills. They also paid their teachers better wages. According to the union, there was a danger that the public education system would be dismantled in favour of these private institutions.

For most of 1993–1994, legislative and other political processes concentrated on the election campaigns. In 1995, the new Government may have to respond to the trade unions' demands in a more serious way, if it wishes to maintain the relative calm that prevailed in mid 1994. The new Supreme Soviet has some trade union representatives, notably Alexander Stoyan and six other FPU leaders, as well as some from the new trade unions. Their role may be important, for the future of trade unionism and for the development of the tripartite mechanism for social and labour policy.

4.2. Other Trade Union Confederations[5]

An alternative Ukrainian trade union movement emerged in the late 1980s, when Ukraine was still part of the Soviet Union. The old system of the VZSPS, appeared among the most conservative as well as most stable of the Soviet structures. Bearing no strong ideological features, it survived after the collapse of the Communist system.

In 1989, many groups of workers started to establish strike committees, and later many of these evolved into free trade unions. It has been widely claimed that they were not aiming to break the official trade union system, but to fight for their rights, for the welfare of their families and for their dignity. Strike committees emerged first in sectors where working conditions were most dangerous, in risky professions where the threat of a strike might have a serious impact on the employer (typically the state): coal mining, railways and air traffic. The biggest strike movement, which led to the creation of a free trade union, was started by miners. Within Ukraine, the following twelve free trade unions seem to represent the main organisations to emerge.

4.3. Coordinating Council of Free Trade Unions of Ukraine (KRVPU)

In July 1992, trade unions of pilots, locomotive drivers, miners and air traffic controllers convened to create a free trade union coordinating body, the Coordinating Council of Free Trade Unions of Ukraine (KRVPU). A year and a half later, on November 3, 1993, it was transformed into the

---

[5] In addition to interviews in 1993–1994, this section is based on S. Pikhoshek, *History of Free Trade Unions of Ukraine*, Kiev, 1994, unpublished.

Association of Free Trade Unions of Ukraine. Its members consisted of the the following trade unions.

- Independent Trade Union of Ukrainian Miners (NPHU).
- Free Trade Union of Locomotive Engineers (VPGU).
- Trade Union Association of Ukrainian Civil Aviation Pilots (PALS CA).
- Federation Trade Union of Ukrainian Avia Dispatchers (FPAD).
- Trade Union of Textile Workers (PPTP) as associated member.
- Trade Union of Air Engineers (PITP).

The KRVPU has been an influential and aggressively independent body. In July 1992, all KRVPU members were involved in negotiations with the government on the General Tariff Agreement, when the President called a meeting of the Cabinet of Ministers, requested by KRVPU, to discuss their demands. When representatives of FPU came to that meeting, KRVPU insisted that they took their place next to representatives of the government emphasising their view that the FPU was associated with the government.

Subsequently, KRVPU representatives broke off negotiations, and on July 17, all the chairmen of free trade unions announced a hunger strike at the building of the Cabinet of Ministers. This led to a renewal of the negotiations, but again they were inconclusive. On September 2, a strike started. The government renewed its promises, and after the President guaranteed that no repression would be used against organisers of the strike, it was suspended and the parties returned to the negotiation table. Although the government acted more cautiously, the General Tariff Agreement was not signed.

In April 1993, the KRVPU held an open conference on the General Tariff Agreement. Later there were further negotiations, which finally resulted in the agreement further of July, 1993.

As of mid-1994, the Ukrainian alternative trade union movement was led by the Association of Free Trade Unions of Ukraine, an organisation established on November 3, 1993. As of 1994, its president was O. Mril and its office in the NPGU office.

4.4. Independent Miners' Trade Union of Ukraine (NPGU)

In July 1989, a wave of miners' strikes hit the Soviet Union. This was a period in which many local trade union strike committees were established, largely because the VZSPS was regarded as passive and as having supported the government. After the July 1989 strike, many mining regions decided to maintain strike committees. Then the Central Committee of the *Soviet Trade Union of Miners* decided to call early leadership elections for all leading trade union bodies. Against the hopes of the leadership, most organisations elected members of strike committees. New leaders of regional and territorial committees and mining trade unions were faced with enormous difficulties in their attempts to change old routines.

In early 1990, representatives of strike committees attending the 15th Congress of the Soviet Trade Union of Miners decided to call their own congress of miners. Held in Donetsk, eastern Ukraine in July 1990, most participants in that Congress voted for the creation of a miners' trade union, and decided to call a special congress in October that year, when 680 of the 800 delegates voted to establish the Independent Trade Union of Miners of the USSR (NPG). Three weeks earlier, workers of the 'Tsentralna' mine had established the first independent trade union of miners. O. Mril, chairman, was a delegate at the second Congress of Miners of the USSR from the new organisation. He was elected to the Executive Board of NPG, and he became deputy chairman. Together with A. Sergeev, chairman of NPG, he visited mines and encouraged miners to create new organisations. In December 1990, they participated in the miners' meeting in Donetsk, and the Conference of the Regional Union of Donbass Strike Committees (RSSKD) established the Independent Trade Union of Miners of Ukraine. Although the Executive committee was elected, this body did not survive.

In March 1991, O. Mril led a two-month strike of NPG in Ukraine. After the strike, in July 1991, a conference was called to adopt statutes and appoint the leadership of the NPGU. Mril was elected Chairman. With branches in six regions, it was decided to locate the union's headquarters in Kiev. By mid-1994, the NPGU had grown from 25,000 to 60,000 members, the figures probably being reliable because the union has insisted on payment of affiliation fees. The NPGU has been a member of the Miners' International Federation since 1993.

4.5. Free Trade Union of Locomotive Engineers of Ukraine (VPMU)

In 1991, railway drivers of the Kharkiv and Kiev depots decided to form their own union. S. Karikov, a locomotive engineer, was then Chairman of the strike committee. A founding conference was held in January 1992. In March 1992, delegates from more than 20 depots created the Free Trade Union of Locomotive Engineers. S. Karikov was elected Chairman. At the time, its major organisations were 'primary' depots of Kremenchuk (about 300 people), Kiev-Pasazhyrsky and Lviv-Zakhid. However, it proved difficult to establish a local branch in Kharkiv depot, even though it had initiated the movement.

The VPMU is governed by a Congress. Between congresses, decisions are taken by a Coordination Council, which includes two representatives from each primary organisation, with each organisation having one vote. Daily business of the union is run by the Presidium, which includes a chairman and a representative from each of the railways; six railways delegate one member each to the Presidium.

The VPMU's membership has expanded steadily, and new primary organisations have emerged in various depots. In April, 1994, on the initiative of the VPMU, the Lviv Federation of the Free Trade Union of Railway Engineers, as well as former organisations of the All-Ukrainian Organisation of Worker Solidarity (VOST) acting in the railways, and some new organisations, established the Union of Free Trade Unions of Railway Workers of Ukraine (OVPZU). S. Karikov was also elected its Chairman. This new body united not only locomotive drivers, but organisations of other professionals of the Ukrainian railways.

In 1994, the VPMU managed to have two representatives elected as members of the national Parliament. During the election campaign, several new trade unions were established by efforts of locomotive drivers at Kremenchuk and Mykolaiv depots. VPMU is affiliated to the International Transport Federation (ITF).

4.6. Trade Union Association of Civil Aviation Pilots of Ukraine (PALS CA)

Before 1989, civil aviation pilots belonged to the Trade Union of Aviation Workers of the Ministry of Civil Aviation. On February 25, 1989, a founding congress established an Association of Civil Aviation Pilots of the USSR (ALC CA). Ukrainian pilots played an active role, and after the association was created, independent organisations of LAS CA emerged in Ukraine. In March 1991, a group of pilots held a founding congress of the Ukrainian Aviation Pilots.

The union did not have an easy initial period. In October 1992, at a second extraordinary Congress, Viacheslav Bulashov was elected the first President of the PALS CA. On September 18, 1993, Bulashov died after falling out of a window at the ninth floor of the Kiev Institute of Civil Aviation Engineers. The union survived this troubled period, and began to expand. By November 1993, when the PALS CA joined the Free Trade Unions of Ukraine, its leaders reported that it had grown to 3,000 members.

As of mid-1994, union leaders were considering whether to apply to join the International Federation of Airline Pilots, and the International Transport Federation, and whether to make an agreement with the Russian Trade Union of Pilots.

4.7. Federation of Ukrainian Air Traffic Controllers (FPAD)

In 1989, a strike movement of air controllers developed in the Soviet Union and resulted in the establishment of the Association of Air Traffic Controllers of the Soviet Union. Two Ukrainian delegates attended the founding congress and proposed to establish a Ukrainian trade union body, but the Russians did not agree. A decision to start a strike was made in May 1991. Major demands included salary increases, higher pensions, and more attention to health norms. Minutes before the strike was due to start, the Soviet government promised to meet all the main demands. When the Government failed to keep its promise, another strike was planned for August, 1991. Again, an hour before the beginning, the Government confirmed that the demands had been fulfilled.

A similar situation occurred in Ukraine in February, 1992. The Government twice promised the strikers to fulfil their demands. In the meantime, Ukrainian air controllers held their own founding conference, left the former all-union structure and established the Federation of Ukrainian Air Traffic Controllers (FPAD).

4.8. Trade Union of Engineers of the Ukrainian Airlines (PITP)

In February 1991, aviation engineers in Boryspil and Lviv separately had the idea of establishing a trade union. Initiative groups were created in Boryspil and in Zhuliany. In September 1991, a founding conference was held in Boryspil. Two alternative draft statutes were presented by the Boryspil and Lviv groups. 23 branches of the Ukrainian Airlines sent representatives. There were efforts to establish an association, but most delegates favoured the idea of a trade union.

On the basis of the drafts, the conference adopted statutes and established the Trade Union of Air Engineers (PITP). A second conference, held in July, 1992 approved the decision to join the Coordination Council of the Free Trade Unions of Ukraine.

4.9. Trade Union of Textile Workers of the Donetsk Cotton Factory (NPT)

The Free Trade Union of Textile Workers of the Donetsk Cotton Factory was founded by ten workers during the Ukrainian miners' strike in April 1991, on the basis of a strike committee. By early 1992, the trade union had 2,600 members. Although mass lay-offs from the factory reduced that to 1,780, its share of the factory's workforce increased compared to membership of the FPU trade union.

Since 1991, the NPT has signed two collective agreements, which have included a demand to privatise the factory. With assistance from the Centre for Market Reform, the trade union has worked to prepare the factory for privatisation. The NPT struggles against mass lay-offs in a context of a lack of raw materials and long-suspended work.

In May 1993, driven to despair by the reluctance of the administration and the state committee for light industry to take measures to improve the situation, which was characterised by unwanted and unpaid vacations and delays in wages, six members of the trade union started a hunger strike at the building of the Ukrainian Supreme Council. After six days, agreements were signed.

The trade union agreed with the administration that part of the delayed wages would be paid in fabric. The trade union insisted on dismissing two managers accused of harassment of female workers. Since November 3, 1993, the trade union has been a member of the Free Trade Unions of Ukraine.

4.10. Independent Trade Union of Dockers of the Illichevsk Trade Sea Port (NPPP)

This trade union was established on October 30, 1991. Then it had 900 members, all dockers, although the trade union was called the Trade Union of Dockers and Warehouse Workers. In late 1991, the union had its first victory, when it succeeded in obtaining a wage rise. Gradually the trade union involved workers of other port professions. In May 1993, at its sixth conference, it changed its name due to its expanded and more diversified membership. By mid-1994, its membership amounted to 3,800, which was about half the port's personnel. In May 1993, the trade union joined the KRVPU.

The union consists of four workshop councils – dockers, warehouse workers, machine operators and the port fleet. These Councils consist of trade union groups according to a production principle. The supreme authority of the organisation is its Conference. Power in periods between conferences belongs to the trade union council including the leaders of trade union groups and heads of the workshop councils. The councils convene at least once a quarter. In periods between Councils, the trade union Presidium convenes every month.

On August 1–2, 1993, the trade union held a 24–hour strike, in support of demands that included recognition of the trade union and wage rises. In subsequent negotiations with in Illichevsk, the Minister of Transport and the Sea Transport Department, of the government, it was decided to establish a state commission to consider the strikers' demands. It resulted in the appointment of a new director of the port.

4.11. Association of Free Trade Unions (Yednist)

In November 1991, workers of the Vijtovetsky local communications network announced their decision to leave the FPU trade union. In March 1992, after the 2nd Congress of the All-Ukrainian Union of Workers' Solidarity (VOST) they joined that organisation. Their example was followed by trade unions of the 'Temp' plant of Khmelnytsky, the Volochysky local communications network No. 3, the 'Meteor' plant, and the garment factory in Volochysk.

At that time, VOST existed due largely to enthusiasm of primary organisations in the Khmelnytsky region and their leaders. For instance, these organisations used their own funds to publish extra issues of the VOST's 'Solidarnist' newspaper, apparently without assistance from the VOST leadership. Viewing this organisation as too politicised, they felt obliged to leave the group and create the *Yednist*. When the Free Trade Unions of Ukraine was set up in November 1993, the *Yednist* was adopted as a collective member, and its leader joined its executive committee and became its representative for the Khmelnytsky region.

By May 1994, the *Yednist* had been joined by the following trade unions.

- 'Svemon' Free Trade Union from Khmelnytsky,
- Free Trade Union of the Ternopil Regional Communications Network from Pidvolochysk,
- Free Trade Union of the Ternopil Regional Communications Company (OPZ),
- Free Trade Union of the Starokostiantynivsky Local Communications Network (RVZ) from the Khmelnytsky region,
- Free Trade Union of the Shepetivka Local Communications Network.

Hence, most organisations belonging to the 'Yednist' represent communications workers.

In May 1994, the Founding Conference of the Free Trade Union of Communications Workers (VPSZU) was held in Volochysk, involving trade unions of the Khmelnytsky regional communications company, 900 members from the workforce of 9,000, according to the union; of the Ternopil regional communications company (100 out of 6,500); and the 'Svemon' joint-stock society (Ukrainian communications builders), which had about 110 members in the Khmelnytsky region. The *Yednist* as a regional association continued to unite all trade unions in the field of communications.

4.12. Solidarity Trade Unions of Ukraine (SPU)

The group Solidarity Trade Unions of Ukraine (SPU) was established in March 1990 and was built according to territorial and production principles. By January 1993, it united 106,000 members, of which 86,000 were only members of the SPU, and 20,000 had double membership with other trade unions. According to the union's president, by mid-1994 it had over 150,000 members. About half of SPU members are professional employees, engineers, doctors, journalists, etc., about a third are industrial workers and about 12% are employed in services.

Local committees comprise city or regional SPU councils, and heads of regional SPU councils form the national Coordination Council. A union Congress elects the SPU President and Secretary General. The President is A. Sheikin. The SPU publishes a national newspaper *Volia* (Freedom) in Ukrainian and a local Mariupol newspaper of the Azovstal Free Trade Union of Steel Workers. The SPU is a collective member of the Free Trade Union of Ukraine and is a member of the SOTSPROF structure based in Moscow. The SPU orients its members towards market relations and changes in forms of property, stands for maximum privatisation of the state sector, private ownership of land, etc. In December 1992, the second SPU Congress adopted a decision uniting the SPU as an organisation that did not attribute priority to any political force in Ukraine.

4.13. All-Ukrainian Union of Workers' Solidarity (VOST)

The All-Ukrainian Union of Strike Committees emerged during the 'perestroika' period of the Soviet Union, and in 1990 the All-Ukrainian Union of Workers' Solidarity (VOST) was established, at a founding congress in Pavlohrad in the Dnipropetrovsk region. Since there was no proper legislation on trade union issues, it was registered at the Ministry of Justice as a civil society. The emergence of the VOST was immediately made public by round tables with its leaders shown on TV, and this led to a mass transformation of strike committees into trade unions.

Since those early days, the group has focused much more on political issues than on the immediate concerns of working people. Although little attention has been paid to establishing branches, their number did steadily increase. In March 1992, the VOST held its 2nd Congress, which attracted more members and by the 3rd Congress in April 1993 it had 2,450. Then the organisation was challenged by splits at its 3rd and 4th Congresses. In December, 1993, member organisations dissatisfied with activities of members of the union's Presidium convoked an early 4th congress and elected a new Presidium and Control Revision Commission, as well as a new Chairman. These developments had their impact on the size, influence and viability of the organisation. It started losing members, and the VOST of mid-1994 had only a small influence on the Ukrainian trade union movement. VOST is affiliated to the World Confederation of Labour (WCL).

In September 1994, ILO-CEET was approached by two separate groups, both of whom claimed to represent VOST leadership. With available information, their credibility can not be confirmed, but the 'main' structure, headed by president O. Dzhulik, maintains the international relations, including those with WCL.

4.14. Independent Trade Union of Ukrainian Military (NPVU)

The organising committee responsible for establishing this trade union was created by nine people in Kiev in February, 1993. This unprecedented case was provoked by the poor conditions of the Ukrainian military, especially conscripts, sergeants and junior officers, and by the perceived need for retraining and jobs of retired military personnel, especially officers returning from Eastern Europe.

The Independent Trade Union of Ukrainian Military (NPVU) was created at a founding congress in May, 1993, when it had only 24 members, all from Kiev. Yet it grew through efforts to redress the increasing social problems faced by servicemen and women. The NPVU held its first meeting of protest against social injustice in the Ukrainian Armed Forces in June 1993, at Maidan Nezalezhnosti. A majority of the participants were homeless officers and Afghan war veterans. The meeting criticised the attitude of the Ukrainian leadership to the Black Sea fleet issue. The union's second Congress was held in September 1993. In January 1994, the NPVU was registered as a member of the Free Trade Unions of Ukraine.

By mid-1994, the union had 15 branches in 13 regions and had increased its membership to 4,027 officers, from senior sergeants to colonels, of whom about 100 were serving at the National Guard of Ukraine. NPVU nominated and registered 36 candidates for local Councils; 20 of whom ran for seats at the Kyiv Council, 1 in Ternopil and 15 in Kherson.

In May 1994, to protect its members' money from inflation and to provide for the financial stability of the trade union, the NPVU initiated a limited liability joint stock society to operate commercially. Time will tell how this non-traditional way of supporting collective social security will function. In mid-1994, the primary concern was to obtain repayment of what they saw as debts to servicemen due to the non-provision of food rations between December 1991 and September 1993, and due to the fact that many had to rent accommodation even though housing was supposed to be provided under the law.[6]

---

[6] *Intelnews*, June 8, 1994, p. 6.

5. Regional Trade Union Development

Regionally, trade union developments have varied, with the FPU being more active in some areas than elsewhere. For instance, in Crimea an important step was taken by the FPU when it begun organising workers in private enterprises, especially in Simferopol, and there the FPU has remained by far the largest union body. It is organised on traditional lines, through branch federations. It gives priority to its members' social needs, and worries that social funds built up in enterprises might be siphoned off by the central government in Kiev, and be devalued by inflation.

This union has focused on relations with the regional government rather than with the employers' organisations, and offers members much higher wages than the other major trade union, seemingly because it has better ties to the government and thus does not depend as much on what the economic development of the enterprises allows. Almost certainly, this latter focus will have to change if the FPU is to remain a major influence in the process of privatisation.

The main alternative on the union side in the republic of Crimea is called *Yedinstvo* (the Russian word for unity). *Yedinstvo* is the regional chapter of the Ukrainian Trade Union Federation of Cooperatives, and has about 10% of all organised workers in Crimea. It has no branch structure, and its leaders claimed it did not intend to form one. It is more oriented towards a tripartite relationship government–unions–employers than its rival, striving for a regional social pact, with minimum wage guarantees. It has managed to ensure that the social fund built up for its members remains administered by themselves, and has so far withstood demands from the central government to hand over that management. It has links with the Kiev union structure, but also with the CIS union movement in Moscow, whereas FPU's regional chapter, the Independent Union Federation in Simferopol has no contacts with Moscow or CIS trade unions other than through Kiev.

95% of Yedinstvo's members are workers and 5% managerial employees. *Yedinstvo* represents 4,000 establishments employing 80,000 persons, of the 7,000 private and 5,000 state enterprises in the republic, with a total labour force of about 1,1 million, of which about 10% are unemployed, according to local union leaders.

In the competition between the two union bodies, the FPU in Crimea has concentrated on keeping as many members as possible in jobs. In this it has foreseen extraordinary difficulties. In March 1994, it forecasts that latent unemployment would reach abysmal levels in some industries by the end of 1994, forecasting 50% in the chemical industry and 70% in textiles. Generally, workers' social needs are given priority, but wage demands (or promises, to attract members) are kept considerably higher than what *Yedinstvo* deems possible, up to double – as the FPU union seems to retain the belief that government subsidies will remain, and that there is no need for individual enterprise to make a profit, especially given that the State, both Ukrainian and Crimean, continues to control production at enterprise level.

An interesting development has occurred in Sevastopol, which used to be organised as a region before Crimea's status as an autonomous republic was further elevated in January 1994. It has its own chapter of the FPU, which organises workers from 1,070 enterprises. By early 1994, it seemed that it was more active in the private than in the (Crimean) state sector. This seems to reflect the fact that much of the state sector employment is actually part of the military labour force employed by the Russian federation and much of the remainder is employed in the naval base and related installations operated there by the state of Ukraine. High on the union's agenda was the issue of amalgamating the Sevastopol chapter with the Crimean Trade Union Federation in Simferopol.

The Sevastopol Union keeps many options open. They cooperate with the Crimean union as well as with Kiev, but also maintain independent relations with the CIS union structure in Moscow, not via Kiev but in parallel. Their main explanation is that they refuse to be restricted by the governance from Kiev. They claim that by this balancing of relations, they have managed to keep part of their social contributions under local control, and also to have staved off several unwanted Kiev proposals.

As yet, there has been little bargaining with private employers, even though many of the union's members work in their enterprises. In 1993, only one union member asked for assistance in a wage conflict with his private employer. The union has engaged in labour conflicts in the private sector, and has tried to achieve working relations with those employers.

Although the authorities in Crimea have not had time to formulate or implement many new policies, they have tried to introduce changes, on such matters as the minimum wage and incomes policy. They have also approached the employers (the Business Union of Crimea) and have supported efforts to improve the financial stability of enterprises. Most important was that the Business Union managed to persuade the Government to go through with a much needed tax reform, in April 1994.

An effort to reach a General Agreement in 1994 was partly successful, in that the trade unions and employers accepted the outcome, but the Government that still directly employs half the total workforce refused to ratify it, on the grounds that it would be too costly for them, and that the labour protection scheme proposed by the Business Union must first be financed.

Other Crimean Trade Union priorities are labour legislation generally, combating the high hidden unemployment, and improving industrial and social relations.

Major local issues are the future of the Black Sea fleet and the political future of Sevastopol, which this union would like to see remain in Russian hands. Another long-term challenge is the disproportionate number of pensioners in Crimea (and Lviv), especially in Sevastopol, which is a reflection mainly of the privilege granted in the Soviet era by which workers in certain professions, such as the military[7], and workers in certain regions, especially the Arctic and Siberia, were allowed to choose where to live as pensioners. That problem has been compounded by the substantial and growing number of redundancies among the Russian military stationed in Crimea.

The central authorities of Ukraine compensate Crimea for the high proportion of general pensioners, while the Russian Federation finances military pensions, but the latter has not been able to provide social security for the many thousands of military personnel who have become unemployed.[8]

6. Roles and Functions of Employers' Organisations

6.1. Before Independence

As noted earlier, no employers' organisations existed in the USSR. Nor could any exist, as there could not be any independent or opposing interests, and accordingly no need for separate organisations expressing dissenting points of view.

Under the Soviet system, functional interests of enterprises and other production units were taken care of by the authorities under the leadership of the Central Committee of the Communist Party. All these instances were structured in a strict hierarchy, where a lower unit had to follow instructions issued by a higher one. There did exist a Ukrainian level, but its main purpose was that of a transmission belt, passing on orders and presenting production statistics in the opposite direction. When more than one instance were involved on the same hierarchical level, the appropriate Party committee always took the lead.

---

[7] Military employed by the Soviet Union became entitled to pension privileges after 20 years of service and 45 years of age, civilians employed by the Soviet military from 60 years of age.

[8] To help compensate for the lack of social protection for this category who are mostly not Ukrainian citizens, a private initiative beginning in 1991 led to the establishment of an independent Social Fund called 'PAFOS', which helps finance various support schemes, such as employment services, labour market training, unemployment support, health care, and counselling . 'PAFOS' finances all this through voluntary contributions, gifts from individuals and authorities, and by operating twenty commercial enterprises in a variety of branches. This is lucrative thanks to the tax-exempt status of the Fund as sole owner of these enterprises. The Fund is chaired by the Commanding Admiral of the Black Sea fleet.

Before Independence, Ukrainian enterprises being both State owned and part of the central command structured production organization, there existed practically not even marginal room for local initiative. In fact, Moscow central control seems to have been harder and more strictly imposed in the 'independent republics' than in the regions of the then Russian Soviet Republic.

6.2. After Independence

The resultant passivity seems to remain a major obstacle since many Ukrainian managers still wait to be told what to do. This relates to many issues they should handle directly as businessmen, such as marketing and selling their products, and as employers, such as all aspects of organising production, regulating the workers' terms of employment and conditions of work, handling grievances and settling disputes and furthering industrial relations and social dialogue, especially on the local level.

However, even more critical than the usual passivity of Ukrainian managers is the extremely low level of officially registered private enterprises and business ventures in Ukraine, (see Figure 6.2). To make matters worse, the numbers grow only very slowly. Even granted the uncertain data used, it is clear that Ukraine should need immediate and colossal infusions of new, private companies. For Ukraine to reach anywhere near the proportions of private enterprises even of the neighbouring ex-communist countries, it would need anywhere from ten to twenty-five times the present number! The worst of it, however, is the near total incomprehension of this fact, rather than the proportions as such.

Yet again, the unusually low propensity to engage in enterprising and business activities – indeed to show any form of initiative publicly – has historical explanations that have to be at least indicated. In fact, until the breakthrough of *glasnost* and *perestroika* ten years ago, such behaviour had dire consequences, which the Ukrainian people learned to avoid the hard way.[9]

Ironically enough, the very suppression of all forms of open initative helped foster a very different form of entrepreneurial talent, especially in

[9] Through many decades, Ukraine's whole population but particularly its more enterprising groups have suffered more than most other peoples of the region from repeated use of the most exceptional methods of curbing initiative and independence. These draconic visitations began in the mid-1920's. The first decade saw the literal extermination of the *Kulaks* – independent farmers – which together with the terrible famine that followed from the Party's brutal enforcing of NEP – Lenin's New Economic Policy – took five to ten million Ukrainian lives. During the next decade many more millions perished, from Stalin's purges and of course from the War when armies marched back and forth across Ukraine, alternately trying to live off its rich resources, and destroying its land and people alike. Through the next four decades, the Gulag archipelago did little to encourage initiative.

Table 6.1 Relative proportions of private enterprise

Country	Population (millions)	Registered private economic activities		
		enterprises	crafts, farms etc.	total
Bulgaria	8.5	(100 000)	260 000	350 000
Hungary	10.5	180 000	(600 000)	780 000
Slovenia	2	48 000	68 000	116 000
Sweden	9	250 000	320 000	570 000
Ukraine	52.5	50 000!		
Crimea	2.5	7 000		

Note: Information is used from 1990–93. Anywhere near accurate data are extremely hard to find, especially as definitions vary a great deal. Examples: The Slovenian data refer to registered enterprises whether active or not, whereas the Ukrainian only show the number of registered and active enterprises; the Hungarians obviously count the number of farmers, not the number of farms; and so on. The figure is intended to indicate proportions.

the women, namely that of managing the literal survival of the close family. Today these two impulses tragically oppose each other – the one trying to surface and show the world what it can accomplish, the other still necessarily securing survival in troubled times through covert operations that do little to support the emergence of a viable mainstream economy.

As noted in Chapter 5, as of 1994, the legislative basis for independent employers' organisations is only partially in place. The work of redrafting the *Labour Code* has proven a burden for the Ministry of Labour, but the delays were caused mostly by the prolonged absence of a functioning parliament and government. The main obstacle for the emerging employers' organisations seems to have been the negative or uninterested attitude among both administrators and politicians towards political and institutional pluralism. As Ukraine's independence was not due to protest against the past regime nor the result of struggle, awareness of the need for fundamental democratic and social reforms has taken longer to develop than in the central European nations. The main factors that have prompted reform stem from the economic chaos rather than from moral or political conviction – but as there seemed little appreciation of the need for economic reform until 1994, the establishment of tripartism and a pluralistic institutional social infrastructure were not given much attention.

There is an emerging organisational pattern pointing towards national cooperation, but as to what new roles the employers' organisations ought to fulfil, the only consensus so far seems to be on the lobby function. Bargaining, industrial relations, social dialogue, joint efforts to handle working conditions and environmental issues are all more or less on the agenda, but not much more than that. These role models cannot be formed by employers alone. They are dependent in part on what happens to the trade unions, both by what roles they assume and to their representative character. And without the fundamental consent of the government and its administration, there is little the other two partners can achieve in promoting tripartism, even jointly.

A further complication is the generally low degree of organising new, private enterprises, both by unions and employer organisations; this extends to those in enterprises that have been privatised. In the private sector, it seems that the employer side is more active, perhaps not in organising as traditional counterparts to trade unions, but rather in forming lobby groups trying to influence the politicians and promote better terms for free enterprise. As the private sector grows, much will depend on what course of action the unions take – moving with the labour force across to new forms of activity, or concentrating on state-owned enterprises.

Although almost two-thirds of the labour force still are union members, unions face three fundamental long-term challenges.

• Low and sinking confidence in trade unions generally.
• Disinterest or inability of the unions in organising workers in private companies.
• Actions of unions in support of unemployed workers.

7. Employer Developments in Ukraine[10]

The first employer organisation to emerge in Ukraine was the Business Union of Crimea, which was founded as early as February 1989, organising primarily private businessmen and entrepreneurs, but gradually also representing industrial enterprises of this region. Through the following two years, in various parts of Ukraine, a surprising number of interest groups formed associations of various kinds – mainly on branch and regional levels – from seaports and municipal enterprises to economic funds and unions of economists and lawyers. Some of these were based on scientific and other societies that were part of the communist infrastructure, but many emerged separately. Given the interaction between the various groups, a more comprehensive analysis than is possible here would be necessary before one could understand the relationships in this shifting kaleidoscope.

Especially confusing is the practice of companies joining more than one organisation. This is rather traditional more than anything caused by the

---

[10] Text based on visits, interviews and material from the respective organisations through the spring of 1994, and on information from the National Council for Social Partnership.

transition. 'Hedging one's bets' is prudent in a society where little infra-structural support has ever been available for the individual, or for individual enterprises regardless of ownership.

Another ambiguity is the application of terms such as private, in the names, ambitions and functions of the organisations. Who is really private, and how private? Is a leaseholder a private entrepreneur, a worker with a share or a bulvan for some state bureaucrat or worse? And are lease arrangements genuine or a facade intended to maintain the power of traditional management groups, or other hierarchies behind them? And is an industrialist a private entrepreneur or a manager of a state industry? Who is to be trusted as an employer – the state manager with 47,000 unionised employees, or the private entrepreneur with one or two unorganised part-time assistants?

Can organisations dominated by state enterprises be believed when claiming to promote privatisation and the introduction of market mechanisms generally? And, given the ambiguities, what organisations should be accepted as belonging to the employer camp?[11]

In the second section of this chapter, it was indicated that the issue of how, and by whom, the various employers' association were initiated – top-down or 'democratically' – remains sensitive. The reason for this is the suspicion that top-down initiated organisations could remain more dedicated to – or dictated to by – state and 'big-business' interests, than to any genuine concern for their members. Which actualises the question of the representativity of the various associations and organisations.

Answers to these questions must not be dictated by external experience and examples, but be sought by the Ukrainian business community itself if its institutions are to become representative and trusted by emerging enterprises and by the other social partners, as well as by the general public. The quicker answers are provided, the better.

After the spread of new interest groups in the wake of the establishment of the Business Union of Crimea, the next, second organisational step in the structural development of organising Ukrainian employers was to form groups of organisations. This process began in 1989 with the founding of the first of the three groups that were to dominate the scene by mid-1994 – ULIE, the Ukrainian League of Industrialists and Entrepreneurs. Two others followed – ULEU, the Union of Leaseholders and Entrepreneurs of

[11] The National Council for Social Partnership has 22 seats for employers and workers, respectively. The list does not always indicate which organisation the individual member represents or its character. The secretariat claims there are ten employer organisations represented, but many of these are members of one or both of the two dominant blocks, leaving just one seat for the third, independent organisation. And, although all the various groups are having increasing numbers of private enterprises as members, only one can yet be said to represent predominantly private sector perspectives and interests.

Ukraine, in 1990, and UNAE, the Ukrainian National Assembly of Entrepreneurship, in 1993.

This second phase in the organisational development remains partially obscured by the 'Ukrainian survival practice' mentioned earlier: not only do many enterprises join several associations, but the associations seem to join each other to an unusual degree. And not only that, but also these three main groups of associations are largely intertwined! This is obviously confusing even to the Ukrainians, and it certainly makes our descriptions less than precise, our observations somewhat doubtful, and our conclusions open to questions.[12]

In early 1994 talk began of taking the third organisational step, that of forming a national confederation to represent all Ukrainian employer organisations internationally and in the tripartite consultations. The ULIE, dominated by state-owned industrial enterprises, and UNAE, with its focus on private business, are already cooperating quite closely. Now that the Presidential and Parliamentary elections are over, further developments can be envisaged.

In Ukraine, the process of forming a pluralistic infrastructure has not progressed far enough for the emerging institutions to become sufficiently independent or to be respected as such. This is clear in the government's attitude towards both employers' and trade union organisations, and is reflected in their involvement in the political process. Symptomatically, when Ukraine's President in September 1993 dismissed his Prime Minister Mr Kuchma, the latter became president of the ULIE, and the then incumbent ULIE president Vitaly Yevtukhov became Vice Prime Minister. When Mr Kuchma was elected President of Ukraine in June 1994, Mr Yevtukhov again became president of ULIE.

The ULIE lobbied the President, Government and Parliament in the critical months preceding the March/April 1994 general elections. In late January, it presented a 'comprehensive and systematic list of emergency economic measures' for 'joint review at the session of the Cabinet of Ministers of Ukraine', and approached the President on those issues.[13] ULIE canvassed for independent candidates running for election and some leading ULIE members were candidates themselves, some of whom were

---

[12] So do ULIE and UNAE share several member organisations. ULEU is a founding member of ULIE from its reorganisation in 1991. Both the ULIE and ULEU Presidents are Vice-presidents of UNAE, together with the President of the Ukrainian Trade Union Federation of Cooperatives (who is at the same time Workers' Co-Chairman of the National Council for Social Partnership). Finally, the UNAE President is Vice-president of ULIE.

[13] The programme contains eight priority issues where ULIE wants to see immediate action. In discussions with ILO-CEET, in February 1994, the then ULIE president Leonid Kutchma grouped them into three: current assets of enterprises, currency regulations and the system of taxation.

remarkably successful. Also the ULEU decided – in November 1993 – to participate in the elections of 1994.

What is still conspicuously absent in the running of the Ukrainian employers' organisations when compared with the ingredients that dominate the working of most employer organisations, is any major involvement in collective bargaining whether directly, in an advisory capacity, through training or otherwise. This has a very simple explanation: the collective agreements[14] still result from negotiations between the *Ministry* responsible for the respective branch of industry and the branch union. There is as yet no recognised role for independent employers' organisations in the state owned sector – and in the private sector there is as yet little trade union activity.

8. Groups of Employer Organisations

As of mid-1994, there seemed to be three discernibly separate groups of employer organisations. Most if not all other sectoral and local associations were affiliated to one or more of these three groups. Outside this structure some smaller organisations were reported to remain, whose existence and/or affiliations need to be clarified.

8.1. Ukrainian League of Industrialists & Entrepreneurs (ULIE)[15]

Ukrainian League of Industrialists & Entrepreneurs (ULIE) was started by 99 large enterprises in 1989.[16] It got its present name and format after a reconstruction in late 1991. ULIE has regional units in all 25 regions of Ukraine. In 1994, about 14,000 enterprises were affiliated, plus a growing number of other associations of employers and some individuals who had held or were still holding political or public offices. In its long-time strategy, ULIE is preparing to become the national confederation, and from 1994 both other groups were included in its national membership structure while retaining their separate identities. The leaders of all three underlined that this is a process that must be given time to find its balance; also, some enterprises have not found what they expected from being members of an organisation, and keep turning to others, or refrain from organising again.

---

[14] In 1993, 54 branch level and 10 regional collective agreements were concluded and duly registered. See also Chapter 5, section 3. 'Labour legislation reforms: Collective bargaining'.

[15] Ukrainskij Sojus Promislovciv i Pridpriemciv, USPP. Text based on material provided by the organisation and on interviews with ULIE representatives in December 1993; President Kuchma and Executive director Ryzhkov in February 1994; director Ryzhkov in May 1994; Vice-president Mayko in June 1994, and President Yevtukhov in September, 1994; plus with President Dudko of the ULIE member organisation in Crimea, in December 1993 and March and September 1994.

[16] 1990, according to other sources.

ULIE claims to represent one-third of total industrial production. Leaseholding enterprises form half the membership, 40% are state owned, 10% private. The dominant group consists of military-industrial enterprises. In 1994, ULIE had a three-tiered structure.

- The national level,
  - 9 all-Ukrainian leagues, associations and unions.
- The regional level,
  - 25 regional plus a number of city divisions and associations.
- The branch level,
  - mix of state branch associations and associated members, banks, exchanges, seaports, the Azov Shipping Company, educational institutions, the Ukrainian House of Economic, Scientific and Technical Knowledge, and state-owned enterprises, parastatal (mixed) enterprises and privately owned enterprises.

The ULIE's main activities include political and governmental contacts, financial and trade promotion, support of foreign investment and joint ventures, economic and legal services, press contacts, information and advertising. It has its own Central Bureau of Statistics and Information.

Since 1991, ULIE has dominated the employer side of the tripartite National Council for Social Partnership, but has had little direct involvement in industrial bargaining, which is mainly handled by the State Branch Associations that form one dimension of ULIE's membership, nor in industrial relations, which are developing mainly at the enterprise level.

The ULIE's highest authority is its Conference with its twin Control organs, a Control and Auditing Commission and a Mandate Commission. Between Conferences, the 58 member management board and the 15 member Presidium provide guidance to the President and five Vice Presidents.

8.1.1. Business Union of Crimea[17]

The Business Union was founded in February 1989 and was thus one of the first independent employer organisations to emerge in central and eastern Europe. In 1994, it was still the only employer organisation operating in Crimea, and through its affiliation to ULIE constitutes their regional member for Crimea. Through 1994 the Business Union has developed closer relations also with UNAE.

The Business Union originally focused on promoting better conditions for the conduct of private business, trade and investment. It has gradually developed good relations with the two regional trade unions, the Crimean

[17] Based on interviews with the President, Alexander Dudko, in December 1993 and February–March and September 1994, plus meetings with Board members and representatives of member enterprises in February–March of 1994.

government and the Ukrainian government and organisations. It has come to represent state enterprises as well, and thus covers employer interests more generally. Its most important achievement to date has been the securing of a tax reform.[18]

Through its President, the *Business Union* has been active in the Ukrainian tripartite consultations and also in the efforts of the Crimean authorities to establish a republican tripartite council and through that reach agreement on a social charter as well as a regional wage agreement.[19]

8.2. Union of Leaseholders and Entrepreneurs of Ukraine (ULEU)[20]

Union of Leaseholders and Entrepreneurs of Ukraine (ULEU) founded in July 1990, claims to be the only wholly democratic employers' organisation, representing private employers and being financed exclusively from their membership fees. By April 1994, ULEU represented 450 member enterprises, institutions, associations of employers and individuals, with together some 7,500 companies covering 27% of the industrial labour force (some 2.5 million employees) and about 25% of all leaseholders.[21] Its president is vice chairman for the employers' group in the National Council for Social Partnership, but obtained that post when he was still vice president of ULIE, which he left in late 1993.

The Union has been active in building up its organisation nationally and regionally and in holding meetings of members to discuss policy. Its main activities have been political lobbying, giving legal service to its members and providing advice – directly and through seminars – on accounting, auditing, legislation, privatisation, taxation and so on. It has also organised management courses. In 1993, a department for foreign economic relations was set up, promoting trade contacts plus management and young entrepreneurial training sessions abroad.

At a general meeting in November 1993 a declaration was adopted concerning the participation of leaseholders and entrepreneurs in the 1994 elections, and the support from the organisation in organising nominations,

[18] Crimea followed Ukrainian tax and fiscal regulations until April, 1994, when the Business Union persuaded President Yuri Meshkov and Finance Minister Galina Kulishko to introduce a more rational system. The progressive personal taxation range was reduced, from 12–90% to now 0–30%. The corporate tax base was reduced (from profits + wages to profits only) and lowered, from 90–150% (or above!) to a uniform 30%. According to Business Union President A. Dudko, this has proven highly successful, with State revenues rising sharply and a substantial budget deficit turning into a corresponding surplus. Interview with A. Dudko September 1994.

[19] See also section 5 of this chapter, 'Regional Trade Union Development'.

[20] Spilka Orendariv i Pidpriemciv Ukrajini, or SOPU. Text based on material provided by the organisation and on interviews with President Khmelyevsky in February and September 1994.

[21] This definition covers lease-held enterprises rather than individual leaseholders. Among state enterprises that have been leased out many are very large, with up to 50,000 workers.

assisting with media contacts and participating in the elections. ULEU's continued membership of ULIE has been discussed at several meetings, but no decisions seem to have been taken.

ULEU advocates privatisation and liberalisation of state property, but warns that the situation is so complicated that close cooperation of all interested parties is necessary in order to enable peaceful and constructive solutions, not least through constructive domestic capital formation and its productive investment.

8.3. Ukrainian National Assembly of Entrepreneurship (UNAE)[22]

Ukrainian National Assembly of Entrepreneurship (UNAE) was founded in March 1993 by All-Ukrainian unions of, respectively, Farmers, Co-operators, Small businesses and Joint ventures, and by National Associations of Lawyers, Auditors and Quality experts on all-Ukrainian and regional levels. Later the Exchanges Union joined. UNAE aims at consolidating private manufacturers of products, goods and services but welcomes cooperation of associations of state enterprises.

UNAE has concentrated on promoting conditions necessary to support entrepreneurship, providing training and services to entrepreneurs, and lobbying the political instances.

It gives priority to the development of a national entrepreneurship support network, which includes the following services:

* Training.
* Consulting.
* Legal and auditing expertise.
* Quality systems implementation.
* Technical assistance.
* Credits and commodities procurement.
* Incubation of small enterprises; and commercial information.

UNAE participates in the National Council for Social Partnership, but has no other relation with the trade unions at the national level.

UNAE has member associations in all 26 administrative sub-divisions of Ukraine, and strives to achieve regional consolidation of private enterprises and help them to interact with experts, consultants, auditors and other professionals and to participate jointly in the processes of privatisation, conversion and small business development.

---

[22] Ukrainska Nationalna Asambleja Pidpriemnitsva, UNAP. Based on material provided and interviews held with UNAE representatives in December 1993, its President Sumin in May 1994, and from the participation of Joseph Prokopenko, of the ILO, in the March 1994 meeting of UNAE's Coordinating Council.

In March 1993, there were 60,000 individual members – owners, farmers, leaseholders, professionals – of the seven associations then forming the UNAE. There have been discussions about possible affiliation of other associations such as commercial banks, business press and insurance companies. UNAE is led by a Coordinating Council consisting of the presidents of the member organisations, and by an Executive Committee.

As of early 1994 at least three[23] of UNAE's eight member associations were also members of the ULIE. The chairman of UNAE's Coordinating Council was one of ULIE's Vice presidents, and both ULIE's and ULEU's Presidents were UNAE Vice presidents.

8.4. Other Employers' Organisations

By mid-1994, all other organisations seem to have been recruited by one or more of the three main groups, on the national, branch or regional levels. There have also been efforts by an Association of Leaseholders and the Ukrainian Financial Group to organise an All-Ukrainian Union of Entrepreneurs, which in early 1994 claimed to represent 90% of all entrepreneurial structures. These efforts did not result in any registered organisation, and the Ukrainian Financial Group remains one of ULIE's member organisations.

9. The Ukrainian Trade Union Federation of Cooperatives: An Hybrid Organisation[24]

This Trade Union Federation organises cooperatives and small businesses which has made it into a kind of in-between 'third force', as its membership encompasses both owners and workers. Both in cooperatives and small businesses, the same person is often both owner and worker, but quite a few such enterprises also have employed workers. This makes it quite difficult to distinguish between the traditional roles of employer and employee. Accordingly, the Federation has become active on both sides. Its President holds the post of Workers' Co-Chairman in the National Council in the National Council for Social Partnership – and is also one of the Vice presidents of UNAE, one of the three main employers' organisations.[25]

---

[23] The Union of Lawyers, the League of Companies with Foreign Capital and the Association of Cooperators and Entrepreneurs.

[24] Text based on interview with President Vasyl Kostritsa in September, 1994.

[25] This unclear status makes the Federation quite controversial, but it is irrefutable that it both represents a considerable number of regular employees and a large group of enterprises. The election of the Federation President as Workers' Co-chairman of the NCSP has also to do with the tensions between the main trade union groups, since neither could accept anyone from the other group for this post.

9.1. 'Yednanniya' – the Kiev Chapter of this Federation[26]

The *Yednanniya* is one such trade union of small and medium businesses. In this it is quite unusual, although there are parallels in some other central and eastern European countries. It is not a traditional trade union representing workers, nor a traditional employers' organisation bargaining with trade unions. Yet it participates in the National Council for Social Partnership, on the trade union side. As its focus is on small and medium sized business enterprises, it should be compared to the numerous service and lobby organisations that cater to such enterprises in market economies and, increasingly, in countries such as Bulgaria, Hungary and Russia.[27]

Ukraine's independence was followed by developments that left legislators behind in trying to adapt existing legislation and/or introduce new conditions, for the citizenry at large as well as for businessmen. It seems that when, on top of this, the existing trade union did not recognise cooperative-type enterprises' need for social protection, a group of entrepreneurs that ran such cooperatives were prompted into action. Their initiative was to form an organisation to handle social insurance issues.

Yednanniya affiliates whole enterprises – all owners/partners and employees. Should conflict arise between these, which has proven rare, the organisation tries to mediate. The Kiev chapter of *Yednanniya* has about 3,000 affiliated enterprises.[28] The largest has about 300 employees, though the average is about 10. Thus they represent about 30,000 individuals.

The *Yednanniya* provides an impressive range of services for its members, at cost, such as business consultations, general advice, accounting via central databases, data processing, searching for business partners and assistance with paper work required by various authorities. The *Yednanniya* runs a pension fund for its members, and has founded an insurance company. The main challenges come from the government and its authorities, which have caused the *Yednanniya* to give high priority to issues concerning the rights of its members, legal support for them, and to try to influence policy lobbying government and other public bodies.

About half of the member enterprises were privately owned businesses or cooperatives from the start. By mid-1994, another 20% represented leaseheld or privatised state enterprises. As there was then still a sizeable

---

[26] Text based on interview with President Koshevina of *Yednanniya*, the Kiev chapter of the Ukrainian Trade Union Federation of Cooperatives, and her colleagues, in Kiev in February 1994.

[27] Bulgarian examples: the Employer Union for Private Enterprising and the Trade Union of Business; Hungarian example: the National Association of Entrepreneurs; Russian example: the Medium and Small Business Workers' Union.

[28] Many of these are cooperatives, both agricultural, industrial, arts and crafts, and services.

proportion of non-private members, the emphasis was not on form of ownership but on the conditions necessary to promote profitability, which was at that time especially low in industrial production. Although the defence sector dominates, about one-third of the *Yednanniya* member enterprises were builders and contractors in data processing and programming, with 20% described as 'innovation enterprises'.

A major issue for the *Yednanniya* has been Ukrainian taxation.[29] The heavy taxes clearly deter production, and have led to a situation in which an increasing number of enterprises pay only the minimum wage, or refrain from declaring its activities altogether. According to *Yednanniya*, this is causing increasing numbers of small businesses to give up, but also results in a considerable membership growth, which in part is explained by *Yednanniya's* advice and support to member enterprises threatened by bankruptcy. The final irony is that, apparently, trade unions are now losing members to *Yednanniya*. In short, the organisation straddles the normal divide between workers and employers and could evolve as a group representing the self-employed and small businesses.

10. International Cooperation

10.1. Employers

Little international support for Ukrainian employers' organisations has been arranged this far. However, the ILO and the International Organisation of Employers (IOE) have ensured that those reporting that they represent Ukrainian employers have participated in the following projects:

- An ILO/IOE Seminar on the Role of Employers' Organisations in a Market Economy, held in Moscow on April 28–29, 1992, in which three Ukrainian employer organisation representatives participated.
- An ILO/BDA[30] Study Tour on the Role of Employers' Organisations in a Market Economy, to Germany and Brussels, with contacts with major EU institutions in 1993 – with five senior Ukrainian participants.
- An ILO/IOE Training Workshop for Central and Eastern European Employers' Organisations, held at the ILO Training Centre in Turin, in May 1994, in which two Ukrainian delegates participated.

[29] The situation cannot be described as a tax system, since ministries and authorities at different levels do not coordinate their various onera and levies. An example is the 52% corporate 'profits' tax levied on the sum of an enterprise's profits and its wages, making this levy alone average 210% of profits. In February 1994, an additional 22% tax on the wage bill was announced, purporting to help finance social security.

[30] BDA = Bundesvereinigung Deutscher Arbeitsgeberverbände – i.e. the German Employers' Confederation.

• An IOE Seminar for leading Ukrainian employer representatives in Kiev in September, 1994, conducted by IOE's Chairman, Jean-Jacques Oechslin.

The ILO's Entrepreneurship and Management Development Branch has assisted the Ukrainian Employers' Organisations and Government in establishing the Ukrainian Management and Entrepreneurship Development Centre. This may turn out to be the most tangible and lasting form of assistance, and it is to be hoped that the international organisations of employers will become more active in 1995.

10.2. Trade Unions

Within Ukraine, there are no official restrictions on the right of unions to affiliate with international trade union bodies. The NPGU is a member of the Miners' International Federation (MIF), and the Nuclear Power Workers' Union is affiliated to the International Federation of Chemical, Energy and General Workers' Unions (ICEF). Two FPU branch unions have applied for membership in the Public Services International (PSI). Several unions are in contact with other International Trade Secretariats that are associated with the International Confederation of Free Trade Unions (ICFTU).

The American AFL-CIO and the Free Trade Union Institute have a permanent representative in Kiev. They give strong support to the Ukrainian Association of Free Trade Unions, and organise education for local trade union activists. They channel support for the magazine MOST ('Bridge') that is published every two weeks in both Russian and Ukrainian and is oriented towards the new trade unions.

FPU has had a good working relationship with VKP, the General Council of Trade Unions based in Moscow, which consists mainly of CIS and other former Soviet trade unions. At their Congress on June 29, 1994, FPU decided to join VKP. Most FPU branches belong to VKP branch structures. The FPU does not belong to the World Federation of Trade Unions (WFTU), but it has participated in some of their meetings as an observer. Several FPU affiliates belong to the WFTU associated Trade Union Internationals. All-Ukrainian Union of Workers' Solidarity (VOST) is affiliated to the christian democratically oriented World Confederation of Labour (WCL).

Ukrainian trade unions are gradually establishing closer links with their European counterpart organisations. These contacts are important for ensuring further development towards strong, independent and democratic unions.

11. Conclusions and Recommendations

The former Soviet structures and practices continue to have an impact on the development of Ukraine's trade unions and employers' organisations. The latter must find ways of establishing new functions and relations among themselves as well as relations with the legislative and administrative authorities.

A precondition for well-functioning labour markets and relations among the main organisations of the labour market is that their own organisations are independent and democratic representatives of their membership. This requires mutual respect and some degree of trust. Already, relations among several organisations appear to be constructive and positive. We recommend that trade unions and employer organisations continue to maintain and expand their dialogue and seek ways of establishing common information sources that would enable them to negotiate and conclude collective agreements and other ways of improving the functioning of the labour market. They should seek common positions on the legislative basis of collective bargaining and conflict resolution, as well as ways of implementing that legislation and sustaining the agreements that are reached.

Based on the bipartite relationships between employers and unions at national, branch and enterprise level, a tripartite relationship should be sought with authorities at various levels. The most urgent needs relate to policy making and implementation levels, where the national tripartite bodies should be strengthened. Their main task should be to promote genuine consultation on social, economic and labour legislation, and to support social consensus on the development of Ukrainian market economy.

The ratification by the Government in May 1994 of *ILO Convention No. 144 on Tripartite Relations* (International Standards) and the *Collective Bargaining Convention No. 154* should offer a new opportunity to enhance the relationships among the government, employers and trade unions. Ratifying the *Workers' Representatives Convention C.135* would also provide additional support to the development and functioning of the necessary structures. They would also be helpful in drafting new and amended legislation on these issues.

Having been a titular country of ILO during the Soviet era, Ukraine ratified 45 ILO Conventions between 1956 and 1993.[31] However, implementation was the exclusive responsibility of Soviet structures, and Ukrainian Republican bodies had only low-level administrative functions. Thus, a new analysis of the ratified conventions and their application in national legislation is desirable.

---

[31] Because of denouncements, the number of ratifications in force in April 1994 was 38.

Especially important and sensitive is the issue of the state's dual role as owner and employer in most enterprises. There should be a more distinct separation of the different roles. State owned industry should be represented by employers' organisations that have independence from governmental control and management of their activities.

The international organisations of employers and trade unions should provide their experience and contacts to their Ukrainian partners. An initially important iniatiative would be support to their capacity to manage information.

Finally, although many of the leaders and officials in all kinds of employers' organisations and trade unions have considerable expertise and experience, it would be widely expected that many officials would benefit from training, particularly to bring their knowledge into line with that found in other countries. Organisations at different stages of independent development have specific requirements. A separate needs assessment is required to develop technical cooperation programmes.

7

The Challenge of Social Protection

1. Introduction

From 1919 to 1991 the country's social protection system was set by the Soviet Union. The Soviet history of formal social security or social protection systems covering a major part of the population dates back to the post-revolution era. Free state financed medical care was introduced in the early years of the Soviet Union. The first general pension law entered into force in the late 1920s. During the following decades, the range of benefits provided and the population coverage were steadily extended. In 1944, the first family benefits were introduced, and in 1964, pension scheme coverage was extended to workers on cooperative farms, thus closing the last gap in population coverage.

The Gorbachov era brought the first recognition of the existence of poverty and consequently a reform process of the social protection system commenced. In order to alleviate poverty, family benefits were extended and pensions were adjusted. The latter change recognised the existence of inflation, which had been denied for decades. After an extensive period of deliberations, a new pension law for the Soviet Union was promulgated in May 1990. Apart from benefit improvements, it marked the transition from a basically general revenue financed pension system to a social insurance system by creating the Pension Fund, which collected for the first time payroll contributions linked to the volume of benefits. But from the beginning the effort was doomed. Contribution collection remained low as the financially stronger republics only reluctantly transferred resources to subsidise weaker ones.

During the months following the declaration of independence in August 1991 the present legal basis for the Ukrainian social protection system was established. Already in 1991, Ukraine introduced its own pension law and the Pension Fund commenced operations in early 1992. The reform process did not stop there. Family benefits were modified, pension adjustment procedures introduced and decrees concerning social assistance issued. The

Employment Service, which also manages the Unemployment Benefit Fund, was introduced in 1992.

The situation is still in a state of flux. Rapid inflation demands quarterly adjustment of pensions and mass open unemployment looming beyond the economic horizon demands anti-poverty measures and a realignment of the financing of social services and social assistance. The Government realises that stop-gap reactions to the changing needs are economically inefficient, not socially acceptable and contribute to a further complication of the present public finance jungle in the country. It has called for a complete over-haul of the entire social protection system.

The present social protection mechanisms and the reform concept pro-posed by the Government in 1993–1994 are analysed in more detail in the following sections. But before the effectiveness or efficiency of present or planned social protection mechanisms can be judged an assessment of the present social conditions in the country has to be attempted.

2. Living Standard, Poverty and Social Protection

As the standard of living is difficult to measure, assessments of whether or not it is adequate are inevitably open to subjective judgements. There are good reasons to believe that standard of living measurements for the for-mer planned economy countries were not compatible with similar mea-surements in other industrialised countries.

However, one can try to trace the changes in the standard of living and quality of life indicators for Ukraine during the recent economic downturn. As in other planned economy countries, the Ministry of Labour had defined a 'minimum consumption budget' (MCB), which was regarded as the per capita expenditure that would allow an individual to have a socially meaningful life. The MCB was calculated for 16 different demographic groups based on determinants like civil status, age and urban or rural area of residence. *Figure 7.1* displays the development of the relationship of the average wage and average income (from all sources including wages) to the MCB for an adult. Whereas the average wage was 2.2 times the MCB in 1991, it dropped dramatically in 1993, following the price liberalisation, and was about 50% of the MCB in March 1994. In the same month, the average per capita income dropped to 40% of the MCB and average per capita consumption to a mere 27% (*Table A7.1* in *Annex III*).

Measured by the above indicators, the standard of living in Ukraine fell in 24 months (from November 1991 to November 1993) by almost 80%. This highlights in a very condensed form the dramatic social consequences of the structural economic crisis in the country. As recently as in May 1992, the food component in the MCB for an adult exceeded the amount of the minimum wage by 42%.[1]

In December 1992, the cost of the food component exceeded the minimum wage by no less than 1,131%. In compensation for the loss in purchasing power of their money income, the population might have been able to find other income sources (e.g., by increasing reliance on self-production of food). But the magnitude of losses in such a short spell is likely to be beyond the level that could be compensated. The quality of life must have deteriorated dramatically and poverty increased.

Quality of life can only be measured schematically, but *Table 7.1* provides indicators that clearly point to a declining quality of life (life expectancy at birth, housing space per person, number of new housing units) and also indicate a declining confidence in the economic and social development of the country.

Other indicators could have been chosen, but these indicate that the quality of life started to decline around 1990. All these are 'slow indicators', i.e. they react to rapid changes in the political, social and economic environment with a timelag ranging from several years (like life expectancy) to one year (natality, abortions, construction of housing units) or even less (household spending). *Table 7.1* also shows that until 1992 the provision for essential public services, like health services followed the downward trend in overall living conditions. The impact of the sharp fall of incomes in January 1993 cannot yet be measured but it must be expected that the negative trends in quality of life will accelerate.

The most commonly used indicator of social conditions in a society is poverty. But as in the case of all others, poverty indicators are subject to definitional and normative debates. The main poverty descriptor is the proportion of the population with incomes under the poverty line. That line has to be defined and the set of income items by another definition.

Ukraine has no official poverty line. The MCB is regarded by some critics[2] as being far too lavish to be a real poverty line. The Government has defined 'a social assistance intervention line' (SAIL), which is considerably lower than the MCB. The amount for food in the intervention line basket in mid-December 1993 was about 27% of the food component of the MCB for an adult, excluding housing expenditure. The welfare offices in the country use this line to establish entitlement to social assistance benefits. Persons with per capita income under the intervention line should receive

[1] The 1992 composition of the MCB was taken from IMF, *Ukraine: Budgetary Implications of Social Safety Net Options*, Washington D.C., November 1992, p. 68. The composition of the December 1993 MCB was provided by the Federation of Trade Unions of Ukraine. The compositions vary slightly.
[2] IMF, 1992, op. cit.

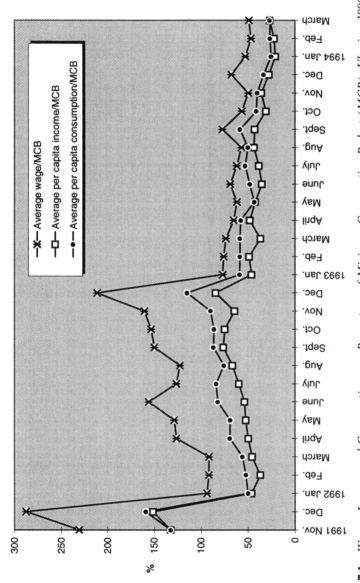

Figure 7.1 *Wages, Incomes and Consumption as a Percentage of Minimum Consumption Budget (MCB), Ukraine, 1990–1993*

Source: Ministry of Labour, 1994.

Table 7.1 *Selected Indicators of Quality of Life, Ukraine, 1994*

	1985	1990	1991	1992
Life expectancy at birth				
males	–	66	–	64
females	–	75	–	74
both sexes	–	71*	69**	–
Live births				
per 1,000 women of age 15–49	59	53	51	48
Abortions				
per 100 live births	149	155	152	156
Suicides				
per 100,000 persons	22.3	20.6	20.7	22.5
Health workers				
per 10,000 persons	152.4	161.5	163.8	159.6
Teachers				
per 100 students in basic state schools	6.9	7.7	7.8	8.1
Constructed flats				
per 1,000 persons	6.7	5.6	4.5	4.4
Expenditure on culture/leisure				
average share of household	8.3	8.0	6.3	4.6

*1989/1990.
**1990/1991, part of the difference might be explained by increasing mortality due the Chernobyl accident.

Source Ministry of Statistics, *Statistical Yearbook 1992, Demographic Yearbook 1992.*

the difference between their income and the actual intervention line as a social assistance payment, as discussed later.

SAIL does not make any difference between age, sex or urban/rural population, although there are substantial differences in the cost of living, between regions for example. The cost of living level (measured as the cost of the basket of goods for the intervention line) in Kiev is, according to the calculations of the Federation of Trade Unions, 16% higher than the national average and about 37% higher than in the cheapest rural region. It is also not clear whether any form of 'adult equivalent' that took into account the age of children is used to determine the per capita income in needy families.

Figure 7.2 shows differences in the levels of MCB and SAIL and *Figure 7.3* differences in their composition (*Table A7.2* in *Annex III*). The figures highlight the distance between the MCB and the SAIL and the changing share of expenditure for food at the two poverty indicators. A food share of over 80% and more is commonly observed in poverty lines that merely guarantee a physiological minimum. *Figure 7.2* demonstrates the dire effects of a delay of only one month in the adjustment of the SAIL in

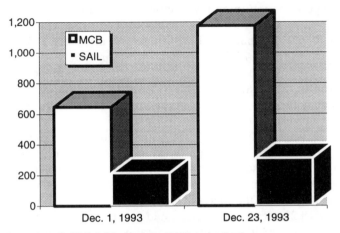

In less than a month SAIL fell behind the MCB dramatically

Figure 7.2 *Level of the Minimum Consumption Budget (MCB) and Social Assistance Intervention Line (SAIL), Ukraine, 1993* (thousand karbovanets)*

*MCB is no longer used officially and the December 1993 calculation was made by the Federation of Trade Unions using the official weights. It also calculated a SAIL for December 31, 1993, taking December inflation into account.

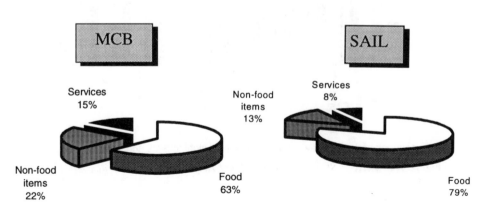

Food has a much bigger share in SAIL

Figure 7.3 *Composition of the Minimum Consumption Budget (MCB) and Social Assistance Intervention Line (SAIL), Ukraine, 1992–1993*

Source: IMF, 1992, op. cit.; Federation of Trade Unions, 1993, ILO-CEET calculations.

periods of hyper-inflation (monthly inflation in December 1993 was about 100%).

Correspondingly the share of those whose incomes were 1–3 times the minimum wage fell from 77.7% in 1990 to 36.1% in 1992.[3]

Figure 7.4 demonstrates the difference in the food component between the MCB (for an adult) and the SAIL (*Table A7.3* in *Annex III*). Except for bread and potatoes, the SAIL requirements permit little more than physiological survival.

The average wage in November 1993 was about 42% higher than the SAIL and the December minimum wage amounted to only 28% of the average wage. As discussed in Chapter 4 there are two main trends in the development of wages and incomes in Ukraine: the falling real level of incomes and wages and the increasing spread of the income distribution. In 1990, only 18.2% of the population had incomes lower than MCB. In 1992 their share was 63.9% and in 1993 already 85% (estimated).

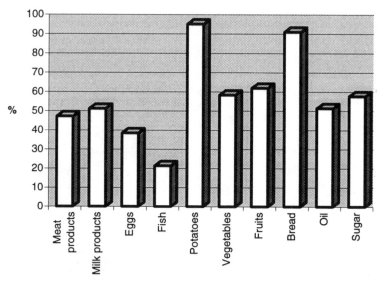

Only potatoes and bread have almost the same weight in SAIL and MCB

Figure 7.4 *SAIL's Share of MCB in Food Requirements for Adults, Ukraine, 1993*

Source: Federation of Trade Unions, 1993.

[3] The data stem from various sources and should only be considered as indicative. 1990 and 1992 figures are from the Ministry of Labour and 1993 figures from Federation of the Trade Unions.

The percentage of wage earners under the SAIL can only be a proxy for the overall assessment of the poverty level. First, households have other incomes than wages. According to the 1992 household and expenditure survey, the average household derived only 56% of the income from wages, 14% from pensions and benefits and about 30% from other sources.[4] But these figures do not provide information on the specific situation of worker and pensioner households. Average per capita income in November 1993 was about 19% lower than the average wage, due to the persons in the households who do not earn any income.

The available data only permits a crude estimate of the poverty level, but the proportion of the population with per capita income under the SAIL should be higher than 55% and probably well in excess of 60% of the total population. In 1992, before the sharp decline in standard of living in January 1993, UNICEF data provide a poverty estimate in the order of 35%.[5] Poverty has reached levels that exceed estimated poverty proportions in many developing countries. The share of the population with incomes under the MCB indicates that the number of people below the poverty line probably quadrupled between 1990 and 1993. In December 1993, the SAIL was fixed at 197,000 karbovanets.

The difference between the average wage and the SAIL has increased and poverty levels have probably been slightly reduced. The statutory minimum wage was increased in April 1994 to 108,000 karbovanets as a mere accounting unit for some social protection benefits, notably family benefits. But even the entry level wage for the lowest grade in the public sector pay scale (120,000 karbovanets) could ensure mere subsistence.

Mass poverty might be a transitory phenomenon but for the 1990s it will remain the key problem for the social protection system. But social protection systems have several functions in a modern market economy: notably poverty alleviation (also called the curative function) and poverty prevention (the preventive function). The second function should ensure that during their active lives employees can build up social security entitlements that will guarantee an economically adequate standard of living for them or their dependants during their retirement. This, for example, consists of entitlements to unemployment benefits, sickness benefits entitlements or pensions, all of which should provide a decent income during periods or phases in life without income from employment or self-employment. The benefits paid under this function should exceed benefit levels that sheer poverty alleviation would require.

In times of economic distress, when there is a massive poverty problem,

---

[4] Ministry of Statistics, *Statistical Yearbook of Ukraine*, p. 43, Kiev, 1992.

[5] This estimate refers to a poverty line of 118 rubles per month. UNICEF, *Public Policy and Social Conditions*, Regional Monitoring Report No. 1, New York, November 1993.

a delicate balance between the two functions has to be found. If a country chooses to allocate all resources to poverty alleviation, the acceptance of the financing burden by the better off might be at risk. If, on the other hand, large population groups are left in poverty, public acceptance of the economic and societal system or the transition process itself might be at risk. The following sections analyse how the present social protection system in Ukraine copes with this double challenge and how envisaged reforms might affect the performance of the social protection system.

3. The Present Social Protection System

The social protection system of the Ukraine is still characterised by structures inherited from the system of the former Soviet Union, which during 1991–1993 had to be complemented by additional benefit provisions introduced in response to the stress placed on the system by the challenges of economic transition. As a result the present social protection system shows a classical three-tier structure.

- Employment related social security schemes (pensions, short-term cash benefits) to which unemployment benefits were added recently.
- Universal benefits systems providing benefits for the total population (i.e. the family benefits system and the National Public Service Health Care System).
- A largely embryonic social assistance scheme.

An additional component of the overall system and a peculiarity of Ukraine is the Chernobyl Fund, which tries to alleviate the dire effects of the Chernobyl nuclear accident in 1986. The following sections describe key characteristics of the different subsystems of the social protection system and briefly analyse their benefit experience.

3.1. Social Security Systems

All social security systems cover the complete working population and their dependants. Some professions enjoy special provisions (teachers, scientists, doctors, artists, aviators, etc.). Ukraine has not yet ratified any of the major social security conventions of the ILO.

The pension scheme has the same double-track administrative structure as the Russian pension scheme, both being based on Soviet legislation of 1991.[6] The Pension Fund, through its network of local offices, collects the

---

[6] Compare L. Liu, Income Security in Transition for the Aged and Children in the Soviet Union and in the Russian Federation, *Social Security Bulletin*, Vol. 56, No. 1, Spring 1993.

'contributions'. Benefits are administered by 800 local and 26 district offices of the Ministry of Welfare. The district offices establish pension entitlements of applicants and calculate the benefit. The amount of benefits and the addresses are reported to local Pension Fund offices, which in turn inform the Central Office of the Pension Fund about its total financial obligation of each month. The list of recipients is sent to the Ministry of Communications, which also receives the total pensions amount and makes payments through local post offices (*Figure 7.5*). Until recently, the Pension Fund reported directly to Parliament, whereas the benefit branch of the pension system reported to the Ministry of Welfare. In early 1994, after financial problems in the Pension Fund, it was placed under the supervision of the Ministry of Finance.

There is anecdotal evidence that the benefit administration is cumbersome. The calculation of pensions, insurance periods and reference incomes are still determined with the help of the workers' workbook and employer certificates. The processing time between claiming pensions and their first payments might take six months. Short-term cash benefits are administered by the Social Insurance Fund, which is operated by the Federation of Trade Unions. Benefits payments are made at enterprise level.

The pension scheme and the short-term benefit scheme are financed by a payroll surcharge (or a social tax) of 37% plus a 1% contribution by firm's employees. Of the 37%, the Pension Fund apparently receives 88% (or 32.56% of the wage fund) plus the 1% employee contribution. Short-term benefits (mainly sickness and maternity benefits) are financed through the remaining 12% of the contribution income (or 4.44% of the Wage Fund).

Prior to the introduction of the Pension Fund, as in other former planned economy countries, there used to be a direct link between the social security accounts and the state budget. Surpluses and deficits were in theory automatically absorbed by the state budget. The introduction of separate Pension Funds, collecting and managing their own resources, should have severed the budget link. But in practice the Government subsidised the Pension Fund when it ran into cash flow problems at the end of 1993. The Government provided a loan at very favourable terms, probably at an interest rate well below inflation.

As discussed in Chapter 3 the unemployment scheme is administered by the network of about 700 employment offices of the Employment Service (ES). The local offices are responsible for providing a set of services for the unemployed including job placement, labour market measures and unemployment benefits.

The Chernobyl Fund is managed by the Ministry of Chernobyl, which has only a limited own benefit delivery system and capacity. It thus uses the delivery system of the social security system. The financial and

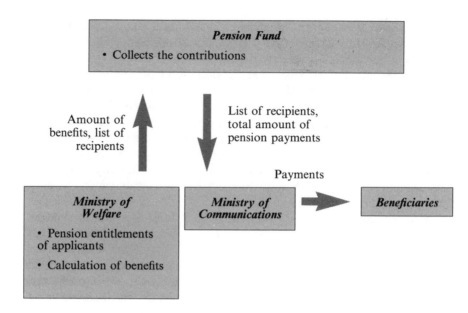

Figure 7.5 *Administrative Structure of the Pension Scheme, Ukraine, 1994*

administrative interrelations between the different social protection systems apparently lack transparency.

3.1.1. The Pension Scheme

As with most social security pension schemes, the pension system provides old-age, invalidity and survivors' pensions (*Table 7.2*).

The replacement rate for old age pension is proportionally reduced for people having reached pension age without fulfilling the required years of service. The replacement rate is increased by one percentage point for each year of service after the minimum, up to a maximum of 15 additional years. The maximum theoretical replacement rate is hence 70%. But this replacement rate can only be reached by long serving, low income wage-earners, due to the definition of the reference income.

The reference income is defined as an average of the last two years' earnings or alternatively as an average of any continuous five-year period during the career of a beneficiary. Reference earnings are defined as a sum of percentages of up to ten income bands. Each band represents one times the minimum pension. In determining the reference 100% of the income up to four times the minimum wage is taken into account, 85% of the 'fifth minimum wage', 70% of the sixth, and so on to 15% of the tenth. Income over

Table 7.2 *Benefit Conditions of the Pension Scheme, Ukraine, 1993–1994*

	Beneficiaries	Formula
Old age pension	• Men at age 60 on a normal job and at age 50–55 years on hazardous and unhealthy job. • Women 5 years earlier (55, 45–50) in both cases.	• 55% of reference earnings plus 1% for each year of service in excess of 25 years (men) or 20 years (women); maximum for this extra being 75% of the pension. • Minimum pension was 120,000 karbovanets per month in April 1994. Maximum pension is 3 times the minimum pension, but there are special higher ceilings for certain categories of workers (miners, Chernobyl victims).
Partial pension	Persons with less than required number of years for full pension.	• Pro-rate-tempore of full pension. • No less than 50% of minimum old age pension.
Social pension	Persons who can not fulfil the conditions for a contributory pension.	• 50% of minimum old age pensions for old age. • Between 30% and 200% of minimum old age pensions for invalidity and disability depending on the degree of disability.
Invalidity pension	Persons who have partially or totally lost their working capacity. The disabled are categorised into three groups according to the degree of capacity loss.	• 70% of reference earnings for category I. • 60% for category II and • 40% for category III • Maximum 3 times the minimum pension. • Minimum 0.5 times the minimum pension.
Survivors' pension	Deceased breadwinner's dependants.	• 30% of reference wage per dependant but no less than the minimum pension.

Source: International Social Security Association (ISSA), *Social Security Systems in Central and Eastern Europe*, Geneva, 1993; World Bank, 1992.

ten times the minimum is not taken into account. The system hence creates income replacement rates that decline as the income level rises. At the same time, it makes pension levels dependent upon discretionary government decisions about adjustment of the minimum wage.

Since the previous economic and political system denied the existence of inflation, the pension legislation – as in all other Central and Eastern

European countries – does not contain provisions on automatic indexing or adjustments of pensions. The effects of the inflationary waves during 1991–1993 thus had to be compensated by ad hoc adjustments of pensions. They were adjusted by a factor of 2 in January 1993, by a factor of 3 in June 1993, by a factor of 2.9 in September 1993 and by a factor of 3 up to the normal maximum in December 1993. For special pensions a factor of 2 up to 400,000 karbovanets was used in December.

Benefit Experience   The benefit experience of a pension system can be summarised by its demographic burden, i.e. the ratio of the number of pensioners or pensions to the number of contributors (the demographic ratio) and the ratio of the average pension to the average insurable earnings of the contributors (the financial ratio).

Figure 7.6 describes the development of the demographic structure of the pension scheme (*Table A7.4* in *Annex III*). In early 1994, the scheme had

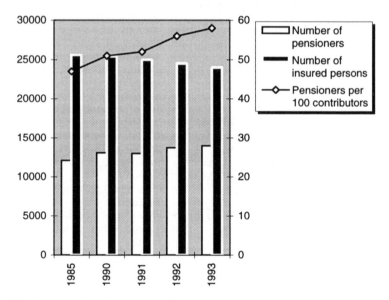

In 1993 there were less than two contributors per pensioner

Figure 7.6   *Pensioners, Insured Persons (thousand) and the Demographic Ratio, Ukraine, 1985–1993**

*Statistical sources and definitions concerning the number of pensioners vary slightly; in particular the distinction between pensions in payment and pensioners is not always made. Total number of insured persons is estimated as equal to the number of employed persons at mid-year.

Source: E. Libanova and O. Paliy, 1994; Ministry of Social Protection, 1994; ILO-CEET calculations.

14 million pensioners, of which 10.9 million were old age pensioners, 1.5 million disability pensioners, 1.1 survivors' pensioners and 0.5 million social pensioners. The number of insured persons was 24 million. The demographic burden of the scheme was hence about 58 pensioners per 100 contributors.

At the end of 1993, only about 416,000, or about 3.8% of all old age pensioners received a minimum pension. Only one year earlier this proportion had been twice as high. A year earlier, at the end of 1991, no less than 57% of all pensioners had received the minimum pension. The latter indicated that the pension scheme had served as a redistributive mechanism, providing high minimum pensions at a relative early age for a considerable number of persons.

Large-scale redistribution has been scaled back through the adjustment system. Pensions have been frequently adjusted on an ad hoc basis by applying a factor to pensions, while minimum pensions were adjusted less frequently.

Minimum pensions would be received primarily by new pensioners, joining the 'pension force' with new minimum pensions. Hence the number of pensioners receiving the minimum pension decreased dramatically, which does not mean that the number of poor pensioners decreased. The total number of old age pensioners – i.e., the sum of recipients of earned pensions and recipients of old age social pensions – amounted to 97.3% of all persons older than normal retirement age in early 1993.[7] This might serve as an indicator that the population coverage of the pension scheme is virtually complete.

The demographic burden of the scheme increased between 1985 and 1993 by about 10 percentage points. The increase of the demographic ratio can be attributed to the growth of old age pensions, which increased between 1985 and 1993 by about 27%. This increase cannot be explained by demographic factors alone. *Figure 7.7* displays the financial component of the overall cost of the pension scheme (*Table A7.5* in *Annex III*).

Even if the data before and after independence were not completely comparable, the increase in earlier retirement in privileged 'job categories' must have played a considerable role. The drop in the employment level explains only about 3%-points of the 10%-points increase of the demographic ratio.

In early 1992, the average replacement rate for old age pensions was only slightly higher than for all pensions. By the end of 1993, the overall replacement rate had fallen to 37% (or by about 16% in relative terms), indicating that pension adjustments had been insufficient even to keep the pensioner's

[7] Census data for 1989. About 70% of all old age pensioners were women. The reasons for the unbalanced sex composition are the earlier retirement age for women combined with higher life expectancy and male age cohorts decimated by World War II. This led to the fact that 88% of single person pensioner households were single women.

standard of living in line with the declining standard of living of the active population.

The drop in the replacement rate for average social pensions was even more dramatic. The average social pension was worth 13% of the average income, or about 52% of the official subsistence minimum, by the end of 1993. This indicated that the pension scheme was moving away from supporting a broadly based income redistribution.

At the same time, the distribution of pensions has become more compact, since minimum pensions and hence maximum pensions have not been raised in line with average pensions.[8] The consequence was that the average pension was rapidly closing in on the maximum. Hence, the average pension has moved away from the minimum towards the maximum bound (*Figure 7.8 and Table A7.5 in Annex III*). As such, the income replacement rates for workers with higher incomes has fallen (*Figure 7.9*). At the end of 1991, the 'normal' maximum pension (three times the minimum) was 7%

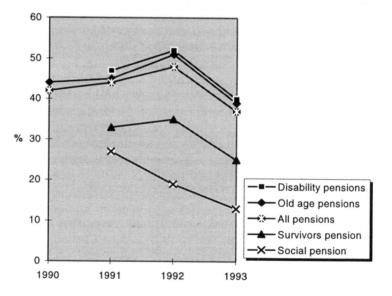

Social pension's replacement rate has dropped most dramatically

Figure 7.7   *Replacement Rate for Pensions, Ukraine, 1990–1993**

*Disability pensions include only general disability pensions.

Source: E. Libanova and O. Paliy, 1994; Ministry of Social Protection, 1994; Ministry of Labour, 1994; and ILO-CEET calculations.

---

[8] On January 1, 1993, about 13% of old age pensions exceeded the 'normal' maximum of three times the minimum pension.

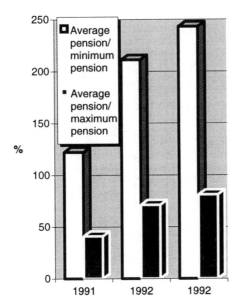

Minimum and maximum pensions have not been raised in line with average pension

Figure 7.8 *Average Pension as a Percentage of Minimum and Maximum Pensions, Ukraine, 1991–1993*
Source: Ministry of Social Protection, 1994, ILO-CEET calculations.

higher than the average wage. By the end of 1993, the maximum pension only reached 45% of the average wage.

Hence, inflation has eroded real pensions levels to a dramatic extent[9] and without a deliberate policy correction the scheme will continue to move towards a de facto flat rate scheme. But it is understood that the Ministry of Social Protection is preparing legislation aiming at increasing the differential between the minimum and the maximum pension.

One reason for the introduction of the subsistence minimum guarantee (see Chapter 3.4.) was to compensate the loss of real income of social pensioners and other pensioners with low pensions and low income.

Since December 1993, the means test of the local welfare office has certified that pensioners can receive additional payments up to the minimum subsistence level (SAIL) of 197,000 karbovanets. As citizens, they are also entitled to cash compensation for former food subsidies (called 'bread

---

[9] Alternatively, one could interpret the figures as implying that inflation has been used to reduce the cost of the pension scheme by reducing the real level of protection of present and future pensioners.

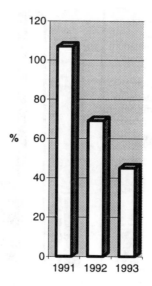

Replacement rate for workers with high incomes has fallen

Figure 7.9 *Maximum Pension as a Percentage of Average Wage, Ukraine, 1991–1993*

Source: Ministry of Social Protection, 1994 and ILO-CEET calculations.

money'). In theory, the measure compensates low income pensioners for the fall in the standard of living between the end of 1991 and the end of 1992 (*Table 7.3*).

The replacement rates in *Table 7.3* indicate that in spite of a differential between minimum pensions and maximum pensions of a factor of 3, the real maximum differential of the money income of old age pensioners was only 1.67 (maximum normal transfer income divided by minimum transfer income in cases of need). In January 1994, the pension scheme paid addi-

Table 7.3 *Value of Social, Minimum and Maximum Old Age Pensioners, Ukraine, December 1993 (karbovanets)*

Type of transfer	Social pension	Minimum pension	Maximum
Pension	60,000	120,000	360,000
Social assistance	137,000	77,000	–
'Bread money'	44,000	44,000	44,000
Total transfer income	241,000	241,000	404,000
% of average income	30.3	30.3	50.9

tional social assistance to 1,364,864 pensioners (about 10% of all pensioners), i.e. at an average rate of 42,463 karbovanets. This appears to be low,
given that at least four million old age and social pensioners had a pension
lower than the SAIL in accordance with the distribution of pensions on
January 1, 1993.

Together with the demographic ratio (59%), the overall financial ratio
(37%) should translate into a pay-as-you-go contribution rate of 22%. A
year earlier, the pure pay-as-you-go cost was about 27%. The scheme has
thus been consolidated and the rising demographic burden overcompen-
sated by decreasing real pension levels. Major reasons for the difference
between the relative costs of pensions and the allocation of funds are the
following.

- The budget is not fully compensating the Pension Fund for its expenditure on behalf of the budget (military pensions and some child benefits)
  according to the statement on expected income and expenditure for 1993
  provided by the Pension Fund.
- The Chernobyl Fund is not fully compensating the Pension Fund for its
  expenditure for Chernobyl victims according to the statement on
  expected income and expenditure for 1993.
- The scheme does not collect the full amount of due contributions: for
  1992 the 'contribution gap' was about 18%.[10]

Even then, the fund was able to transfer about 28% of its 1992 income
to its reserve. For 1993, the Pension Fund's budget envisaged a transfer of
only 1.2% of its current income into the reserve. In fact, the fund ran into
a liquidity crunch at the end of 1993 and was placed under the control of
the Ministry of Finance. Liquidation of the 1992 reserve increase would not
have helped since inflation had eroded the reserve, which amounted to 28%
of the 1992 income to 1.1% of the 1993 income, and the earned return on
investment was only modest.[11]

The reason for the liquidity problem at the end of 1993 was a simple
timelag. Pensions had been increased by a factor of 2.9 in September and
a factor of 3 in December, i.e., by a composite factor of 8.7, while average
wages increased by a factor of only 4. Together with a reserve wiped out

---

[10] The contribution gap is the difference between the contribution income and the product
of the estimated annual average number of employed persons multiplied by the annual average wage times the contribution rate charged for the pension scheme (together with the
employee share 32.8% of total insurable earnings). The contribution gap might be due to
administrative inefficiency or to the fact that enterprises are simply not able to pay contributions, or due to the fact that a considerable proportion of the workforce were on unpaid leave,
during which no contributions are paid. Without a major investigation the relative weight of
the different reasons cannot be clarified.

[11] This demonstrates once again that the build-up of a technical reserve for pension financing in times of high inflation is useless.

by hyper-inflation and the usual one month grace period for the payment of contributions, this resulted in a 'classical' cash crunch. In stable economic conditions, this would not have happened.

3.1.2. The Short-term Cash Benefit Systems

In Ukraine, the main short-term cash benefits are sickness and maternity benefits. Sickness benefits are paid at a rate varying with the length of a past employment, ranging from 60% of previous earnings for workers with less than three years of service to a 100% replacement rate for long-serving officials, after eight years of service. There is no waiting period and benefits are paid for a maximum of four months per case (a maximum of six months per year) or pension receipt. Sickness benefits are also paid to a working parent for the care of a sick family member (usually a child) for up to 14 days per case.

A maternity grant is payable and recurrent maternity benefits are paid at a rate of 100% of earnings for ten weeks prior to the expected date of confinement and normally eight weeks after the confinement (a total of 126 calendar days). After the expiration of the maternity benefits one parent can opt for parental leave (receiving a flat rate benefit) until the child reaches the age of three years.

While the provision for maternity and parental leave can be considered normal by European standards, the sickness benefit provisions for longer-serving workers are generous. But reported sickness days per employee have been fairly stable over the last fifteen years: in 1992, 9.82 calendar days per employee, about 11.5% of which were reported as sickness days for the care of sick family members. Hence, the sickness rate was only 2.7%, which in an international comparison is a low level.[12] Statistics on the exact costs of these benefits could not be obtained. The benefits (maternity benefits without parental leave and sickness cash benefits) are financed by an allocation of 12% of the total social insurance contribution. The cost of parental leave is financed out of the allocation to the Pension Fund. Based on the benefit experience for the sickness benefit and a declining birth rate, the allocation of 5.2% of the payroll appears to be an acceptable order of magnitude but it leaves room for some other benefits (for example cures at spas) to be provided on a discretionary basis by the trade unions administering them.

3.1.3. Unemployment Benefit System

Unemployment benefits, labour market measures – such as training and retraining of unemployed – and job placement services are provided

---

[12] Ministry of Statistics, *Statistical Yearbook of Ukraine*, p. 206, op. cit.

through the Unemployment Fund. The fund is administered by the Ministry of Labour through a network of local employment offices. It is financed by a 3% payroll surcharge paid by employers and budget transfers, if needed. In 1993, 90.7% of the fund's income stemmed from contributions and 8.4% from 'commercial activity revenue' (for example returns on the investment of reserves). Unemployment benefits differ by category of unemployed. Eligibility criteria and the resultant registration propensities are reviewed in Chapter 2 and Chapter 3.

According to unofficial estimates of the Employment Service, hidden unemployment might presently be about 30%. This demonstrates the threat that looms beyond the horizon for the Unemployment Fund. As many of the hidden unemployed receive neither wage payments nor any benefits, there is mounting political pressure on the Ministry of Labour to introduce a benefit for under-employment or partial unemployment. If benefit provisions for that are not drawn up very restrictively, this might release a flood of benefit applications, which would exhaust the recurrent income and the contingency reserve of the Unemployment Fund in a very short time. Enterprises would simply use the opportunity to delay bankruptcy, and the inertia of the industrial restructuring would simply be prolonged. The result might be that the society ends up paying both unemployment benefits and 'lost' subsidies to inefficient and redundant enterprises.

Benefit Experience   Registration of unemployed persons began on July 1, 1991. The first benefit were paid at the same time.

Figure 7.10 shows the benefit delivery and unemployment trends (*Table A7.7* in *Annex III*). The decline of the beneficiary rate is a typical phenomenon during times of rising unemployment, which usually coincides with increasing average duration of unemployment. Thus an increasing number of beneficiaries exhaust entitlements notably because a considerable number enjoy only a maximum benefit duration of six months. In addition, the Employment Service can delay payment of benefits for persons who have voluntarily left their jobs and might also discontinue benefit payments if the unemployed refuses two 'suitable' offers and for some other reasons. The beneficiary rate is low. Persons on severance pay and persons in retraining programmes are not counted as registered unemployed, so their number cannot help to explain why more than half of the unemployed do not receive benefits. An analysis of benefit delivery and the statistics of registered unemployed and beneficiaries is necessary, as emphasised in Chapter 2.

Benefit levels are acceptable for medium and higher income earners laid off during their first six months of unemployment. The long-term unemployed (those out of work for more than six months), even with average

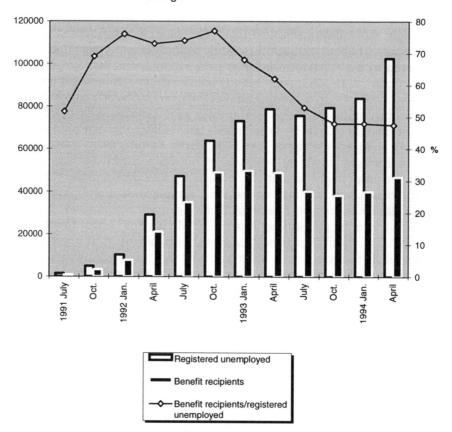

The beneficiary rate has been declining since October 1992

Figure 7.10   *Number of the Unemployed and Benefit Recipients and Benefit Recipients' Share of the Unemployed, Ukraine, 1991–1994*
Source: E. Libanova, 1994; Employment Service, 1994.

reference income (the income of the two months prior to unemployment), merely reach benefit levels in the order of the minimum wage. Virtually all long-term unemployed with lower than average incomes are thus receiving benefits under the subsistence level. Contrary to the practice in the pension scheme, the Unemployment Fund does not top up calculated benefits to the level of SAIL. Local welfare offices apparently also do not provide for the difference between the unemployment benefits and the SAIL. The only extra payment that the unemployed are entitled to is the cash compensation ('bread money') of 63,000 karbovanets, which is paid to every citizen.

In March 1994, the average monthly unemployment benefit was 169,066 karbovanets or about 20% of the average wage at the time. This 'financial' ratio is extremely low and can only be explained by less than full indexing of benefits (in line with inflation) and a large proportion of beneficiaries receiving minimum benefits. Again, a more detailed investigation is necessary.

To sum up, the benefit system does not reach more than half of the registered unemployed and those who are reached are on the average supplied with meagre benefits. The demographic ratio of the fund and the financial ratio would lead to a total cost of unemployment benefit of under 0.1% of total wage income of the employed. Collected contribution are, however, 3%.

According to the estimate for 1993, the fund spent of its total income of about 608 billion karbovanets:[13]

 1.9% on unemployment benefits,
 7.4% on job creation measures,
 1.4% on training and retraining programmes,
 1.0% on public works,
 7.3% on administrative expenditure,
 10.6% on transfers to the Central Employment Fund,
 7.1% on loans to enterprises,
 62.6% on the build-up of reserves and
 0.7% on other expenditure.

In the meantime, the Unemployment Fund built up a reserve, which at the end of 1993 was equal to 75% of its total income for 1993. While the building up of a reserve is understandable, in view of the major financial commitments that must be expected, given the very real possibility of mass open unemployment in the near future, non-use of almost two-thirds of the income of the fund is a questionable order of magnitude. The example of the Pension Fund demonstrates that the build-up of a reserve is not a rational strategy in a hyper-inflationary environment. Inflation has eroded a major share of the reserve, which could have been used in 1993 for a big 'employment creation and retraining campaign' and for the upgrading of meagre benefits in times of rampaging poverty. The fund could afford to top up benefits of unemployed to the minimum subsistence level and increase the beneficiary ratio. It would be better to spend the money for the preparation of the workforce for the new challenges on the labour market than to build up a financial reserve with a rapidly eroding real value.

If mass open unemployment arrives, the contribution rate will have to

[13] Employment Fund: Statement of income and expenditure of the State Fund for the Promotion of Employment, Exercise, 1993. The percentages refer to the total income of the local employment funds only. Local employment funds transfer about 10% of their income to the Central Fund to cover national expenses and ensure funds for the equalisation of different financial burdens between the regions. The Central Fund has very little direct income, which is neglected here.

increase. At present, when the average replacement rate and beneficiary rate are low, the contribution rate of 3% could cater for an unemployment rate of 18%, even under the assumption that 25% of the income would be spent on labour market policy measures and on administration. Even in transition such a level is not reached overnight and, because of that, there would be ample time to increase the contribution rate before the scheme would run out of funds.

3.2. Universal Systems

The universal benefit systems consist mainly of family benefits and the public service health care system.

3.2.1. The Family Benefit Scheme

Ukraine has an extraordinary array of family benefits. They are administered and financed from various sources (Pension Fund, budget of the Ministry of Social Protection and local government budgets). The sharing of the financing between local government and the central government is not clear. Most benefits are supposedly financed by the central government through transfers to local budgets. Yet, it is not clear whether the local governments receive earmarked funds for all or some of these benefits, or whether they are just obliged to finance these benefits out of the budgetary allocation from the state budget.

In November 1992, the Government and Parliament codified all family benefits in the Law on Assistance to Families with Children. The family benefit systems combined features of a classical universal benefit scheme with features of a social assistance scheme. Apart from the maternity and parental leave benefits, which are financed by social security, they consist mainly of around 10 major benefits. These are either income support benefits for low income families or benefits that depend on other conditions, like raising children during parental leave.

A list of the main family benefits is provided in *Annex I*. One family can receive more than one kind of benefit, depending on eligibility. The income support payments are tied to a means test. Most are payable in full to families with a total income of no more than three times the minimum wage. Due to the low income ceiling (three times the minimum wage was in December 1993 less than the subsistence minimum) a declining number of families should be eligible for these means tested benefits. In general, the benefit package seems to be designed to enable couples or single persons to have families in spite of low income levels.

Benefits are tied to the minimum wage. This implies that they used to be generous. But recently the minimum wage has deteriorated to such an extent that it is now merely serving accounting unit. Real benefits have thus deteriorated sharply, particularly during 1993. A parent taking parental leave received a benefit worth about 30% of the average wage in January, but by December the same benefit had deteriorated to 7.6% of the average wage.

The linking of family benefits to the minimum wage also has a disadvantage for low income workers. In time of scarce resources, the Government will tend to hold the minimum wage down in order to avoid increasing budgetary expenditure for family benefits. It would be advisable for the protection of real benefits as well as the protection of real wages of low-income workers to disconnect social protection benefit levels from the minimum wage. Linking benefits to the average wage and, hence, in some way to the volume of income tax and social security contributions would be preferable from a social policy point of view.

According to IMF estimates, total expenditure for tax-financed family benefits was in the order of 2% of GDP in 1992.[14] Due to the deterioration of real benefit levels and the decreasing number of families eligible for means tested benefits, the Ministry of Finance estimated during the budgeting exercise in late 1993 that the cost for the scheme in 1993 was only 0.8% of GDP and, after an upward revision of the minimum wage, would be 1.2% of GDP in 1994. In effect, inflation has helped to 'consolidate' social expenditure.

3.2.2. The Public Service Health Care Scheme

The health system is basically the classical public system still prevailing in most former planned economy countries, although these are undergoing reforms in virtually all countries of the region. The public system – the backbone of health care delivery – is a branch of the civil service.

The Ministry of Health is operating tertiary care hospitals (national referral centres), research centres and medical schools. Only technically does it supervise the oblast medical delivery systems, whose chief medical officers report to the oblast administration. Since 1992, the oblast delivery systems have been financed from the oblast budget, whereas the national institutions have been financed directly from the state budget through the Ministry of Health. The facilities are now preparing their own budgets and submit them either to the oblast government or the Ministry of Health.[15]

As in most other countries of the region the health care infrastructure appears extensive compared to European standards. In 1993, the country had 4.4 physicians per 1,000 persons (compared to 2.8 in the former West Germany and 1.4 in the United Kingdom in the late 1980s) and 13.5 hospital beds per 1,000 persons (compared to 11.0 in Germany, 6.8 in the UK

[14] IMF, 1992, op. cit., p. 4.
[15] World Bank, 1992, op. cit., Chapter 9.

and 5.3 in the USA in the late 1980s). Ambulatory care is provided by about 6,500 polyclinics and similar and affiliated outpatient care units and inpatient care by a network of 3,800 hospitals. Utilisation data indicate extensive use of facilities (for example, 4.0 hospital days per person). Performance indicators also suggest that delivery is less than efficient. For example, average length of stay is 16.5 days.

In addition to the Ministry of Health and oblast facilities, bigger enterprises and agencies still operate their own facilities, polyclinics and even hospitals. The quality of care in these facilities is reported to be superior to the care provided in public facilities. Private dental care facilities have always existed in a limited form, involving about 5% of all dentists, and other types of private health care facilities are developing, albeit slowly due to the lack of affluent patients.

All state-run health care services used to be essentially free. But the difficulties the country faces in obtaining cheap pharmaceuticals have led to tough rationing of the drug supply. The main former supply channels from countries like the Czech and Slovak Republics, East Germany, Hungary and Russia have virtually evaporated since these countries trade their goods overwhelmingly in hard currency. Drugs are today free only for children under the age of one and for certain categories of seriously or chronically ill persons. For other groups, the purchase of drugs has become a predominantly private affair, even for persons with low incomes. The choice of providers had been strictly limited due to administrative allocation of patients to local providers. Only now the range of choice is slowly widening.

The system seems to suffer from the symptoms that can be observed in other countries, i.e. a lack of allocative and productive efficiency indicated by poor quality of care provided by unmotivated staff in badly maintained facilities. These symptoms are triggered by a combination of chronic and acute underfunding of the over-dimensioned delivery system. Salaries of health care professionals are low. Experienced doctors, for example, earn only slightly more than the national average wage. For a number of years, the system has experienced a critical shortage of non-staff inputs, such as drugs and other types of medical technologies. The present economic and budgetary situation has aggravated shortages, and the mismatch of staff and non-staff inputs has become worse. Hence, access to appropriate health care is deteriorating. Declining health status indicators also point to low effectiveness of the delivery system, although part of the deterioration in health status can be attributed to the impact of the environmental disaster of Chernobyl.

Public expenditure for health care was about 4% of GDP in 1992. It was in the order of 5% of GDP if private outlays for the purchase of drugs, so-called gratitude payments by patients to health professionals, incomes from the Social Insurance Fund (for example, through treatment in sanatoria) and the Chernobyl Fund are taken into account. Public expenditure in 1993 was 4.8% of GDP and should increase to 6.8% of GDP in 1994, according to Ministry of Finance estimates. This is due to a fall in GDP rather than to a real increase of resources for health.

3.2.3. Other Schemes

In 1992, the Government abolished much of the budget subsidies for consumer goods. Between 1992 and 1991 subsidies were reduced from 19.3% of GDP to 11.5% of GDP. The majority of subsidies were abolished when consumer prices were liberalised on June 10, 1992. In 1992, the government introduced a cash compensation scheme for low income families, notably households with pensioners and small children, for loss of disposable income due to the abolition of subsidies for essential food products.

In 1994, the following amounts were paid per month:

- 63,000 karbovanets to persons of active age,
- 44,000 karbovanets to persons in pension age and
- 24,000 karbovanets to children.

The income limit for this benefit is 20 times the minimum wage, which means that virtually every resident is eligible. Means tested benefits should become part of the social assistance scheme in the long run. In the market economy, wages will be determined in such way as to cover the cost of a certain consumption basket at market prices. General monthly transfer payments for the purchases of certain goods, which are financed from general taxation, should be a transitory phenomenon. This implies that the level of tax financed cash benefits, notably family benefits, should be reviewed with a view to incorporation of 'bread money'. Earnings related benefits would need increments until the new earning levels have had their full impact on benefit levels.

In 1992, the scheme was supposed to cost about 1.6 % of GDP.[16] Due to inflationary developments, the cost in 1993 may have been considerably lower, about 1% of GDP according to Ministry of Finance estimates.

3.3. The Chernobyl Fund

The Chernobyl Fund was introduced to finance compensations and ongoing clean-up activities related to the nuclear disaster in Chernobyl in 1986. After independence, the Government of Ukraine was left with the financing of the bulk of Chernobyl related benefits and services on its territory. The fund provides an array of cash benefits for victims of the catastrophe.

[16] IMF, 1992, op. cit.

- Benefits replacing income (like invalidity pensions or invalidity pension and old age pension increments).
- Payments with the characteristics of damages.
- Income support measures.
- Lump-sum compensations, for example for relocation expenses.

The fund also covers wage supplements for persons still working in contaminated areas and expenses for the ongoing clean-up of the reactor and the area. It is also funding research needs for the latter activities. A list of the main benefits is given in *Annex II*. The fund is financed by a 12% payroll surcharge provided by employers. It uses the pension scheme as a 'handling agent' for some of its benefits.

Although the Pension Fund was not fully reimbursed for all Chernobyl-related expenditure channelled through the local welfare offices, the scheme was financing about 650,000 old age pensions (supplements to old age pensions), 76,000 invalidity pensions and about 41,000 survivors' pensions in January 1993. The number of pensions and pension supplements is still growing as affected persons reach retirement age and disabilities become apparent.

Chernobyl old age pensions were on average about 8% higher than the general average old age pensions. Invalidity pensions were 47% higher and survivors' pensions were about 8% higher than the general average pension in the respective categories. There is evidence that eligibility conditions for Chernobyl benefits, notably old age pension supplements, are liberal and that targeting the benefits to the most affected persons is not necessarily very efficient. It is also not certain that all in need and entitled have applied for benefits. It appears that within the review of special protection benefits the adequacy, allocation and delivery of Chernobyl benefits deserve special attention.

The cost of the scheme was about 5% of GDP in 1992. The relative cost for 1993 is estimated to be lower, again probably due to incomplete indexing of benefits. The Chernobyl cost is thus in the same order as the overall national health expenditure.

The financing of benefits should be viewed as a state affair or maybe even an affair of the CIS. The IMF is questioning the financing of the benefits through a payroll surcharge in the context of future privatisation.

3.4. Social Assistance Benefits

Social assistance benefits in the Ukraine consist of income support benefits in cash and in kind and social care.

3.4.1. Income Support Benefits

So far, social assistance benefits have played only a minor role. The formal full employment policy has avoided a sizeable number of persons becom-

ing dependent on social assistance. Presently, social assistance cash benefits are still mainly provided on an ad hoc basis as aid to the needy by local
welfare offices. At an early stage of the reform process, a limited general
cash income support system was introduced. It provided limited payments
to families with per capita incomes under 50% of the minimum wage. The
benefits are 200% of the minimum wage for adults and 100% of the minimum wage per child. The scheme is financed by local government. Benefit
take-up was apparently very low, which might in part be explained by the
very low benefit levels.[17] There are anecdotal reports that local welfare
offices are increasingly paying benefits to persons on hidden unemployment
(i.e., those on unpaid leave for several months). Hence, financing unemployment through the rudimentary social assistance mechanism is already
'creeping' in.

In June 1993, the scheme was complemented by an income support
scheme for pensioners and low-income persons by a Decree of the Prime
Minister[18] and by a Joint Executive Order of the Ministries of Social
Protection, Labour and Finance.[19] Persons on other state benefits were
explicitly excluded, in particular children covered by the Law on State
Assistance to Families with Children and also persons receiving unemployment benefits. The system consists of two parts:

a) For old age, invalidity and survivor pensioners and disabled persons a
   minimum income guarantee at the amount of a social assistance intervention line (SAIL[20]) was established. It amounted to 197,000 karbovanets in December 1993. If the per capita income of a household is
   lower than the SAIL, the scheme tops up the per capita income for family members with personal income under the SAIL up to the poverty
   line. The financing of this scheme is delegated to the Pension Fund and
   local authority budgets. Local welfare offices are charged with the
   administration of the benefits.
b) The Decree recommended that local authorities ensure, within their
   financial possibilities, similar support to low-income families and that
   they complement those benefits with cash payments or loans for specific
   needs.

Data on the benefit experience are not yet available. It can be expected
that the pension scheme is complying with its obligations and that a major
part of the cost of the scheme will be 'hidden' in the total expenditure of
the pension scheme. It is also to be expected that the recommendation

[17] E. Libanova and O. Paliy, 1994, op. cit.; World Bank, 1993, op. cit.
[18] Decree No. 394 on Targeted Cash Benefits to Low Income Persons, June 1993.
[19] Decree of June 14, 1993.
[20] The SAIL is also called 'poverty line' but given its small amount the name poverty line
might be misleading.

concerning local authorities in times of dire financial distress will have a very limited impact on the well-being of the poor.

This arrangement burdens the social security pension scheme with a social assistance function and demonstrates that separation of social assistance from the responsibility of Government for social security is a fiction.

The income support system also has the following deficiencies.

* The actual allocation of benefits within a needy family is not clear. The SAIL does not seem to be differentiated by age or region.
* The definition of income is not clear when calculating the average income per capita. Chernobyl-related allowances are for some reason excluded.
* The procedure for means testing is not elaborated.
* There are coverage gaps. For example, unemployed persons are excluded from additional income support, no matter how low their benefits.

While the system was necessary as a stop-gap measure, its inconsistencies indicate the necessity of an overhaul and streamlining of social assistance and an allocation and guarantee of sufficient financial means for the provision of equal benefits to the poor throughout the country. Social assistance benefit levels cannot be designed by financial means available in local budgets. This leads to a state where the poor in 'poor' regions will always be worse off than the poor in more affluent regions.

3.4.2. Social Care

The Ministry of Social Protection through its network of 26 district and 800 local welfare offices also operates and maintains facilities for institutional care (about 61,000 persons in 1992) and home care (about 270,000 persons in 1992), including sanatoria and sheltered workshops. The costs are covered by state and local budgets. Rules concerning the sharing of financial burden between the state and local governments are not clear. This is the case also in local offices, where lines of command with respect to local governments and the state government are not clear.

The total expenditure for social assistance is hard to estimate, but according to a very rough guess it could be in the order of 1% of GDP for 1992 and 1993, excluding the share covered by the pension system.

3.5. Social Protection Through Charities and Non-Government Organisations

With the exception of churches, Non-Governmental Organisations (NGOs) are a new phenomenon in the Ukraine. The societal and political structure of the previous regime did not leave room for such activities. Following independence, there was a rapid growth in the number of NGOs. Most are professional or ecological pressure groups. NGOs that provide social services are still not well developed.[21] But the emerging poverty has triggered a variety of initiatives from private individuals and groups trying to fill the gap in social protection inevitably neglected by the state social protection system. Data on their activity are not available.

It would be a mistake to believe that NGOs and charities could develop into the backbone of social protection activities in a modern industrial society. Social protection needs legal guarantees and implies long term social and financial commitments. NGOs and charities do not have the degree of public accountability and long term stability that social protection schemes need but they play an important role in a pluralistic social protection system. As pressure groups, they can help to further or safeguard social rights of special groups, such as pensioners. They might also deliver social services that cannot be provided by the public social protection machinery. However, even good intentions need supervision, protection and help from authorities. A regulatory mechanism for non-profit organisations is urgently needed.

3.6. Other Benefits

The above categorisation of social protection benefits only includes benefits provided by social protection institutions and agencies, with the exception of NGOs. These institutions or agencies provide basically statutory benefits defined and mandated by a legal framework. In addition, there is a variety of other benefits provided by enterprises and local authorities. In the absence of comprehensive data, the extent of such local or enterprise based arrangements cannot be determined. There are, however, indications that as a consequence of financial constraints the 'non-statutory' engagement of local authorities and enterprises is declining.

Data on the recent extent of social expenditure in enterprises are scarce. European Union sources quote figures of 30% as the average social expenditure's share of the total costs of enterprises. But apart from the social security levy, these costs are fringe benefits rather than real social expenditure. Social benefits (like enterprise based health care, stays in sanatoria and company resorts) can be considered as a part of the remuneration package of workers.

The government still provides subsidised low-cost housing. Presently, the share of the average household income spent on housing is still negligible (0.8% in 1992).[22] According the Council of Ministers, the ratio increased

[21] United Nations, *Draft Report on the Status and Definition of NGOs in the Ukraine*, Kiev, 1994; and UNICEF, *Possibilities for an Agenda for Children in the Ukraine*, Report of a UNICEF mission to Ukraine, February 1994.
[22] Ministry of Statistics, *Statistical Yearbook of Ukraine*, 1992, op. cit., p. 43.

during 1993 as rents were raised. In addition to subsidised housing, invalids and other special groups are provided with a rental subsidy financed by the general revenues and heating subsidies financed by local budgets.[23] Overall expenditure for this benefit, which would include a part of the depreciation of the apartments provided by the Housing Authorities at below cost rents, is impossible to account for. There are plans to accelerate privatisation of housing and to increase the cost for state owned houses for renters substantially. The latter measure would reduce the purchasing power of the average household.

4. Overall Social Expenditure Level and Economic Constraints

The latest available, fairly reliable social expenditure figures were for 1992. Even these figures are fraught with definitional problems and most of them are not more than estimates. However, the level of social expenditure seems to be in the upper range of the social expenditure levels in OECD countries (*Figure 7.11* and *Table A7.8* in *Annex III*). The estimates for total expenditure might not be excessive for an economy in distress, but one cannot overlook that its levels far exceed those in other countries of the region, which are below the 20% mark, as in Bulgaria and Russia. One major reason for the difference is the substantial expenditure on Chernobyl victims.

As mentioned previously, the reduction of the overall cost in 1993 is due largely to the effect of inflation, which reduced the real value of many benefits. The 1993 data have to be interpreted with extreme care. The estimate is clearly affected by uncertainties on the expenditure side as well as the GDP estimates used in an hyper-inflationary environment. The Ministry of Finance expects that social expenditure will be about 30% of GDP in 1994.

The country's social budget has thus apparently been kept under control. The country has paid for it by increasing poverty and a declining standard of living and probably also by a declining health status. This estimate of the country's social budget also indicates some structural deficiencies. Expenditure on an inefficient health system and expenditure on pensions account for more than half of total expenditure whereas social assistance expenditure even in times of dramatically rising poverty remains at or even below the 1% of GDP level. The allocation has a clear bias against anti-poverty mechanisms even if the social assistance expenditure hidden in the pension scheme is taken into account. These social pensions and social assistance payments up to SAIL are less than 1% of GDP.

The 1993 data are based on estimates of the annual expenditure of the

---

[23] E. Libanova and O. Paliy, 1994, op. cit.

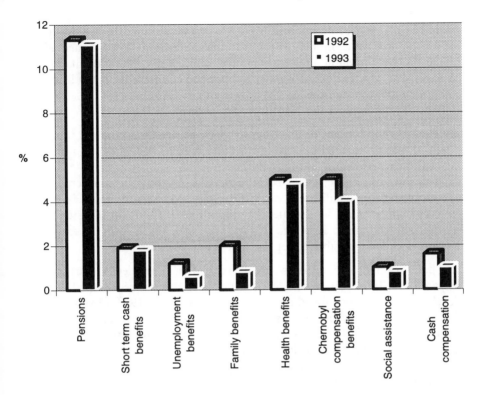

Social expenditure was 29% of GDP in 1992 and 24.9% in 1993

Figure 7.11   *Items of Social Expenditure as a Percentage of GDP, Ukraine,*
1992–1993

Source: figures for 1992 are calculations of IMF and ILO-CEET and figures for 1993 are
estimates of Ministry of Finance, Pension Fund and Unemployment Fund and calculations
of ILO-CEET.

Pension Fund and the Employment Fund and on Ministry of Finance estimates for state financed benefits (compiled during the budgeting exercise
for 1994). Due to the uncertainty about the GDP data and the hyper-inflation, all public expenditure estimates in the Ukraine have to be interpreted
with caution. Hence, the estimated structure of the overall national social
expenditure can only be of an indicative nature.

5. Effectiveness, Efficiency and Affordability

One could describe the present social protection scheme of Ukraine as
being in a half-way stage between the social protection system inherited

from the planned economy and a pluralistic one adapted to the demands of a social market economy. Major reforms still have to be implemented to make the system viable in social and economic terms. The present system is expensive. Up to 1992, it was well above the comparable expenditure of other countries in the region.

Two factors explain the high expenditure level.

a) The growing burden of the Chernobyl Fund, which accounted for 17% of all social protection expenditure and cost as much as the national health care system already in 1992.

b) The shrinking GDP. While social expenditure should be countercyclical (more social expenditure is needed during recessions) to some extent, a very high level of social protection might reduce funds for investment in the new economic structure. Conversely, too low a level of spending would endanger public acceptance of the reform process.

There are indications that a 'quick fix' has been applied to curb social expenditure. Implicitly hyper-inflation has been used to reduce real benefit levels. Expenditure dropped at least by 4% of GDP in 1993. Given present benefit levels, however, this can be done only once. Structural reforms together with efforts to streamline the benefit systems are necessary. A proper social reporting, evaluation and budgeting device should be established in order to ascertain that the impact of emergency measures is shared in a fair way between different population groups. Such a system does not exist.

The pension scheme presently finances a large number of pensioners due to very early retirement ages and very low pension levels. If the scheme is kept on 'auto pilot' (i.e. if maximum benefit levels are not adjusted), inflation will soon turn it into a flat-rate benefit system with only subsistence level benefits. This type of scheme will be unattractive and employees will see little incentive to contribute. Consequently, evasion of contributions will become even more widespread. Private schemes for the better off will spring up, with the likely effect of depleting even further the resources available for the public scheme and, hence, the redistribution of income.

Health services are apparently of low quality due to the shortage of non-staff inputs, while resources are wasted in a too extensive, inefficient and ineffective provider network.

The new cash benefit schemes, social assistance and unemployment are leaving wide gaps in coverage. Considering the extent of poverty, social assistance spending is insufficient. Compared to average income, family benefits – once generous – have lost 75% of their value, leaving needy single parents in an increasingly difficult situation. At the same time, Chernobyl benefit expenditure keeps rising. Reserves are permitted to accumulate in the Pension and Employment Funds, which are simply wiped out by inflation and could have been used for human resource investments to prepare the workforce for the transition to a more performance oriented economy.

The major longer term structural problem of the social protection scheme is how to consolidate the pension scheme in the context of an ageing population. In the near future, a combination of a social emergency package and a long-term structural consolidation of the social protection system is needed. However, given the level of incomes and pensions the room for manoeuvre is small. Obtaining additional funds for social protection is unlikely. Hence decisions will be painful and the social protection system will have to focus its activities. It might be difficult to avoid social tensions. But if the present half-way scheme is allowed to deteriorate indiscriminatorily, public confidence will continue to erode and social tensions will be inevitable.

6. Reforms under Discussion

The Government has launched an overhaul of the social protection system, trying to adapt it to the new demands of a more market oriented economy. The process is characterised by a careful exploratory approach to the reorientation and restructuring of the financing system, which redistributes about 30% of GDP and is thus in itself a major economic force. The following major steps were already taken and/or were envisaged by the Government in 1993.

6.1. Development of a Comprehensive Concept for Social Protection Reform

In early 1993, the Cabinet of Ministers charged the Ministry of Labour, the Ministry of Social Protection, the Ministry of Finance, the Ministry of the Economy and the Ministry of Public Health to develop jointly a concept of reform for the Social Protection System (called here the concept). The concept was accepted by the Cabinet of Ministers on April 5, 1993. The Minister of Labour presented the Concept of Social Security of the Population in Ukraine as a comprehensive reform of the national social protection system to a National Conference on Population Social Protection in Conditions of Economic Reforms in Ukraine in May 1993.[24] In April 1993, the concept was submitted to Parliament (Verhovna Rada).

[24] ILO-CEET, *Mission Report*, Ukraine, May 1993, decision of the Cabinet of Ministers No. 26 – 837/4 of April 17, 1993.

Parliament approved the concept on December 21, 1993. During the whole process, the Government placed great emphasis on achieving national consensus on the basic principles of the reforms before starting the drafting of a legislative framework. The new Rada elected in June 1994 has decided to develop its own concept. So far, only the general guideline ('Preserving social stability') is known. An informal working group which involves the social partners will assist the Social Committee of the Rada to develop the new concept. It is not clear to what extent the new concept will differ from the previous one. It may be assumed that some elements will be similar. It is hence useful for the coming debate to analyse the principal elements of the previous concept (here called the December 1993 Concept).

The December 1993 Concept encompassed four branches of social security (unemployment benefits, health care benefits, employment injury and employment related disease benefits, pension benefits), safeguards against the loss of income due to inflation, provides social assistance to the disabled and poor and provides benefits for victims of technological, environmental and natural disasters.

The concept aimed at a clarification of the respective responsibilities of the state, employers and individuals for social protection of the population. According to the key principles, the state will have the role of guarantor of a minimum level of protection. This implies that it would remain responsible for determination of minimum protection norms, such as minimum wages, minimum pensions and the minimum subsistence levels (or the SAIL). It would also finance some family benefits but its main financial contribution would consist of the financing of social insurance benefits for the disabled and the poor.

Employers, employees and, to a lesser extent, self-employed persons would be the main financiers of the social security component (i.e., the system of all benefits for persons who are in the labour market) of the overall social protection system through introduction of social insurance financing principles. While reflecting new economic and social realities, the reform proposal was, hence, also – as most other national social protection reform concepts in the region – an attempt to shift a major proportion of the social protection expenditure 'off budget'.

The concept established a set of rules governing the population coverage and the mandate for the following four independent Social Insurance Funds.

- Pension Insurance,
- Health Insurance (also providing short-term cash benefits in case of sickness and maternity),
- Unemployment Insurance and
- Employment Injury Insurance.

The basic principles which were supposed to govern all four branches of social insurance are listed below.

- Compulsory coverage of all employees.
- Right to cover self-employed, artists, farmers and members of co-operatives.
- Right to introduce an additional insurance for all those who are compulsorily insured.
- Sharing the contributions between employees and employers, except for the occupational injury scheme, for which contributions will be paid exclusively by employers.
- Contribution amounts according to the individual ability to pay them as percentage of earnings subject to contributions.
- State contribution to unemployment insurance which will also provide selective labour market measures (job placement services, training and retraining, etc.).
- State guarantee for benefit levels and the financial viability of social insurance schemes.
- Autonomous management of the schemes by trade unions and employers, but subject to state supervision.

The December 1993 concept stipulated in broad terms the range of benefits to be provided by the individual branches of social insurance as well as their sources of funds (*Table 7.4*). The determination of benefit levels will be subject to later legislation. Parallel to the social insurance approach, the concept outlines a complementary social assistance scheme, Social Assistance to Disabled and Poor. According to this, the scheme was supposed to maintain the present functions of social assistance (providing benefits to families raising children, providing benefits in kind to the poor, providing nursing homes or old age homes for pensioners and disabled persons, and providing social pensions for those without entitlement to old age pensions). But means tested cash benefits to the poor were be added to the portfolio of the scheme. The financing share of local budgets is assumed to increase gradually.

The concept also stipulated that a system of interconnected measures should be devised to protect the population to some extent against the loss of standard of living due to the rise of consumer prices. These measures seemed to consist of a system of guarantees rather than real cash transfers. It appeared that the government would ensure that the minimum levels of wages, pensions and subsistence were regularly adjusted in line with inflation, whereas incomes policy in general was to strike a balance between the need to protect the real standard of living and the macroeconomic goal of containing inflation. No concrete measures to achieve the above goals were spelled out.

Table 7.4 *Benefits and Sources of Funds for Four Envisaged Social Insurance Branches, Ukraine, 1994*

Branch	Benefits	Sources of funds
Unemployment insurance	Active labour market measures: • occupational counselling, • training and retraining of unemployed, • job placement services, • organisation of public works programmes and • payment of unemployment benefits.	Contributions from • employers and • employees Subsidies from • state and • local government. Donations from • enterprises and • individuals.
Health insurance	• Medical care for insured persons and their dependants. • Cash benefits in case of sickness of insured persons. • Care for sick children. • Maternity, birth and funeral grants. • Cures in sanatorium and spas. • Parental leave benefit till age three of a child. • Medical care for the non-insured.	• Contributions from employers. • Donations from various sources.
Insurance against employment injuries and diseases	• Short-term and long-term cash benefits in case of employment related injuries and diseases. • Indemnities for health damages and loss of breadwinner. • Incentive payments to enterprises in order to reduce the level of accident and health risks.	• Employers' contributions.
Pension insurance	• Old age pension. • Survivors' pension. • Invalidity pensions. (based on contribution payments and, hence, individual incomes during entire working life).	Contributions from • employers and • employees.

The last major component of the reform concept was the setting up of a scheme for the protection of individuals against damages (notably physical impairments) incurred by technological, environmental and natural catastrophes. This component reflected the country's traumatic experience with compensation of individual victims of the Chernobyl disaster. The scheme was to be funded by contributions from the state and local budgets, enterprises and individuals but no details are given on the possible benefit package.

With respect to the complementary roles of social insurance and social assistance, the overall structure of the suggested social protection system strongly resembled those operating in central and western Europe, notably the one in the Federal Republic of Germany.

The concept envisages that the transition to the new social protection system has to proceed in careful steps so as not to overwhelm the population with measures that they would perceive as renunciation of achieved social rights (for example the substitution of the right to employment by the right to benefits in case of unemployment). The provisions on the exact functioning of the branches of social security are expected to be regulated by up to 10 specific laws, one of which was to be a 'basic law on social insurance'.

The basic Law on Social Insurance has been drafted by the Ministry of Labour. It aims to achieve the following.

- Establishing the four different social insurance schemes.
- Defining their population coverage (compulsory and voluntary).
- Establishing the principle of self-governance for the four schemes.
- Establishing the mandate of the representative assemblies of the schemes and the procedure for the election of the members.
- Determining the mandate and establishment of the governing board of the schemes.
- Defining the state supervision of the schemes.
- Defining the sources of funds for the individual schemes and regulating the procedure for the determination of the contribution rates and the payment of contributions.
- Setting the frame for accounting and reporting procedures.
- Requiring the provision of a unique social insurance number to each insured person.
- Defining the range of benefits to be guaranteed by the four insurance schemes.

This draft law has been discussed with the trade union and employer bodies. The trade unions disagreed with some points. The major point of disagreement was the integration of today's Social Insurance Fund (i.e., the short-term cash benefit scheme, as well as cures at spas and sanatoria) into the health insurance and, hence, its removal from direct trade union control. This issue might turn out to be a major stumbling block for social protection reform. Autonomous trade union administration of short-term cash benefits may be incompatible with privatisation, especially if fragmentation of the unions would continue and their membership levels would decline. But fundamental social protection reforms have to be based on wide societal consensus. No consensus will be reached without the unions and therefore a compromise has to be achieved consolidating the interests of the unions and the government.

The new Reform concept will have to be worked out in a constructive spirit between between the Government, the Rada, the government and social partners. So far, only the Council of Ministers has formulated clear clear requirements for the reform process. These requirements are:

- The public encouragement of various forms of 'self-protection' of the population.
- Implementation of an effective social assistance scheme.
- Encouragement of additional 'voluntary social insurance systems' providing complementary benefits.
- Improvement of the operations of the present social security system, notably by the enhancement of its contribution collection capacity (inter alia by more inherent collaboration with the tax authorities).
- Reorganisation of the management of the Social Insurance Fund.
- Introduction of greater individual differentation of Pension Amounts.

The outcome of the decision making process between the main stockholders in the social protection system (Government, Parliament and social partners) remains to be seen. The key elements of reforms presently discussed for the benefit structure of individual components of the social protection system are discussed in the following sections.

6.2. Pension Reform

As far as pensions are concerned, the discussion on benefit reforms has concentrated on raising the retirement age to ease the demographic burden of the pension scheme and on the prohibition of simultaneous employment and receipt of pensions or at least the creation of financial disincentives for it. A phased raising of the retirement age is also discussed and the benefit formula for pensions will be reviewed.

The Ministry of Labour has contemplated abolishing the 'band approach' in the calculation of reference earnings. Reference earnings should be the average revealed lifetime earnings of an employed person.

The Ministry assumes that the present legal replacement rates (55% plus 1% for each additional year in excess of 25 respectively) can be maintained. Employer and employee contributions will replace the present combination of employer provided payroll surcharges and state subsidies.

Participation of employees in the financing of the schemes is controversially debated, notably since plans of the Government do not foresee a compensatory increase of wages. The unions do not accept an unconditional introduction of employee contributions. They would accept employee contributions into individualised accounts, whereas employer contributions could finance a statutory pension scheme. While this appears to have all elements of a two-tier scheme, with one component being de facto the provident fund, the exact concept has not been spelled out.

6.3. Health Care Reform

The Ministry of Health drafted an outline for reform of the health care delivery and financing system in early 1993. The main component on the delivery side was the introduction of the family doctor system in order to put more emphasis on personal primary health care. The key element on the financing side is the introduction of health care services through compulsory insurance. The Ministry of Health has received advice from a range of international agencies and consultants, notably the World Bank and a group of Canadian health care consultants.

The National Institute of Health drafted a Law on Health Insurance which described the broad principles of the new system. The scheme was based on a National Health Insurance approach to cover the whole population in principle. A National Fund for Health Care was to collect contributions (initially 4% of wages which appeared low) and to allocate them according to a formula (applied to variables like age structure, gender composition and regional indicators) to different insurance carriers to be selected by the population.

Insurance carriers, whether public, private or statutory, would have to practice open enrolment. They were to finance non-capital costs of services for their members. For the time being, the capital cost will still be met by the public budget. The latter is mainly due to the fact that the government did not expect rapid privatisation of the health care delivery system. The present reform discussion also envisages payment of GP services on a capitation basis and payment of hospital services on the basis of DRG principles. The number of DRGs discussed (about 2,500 across hospitals of all categories and regions) is high and could easily turn the payment system into a fee-for-service system. The financing part of this proposal, i.e. reliance on managed competition between insurance carriers, showed characteristics of the health care reform under discussion in the Nether-lands.

In the meantime, the financing elements of the reform proposals have been modified considerably by the December 1993 Concept for social pro-tection reform, which envisaged a social insurance financing system poten-tially complemented by a complementary and voluntary private insurance. The Ministry of Health now envisages that insurance carriers for basic insurance will be exclusively statutory social insurance funds governed by a board composed of employer and employee representatives and organ-ised on a local basis. Smaller localities might jointly create a single fund. The total number of individual funds could still reach 300.

All funds should join a National Health Insurance association, which will supervise the operations of the local funds and initially also play a con-siderable role in the management of the local funds. The main financial function of the National Association will consist of the operation of an equalising fund, which will compensate for disadvantages of local sickness funds (which would normally have higher contribution rates) for specific risks (for example high share of old people, or certain health risks like AIDS cases etc.).

6.4. Unemployment Benefits

A Law on the Unemployment Fund has been discussed by the Ministry of Labour and the Employment Service. The deadline for the first draft of the law was apparently the end of 1994, but might now be delayed depending on the provisions of the new social protection reform concept.

One of the major elements of the benefit modification will be the increase of the minimum benefit, which should be linked to the SAIL rather than to the minimum wage. This would abolish the social anomaly of unem-ployment benefit recipients receiving benefits below the minimum subsis-tence level defined by the social assistance scheme. No major other modifications of the existing benefit provisions are presently discussed.

However, provisions on benefits for under-employment (partial unem-ployment) might have to be incorporated. There are indications that eligi-bility conditions for benefit receipt might be tightened and replacement rates might be modified, but no details are known.

6.5. Other Elements of Reform

In spite of being singled out as top priority by many experts, the future shape and functioning of the social assistance scheme still seems less clear than that of the social security benefits. The Ministry of Social Protection has just started to develop the concept. The plans in the Ministry of Health for health care reform and the Ministry of Labour for pension and other social security benefits appear more advanced. No details are known of any potential reform of the family benefit system.

A streamlining of the benefits and the operation of the Chernobyl Fund appears likely. No details are known.

7. Conclusions and Recommendations

The population faces dramatic social and economic uncertainty. Poverty is on the upsurge and the social protection system provides (inflation eroded) benefits not even to all in need. Does the reform process provide any signs of hope?

The answer, in spite of all obstacles, is yes. Yes, under certain conditions. These conditions as well as the strengths and weaknesses of the current reform process are spelled out in the following observations on specific characteristics of the reform process. While the section tries to avoid to be prescriptive some key recommendations for further consideration of policy makers presently charged with developing a new reform concept are also developed.

7.1. General Observations

There is no guarantee of success but most of the reform elements presently discussed appear to point in the right direction. Above all, the willingness of the government and the Rada to develop as a first priority a comprehensive reform concept which should ensure that the individual subsystems of the overall national social protection system are compatible with each other deserves to find the national consensus and support which it requires.

It cannot be judged to what extent the reform plans which have been discussed up to now, will outlast the review which the new Rada has just started. However, it is expected that – while a new round of discussions will concentrate on future benefit levels – the basic structural elements of the reform have a good chance to be maintained by the parliamentary majority and the government.

It is apparently well understood that the transition to a social insurance financing system will have to stretch over several years. Social protection experts in the Ministries of Labour, Social Protection, Health and the National Institute of Health are aware that the transition from one system to the other has to progress in a series of careful steps and has to be kept in tune with the overall social protection reform. This is a positive departure from the situation prevailing in other countries of the region.

In spite of debate about the competence for the drafting of the reform of the pension and short-term cash benefits, there seems an ongoing debate between the Ministries, the Supreme Soviet and unions and employer organisations on conceptual issues of the reform of the social protection system. Such a debate is the prerequisite for achievement of a national consensus. And that consensus is in turn a prerequisite for far reaching social policy reforms which impact on the lives of more than one generation. The necessity of an – as complete as possible – national consensus on social protection reforms appears to be accepted by all 'stakeholders'.

If the present consultation process continues there is a good chance that the conceptual framework for the social protection reform will be developed in a consolidated, comprehensive and coherent way. This again is a positive departure from other approaches in the region.

7.2. Observations on Specific Reform Elements

7.2.1. Consensus and Governance

A new system of governance for the social protection scheme in general and its individual subsystems has to be established. The system of governance encompasses all elements of social protection design, management and administration. It ranges from the establishment of mechanisms to obtain national consensus on planned reforms, mechanisms to govern individual schemes through performance monitoring by 'stakeholders' down to administrative and management control and auditing. The system of governance ultimately determines how well a social protection system functions.

Sound governance should first ensure national consensus on the basic structure and level of protection offered by the overall national social protection system and its component parts. The trade unions will hold a key role in the shaping of a national consensus. They should play an important albeit new and different role in this new system of governance. But autonomous trade union administration of short-term cash benefits could soon become incompatible with the new industrial structures brought about by structural change and privatisation. Increasing union fragmentation and declining 'unionisation' of the labour force also make union administration of a social protection scheme difficult. No consensus will be reached without the unions, and hence a compromise will have to be achieved consolidating the interests of the unions and the government.

Instead of operating one scheme (short-term benefits), which gave them some leverage (which for obvious reasons is difficult to give up) and influence on workers, unions will now have to be an active partner in the national and subsystem supervision and management of social protection. They will have to represent the interests of the protected persons on the governing and managing boards of all social security systems (not only the short-term benefit system). In order to make the change acceptable for the unions it might be necessary to maintain enterprise based 'social services funds' which could remain under union control but would no longer provide short-term cash benefits. The funds could provide the non-cash benefits like cures at a spa and other recreation benefits to the workforce of the respective enterprise, which are presently provided by the Social Insurance Fund. Compromises also come in packages. It might not be possible to ask the unions to give up control on one fund and ask them to accept not fully compensated increased employee contributions for social insurance at the same time. There seems to be room for manoeuvre and a chance that the unions will accept a new role in a modern social protection systems. It is hoped that the reform process will not be made a battleground for short-term politicking.

7.2.2. The Benefit Debate

One of the central elements of the present debate is the pension reform. The financial weight of the system (it accounts for almost 45% of all social protection expenditure) justifies this focus to some extent. The discussed main elements of the reform, i.e a step-by-step increase of the retirement age and a modernisation of the pension formula, are definitely necessary. But the structure of the benefits, eligibility conditions as well as the phasing in of the reform have to be aligned with reform efforts in other social protection subsystems notably other cash benefits, for example the social assistance scheme and the unemployment benefit system. A discussion on the overall structure and interaction of all cash benefits is necessary. This is the politically most sensitive aspect of the reform process. National consensus will ultimately hinge on consensus on the envisaged benefit levels and hence on the redistributive nature of the social transfer system.

No social protection system operates in an economic vacuum. The present debate on the structure and level of (notably cash) benefits often appears to be strangely aloft of economic constraints.

Social protection benefits have to some extent be adapted to the actual and expected longer-term economic environment. The structure, composition and level of social protection benefits has to be planned based on short and longer-term economic and labour market scenarios. The main characteristics of the latter are presently acute shortage of financial resources and uncertainty. The benefit structures have to reflect this. Cash benefits for almost all contingencies (except of social assistance benefits) could thus consist of a basic layer to combat poverty and a social security layer which allows the building up of additional protection in the longer run. The two benefit components could be adjusted at two speeds: the basic layer should follow inflation or average wage and the second layer could be adjusted in line with the general economic development. The second tier adjustment could hence implicitly reflect the ability of the respective social insurance funds to finance benefit adjustments. Thus efforts to protect the real value of basic layer benefits and simultaneously adjust the overall national social expenditure (including the second tier benefit expenditure) in times of economic distress could be facilitated. Benefit systems in uncertain economic environments should hence contain social and financial stabilisers which permit a sensible 'targeted' adjustment of social expenditure to economic developments.

7.2.3. The Financing Reform

The presently favoured financial reform envisages a redistribution of the financing shares for social protection between employees, employers and the state. It appears to be also necessary to design a financing system which on the one hand does not overcommit the state budget and on the other hand does create a level of labour cost which hampers formal employment. While the overall labour cost in the country are still low due to low wages, the present differential between the gross wage and the costs of a worker for an employer is considerable. Only the social security contributions amount to 52% of the average wage (presently paid from the enterprise wage fund).

This differential provides a clear incentive for employers and employees in small enterprises to avoid formal employment. With a greater diversification of employment structures, one can expect increasing compliance problems at least on the 'borders' between the formal and informal labour market. In this context the discussed financing of apart of the health services through contributions as well as the continuation of the financing of the Chernobyl fund through payroll taxes has to be reviewed. A greater employee share at social insurance contributions might be helpful to reduce the difference between gross wage and overall labour cost. It would also indicate the responsibility of workers for the financing of their own social security systems. But – given the low wage levels – it would be unrealistic to increase the employee share of the overall financing of social security without wage compensation. This would initially make the introduction of the social employee share almost cosmetic, but would help to distribute future cost increases between employers and employees. As mentioned above the financing system also needs a series of 'stabilisers' which will help to keep the system in financial equilibrium if the economic situation dete-

riorates even further. The overall 'financing plan' for the social protection
system still needs to be worked out in more detail.

7.2.4. The Sequencing of the Reform Process

The December 1993 reform concept established a priority for rapid deployment of anti-poverty mechanisms in a social assistance scheme. The
deficiencies of the present social assistance system make this urgent.
Consolidation of the unemployment benefit system which will have to bear
the brunt of the social impact of faster privatisation should enjoy the same
priority. It appears that the reform of other branches of social protection,
notably the health financing system, is not of the same importance. In particular, a possible implementation of a health insurance scheme has to be
prepared carefully. A streamlining of the public delivery system should be
undertaken first. Tough decisions on the downsizing of the provider structure will have to be made. They should be made now. A possible new social
insurance scheme will be overstretched when asked to trigger a restructuring of the delivery system through provider payment systems and contractual arrangements, the functioning of which it does not fully understand.
Burdening a new health insurance system with an oversized public provider
system would almost certainly lead to a cost explosion in the health sector,
which in turn might crowd out resources available for other parts of the
social protection system.

A further set of difficult decisions is probably due in the Chernobyl
Fund. The Fund consumes as much national resources as the overall health
care system. In view of the overall level of social protection spending, the
range of benefits as well as the operations of the Fund have to be reviewed.
The issue is no doubt politically sensitive but needs to be addressed.

7.2.5. The Implementation Procedures

The key to success of the reform will be proper planning of the implementation. Concepts and laws are quickly written. It is the deployment of
proper management and administrative structures that decide whether 'well
meant' intentions can be put into 'well done' practice. The first thing to
ensure is proper management of change, i.e. ensure that the process follows
a proper development path. A clear locus of overall responsibility for the
process has to be defined. This is apparently lacking. Second, the administrative structure for the new schemes should be prepared now. This means
that a sufficient number of experts should be trained in social assistance
management and administration (for example, in techniques to identify the
needy) and social insurance managers must be trained. Only well prepared
and highly motivated staff can successfully implement new schemes.

The design of sustainable social protection systems implies that sound financial and economic studies must be undertaken to assess whether the country can afford a certain level of protection in the short-term or long-term. No economic and actuarial analysis of the impact of alternative models of benefit and financing reforms seems to have been undertaken. Although actuarial and economic assessments are difficult in highly inflationary situations, that cannot be an excuse for not undertaking such studies, at least in the form of best case and worst case scenario analyses.

If (and only if) such preparations are made and an additional element of credible flexibility is introduced into the new reform concept, which would allow to concentrate all efforts on the avoidance of a social catastrophe due to a worsening of the economic crisis, there is a chance that the reform process in Ukraine will lead to a sustainable and rational social protection system that could safeguard the reform process and provide acceptable social security to the population in the long run.

8. Present Technical Assistance and First Assessment of Additional Needs

8.1. Ongoing Assistance

Compared to other countries, the engagement of international technical assistance agencies in the social protection system has been rather limited. The following are the main technical assistance activities that have been completed, are in progress or are in the pipeline, as of early 1994.[25]

World Bank   The World Bank conducted an extensive study of the social protection system in Ukraine in 1992.[26] Apparently as a follow up, it has just started a project to strengthen the performance of the social assistance scheme. In a recent Aide Memoire, a host of further projects are mentioned. It has also commenced investigation of investments into the EDP software and hardware of the social security schemes. A health sector mission in January 1994 explored the possibility for further projects in health care. A major health care infrastructure and financing projects appears possible. In general – according to World Bank economists – major financing (in the three digit million dollar range) of social protection projects through World Bank Loans could commence after two to three years. World Bank sources have expressed a clear preference for the upgrading of the 'basic social safety net' component of the social protection system. But major preparatory work for loans would need to be initiated soon. Concrete

[25] The following list of ongoing technical assistance activities was provided by the MOL (Deputy Minister Malish) in early 1994.
[26] World Bank, 1994.

government requests are a prerequisite. Such requests, however, will depend on the characteristics of the new concept for social protection reform.

International Monetary Fund   The IMF conducted a fairly comprehensive inquiry into social expenditure as a component of their public sector expenditure studies. Concrete projects have not yet resulted from this activity. However, the government is presently negotiating a major adjustment loan with the Fund. Conditions for the loan are likely to include fiscal measures which will no doubt affect the social protection system. Legislative activities in social protection will hence be triggered during the fall of 1994. It is hoped that these activities will be compatible with the development of a new overall social protection concept.

German government   The German government (and the State government of Bavaria) provided the Ukrainian government with comments on the draft social protection reform concept and is providing legal drafting assistance for the formulation of the social security framework law.

French government   The French government is collaborating with the Ministry of Statistics to improve the statistical reporting on the social sector.

8.2. Technical Assistance Needs

The present scope of ongoing or planned technical assistance leaves room for a variety of further technical assistance projects in the field of social protection. The following observations are only of a preliminary nature. A more detailed assessment of technical assistance needs would require a more detailed analysis of the administrative, economic and financial aspects of the social protection system in Ukraine.

There is a need for a complete strategic, administrative and financial review of the social protection system as well as the reform process. According to our analysis, some elements of the present scheme are well developed but too complex (for example family allowances), others are underdeveloped (unemployment benefits and social assistance), others have structural, systemic and conceptual problems (pensions, health, Chernobyl Fund). The reform proposals presently discussed are offering solutions for a number but not all of these deficiencies. In particular the economic and financial analyses would need to be upgraded by impartial international advice. The UNDP and ILO have agreed to undertake such a review (under the UNDP's TSS1 arrangements). The main result is expected to be a relatively detailed Technical Assistance Plan for the social protection sector in the Ukraine. The mission will take place in November/December 1994 and will also be ready to assist government agencies with ad hoc advice concerning legislative measures expected for this fall.

Without prejudice for the outcome of the above review (but based on the limited analysis of the present social protection system and the reform proposals) further technical assistance could have three major aspects:

- Assistance appears to be needed in the design of social assistance benefits, the health care financing and delivery system, and the overhaul of the Chernobyl Fund, unemployment and family benefits as well as the lay-out of the overall financing plan for social protection (i.e. the appropriate mix between employer and employee contributions and general and local tax financing).
- Support is needed for the management of all branches of social security which could be financed on a social insurance basis. The need for staff training is crucial. The rapid transfer of skills and methodological tools for general and financial management is crucial.
- There is a need for assistance in legal drafting (for the drafting of detailed social protection laws in particular with respect to ILO standards) and the analysis of the financial and economic impacts of planned social security reforms.

Annex I *List of Family Benefits, Ukraine, 1994*

	Amount	Delivery Agent	Financed through
Parental leave			
a) Employed women, with			
• one child under age three.	MW	Employer	PF
b) Unemployed women, with			
• one child under age 2	0.5 x MW	LWO	GR through LB
• one child between 2 and 3	0.5 x MW		GR through LB
(family monthly income under three times the minimum wage).			
Benefits for large families			
• Three children under age 16.	MW	Employer or LWO	GR through LB
• Four and more children under 16.	2 x MW		LB through LB
Benefit for caring for a disabled child under age 16	MW	LWO	GR through LB
Income support for low income families with children under age 16 (less than LWO 3 minimum wage, age under 18 if in education).	0.5 x MW	Employer or LWO	GR through PF
Benefit for single parents with children under age 18			
• General benefit.	0.5 x MW	LWO	GR through LB
• Benefit for a parent raised in orphanage.	MW	LWO	GR through LB
Persons in military service	MW	LWO	GR through PF
Children in foster care if total benefits less than 2 x MW	2 x MW	LWO or Educational Institution	GR through LB
Benefit for children without alimony	0.5 x MW	LWO	GR through LB

Acronyms: MW, minimum wage, GR, general revenue, LB, local budget, LWO, local welfare office, PF, Pension Fund

Source: E. Libanova and O. Paliy, 1994; Ministry of Social Protection; 1994, World Bank, 1992.

Annex II *List of Main Chernobyl Benefits, Ukraine, 1994*

Type of benefit	Amount of benefit/conditions
Employment subsidies	
• Wage supplements for people working in contaminated areas	• 20 to 100% of wage depending on contamination level.
• Additional paid vacation	• 14 to 42 days depending on contamination.
• Business start-up loans	• level as required, for people evacuated from the area.
Evacuation benefits	
• Rental subsidy	• flat rate allowance for persons having to rent housing outside the contaminated area.
• Moving expenses	• as necessary.
• Relocation allowance	• 3 x MW.
• Wage payments while moving	• 0.5 x previous monthly wage.
Compensation	
• Contaminated household goods	• as necessary.
• Persons still living in contaminated areas	• 0.3 x MW to 0.5 x MW.
Short-term and long-term social security benefits	
• Temporary disability benefits	• 100% of previous wage.
• Supplement to old age pensions	• depending on degree of exposure to radiation, up to 100 % and more of minimum pension.
• Supplement to invalidity pension	• depending on the degree of exposure.
• Survivors' pensions	• 50% of minimum pension.
• One-time compensation for loss of breadwinner	• lump-sum (10,000 rubles in 1992).
Other benefits	
• Tax exemptions	• exemption from all taxes and duties for all persons affected by the catastrophe.
• Free transportation/cars	• all seriously affected persons.

Source: World Bank, 1992; Ministry of Labour, 1994.

Annex III *Tables*

Table A7.1 *Average Wage, Average Income and Average Consumption as a Percentage of Minimum Consumption Budget (MCB), Ukraine, 1991–1994*

	MCB (rubles, coupons, karbovanets)	Average wage (%)	Average income (%)	Average consumption (%)
1991				
November	355	230.7	132.6	132.5
December	452	287.6	159.1	151.3
1992				
January	1,766	93.8	50.1	46.3
February	2,015	91.7	52.2	37.0
March	2,260	91.5	55.9	45.7
April	2,430	126.3	69.3	49.8
May	2,775	128.7	69.0	52.4
June	3,509	155.7	82.2	53.9
July	4,300	126.5	83.9	59.9
August	4,650	122.7	75.7	66.8
September	5,135	149.7	86.7	76.2
October	5,720	153.2	86.3	74.8
November	7,060	160.3	90.0	64.5
December	9,500	211.3	114.9	84.6
1993				
January	19,700	77.0	59.1	46.4
February	25,530	76.0	58.6	49.0
March	31,100	73.7	58.8	37.1
April	38,500	65.3	57.8	48.3
May	49,100	62.0	43.6	42.6
June	84,250	69.2	48.3	35.6
July	116,000	62.1	53.2	38.7
August	141,100	57.2	50.3	43.8
September	245,500	77.4	58.7	43.2
October	423,000	56.7	41.5	31.3
November	615,200	49.9	40.5	36.1
December	1,173,000	67.8	33.7	28.2
1994				
January	1,439,900	53.0	25.7	21.1
February	1,612,700	47.1	27.0	22.5
March	1,720,800	49.2	27.1	27.1

Source: Ministry of Labour, 1994.

Table A7.2 *Level and Composition of the Minimum Consumption Budget (MCB) and Social Assistance Intervention Line (SAIL), Ukraine, 1992–1993*

	MCB* May 1992 IMF	MCB* 12/1/1993 Government	MCB* 12/23/1993 FTU	SAIL 12/1/1993 Government	SAIL 12/23/1993 FTU
Monthly amount (coupons, karbovanets)	31,590	645,313	1,176,161	216,000	311,848
Composition (%)					
Food	48.6		62.7	76.6	79.1
Non-food items	32.6		22.4	12.3	12.9
Others (services, payments etc.)	18.8		14.9	11.1	8.0
TOTAL	100		100	100	100

*MCB for adults

Source: IMF, 1992; Federation of Trade Unions, 1994; ILO-CEET calculations.

Table A7.3 *Annual Food Requirements for Adults in the Minimum Consumption Budget (MCB) and the Social Assistance Intervention Line (SAIL), Ukraine, 1993*

Items	MCB	SAIL	SAIL as a % of MCB
Milk products	336 litres	172 litres	51.2
Eggs	270	104	38.5
Butter	5 kg.	–	–
Meat products	50 kg.	23.6 kg.	47.2
Fish	15 kg.	3.2 kg.	21.3
Potatoes	105 kg.	100 kg.	95.0
Vegetables	120 kg.	70 kg.	58.3
Fruits	42 kg.	26 kg.	61.9
Bread	110 kg.	100 kg.	90.9
Oil	7 kg.	3.6 kg.	51.4
Sugar	33 kg.	19 kg.	57.6

Source: Federation of Trade Unions, 1993.

Table A7.4 *Demographic Structure of the Pension Scheme, Ukraine, 1985–1993 (thousand)*

	1985	1990	End of year 1991	1992	1993
*Number of pensioners** (with pensions in payment)					
All	12,038	13,084	12,997	13,728	14,001
Old age	8,541	9,713	10,294	10,737	10,865
Invalidity	1,352	1,313	1,329	1,362	1,452
Survivors	1,522	1,209	850	1,069	1,145
Social pensions		318	500	532	501
Others	623	531	24**	28	38
*Number of insured persons***	25,600	25,400	25,000	24,500	23,900
Demographic ratio Number of pensioners/ Number of insured persons	0.47	0.515	0.52	0.56	0.59

*Statistical sources and definitions vary slightly; in particular the distinction between pensions in payment and pensioners is not always made.
**In 1991, only early retirement pensions for full time employement are listed as other pensions. The difference is probably due to military pensions paid from other budgets than the pension scheme.
***Here estimates are equal to the number of employed persons at mid-year.

Source: E. Libanova and O. Paliy, 1994; Ministry of Social Protection, 1994; ILO-CEET calculations.

Table A7.5 *Financial Structure of the Pension Scheme, Ukraine, 1991–1993 (rubles, coupons, karbovanets)*

	1985	1990	End of year 1991	1992	1993
Average monthly pension					
All	68	104	540	9,735	292,071
Old age	73	110	555	10,204	306,902
Invalidity	57*	89*	583	10,469	317,445
Survivors	42	58	412	7,036	200,830
Social	–	–	332	3,773	102,349
Others		–	480	10,577	331,415
Average monthly income of insured persons subject to contributions	–	248	1,237	20,073	792,797
Financial ratio (Average pension/average income)					
Overall	–	0.42	0.44	0.48	0.37
Old age	–	0.44	0.45	0.51	0.39
Disability	–	–	0.47	0.52	0.40
Survivors	–	–	0.33	0.35	0.25
Social	–	–	0.27	0.19	0.13
Others	–	–	0.39	0.53	0.42

*General disability pensions only.

Source: E. Libanova and O. Paliy, 1994; Ministry of Social Protection, 1994; Ministry of Labour, 1994; ILO-CEET calculations.

Table A7.6 *Indicators of Distribution of Pensions, Ukraine, 1991–1993*

	Average pension/ Average social pension	Ratio in the end of the year Average pension/ Minimum pension	Average pension/ Maximum pension	Maximum pension/ Average wage
1991	1.63	1.22	0.41	1.07
1992	2.58	2.11	0.71	0.69
1993	2.85	2.43	0.81	0.45

Source: Ministry of Social Protection, 1994; ILO-CEET calculations.

Table A7.7 *Registered Unemployed and Benefit Recipients, Ukraine, 1991–1994*

	Employed	Registered unemployed	Benefit recipients	Benefit recipients as a % of the employed	Benefit recipients as a % of registered unemployed
1991					
July	25,000,000	1,400	700	0.00	52
October	–	4,900	3,400	–	69
1992					
January	–	10,300	7,800	–	76
April	–	29,100	21,100	–	73
July	–	47,200	35,000	–	74
October	24,000,000	63,900	49,000	0.20	77
1993					
January	–	73,200	49,900	–	68
April	–	78,800	48,900	–	62
July	–	75,800	40,200	–	53
October	–	79,500	38,300	–	48
1994					
January	–	83,900	40,000	–	48

Source: E. Libanova, 1994; Employment Service, 1994.

Table A7.8 *Estimated Social Budget, Ukraine, 1992–1994**

Expenditure item	Estimated cost as a % of GDP	
	1992	1993
Pensions	11.3	11.1
Short-term cash benefits	1.9	1.8
Unemployment benefits	1.2	0.6
Family benefits	2.0	0.8
Health	5.0	4.8
Chernobyl compensation	5.0	4.0
Social assistance	1.0	0.8
Cash compensation	1.6	1.0
Total**	29.0	24.9

*The 1992 and 1993 estimates are based on data available in June 1994. In late 1994 the nominal values for the 1992 and 1993 GDP were revised upward and hence latest estimates of the SERS are about 10–15% lower.
**Expenditure for military pensions is neglected here. It might be 0.7% of GDP.

Source: For 1992 IMF and ILO-CEET calculations. For 1993 estimates of the Ministry of Finance, Pension Fund and Unemployment Fund and ILO-CEET calculations.

8

Social and Labour Policy Priorities

1. Introduction

There have been complaints that, compared with other countries undergoing similar restructuring upheavals, Ukraine has been relatively neglected in the allocation of financial and technical assistance by the international community. If one considers its size and the depth of its social and economic problems, one can only agree.[1]

Without financial and technical assistance the inadequate conditions would become worse

---

Some might argue that the conditions to justify much greater financial and technical assistance have not existed. But this could become a vicious circle. Without assistance, perhaps the inadequate conditions would merely become worse, further undermining the ease of providing assistance. Technical assistance must be targeted at breaking the constraint to the development and implementation of effective social and labour policies.

Developing public administration should be given a priority in technical assistance

---

If there were just one area of technical assistance to be given priority from abroad, it would have to be assistance in developing an effective system of public administration. Although the size of the public administration is small, it has been criticised for being excessively rigid and

---

[1] The first US Ambassador to independent Ukraine (from June 1992 to July 1993) admitted that this complaint was well-founded. He attributed the neglect to (i) 'our own (US) economic problems', (ii) 'the failure (of Ukraine) to arrive at an economic plan with the IMF', and (iii) 'Washington's preoccupation with Russia.' R. Popaduik, 'Building American–Ukrainian Partnerships', address at Georgetown University, Washington D.C., October 9, 1993.

hierarchical, with most decisions having to be made at high level. This has apparently contributed to technical and financial assistance bypassing central government, deliberately so in at least the case of the United States Agency for International Development (USAID), which has concentrated on working with the regions.[2] This has certain merits. Yet it may lead to an uncoordinated and ultimately even contradictory or competing approach by foreign donors and regional authorities.

In the preceding Chapters, many policy recommendations have been made, and we will not attempt to repeat them all. Rather, this final Chapter attempts to set out a few priority issues that seem to deserve high priority in technical and policy formulation work in 1994–1995.

International meeting of donors should be convened

It is proposed that, as soon as practicable, the Ministry of Labour of Ukraine, in collaboration with the ILO and the United Nations office in Kiev, convene an international meeting of donors and technical agencies to review and expand the provision of social and labour market policy assistance. If possible, this should involve all heads of ILO technical departments.

2. Labour Markets and Labour Market Policies

Coherent labour market information system is needed

Labour market and employment policies can only be effective if developed in the context of a coherent macro-economic policy stance, preferably backed by an industrial and restructuring strategy. In Ukraine, the first need is better labour market information and more thorough analyses of the dynamics of the labour market. Fortunately, the Ministry of Statistics has a good professional base – to which we can testify, having worked collaboratively with it in carrying out the Ukraine Labour Flexibility Survey (ULFS) – and has developed and applied surveys suitable for monitoring labour market developments. Now, the need is to develop a coherent labour market information system, involving the Ministry of Statistics, the Ministry of Labour, including the National Employment Service, and the Ministry of Social Protection, as well as a network of academic specialists. The ILO is ready to assist in the development of that system.

[2] R. Popaduik, 1993, op. cit.

The Employment Law should be revised

In terms of policy, revisions are recommended in the Employment Law, notably in relationship to the process of registration of the unemployed and of entitlement to unemployment benefits. Also, regulations for dealing with mass lay-offs and for avoiding the misuse of administrative leave should be reviewed as a matter of some urgency. It is recommended that a working group be set up within the Government and that financial assistance secured to enable a small international group of specialists to be assembled to draft amendments to the Law to bring the regulations in line with good international practice. In particular, severance pay should not be a blockage to receipt of unemployment benefits in the first three months of unemployment.

The National Employment Service has progressed considerably since 1991. Although some labour market policies have already been introduced, their range, design and effect should be significantly strengthened. For instance, the programme of social (public) works should be associated with large investments into infrastructure so as to promote economic restructuring and growth. Participants should be offered retraining and appropriate utilisation of their skills in order to give them better future job prospects. Also policies promoting small businesses and self-employment should be expanded. Employment restructuring should be widely stimulated by such labour market policies as job creation schemes, training and retraining, assistance in restructuring of viable enterprises, etc. which should cover not only jobless workers but also those on 'administrative leave' or shorter working hours, or those threatened by unemployment.

Foreign donor partners should be enlisted to help in establishing a model employment centre

The Ministry of Labour would like to establish a 'model' employment centre, as a demonstration project, following the German Government's effort to set up such a service in Kiev. If this were to be done, it would be advisable for the Ministry to enlist at least two foreign donor partners, to ensure that a cross-section of national experiences in establishing model employment offices is taken into account, and to ensure that no single national donor is shouldering the entire burden. The Ukrainian authorities may gain in this regard from drawing on similar work done in other central and eastern European countries by the governments of such countries as Germany, the United Kingdom and the United States of America.

Tripartite mechanism should be established to advise on the development of the employment service

---

It is also recommended that the authorities, trade unions and employer organisations examine the feasibility of setting up a tripartite mechanism to govern and advise on the development of the employment service, according to lines laid down in ILO Convention No. 85. This would have many advantages, including the important one of legitimising its functions more effectively with both workers and employers throughout Ukraine.

The importance of regional policy will become more apparent in 1995, when we expect open unemployment in some regions to rise sharply. In terms of labour market policy, it is recommended that the authorities select one local area for a pilot project in developing a local labour market adjustment strategy. This would entail bringing together local groups, most notably the local authorities, the local employment service, the local trade unions and local employer organisations, to work out a comprehensive strategy for achieving employment restructuring and for responding to unemployment with policies at the local level. A great deal can and should be done to prepare for employment and labour market restructuring, and only if all the main groups are involved will local communities be able to come to terms with what is required.[3]

The growth of non-regular employment should be encouraged

In the area of employment policy, it is recommended that the authorities examine the feasibility of encouraging the growth of some forms of non-regular employment, including self-employment and small-scale businesses, including networks of small-scale and larger enterprises. It is also recommended that the authorities should consider ways of promoting part-time employment, which comprises a very small share of employment in Ukraine. With growing unemployment and a likely cut-back in state support of child care facilities, as well as the difficulty of maintaining full-time employment of older workers, it might be desirable to facilitate a growth of part-time employment, as long as it is voluntarily chosen by the workers. Those in part-time jobs should have similar rights and forms of protection as other workers, in accordance with conventional practices in many parts of western Europe.

[3] For such a pilot exercise in the Czech Republic, see A. Nesporova and R. Kyloh, *Economic and Social Dialogue in the Ostrava-Karvina Region*, ILO-CEET Report No. 5, Budapest, February 1994.

Workers with disabilities should be treated within the regular Employment service

Among the socially vulnerable groups affected by employment restructuring and rising unemployment, workers with disabilities have probably been most disadvantaged. We believe it is unfortunate that policies for dealing with their employment have been separated from employment policies for all other groups, and strongly recommend that as far as possible they should be treated within the regular employment service, and that appropriate policies for ensuring that they return to the mainstream of the labour market are developed. It is hoped that the Ministries of Labour and Social Protection will be able to draw on the advice and assistance of the ILO's Vocational Rehabilitation Branch and on the various international organisations with extensive experience with ensuring that workers with disabilities have equal opportunities and rights in the labour market.

Cooperative forms of employment should be regenerated

Finally, it is recommended that the regeneration of cooperative forms of employment be explored, particularly in agriculture through cooperative farms (some good experience has already been made with the so-called associated cooperatives which should be replicated in other regions of Ukraine). The ILO's Cooperative Branch should build on its work with the Ministry of Labour in 1993.[4] As the Minister of Labour stated at the time, cooperatives have played an important role in providing employment for those with limited labour market mobility, and they could be a vehicle for preventing the marginalisation of vulnerable social groups and be a means of promoting small-scale enterprises, as long as the legislative basis for cooperatives is established on a sound basis.

3. Wages and Incomes Policies

As far as wages and incomes are concerned, there are many aspects that deserve reform, and we recommend that five issues should be given top priority in 1995.

---

[4] International Labour Organisation and Ministry of Labour of Ukraine, *Economies in Transition and the Employment Problem: The Role of Cooperatives and Associative Enterprises,* Report of an International Seminar, Kiev, May 11–14, 1993.

The role of statutory minimum wage needs to be examined

First, it is recommended that the statutory minimum wage be examined to determine what role it should play in the emerging labour market and to determine how it should be set and adjusted. As we have seen, the minimum wage in Ukraine has been detached from reality, providing no income protection for low-paid workers and contributing to impoverishment rather than the reverse because of its role in determining some social transfers and in setting the base of the wage tariff system. We recommend that a commission be established to report to the government within six months on a reform of the minimum wage, and that this commission should have representatives of workers and employers as well as the relevant governmental agencies. It would be advisable to secure some external funding to enable the commission to obtain the services of consultants familiar with the role and effectiveness of minimum wages in international labour markets. The ILO's Industrial Relations Department would wish to assist in the work of such a commission.

The wage tariff system needs to be reviewed

Second, a review of the wage tariff system would be advisable. It is increasingly hard to operate in the context of decentralisation and property restructuring of enterprises, and may be an impediment to enterprise restructuring and to productivity growth. The issue can be linked to other aspects of the wage determination process, such as the high ratio of non-monetary to monetary forms of remuneration, the forms of payment (time rate, piece rate, etc.) and the roles and extent of 'bonuses' and other payments that are not part of the standard wage. We recommend that a special project to examine the wage determination system be launched as soon as possible, to determine how Ukrainian practice can move towards the best practices found in other economies. In particular, we believe it would be appropriate to examine wage reform in the context of considering the feasibility of various forms of economic democracy in the context of the property restructuring of enterprises and the spread of joint-stock companies.

The process of wage indexation should be reviewed

Third, a review of the process of wage indexation is needed to try to break the inflationary cycle that is typically associated with indexation procedures. This should be done carefully and systematically, so that the equity objectives of indexation are not sacrificed.

The tax-based incomes policy should be examined

Fourth, the tax-based incomes policy should be examined with the objective of introducing a reform to overcome the drawbacks of that policy mentioned in Chapter 4. Imposing a high tax on wage increases may deter productivity growth and lead to labour market and social policy distortions, notably a shift away from the payment of money wages to 'services' and benefits and to unrecorded, untaxable forms of remuneration.

The tax system should be reviewed

Fifth, the tax system should be reviewed. In the main, this is outside our remit, yet it is clear that many taxes in Ukraine adversely affect the operation of the labour market and hinder production and employment. In particular, the tax on profits should not be applied to the wage bill, but only to actual profits. Also, for many reasons, tax-collecting discipline must be strengthened, and fiscal methods should be considered for encouraging the growth and legitimacy of small-scale business and productive self-employment.

In sum, wage policy reform is vital to the economic regeneration of Ukraine, and much can be done in a reasonably short period to make the wage determination system a much improved mechanism for promoting and rewarding labour productivity while avoiding gross inequalities that come from outmoded, rigid systems that invariably induce abuse from privileged minorities.

4. Labour Legislation and Industrial Relations

A project to review the Labour Code should be developed

The highest priority in the sphere of labour legislation is a fundamental review of the Labour Code. This is not a minor undertaking, given the comprehensive nature of that regulatory apparatus. This too may best be treated by the establishment of a special tripartite commission, which could draw on experts (probably from abroad) on the various subjects covered by the Code, and then make detailed recommendations on the various parts of the Code. In any case, it is recommended that a project be developed, preferably funded by a multilateral or bilateral donor, to review the Code and make very specific recommendations on the sort of reforms discussed in this review, notably in Chapter 5. In the same connection, those responsible should also examine the elements of the Employment Law to ensure compatibility with the new and more flexible labour regulations that should emerge from this exercise.

To establish industrial relations suitable for a regulated market-oriented economy, institutional procedures must be clear and transparent. In that regard, it was a very positive development that in May 1994 the Supreme Council ratified ILO Convention No. 144 on Tripartite Consultation (International Standards) and ILO Convention No. 154 on Collective Bargaining. The relevant technical units in the ILO would be prepared to assist in bringing the legislation and national procedures into line with the obligations under those Conventions.

In particular, it is recommended that the proposed Law on Procedures for Resolving Collective Labour Disputes should be finalised, and the means of reconciling the differences between the Government and the FPU be found. It may be useful if the negotiators invited the ILO to assist in reaching a compromise agreement compatible with ILO standards and international practice.

The National Council for Social Partnership should be strengthened

---

For the long-term development of an efficient, harmonious and socially equitable labour market, the National Council for Social Partnership should be strengthened. It is recommended that financial assistance be sought, perhaps from EU-TACIS or/and the UNDP, to provide a substantial long-term project to develop mechanisms of tripartism in general and to assist the Council members and the technical secretariat to become more technically efficient and effective, based on the experience in western Europe, in particular, and on the valuable experience gained by countries in central Europe since 1989 where tripartite councils have been operating. The ILO Central and Eastern European Team (ILO-CEET), in collaboration with the ILO's Industrial Relations Department, would be prepared to organise a seminar in Kiev in order to bring leading officials from the main tripartite councils of western European countries to advise on the most appropriate procedures to follow.

Training mechanism for trade unionists should be established

It is also recommended that a mechanism be established, perhaps as a component of the NCSP, by which an equal number of employer representatives, trade unionists and government officials dealing with industrial relations should be enabled to acquire training and practical experience of industrial relations and collective bargaining practices in western Europe and elsewhere. In that regard, it would also be desirable to ensure Ukrainian participation in all multinational training courses in the ILO's Training Centre in Turin. And it would be desirable to obtain financial assistance to make it possible to have texts of labour laws and industrial relations material translated and to have texts that already exist in Russian distributed more widely in Ukraine.

Laws concerning industrial disputes should be amended

Finally, in this area, it is recommended that the issue of strikes and other industrial disputes be analysed in detail to determine what should be amended in the laws and in the institutional framework, since it is likely that in the difficult period of economic and employment restructuring labour market tensions will escalate, so that it will be important to ensure that the institutional machinery for resolving industrial relations disputes is well-founded. In particular, the establishment of a national service for the mediation and reconciliation of strikes should be a priority. In that regard, the Ukrainian authorities should be able to draw inspiration from the ILO Voluntary Conciliation and Arbitration Recommendation, No. 92, of 1951, and the many years of experience with refining the conciliation and arbitration machinery outlined in that Recommendation. The relevant specialists in the ILO would be prepared to assist in developing the appropriate procedures and legislation.

5. Trade Unions

The trade unions in Ukraine have a difficult set of responsibilities and enormous challenges to meet in the next few years. As we have seen, it is difficult to make sharp distinctions between 'old' and 'new' unions or types of union, particularly because Ukraine only became independent in 1991. For the future of worker representation in the country, it will be vitally important that mainstream trade unions do not waste their energies and resources on inter-union rivalry and competition, beyond that required to ensure that all unions become more representative of ordinary workers and that membership levels are raised because workers respect and value the union roles.

In the same vein, it will be important that the international and other foreign trade union organisations give constructive assistance and advice to trade unionists in Ukraine, and that no foreign union body contributes to any unnecessary inter-union rivalry, which could have long-term deleterious effects on the level of unionisation in the country.

Practical training should be made feasible

Undoubtedly, all trade unions in Ukraine need greater experience and training in developing and operating trade union affairs. Along with the suggestions made in the previous section, it is recommended that more opportunities be created to enable trade union officials to participate in training courses in Ukraine, and if possible to have periods of work within trade union organisations in a variety of European countries and within the international bodies representing trade unions. It is hoped that donor agencies will make such practical training feasible in the near future. The ILO Workers' Education Branch and the ILO's Central and Eastern European Team are ready to act as conduits for this process.

6. Employer Organisations

In the five years since the emergence of the first organised employer group in Ukraine, a quite representative network of organisations of employers has developed. However, due to lack of legal and political support for the independence of social institutions, as well as ambiguity as to the concept and purpose of the various organisations among their own members and leaders, much remains before the employer side can fully face the expectations and demands of the emerging Ukrainian social partnership, and contribute effectively to Ukraine's transition.

Independence of employers' organisations must be ensured

The first step is necessarily to arrive at a clarity of purpose and achieve a general distinction of the roles and responsibilities of employers and their organisations more oriented to practical promotion of their labour market and production functions, and to re-focus their overtly political lobbying to that of promoting precise reforms fundamental to efficient enterprise.

Secondly trade union and employer organisations must expand their dialogue and seek ways that would enable them to negotiate and conclude collective agreements. By allowing independent organisations of employers to represent also state owned firms and farms, the government can deliver much-needed political support to employers, as well as influence public opinion favourably on their behalf. This is especially important in Ukraine's case since the bulk of economic activity will remain owned or controlled by the state (including lease-held firms and farms) for some time.

In order to promote the development of efficient, professional organisations of employers in Ukraine, the transfer of relevant experience from other central and eastern European countries should be facilitated. In these countries employer organisations have evolved through very similar processes as can be observed in Ukraine. It is recommended that increased financial assistance be provided to the major employer organisations so as to enable them to participate in training programmes, seminars, employer conferences and other events designed to demonstrate how to play a constructive role in tripartite mechanisms of social and labour market policy consultations and in the governance of social protection systems.

Finally, employer organisations must play a constructive role in promoting small-scale and informal enterprise, and in assisting in the difficult process of legitimising much of the informal economy that has been a source of survival and, to a certain extent, of economic dynamism in the early disruptive phase of economic restructuring. It is important that much of the more productive activity in the informal economy is brought into the mainstream economy, and employer organisations could play a major role in ensuring that this occurs without destroying the productive potential that many informal activities possess.

7. Social Protection

The social protection system in Ukraine has been in a state of crisis, in the negative and positive sense of the term. The old system based on full employment and distribution of numerous forms of benefit, mainly through enterprises and the trade unions, has been eroded, such that poverty has become endemic and many people have found themselves exposed to insecurity and the need for social transfers to cover newly-experienced contingencies. At the same time, as Chapter 7 argued, many of the reforms and proposals have been moving the system forward in a constructive manner, so that there is an opportunity to establish an efficient, equitable and comprehensive system of social protection.

The Concept of social protection reform should be developed

A first priority should be the determination of the overall strategy of reform, and in that regard, in the context of the new Parliament and Government, it is recommended that the so-called concept of social protection reform developed in early 1993 should be reviewed and agreed by the authorities as soon as possible. Any delay in developing a viable comprehensive strategy could have disastrous consequences for the evolution of social protection and, most importantly, for the well-being of the people of Ukraine, large numbers of whom have been struggling to survive without proper or assured access to income transfers and social services, including health care, that are required to make their lives tolerable. National consensus on the new concept is a prerequisite for the success of social protection reform and should be sought at an early stage.

The ILO's Social Security Department, assisted by ILO-CEET, would be prepared to provide advice and assistance in this area, always bearing in mind that the design of the social protection system is entirely the prerogative of the Ukrainian authorities. Indeed, with financial assistance from the UNDP, the ILO will be assisting the authorities in refining the reform strategy. Particularly sensitive areas in the latter include clarification of the trade unions' role in the implementation of social insurance.

Upgrading of the Social Assistance Scheme is urgent

The present social assistance scheme shows serious deficiencies. It should be upgraded as a matter of absolute priority and equipped to reach more of the poor. Legal and administrative barriers to access to benefits for the needy should be removed. International assistance would help to benefit from experience in other countries with means-tested schemes.

A socially and economically appropriate social protection benefit structure should be developed

The structure volume and level of social protection benefits has to reflect the social priorities on the one hand and the likely future economic development which determines the ability of the country to finance benefits. An appropriate 'benefit strategy' reflecting the present economic uncertainity – combining urgent anti-poverty benefits with benefits providing 'earned' replacement income – should be developed for all cash benefits.

Unemployment benefit system should be reformed

On specifics, it is recommended that the unemployment benefits system be reviewed and reformed. As emphasised in Chapters 2, 3 and 7, it is clear that the entitlement conditions and the levels and duration of unemployment benefits need revision.

All aspects of the Chernobyl Fund should be reviewed

Another very specific issue requiring reform is the Chernobyl Fund, which has been a valuable and regrettably essential tool of social policy since 1986. It is recommended that all aspects of the Fund be reviewed. As discussed in Chapter 7, the time has come for it to be overhauled, and it would be advisable if a donor agency could provide financial assistance to ensure professional assessment of how to achieve that without adversely affecting the victims of that terrible tragedy.

The health care reform should be prepared carefully

The reform of the health care benefit system needs careful preparation for example through the realignment of the health care infrastructure. Financial risks affiliated with the financing reform are considerable and should be minimised through early preparation of the health care managment staff. Training in international experience with health care financing and management techniques is absolutely necessary.

The desirable pension system should be elucidated

More generally and very importantly, pension reform should not be delayed. It is recommended that to clarify the desirable pension system for Ukraine, a small technical conference of pension specialists be convened in Kiev, under the auspices of the Government and with involvement of international technical and financial agencies, including the International Social Security Association, the ILO, the IMF, the World Bank and the European

Union. This conference should clarify the advantages and disadvantages of alternative pension systems, including the mix of public and private pension provision.

A consensus-based national system of social protection governance should be designed

Another important aspect of the reform of social protection in Ukraine is the mechanisms by which it should be operated. Both the financing and management of a national system of social protection are complex and by their nature easily over-politicised. That is why the system of governance is so crucial. By this is meant the institutional structure and processes by which social protection schemes are designed, implemented, managed, monitored and evaluated. That could be done by an authority, as part of the government, or it could be done through independent tripartite organisations set up specially to oversee the system and be accountable to the various groups in the labour market, which are contributing to the system or likely to be drawing benefits from it.

It is recommended that the Government, trade unions and emerging employer organisations formulate a strategy for reforming the governance of social protection, and in that regard they may wish to secure financial assistance to establish a working group to draw up recommendations for the NCSP and the relevant Ministries on a feasible set of mechanisms and procedures for establishing them. It should be recognised that all three groups – government, unions and employers – would have advantages in establishing a representative body for overseeing the social protection system, as long as groups at the margin of society and vulnerable groups in the labour market are adequately represented.

Rapid transfer of skills and technical know-how needed

With the new role of the social protection system in the society new demands are placed on the general and financial management of the system. Managers and administrators need to acquire new skills and need to employ new management, financing and planning techniques (such as actuarial valuations). Skills and techniques have to be transferred on an urgent basis. No new social protection scheme can function without properly trained staff. The ILO stands ready to assist in the development of a training plan.

8. Concluding Points

A sense of urgency must be sustained. The challenge for Ukrainians in positions of responsibility for reforming social and labour market policies is enormous and daunting. It is almost inevitable that in transforming the old policies, numerous mistakes will be made. That is one reason for valuing social consensus as a vehicle for reform, since only through consultation and negotiation between the authorities and representative groups in the labour market will policy reforms be legitimised. And only if they are legitimised will they have a good chance of being implemented in the local communities and factories and farms and offices across the vast area of Ukraine.

Critics of 'consensual policies' sometimes dismiss the pursuit of consensus on the grounds that the necessary negotiations and incorporation of trade unions and employer organisations in decision-making processes result in rigidities, inertia and excessive compromises. That could be true. Yet without consultation and agreement the policies are unlikely to be implemented or legitimised. And those considerations remain essential to democratic reform.

Conclusions from the International Conference 'Reforming Labour Market and Social Policy in Ukraine'[5]

1. Labour legislation should be refined in connection with
   - severance pay;
   - entitlement, provision and level of unemployment benefits;
   - misuse of administrative leaves;
   - mass layoff procedures.

2. Workers with disabilities should be treated within the regular Employment Service and policies promoting their employment and competitiveness in the labour market should be modified and developed.

3. The programme of social (public) works should be improved in order to promote economic restructuring and offer the participants better job prospects.

---

[5] These were the main conclusions and recommendations drawn from the Conference organised by the Ministry of Labour of Ukraine, ILO and the UNDP Office in Ukraine, Kiev, September 26–27, 1994 and the reports submitted to it. The following 22 recommendations were submitted to the Ministry of Labour for their reflection.

4. Policies promoting small businesses, self-employment and part-time employment should be introduced or expanded. Also, labour market policies promoting employment restructuring, such as job creation schemes, training and retraining, assistance in restructuring of viable enterprises, etc. should be strengthened and should cover not only job-less workers but also those on 'administrative leave' or those threatened by unemployment.

5. The Government should modify the tax system and other relevant legislation in order to bring the informal economy into the mainstream economy while promoting entrepreneurial activities and restructuring in the official economy. Also, tax-collection discipline should be strengthened.

6. Cooperative forms of employment should be promoted, as recommended in the conclusions of the joint ILO–Ministry of Labour of Ukraine conference of May 1993, especially in the form of 'associated cooperatives'.

7. The role of the statutory minimum wage as a base of income protection, determination of certain social transfers and setting of wage tariffs should be reconsidered in tripartite negotiations; the ILO recommends the authorities to disconnect the determination of the level of all social benefits from the minimum wage.

8. The wage tariff system should be reoriented towards more adequate decentralisation with the aim of promoting enterprise restructuring and productivity growth while guaranteeing a social minimum regardless of economic performance of the enterprise.

9. There was an agreement in the discussion that the Government should promote payment systems more closely linked to productivity and enterprise performance. At the same time, the minimum wage has to be adapted to the subsistence minimum, and the ILO recommends the Government's moves in that direction.

10. Wage indexation should be subject to collective bargaining with the aim of providing compensation for price increases without intensifying inflationary pressures.

11. The legislation and national mechanisms for industrial relations should be improved, with adequate international assistance in order to establish an appropriate framework for regular tripartite negotiations at all levels. In particular, the proposed Law on Procedures for Resolving Collective Labour Disputes should be finalised and enacted. The term 'lock-out' should be utilised only for temporary suspension of

contracts by employers in collective bargaining and problems of mass layoffs or closures of enterprises should be solved through appropriate labour legislation.

12. The National Council for Social Partnership should be strengthened to become a real tripartite body representing different interests of all three parties. Representatives of trade unions and employer organisations should be given training in collective bargaining practices in western European countries and should receive relevant information on the legal framework of industrial relations and their development in various countries, including 'economies in transition'. Also, establishment of a regional network of tripartite bodies of social partnership would be advisable.

13. The institutional machinery for resolving industrial relations' disputes should be improved so as to moderate existing and future labour market tensions.

14. Trade unions must be independent from government policy and from enterprise managements, to become strong partners in collective bargaining, in negotiations concerning privatisation and in other issues. They should build their own, independent and solid information base. They should pay appropriate attention to occupational safety and health.

15. It is important to increase the respect of workers for trade unions' activities. International trade union organisations should give constructive assistance and advice to Ukrainian trade unions.

16. As for employer organisations, it is important to achieve a distinction of their roles and tasks concerning their labour market and production functions and orient their activity and influence to promoting reforms fundamental to efficient enterprise.

17. The Government should transfer responsibility to represent state-owned enterprises in tripartite negotiations on independent organisations of employers and managers of state enterprises.

18. Employer organisations should play a constructive role in promoting small-scale business and entrepreneurship and in assisting in the process of bringing the informal economy into the mainstream economy.

19. It is important to find social consensus in reforming social protection systems. The Government, trade unions and employer organisations should formulate a strategy of reforming the governance of social pro-

tection and should control the operation of the reformed social protection system.

20. As the financing and management of a national system of social protection are complex, it is important to establish technical capacities and train staff in managing this system.

21. Ukraine should develop a system of social protection which
    - ensures social stability;
    - gives priority to adequate social assistance benefits;
    - ensures that social benefits are protected to the extent possible against inflation;
    - reflects in structure and level the financial and economic potential of the country.

22. Formulation of any effective labour market and social policies is crucially dependent on a coherent, reliable labour market and social protection information system reflecting relevant changes in the economy. Ukraine has made substantial progress in its development and all the involved institutions should collaborate on its further improvement, with technical assistance from the ILO and other international organisations.

Sources

Articles

M. Baglai, The Creation of a New System of Labour Relations in Russia, *Problems of Economic Transition*, September 1992.

I. Brzezinski and M. Zienchuk, Political Debate in Ukraine, *The Ukrainian Legal and Economic Bulletin*, Vol. 2, No. 1, January-February, 1994.

S. Clarke, Trade Unions, Industrial Relations and Politics in Russia, *The Journal of Communist Studies*, Vol. 9, No. 4, December 1994.

M. Conte and J. Svejnar, The Performance Effects of Employee Ownership Plans in A. Blinder (ed.), *Paying for Productivity – A Look at the Evidence*, Brookings Institution, Washington, D.C., 1990.

Ekonomika Ukrainy u 1993 rotsi, *Uriadovyi Kurier*, No. 14, January 25, 1994.

D. Gregory and L. Hethy, Trade Union Policy, *On Business and Work*, ILO, 1993.

Intelnews, Vol. IV, No. 55, February 25, 1994.

Intelnews, Vol. IV, No 56, February 26, 1994.

Intelnews, Vol. IV, No. 57, February 27, 1994.

D. Jones and T. Kato, The Productivity Effects of Employee Stock Ownership Plans and Bonuses: Evidence from Japanese Panel Data, *Industrial and Labour Relations Review*, 1993.

K. Kiss and V. Sidenko, Ukraine on the Way Toward Economic Stabilisation and Independence, *Eastern European Economics*, Winter 1992-1993.

D. Kruse, Profit-sharing and Employment Variability, Microeconomic Evidence on the Weitzman Theory, *Industrial and Labour Relations Review*, 44, April 1991.

L. Liu, Income Security in Transition for the Aged and Children in the Soviet Union and in the Russian Federation, *Social Security Bulletin*, Vol. 56. No. 1, Spring 1993.

J. MacNeil, Waiting for Change: Notes from the Underground, *Intelnews*, June 26, 1994.

D. Vaughan-Whitehead, Workers' Financial Participation: An East–West Comparative Perspective, *Economic and Industrial Democracy*, Vol. 14, No. 2, May 1993.

M. Weitzman and D. Kruse, Profit-sharing and Productivity, in A. Blinder (ed.), *Paying for Productivity – A Look at the Evidence*, Brookings Institution, Washington, D.C., 1990.

M. Zienchuk, Ukraine in Numbers, *The Ukrainian Legal and Economic Bulletin*, Vol. 2, No. 1.

Documents

Communiqué adopted by members of the round table of the President of Ukraine and the representatives of trade union associations, June 5, 1992.

Decision of the Cabinet of Ministers No. 26 – 837/4 of April 17, 1993.

Decree of the President of Ukraine on the National Council for Social Partnership, No. 34/93, February 6, 1993.

Decree on Targeted Cash Benefits to Low Income Persons, No. 394, Ukraine, June 14, 1993.

Draft Law on Submission of Alterations and Amendments into the Labour Code of Ukraine, Cabinet of Ministers of Ukraine, December 31, 1993, No. 26-2799/4.

Draft Law of the Ukraine on Trade Unions, 1991, based on a English translation of the draft, provided to the ILO by the FTUU.

Employment Fund, Statement of Income and Expenditure of the State Fund for the Promotion of Employment, Exercise, 1993.

FTUU, Resolution No. 11-12-1, Kiev, March 2, 1994.

General Tariff Agreement between the Cabinet of Ministers of Ukraine and Trade Unions of Ukraine, April 30, 1993.

ILO, Labour Law Documents, January 1991.

Law of Ukraine on Employment of the Population (Chelovek i Rabota, Zakon Ukrainy o zanyatosti naselenia), Kiev, February 1993.

Ministry of Labour, Basic Conceptual Issues of Elaboration of the State Programme of Youth Employment for the Years 1994-95 (Osnovni konceptualni polozhenya rozrobki proyektu derzhavnoy programi sprianya molodi na 1994-1995 roki), Kiev, August 1993.

Ministry of Labour, Basic Conceptual Principles of Project Elaboration of the State Programme for Youth Employment Promotion in 1994-1995 (Osnovni konceptualni polozhennya rozrobki proektu cilovoy derzhavnoy programi spriami spriannya zaynyatosti molodi na 1994-1995 roki rik Kiev), August 1993.

Ministry of Labour and State Employment Service, On Execution of the State Programme of Population Employment in 1993 (Pro vikonanya Derzhavnoy programi zaynyatosti naselenija na 1993 rik Kiev), December 1993.

Ministry of Labour, State Programme of Employment for 1993 (Derzhavna programa zaynyatosti naselenya na 1993 rik Kiev), 1993.

Ministry of Labour, State Programme of Employment for 1994 (Derzhavna programa zaynyatosti naselennya na 1994 rik Kiev) approved by the Cabinet of Ministers, February 23, 1994.

Resolution of representatives of trade union associations authorised to negotiate with the government on the summing up of the 1993 General Agreement and enter negotiations for a new General Agreement, April 4, 1994.

Trade Union Associations, Open Letter to the President of the Ukraine, Mr. Kravchuk, April 4, 1994.

Reports, Seminar Papers and Studies

T. Berezanetz, Disabled Workers in Ukraine, paper prepared for ILO-CEET, Budapest, October 1993.

S. Browne, The Transition in Ukraine, United Nations, mimeo, Kiev, September 1993.

Centre for Market Reforms, Ukraine: A Survey of Economic and Social Reforms, Kiev, mimeo, 1993.

O. Havrylyshyn, M. Miller and W. Perraudin, Deficits, Inflation and the Political Economy of Ukraine, paper presented at a Conference on Societies in Transformation: Experience of Market Reforms in Ukraine, Kiev, May 20, 1994.

ILO, *Freedom of Association and Collective Bargaining*, Report of the Committee of Experts on the Application of Conventions and Recommendations, International Labour Conference, 81st session, 1994.

ILO, *General Survey on Freedom of Association and Collective Bargaining*, International Labour Conference, 81st Session, 1994.

ILO-CEET, *Labour Market Dynamics in Ukrainian Industry: Results from the Ukrainian Labour Flexibility Survey*, ILO-CEET Paper No. 7, Budapest, 1994.

ILO-CEET, *Mission Report*, Ukraine, May 1993.

ILO-CEET, *Policy Manual for Disabled Workers*, Budapest, April 1994.

IMF, *Ukraine: Budgetary Implications of Social Safety Net Options*, Washington D.C., November 1992.

Institute of Sociology, Academy of Science, Socioeconomic and Political Situation in Ukraine's Regions, Kiev, mimeo, 1994.

International Labour Organisation and Ministry of Labour of Ukraine, *Economies in Transition and the Employment Problem: The Role of Cooperatives and Associative Enterprises*, Report of an International Seminar, Kiev, May 11–14, 1993.

V. Jatsenko, Employment Policy in Ukraine in 1991-1994, paper presented at ILO Conference on Employment Policy and Programmes, Budapest, June 2–3, 1994.

M. Kaskievich, The Modern State of the Cooperative Sector, paper presented to the International Seminar on Economies in Transition and the Employment Problem: The Role of Cooperatives and Associative Enterprises, organised by the ILO and the Ministry of Labour, Kiev, May 11–14, 1993.

G. Kulikov, *Remuneration System: Reforms and Needs*, Report for the ILO, Institute of Economics, Kiev, ILO-CEET, Budapest, April 1994.

V. Lanovoy, Ukraine: National Strategy for Technical Assistance for Reform, Report prepared for UN, mimeo, Kiev, 1993.

E. Libanova, Ukraine's Demographic-related Economic Problems, draft paper for UN Human Development Indicators Project, Kiev, March 1994.

E. Libanova, *The Ukrainian Labour Market: Problems and Perspectives (Ukrainskiy Reno truda: problemy i perspektivy)*, International Institute of Market Relations and Entrepreneurship, Kiev, 1993.

E. Libanova and A. Revenko, Public Policy and Social Conditions in Ukraine during 1989-1993, paper prepared for UNICEF, Kiev, 1993.

Ministry of Labour, Survey of Collective Agreements and Bargains, March 1993 (unpublished).

Ministry of Statistics, *Labour in the Ukrainian National Economy* (Pracya v narodnomu gospodarstvi Ukraini), Kiev, 1991.

Ministry of Statistics, *Labour in the Ukrainian National Economy* (Pracya v narodnomu gospodarstvi Ukraini), Kiev, 1993.

National Centre of the State Employment Service, *Report on Job Placement and Employment of the Population Turning to the Employment Service of Ukraine* (Zvit pro pracevlashtuvannya i zaynyatist naselenya, yake zvernulosya do sluzhbi zaynyatisti Ukrainy), Form No. 2-PN, Annual Report for 1993, Kiev, January 1994.

National Institute for Strategic Studies, Strategies for the Development of Ukraine: Contemporary Challenges and Choices, Kiev, 1994, mimeo.

A. Nesporova and R. Kyloh, *Economic and Social Dialogue in the Ostrova-Karvina Region*, ILO-CEET Report No. 5, Budapest, February 1994.

S. Pikhoshek, History of Free Trade Unions of Ukraine, Kiev, 1994, unpublished.

R. Popaduik, Building American–Ukrainian Partnerships, address at Georgetown University, Washington D.C., October 9, 1993.

V. Pynzenyk, Ukrainian Economic Reforms: Reflections on the Past and the Future, paper presented at the Conference Societies in Transformation: Experience of Market Reforms in Ukraine, Kiev, May 19–21, 1994.

M. Rutkowski, *Labour Hoarding and Future Open Unemployment in Eastern Europe: The Case of Polish Industry,* London School of Economics, Centre for Economic Performance, Discussion Paper No. 6, London, July 1990.

V. Shamota, An Analysis of the Ukrainian Labour Market and Efficiency of the State Employment Policy, background paper prepared for the Ukrainian COR, Kiev, 1994.

G. Standing, *Developing a Labour Market Information System for the Russian Federation,* ILO-CEET, Budapest, 1993.

G. Standing, Industrial Wages, Payment Systems and Benefits, Conference on Employment Restructuring in Russian Industry, Moscow and St. Petersburg, October, 1992.

G. Standing (ed.), *In Search of Flexibility: The New Soviet Labour Market*, Geneva, 1991.

The Economist Intelligence Unit, *Ukraine, Belarus, Moldova: Country Profiles,* London, 1994.

UNICEF: *Possibilities for an Agenda for Children in the Ukraine*, Report of a UNICEF mission to Ukraine, February 1994.

UNICEF, *Public Policy and Social Conditions: Central and Eastern Europe in Transition,* Regional Monitoring Report No. 1, November 1993.

United Nations, *Draft Report on the Status and Definition of NGOs in the Ukraine*, Kiev, 1994,

D. Vaughan-Whitehead, Interessement Participation Actionnariat – Impacts economiques dans l'entreprise, *Economica*, Paris 1992.

The World Bank, *Ukraine: Employment, Social Protection and Social Spending in the Transition to a Market Economy,* Washington D.C., November 1992.

The World Bank, *Ukraine: The Social Sectors during Transition*, Washington D.C., 1993.

Statistics

Ministry of Statistics, *Demographic Yearbook of Ukraine*, Kiev, 1993.
Ministry of Statistics, *Statistical Yearbook of Ukraine*, Kiev, 1991.
Ministry of Statistics, *Statistical Yearbook of Ukraine,* Kiev, 1992.
Ministry of Statistics, *Statistical Yearbook of Ukraine*, Kiev, 1993.
Ministry of Statistics, *Statistical Bulletin* (*Statistichniy byuleten*), Kiev, January 1994.
Ministry of Statistics, *Statistical Bulletin* (*Statistichniy byuleten*), Kiev, March 1994.
Ministry of Statistics, *Statistical Bulletin* (*Statistichniy byuleten*), Kiev, May 1994.